D0456938

COTTON *and* RACE
in the
MAKING *of* AMERICA

Cotton *and* Race *in the* Making *of* America

THE HUMAN COSTS
OF ECONOMIC POWER

Gene Dattel

IVAN R. DEE
Chicago 2009

COTTON AND RACE IN THE MAKING OF AMERICA. Copyright © 2009 by Gene Dattel. All rights reserved, including the right to reproduce this book or portions thereof in any form. For information, address: Ivan R. Dee, Publisher, 1332 North Halsted Street, Chicago 60642, a member of the Rowman & Littlefield Publishing Group. Manufactured in the United States of America and printed on acid-free paper.

www.ivanrdee.com

Library of Congress Cataloging-in-Publication Data:
Dattel, Eugene R.
  Cotton and race in the making of America : the human costs of economic power / Gene Dattel.
    p. cm.
  Includes bibliographical references and index.
  ISBN 978-1-56663-747-3 (cloth : alk. paper)
  1. Slavery—Economic aspects—Southern States—History. 2. Cotton growing—Economic aspects—Southern States—History. 3. Cotton growing—Social aspects—Southern States—History. 4. Plantation life—Southern States—History. 5. African Americans—Southern States—Social conditions. 6. United States—Race relations. 7. United States—Economic conditions. 8. Slavery—Political aspects—United States. 9. United States—Politics and government—1783–1865. 10. United States—Politics and government—1865–1933. I. Title.
E441.D237 2009
338.1'73510975—dc22   2009001342

For Licia, who shared this journey

Contents

Preface

Cotton and Race in the Making of America is about money and the uses and abuses of power. The story of cotton in America is a dramatic economic tale whose fundamental importance in the nation's history has been largely ignored. Because of its connection with race, cotton is uniquely tainted in American history. "It is the melancholy distinction of cotton," wrote David Cohn in 1956, "to be the stuff of high drama and tragedy, of bloody civil war and the unutterable woe of human slavery. . . . [Cotton was] a 'map-maker, trouble-maker, and history-maker.'" To put it less poetically, slave-produced cotton was shockingly important to the destiny of the United States; it almost destroyed the nation. In many ways this book is also about America's overwhelming attachment to material progress at whatever the human cost. Once we begin following the money trail, we realize that it leads us to the heart and soul of America.

The story begins at the Constitutional Convention of 1787 and ends in the 1930s, when technology finally broke the link between cotton and race with the first successful trials for a mechanical cotton picker. In 1787 cotton production was virtually nonexistent as the delegates met in Philadelphia. The Constitution would have been quite different if it had been written a few years later, after the nascent force of cotton was realized. The Founding Fathers were truly blindsided by cotton. Thus the Constitution protected race-based slavery, cotton's eventual labor pool, because slavery was thought to be already receding.

But slavery in America survived and expanded to satiate the international commercial interest in one crop, cotton. Its primary social by-product, the subordination of black men and women to the cotton economy, shaped the plight of African Americans throughout U.S. history. And as cotton shaped the nation's economic landscape, racial oppression shaped its social landscape. A people and a crop became bonded.

A force of enormous proportions was needed to keep millions of people enslaved at a time when slavery was, as Carl Degler wrote, a "moral anachronism" in the Western world. Only a commercial hurricane could have created the fundamental paradox of the American nation: the simultaneous story of dynamic economic growth and the prolonged devastations of the African-American experience. Cotton was that force and thus the chief cause of commerce's most destructive creation, slavery in its nineteenth-century iteration. Slavery, however, is only the first chapter of the tale. Beginning in 1800, slaves cultivated cotton for sixty years; but *free* blacks were cotton laborers for nearly a hundred years after emancipation. Only the African-American migration to Northern cities during World War I and the mid-twentieth-century technological revolution in cotton production ultimately separated cotton from race.

Cotton stimulated economic growth in antebellum America more decisively than any other single industry or crop. From 1803 to 1937 it was America's leading export, a reign that will likely never be surpassed. On the eve of the American Civil War, cotton comprised fully 60 percent of all American exports. These stunning statistics were wrought primarily from the hands of slaves and later of free blacks—generations of men, women, and children who "chopped" the weeds that surrounded the young stalks, guided the mules through the endless rows of cotton, and stooped to pick the ever-valued crop for market.

Cotton was also the foundation of the Industrial Revolution and thus transformed the economic world. Its significance was not lost upon the twenty-two-year-old political economist Karl Marx, who wrote in 1846 that "without cotton you have no modern industry." For Marx, the relationship between cotton and slavery was similarly unambiguous: "Without slavery, you have no cotton." Cotton brought wealth, power, and prosperity to both America and Europe. Affordable textile garments woven from American cotton improved the quality of life for people throughout the world. But this material progress came with a human cost, for cotton production played the leading role in a tragedy of epic racial proportions.

I view the saga of cotton and race from a racially tinted economic and financial perspective, rather than through a moral lens. I also explore this story from a national and international perspective, seeing cotton for the "history-maker" it was, rather than just a Southern regional phenomenon. Not surprisingly, the cotton epic unfolded in what Europeans viewed as the most commercial of nations, the United States. The quest for money determines what people do and why they do it, and the American pecuniary obsession has remained constant throughout the nation's history. Cotton production in the pursuit of riches swept through the physical, social, and economic terrain of nineteenth-century America with the force of a tornado. The slaveholder and the slave before the Civil War, and the plantation owner and the sharecropper afterward, were all—each in his own way—pawns in the hands of finance.

While one may dwell on the moral and social debacle of slavery and its aftermath, it is important to remember that slavery's existence was based on racially influenced economic facts. Simple concepts such as labor shortages, profit or the expectation of profit, the ability to finance, supply and demand imbalances, monopoly, and the price of cotton combined to form a commercial juggernaut. Cotton offered potential wealth; black slavery solved the labor problem. In the first half of the nineteenth century, cotton was primarily responsible for the enslavement of four million African Americans. Slave-produced cotton connected the country's regions, provided the export surplus the young nation desperately needed to gain its financial "sea legs," brought commercial ascendancy to New York City, was the driving force for territorial expansion in the Old Southwest, and fostered trade between Europe and the United States. No other American commodity achieved such regal status. The moral justification and the political and legal defense of slavery followed in the wake of cotton's march across America.

Northerners played a leading role in the cotton economy of the South and its accompanying racial disaster. Racial animosity and hypocrisy have been an underappreciated but fundamental aspect of the white North, both before and after the Civil War. This racial hatred severely impeded black mobility—physically, economically, and intellectually. To examine racial attitudes in the white North from 1800 to the 1930s will disabuse any wishful thinking about the possibility of black equality after the Civil War. The actions of white Northerners provide a near-perfect guide for the dismal future of the freedman. By creating an inhospitable and exclusionary environment, the North helped entrap blacks in the cotton South. Had the North been otherwise, 90 percent of black Americans would not have lived in the South on the eve of World War I.

In 1930 cotton production bore a striking resemblance to the methods of the antebellum era. Within a few years, successful development of the mechanical cotton picker would render black farm labor useless by the 1950s. The cotton price collapse of the Great Depression toppled King Cotton, which forever after would depend on government subsidies. The beginning of an effective attack on America's firmly entrenched system of legal segregation would come a few years later, and World War II would soon inspire African Americans to challenge America's racial system. The civil rights movement of the 1960s would put an end to legal segregation but not to America's racial dilemma.

Cotton has long since vanished as an economic powerhouse, but the relics of cotton—a black underclass in the North and South, with its destructive behavioral characteristics—remain long after slavery, sharecropping, and legal segregation have disappeared. This is the story of how cotton shaped America, defined the South, and in so doing prepared the ground of our racial quagmire. The tale winds through the interconnected worlds of finance, politics, diplomacy, and technology, and is built upon powerful personalities, the hunger for money and power, and the maelstrom of race.

Acknowledgments

ONE OF THE exciting aspects of writing this book has been the opportunity to talk with and learn from many people whose disciplines range from economic history, finance, agronomics, and the history of race relations to blues musicians and museum curators. They have given generously of their time and perspectives over the last decade in which this book has gestated and evolved. Of those who have been especially helpful, I would like to acknowledge John Harkin, Chester Morgan, John David Smith, Kent Syverud, Robert G. Stanton, and Charles Reagan Wilson. Nevertheless I am solely responsible for any errors or erroneous interpretations.

Along the way, several persons now deceased have had a major impact on my task. I am deeply indebted to Robin Winks for sparking my interest and initiating this study in his Yale seminar in 1962. His embrace of a comparative and global approach to history has led me, and many other Yale students, down some fascinating paths. Roger Malkin, the New York native who transformed the Delta & Pine Land Company from a large cotton farm and seed company into a cutting-edge biotech firm, was a wonderful source of inspiration and energy. This financier represented the finest tradition of American entrepreneurship, perseverance, ingenuity, and colorblind philanthropy. Milburn Crowe provided me a thorough explanation of the history of Mound Bayou.

Many others participated. My brother Richard, with his farming background and his commitment to community service, has been a valuable resource. Allan Hammons, through his impressive involvement with the B. B. King Museum and his creative mind-set, energizes those around him. The blues legend B. B. King gave a generous personal account of growing up as a field worker in cotton country. The New York Historical Society provided valuable experience in allowing me to work on their "New York Divided" exhibition in 2007. Two articles based upon material in this book have appeared under the auspices of the Mississippi Historical Society and its able editor, Peggy Jeanes. Useful material was provided by the Wisconsin State Historical Society and Delta State University. Jody Stovall guided me through the Delta Branch Experiment Station in Stoneville, Mississippi—sometimes referred to as the Silicon Valley of agriculture—and introduced me to their archival treasure trove of photographs.

History is not just about reading books, diaries, and documents or examining census reports and statistical data. To get the feel and texture of a historical situation, it is always enlightening to visit the actual site of an event, walk through a battlefield, or peruse an industrial structure. In this regard I am especially grateful to Rogers Varner, who coaxed me into attending a meeting of what was then called the Liverpool Cotton Association. This led to an excursion to Quarry Bank Mill at Styal, Manchester, a stroll along the dock in Liverpool where cotton was unloaded, a poignant stop at the shipyard where the *Alabama* was built, and a tour led by the dedicated Bob Jones of Liverpool's Civil War–era sites. I gazed at the statute of Abraham Lincoln in Manchester and thought about the juxtaposition of diplomacy, finance, commerce, war, and morality. All of the international connections wrought by the cotton business came alive.

It has been a pleasure and a privilege to work with my publisher and editor, Ivan Dee, who embodies a formidable combination of intellectual curiosity, discipline, and good humor.

G. D.

New York City
March 2009

COTTON *and* RACE
in the
MAKING *of* AMERICA

PART ONE

Slavery in the Making of the Constitution

I know of no country, indeed, where the love of money has taken stronger hold on the affections of men [than in the United States]. . . . The love of wealth is therefore to be traced, either as a principal or accessory motive, at the bottom of all Americans do. . . . [The white Northerner's] acquisitive ardor surpasses the ordinary limits of human cupidity; he is tormented by the desire for wealth, he boldly enters upon every path that fortune opens to him . . . , and the avidity in the pursuit of gain amounts to a form of heroism. . . .
—Alexis de Tocqueville, 1835

CHAPTER ONE

The Silent Issue at the Constitutional Convention

BY MANY ACCOUNTS the Constitutional Convention of 1787 was a profound manifestation of the American passion for liberty and freedom, a hunger that animated the country literally from the beginning. This depiction is easy to accept. Who doesn't wish to believe in the moral, egalitarian, and democratic origins of one's country? But in this rose-colored tale, we have left out a great deal. The Constitutional Convention, far from being an exalted meeting of the minds, was often a fractious struggle where lofty ideals were subsumed beneath the deep anxieties of America's founders. Here we look past the rhetoric—so far removed from today's politicians and celebratory historians and thus easily romanticized—to focus on the far more mundane but revealing realities of the convention. What we find, again and again, is a desire for economic development that trumped almost all else. For this hodgepodge of not often "united" states, the need to make money demanded a semblance of unity and collective purpose. And toward this end, enormous compromises were made, agreements that would make America an economic powerhouse but one with serious social ills. Economic self-interest and national growth complemented each other from the start.

The Constitutional Convention affords an appropriate beginning for the story of cotton and the black experience in America. While there was no cotton production to speak of at the time, within decades the cotton boom would radically redirect the country and become a virulent example of the oft-repeated American pattern of land speculation, settlement, commerce, and economic vitality. In contrast to cotton, the importance of race was apparent right from the nation's colonial beginnings. North and South alike profited from the importation of African men, women, and children. By the time of the convention, many of the delegates believed that slavery was an essential feature of their state, even if some of them claimed to despise the institution and others believed that the sale of persons would eventually disappear. Thus cotton was not even a part of the consciousness of the new nation while the bondage of human beings soon was very much embedded in the American brain (and ledger sheet). Before long, an insignificant crop would become the engine of the American economy, and the thorny practice of slavery, far from dying out, would become even more vital for the expansion of King Cotton. After slavery, white America obliged cotton with another century of black bondage.

Although the cotton phenomenon was years away, the destiny of blacks in the cotton fields resulted from commercial priorities and racial attitudes that were on display at the Constitutional Convention. Slave-produced cotton would find fertile soil in the commercial and racial world of the Founding Fathers. At the convention the issue of slavery was subordinated to union as the delegates confronted a choice: a nation with slavery, or no nation without slavery. But no one at the convention could envision a cotton kingdom that would spawn delusions of a slave empire.

While Americans are taught to revere the Founding Fathers as statesmen with exalted ideals, these men were earthbound and very much concerned with business and economic survival. The convention was largely provoked not by ideals but by the need to impose order on the commercial chaos that resulted from the government under the Articles of Confederation. At the time of the convention, foreign intervention, squabbling among states, Indian occupation, confusion over land ownership, the lust for more land, and a shortage of settlers hampered economic viability. Despite some prosperity, the Federalists who initiated the convention saw the advantages of a strong central government and the perils of state sovereignty. The priorities, fears, hopes, visions, and obligations of the delegates and the states became clear as the Constitution was forged through debate and compromise.

*

Before the Constitution, America's governing document had been the Articles of Confederation, which in 1781 had created a loose association of the thirteen states. The document gave the states supreme power while restricting the central government. Each state had one vote; all measures had to be passed unanimously. The resulting disorder, fragmentation, and competition hampered political and commercial activity. It was state sovereignty run amok, threatening the existence of a fragile union. Foreigners took note of the bedlam. The French diplomat François Barbé-Marbois, an ardent admirer of the United States and a six-year resident, summarized the state of the government under the Articles of Confederation: "There is no Congress, no committee, no President, no minister of any department. All affairs, especially the finances are falling into confusion even worse than in the past." As a result of the chaos, an interstate convention was held in Annapolis in September 1786 to rectify the commercial flaws of the Articles. This commercial convention was the prelude to the Constitutional Convention.*

The statesmen who assembled at the Philadelphia State House on May 25, 1787, were aware of America's potential for greatness. They were equally mindful of, and anxious about, the many obstacles that might sabotage the young commercial republic. The need to raise revenues and quell land quarrels, belligerent squabbling over conflicting

---

*In the midst of disorder, Shays' Rebellion, an insurrection with commercial roots, provoked the urgency that led to the Constitutional Convention. In 1786, Daniel Shays, a Revolutionary patriot, led an armed insurrection aimed at closing the Massachusetts courts in order to prevent land foreclosures and debtors' imprisonment. High state taxes were a particular thorn. The insurrectionists even attacked the federal arsenal in Springfield, Massachusetts. While Shays' Rebellion is merely a footnote in American history, the episode had genuine significance in pointing up the threat of chaos and revolt that preceded the convention. George Washington was ". . . mortified beyond expression" by Shays' Rebellion, calling it a "triumph for the advocates of despotism." The event prompted Oliver Wolcott, then lieutenant governor of Connecticut, to write that the "authority or rather the influence of Congress and the system connected to it, I consider at about an end."

state laws and policies, Indian threats and the condescension of foreign powers—all these concerns demanded a stronger central government. The delegates also had to grapple with the issue of slavery, which threatened the convention's agenda and hence jeopardized the very existence of the United States. Slavery created a sectional divide that threatened to thwart the convention. James Madison clearly outlined the breach: ". . . the States were divided into different interests not by their difference of size, but principally from their having or not having slaves. . . . It did not lie between the large and small States; it lay between Northern and Southern." Madison's motivation for his warning, it has been argued, was his need to divert attention from the big state–small state controversy over proportional representation to another area—sectional strife over slavery. If so, he picked the topic that was sure to create the greatest emotional response.

The sparsely settled colonies and the consequent shortage of workers meant that in the seventeenth century slave labor was ensconced in the economic and social fabric of the Southern states, where it suited the profitable production of staple crops like tobacco, rice, and indigo. By 1787, slavery had proven to be unprofitable in the Northern states, where staple crops were not grown. (At no point in the nation's history were large-scale slave populations used to produce anything other than staple crops.) The census population statistics of 1790 are compelling. Of the roughly 700,000 slaves in America, 642,000 lived in the South, 42,000 in the North. In addition there were 59,466 "free colored" persons. Slaves accounted for approximately 17 percent of the total U.S. population at the time of the Constitutional Convention. A disproportionate 396,463 slaves, or 60 percent of the slave population, lived in the two primary tobacco-growing states of Maryland and Virginia.

But while slaves lived primarily in the South, slavery was a nationwide business. Hundreds of slave ships were based in ports along the East Coast, including Boston and Newport, Rhode Island. The first American slave ship, the *Desire*, had been built in Marblehead, Massachusetts, in 1683. An anti-slavery advocate, William Ellery of Rhode Island, in 1791 described his state's attachment to slave trading: "An Ethiopian could as soon change his skin as a Newport merchant could be induced to change so lucrative a trade as that in slaves for the slow profits of manufactory."

Southern slaveholders, no matter their views on the morality of human bondage, were chained to their slaves by economic necessity. George Mason, the Virginia delegate who excoriated slavery and the slave trade, owned more than two hundred slaves. Slaves, he thundered, "produce the most pernicious effect on manners. Every master of slaves is born a petty tyrant; they bring the judgment of heaven on a country. . . . Slavery discourages arts and manufacturers. The poor despise labor when they see it performed by slaves." Mason, a resident of the largest slave state, blamed the British for introducing the slave trade and also New Englanders, whose "lust for gain embarked on this nefarious traffic."

Yet by 1787 the belief was common that slavery would wither away of its own accord. The long-term health of the slave-grown tobacco business was in doubt. Thomas Jefferson observed in 1781 that "tobacco was fast declining at the commencement of this war, it must decline in return of peace." Tobacco was known to deplete the soil, and a whiff of serious stagnation in tobacco prices had already been detected. The other slave-produced crops, rice and indigo, were small markets.

Thus nothing on the economic horizon in 1787 suggested a massive demand for slave labor. Accordingly, while the price of slaves might be volatile for years at a time, eventually the price would be determined by the profit earned from their forced labor. Without profit or the expectation of profit, slavery could not be maintained exclusively as a social system. Some of the delegates assumed and hoped that slavery would therefore wither away over a period of time. Connecticut's Oliver Ellsworth cautioned against interference, for "Slavery in time will not be a speck in our country." His Connecticut colleague Roger Sherman thought that "the abolition of slavery seemed to be going on in the U.S." and that the "good sense of the several States" would mean the end of the institution. Later, at the Pennsylvania ratifying convention, James Wilson expressed a similar opinion about the eventual demise of slavery: "and though the period is more distant than I could wish, yet it will produce the same kind of gradual change for the whole nation as was pursued in Pennsylvania." This notion of slavery's eventual death, plus the lack of any immediately foreseeable stimulus for slave expansion, gave the anti-slavery delegates comfort in their decisions to compromise.

Regardless of slavery's future, the priority of the Constitutional Convention was to create a framework for an effective national government. The stakes were high. An uncompromising stance in favor of abolition might destroy the possibility of the union itself. As the historian Edmund Morgan wrote, no one "could insist on abolition. To have done so would have ended the convention." The South's "huge investment" and "vested interest" precluded any practical plan for abolition. What labor system would be used to replace slavery, and what would be done with the former slaves?

As the issues of slavery were raised—the slave trade; how to count slaves in apportioning the legislature; import and export taxes on slave-produced staple crops; the protection provided by fugitive slave laws; and assistance for putting down a possible slave insurrection—most of the demands of the South were met. Abolition, gradual emancipation, equality for free blacks, and the removal of free blacks from America were not on the agenda.

The most emotional condemnation of slavery came from Gouverneur Morris of Pennsylvania during debate over whether—and how—to count slaves for the purpose of representation in the legislature. In his oft-quoted remarks, Morris called slavery a "nefarious institution . . . the curse of Heaven on the states where it prevailed. . . . Upon what principle is it that the slaves shall be computed in the representation? Are they men? Then make them citizens and let them vote. . . ." Morris also introduced a motion to limit slavery geographically to the "Deep South." Another delegate from Pennsylvania, John Dickinson, proposed that slave importation be banned in states that had already ended the slave trade. Fear of Southern objection doomed both suggestions. Gouverneur Morris's righteous stand was, however, mere rhetoric. A land speculator, Morris ultimately succumbed to the priority of establishing a union, voted for the Constitution, and was largely responsible for its final draft.

Two ostensibly disparate trading states, Connecticut and South Carolina, provided the key support that allowed the Constitution to be approved at the convention. Connecticut certainly had small farmers who tilled its rocky New England soil, but it also epitomized the commercial spirit of the new nation with its fleet of some three hundred cargo ships. It exported cattle, lumber, and foodstuffs to West Indian slaveholders, a trading volume greater than Boston's and equal to New York's. Like all New England states, Connecticut found the ownership of slaves unprofitable but gained from the slave trade and did a thriving business with slaveowners. In 1784 it had passed a gradual emancipation bill. In the 1790 census, Connecticut's population of 238,141 included 2,759 slaves and 2,801 "free colored." Black slaves were thus a tiny 1 percent of the total population. By contrast, South Carolina's population was 249,073, of which 107,094 were slaves and 1,801 "free colored." Slaves made up 43 percent of South Carolina's population. Its trading economy was built on slave labor, which produced its export crops.

The two most important Connecticut delegates were anti-slavery advocates Roger Sherman and Oliver Ellsworth. Sherman, awkward in appearance and attire, had risen from a poor background to become a gifted lawyer, politician, and judge. A "crafty debater," he spoke 138 times at the convention, more often than all but three other delegates. Ellsworth, Yale and Princeton educated, a lawyer and superb orator, generally followed the lead of his colleague Sherman. South Carolina's delegates—Pierce Butler, Charles Pinckney, Charles Cotesworth Pinckney, and John Rutledge—were all forceful proponents of slavery and pro-slavery legislation. Rutledge famously highlighted sectional differences by declaring that the interests of the North and South are as "different as the interests of Russia and Turkey."

John Rutledge rejected moral arguments. He asserted that "religion and humanity had nothing to do with . . . [the slave trade]. Interest alone is the governing principle with nations. The true question is whether Southern states shall or shall not be parties to the union." His fellow South Carolinian Charles Pinckney was equally blunt: "South Carolina can never [support a constitution] if it prohibits the [foreign] slave trade." He softened his remarks by suggesting that South Carolina might "abolish the importation of slaves, as Virginia and Maryland had done." In any event, he observed, it was South Carolina's choice to "do of herself what is wished." In other words, no state or national government could tell South Carolina what to do. The ultimatum had been delivered.

For Roger Sherman and Oliver Ellsworth, the priority was to create a union and gain advantage for Connecticut. This called for compromise or, more precisely, concessions to the South. Sherman and South Carolina's John Rutledge discussed a bargain over wine and dinner. Rutledge wanted protection for slavery; Sherman wanted land. Ellsworth, Sherman's protegé, set aside moral issues and followed Sherman's lead. He subordinated his anti-slavery views to other priorities—personal, state, and national. It was said of Ellsworth that he "never missed a chance to make a dollar." Indeed, his financial dealings gave him a strong vested interest in producing a Constitution and a national government. He wanted a commercially prosperous nation in which the economic activities of the states complemented one another: "What enriches a part [of the country] enriches the whole and the states are the best judge of their particular [interests]." Sherman believed that the "public good did not require" prohibition of the slave trade. For him, it was expedient to have as few objections as possible to the proposed Constitution. He said plainly that "it was better to let the southern states import slaves . . . if they make that a sine qua non." He thought "it best to leave the matter rather than force them out of the union."

Southerners demanded a union with slavery. New Englanders, led by Sherman and Ellsworth, were concerned above all with economic security and growth. They seemed genuinely to believe that slavery would grow extinct over time. And so the deal was struck. Neither equality for free blacks nor even whether they fit in America was ever considered in the constitutional debates.

After an arduous four months of discussion and debate, in the sweltering heat of a Philadelphia summer, the final draft of the Constitution was presented to the delegates on September 17, 1787. Some of the main provisions that dealt with slavery indicated a Southern victory. As we know, the word "slavery" never appears in the document produced at that historic convention. Instead the delegates agreed upon a series of clauses that offered a rough, indirect, but ultimately lasting set of guidelines to regulate the commercial existence of slavery. The famous three-fifths compromise was derived from an economic rather than a moral calculation. In this concession, five slaves were counted as three people for purposes of determining population and hence congressional representation. The "three-fifths clause" would over time greatly augment Southern power in Congress and in some instances determine presidential elections. Gouverneur Morris opposed the clause but signed the Constitution, a document he had been largely responsible for writing. Alexander Hamilton was also pragmatic. Without the "indulgence" of the three-fifths issue, he declared, "no union could possibly have been formed." William R. Davie of North Carolina, who would later found the University of North Carolina, observed that without the inclusion of the three-fifths concept, North Carolina would "never confederate" and "the business [of the convention] was at an end."

Some delegates wanted an immediate end to the international slave trade; others put forward a deadline of 1800; the South accepted 1808 with a provision for a modest ten-dollar tax on each imported slave. The slaveowner James Madison advocated prohibiting the slave trade consistent with his view of slavery as a "deep-rooted abuse." He thought that extending slave importation another twenty years would "produce all mischief that can be apprehended from the liberty to import slaves." His ownership of slaves was inconsistent with this attitude; his support of the Constitution indicated his true priorities.

Other provisions supported the institution of slavery. No tax could be levied on a state's exports—an important victory for the South, which protected the slave-produced staple export crops of tobacco, rice, and indigo. The fugitive slave provision obligated states to return slaves who had escaped from their owners. The Constitution's clause providing that the militia could be called to "suppress insurrections" was particularly aimed at slave rebellions.

In summary, these provisions accommodating slavery are overwhelmingly commercial in nature. They are both direct and indirect recognitions of economic interests. Slaves and slave-produced products were considered private property in need of protection. The South feared that its economic structure would crumble unless slavery were protected; the North respected this interest and conceded to the South's ultimatum. The South's major concession, a simple majority requirement rather than a two-thirds majority for the passage of navigation acts, was equally commercial. Northern and Southern delegates, individually, represented a complex set of beliefs and motivations, all of which were subordinated to the goals of security and economic prosperity implied in a stronger union. All the delegates managed to suppress the moral issue of slavery.

When the delegates had wrestled with the issues of slavery and had finally produced a document that most agreed was the best possible under difficult circumstances, they expressed relief and resignation. Even though some Southerners were not satisfied, Charles Pinckney of South Carolina was convinced that the Constitution offered sufficient protection for the institution of slavery. The sage Benjamin Franklin's response was read by his fellow Pennsylvania delegate James Wilson. Franklin "agreed to the Constitution with all its faults because I think a general Government necessary for us, and there is no form of Government but what may be a blessing to the people if well administered." He elaborated by citing his experience, flexibility, and judgment.

> Mr. President, I confess that there are several parts of this constitution which I do not approve. . . . I doubt too whether any other convention we can obtain may be able to make a better constitution. . . . It therefore astonishes me, Sir, to find this system approaching so near to perfection as it does; and I think it will astonish our enemies. . . . Thus, I consent, sir to this constitution because I expect no better, and because I am not sure that it is not the best.

Opponents of slavery bowed to economic necessity. Gouverneur Morris expressed his opinion that "The moment this plan goes forth, all other considerations will be laid aside—and the great question will be shall there be a national government or not? And this must take place or a general anarchy will be the alternative." Alexander Hamilton, an anti-slavery advocate, put aside his own objections to the document. He urged all delegates to sign with a compelling rhetorical question": ". . . is it possible to deliberate between anarchy and convulsion on one side, and the chance of good to be expected from the plan on the other?"

John Adams, in a letter to Thomas Jefferson, praised the Constitution as "the greatest single effort of national deliberation that the world has ever seen." Jefferson, of course, objected to the absence of a bill of rights, but he too lauded the delegates' handiwork. The president of the convention, George Washington, sent a copy of the Constitution to the Marquis de Lafayette. Washington seemed relieved in remarking to his French friend, "I wish the Constitution . . . had been made more perfect. But I sincerely believe it is the best which could be obtained at this time. . . . It appears to me that the political concerns of this country are in a manner suspended by a thread . . . and, if nothing had been agreed on by the Convention, anarchy would have ensued."

In the ratification process, states emphasized commerce and security. The issue of slavery presented no barrier in winning approval from the requisite nine states. On July 26, 1788, New York became the eleventh state to ratify the Constitution. The laggards, North Carolina (November 1789) and Rhode Island (March 1790), had no choice but to agree. Despite minor hiccups, this less than idealistic document became the Constitution of the United States, and with it was enshrined a fundamental economic motivation that would shape much of the nation's history.

*

The racial attitudes of the Founding Fathers were to influence the destiny of blacks in the cotton fields. The delegates' thoughts about slavery are well known, their attitudes toward race much less familiar. And in almost all cases their personal ambitions and hopes for their new nation took precedence over their moral strictures.

Benjamin Franklin opposed slavery, but his attitude toward blacks could be harsh. It is generally recognized that he owned household slaves for thirty years, even though as an old man he was president of the Pennsylvania Abolition Society. Interestingly, Franklin's belief in black inferiority contributed to his disdain for the slave trade. Franklin thought that "the importation of blacks . . . might 'darken' the superior beings, namely, 'the lovely white and red.'" He never quite conquered his "fear and loathing of a people of different color" and did not relish the prospect of an "ever-blacker America."

Franklin's notions of inherent racial inferiority were somewhat tempered by visits in 1763 to the charity schools for black children established in Philadelphia by Anthony Benezet. After visiting one of these schools, Franklin "conceived . . . a higher Opinion of the Natural Capacities of the black race, than I have ever before entertained. Their Apprehension [is] as quick, their Memory [is] as Strong, and their

Docility in every Respect equal to that of White Children." In 1774 he wrote that blacks were disadvantaged because of lack of education. Black children, he thought, held promise, yet adult blacks "were still a terrifying people to him." He "hated slavery but could not love slaves." Franklin's experience with a few children could not allay his deep feelings of foreboding about free blacks.

Franklin could also vilify blacks in word and deed. In his 1770 essay "Conversations on Slavery," he cautioned: "Perhaps you imagine the Negroes to be a mild tempered, tractable Kind of People. . . . some of them are so. But the Majority [are] of a plotting disposition, dark, sullen, malicious, revengeful and cruel in the highest Degree." At the time Franklin was representing the state of Georgia in England and was lobbying for British approval of Georgia's slave codes, which he considered "necessary to govern [slaves]." In 1779, Franklin contacted the French police to recapture Abbe, a female slave owned by John Jay, another of his compatriots living in France. (Jay was a founding member of New York's abolition society at a time when he still owned slaves.) The French police found Abbe and imprisoned her until she "repented her ingratitude." Franklin also asked the French government to allow his relative, John Williams, Jr., to keep a slave in France after the French had abolished slavery.

Simultaneously an abolitionist and a pragmatist, Franklin was truly alarmed about the entry of free blacks into a white world. He recommended that a national police pay particular "attention to emancipated black people." Slavery, he wrote in 1789, had so debased the slave that the aftermath of emancipation could be dangerous: "Slavery is such an atrocious debasement of human nature, that its extirpation, if not performed with solicitous care, may sometimes open a source of serious evils." The slave, according to Franklin, had "long been treated as a brute animal [who] too frequently sinks beneath the common standard of the human species. . . . Under such circumstances, freedom may prove a misfortune to himself and prejudicial to society." Freed slaves, he suggested, would operate without "reason and conscience."

On October 26, 1789, Franklin issued his plan for a committee of twenty-four Pennsylvania Abolition Society members who would oversee four subcommittees to deal with emancipated blacks. Franklin,

At the Constitutional Convention and after, Alexander Hamilton, though opposed to slavery, yielded to priorities of union and economics. Without a constitution that acquiesced to slavery, Hamilton recognized, "anarchy and convulsion," rather than union, would result. In 1795 he presciently predicted that cotton would be a "valuable export." *(Library of Congress)*

who feared the consequences of masses of former slaves unleashed on American society, recommended that a special "branch of our national police" supervise emancipated slaves. "A committee of inspection" would "superintend the morals, general conduct, and ordinary situation of Free Negroes." "A committee of Guardians" would find "children and young people" apprenticeships so that they might learn trades; this committee had the "right of guardianship over the persons bound." "A committee of Education" was formed to "superintend the children" of "Free Blacks" who would be trained for the necessities of "future situations in life" and taught "moral and religious principles."

"A committee of employ" would find "constant employment for those Free Negroes who are able to work, as the want of this would occasion poverty, idleness, and many vicious habits." The jobs contemplated would "require but little skill." Apprehensive white abolitionists like Benjamin Franklin wanted comprehensive white regulation of the lives of free blacks after emancipation.

Alexander Hamilton is credited with a more tolerant attitude toward blacks than his contemporaries. Of course, opposition to slavery did not deter Hamilton from having many slaveholding friends, if they were Federalists. He also never publicly condemned slavery at the Constitutional Convention. His priorities were, first, the union of the states and, next, the Funding Act of 1790 that would place the nation on a sound financial footing.

In 1779, when he was in his early twenties, Hamilton wrote a letter that is often cited as proof of his fair treatment of blacks. In it he described the need to recruit black troops in the Revolutionary army as a precursor to emancipation:

> I have no doubt, that the negroes will make excellent soldiers, with proper management. . . . I frequently hear it objected to the scheme of embodying negroes that they are too stupid to make good soldiers. This is far from a valid objection that I think their want of cultivation (for their natural faculties are probably as good as ours) joined to that habit of subordination which they acquire from a life of servitude, will make them sooner become the nearer soldiers than our White inhabitants. . . . An essential part of the plan is to give them their freedom with their muskets. This will . . . have a good influence upon those who remain, by opening a door to their emancipation. . . . The dictates of humanity and true policy, equally interest me in favour of this unfortunate class of men.

Thus Hamilton was keenly aware at an early age of the contempt that white Americans felt toward blacks. He makes a nod toward their equality, as soldiers, and recognizes their characteristic "subordination." Further evidence of his notions about black equality is sparse. Hamilton and his wife, Eliza, may have owned household slaves. He certainly handled legal transactions involving slaves.

Hamilton was a founder of the New York Society for Promoting the Manumission of Slaves. The group elected John Jay, the owner of five slaves, as its president, and more than half its members owned slaves. In 1785, Hamilton attempted to pass a rule that required abolitionist members of the Society to free their slaves, but the proposal was voted down.

Yet when Hamilton was forced to choose between his financial system and slavery, the choice, like that of his fellow Americans, was nearly always the former. By 1792 Hamilton realized that the cotton textiles industry should be promoted in America, noting the "rapidly rising Cotton" manufacturing in England. In 1795 he recognized the potential of cotton as an export commodity.

> [Cotton] . . . has not been cultivated except in a limited degree, and as an article of export rather, in the manner of Experiment than otherwise, . . . from the Expence and Difficulty of separating the Seeds, from the Cotton, we have been [hardly] able . . . to class Cotton among our exports. Its cultivation is said latterly to have become an object of attention in Georgia & South Carolina—still however it cannot yet be considered as a staple commodity. But from the recent Invention of an ingenious, & simple, Machine, for ginning Cotton, It is hoped that the cultivation may be extended, so that not only our own Domestic manufacturers may be relieved from a Dependence on foreign supply, but the catalogue of our valuable Exports inriched by the addition of this inestimable production.

George Washington, as we have seen, did not want the discussion of slavery to retard the growth of American institutions or land expansion. He did provide that his slaves would be freed after both he and his wife died. He loathed the institution of slavery but succumbed personally. In 1786 he advocated a plan "by which slavery may be abolished by slow, sure and imperceptible degrees."

Yet Washington, the consummate businessman, "was one of the least tolerant . . . masters who put himself on record." In 1794 he instructed his "steward," William Pearce, to carefully monitor his overseers. A lax overseer, according to Washington, would encourage "idleness or slight work on the one side and flogging on the other, the last of which besides the dissatisfaction which it creates has in one or two instances been productive of serious consequences." Slaves were accused by Washington of "ruining horses," "embezzling grain," and "lying and malingering in general." Slave carpenters, he wrote, were "notorious piddlers"; and house slaves he considered untrustworthy. Washington thought that slaves feigned "illness" and fabricated reasons for not working: "If they are not made to do what their age and strength will enable them, it will be a very bad example to others." When he pursued the "occasional" slave who ran away, Washington was careful to avoid publicity. In one instance he gave instructions that he would pay expenses for "recovering" the runaway slave "but . . . would not have my name appear in any advertisement, or other measure, leading to it." Washington probably supplied "adequate . . . housing and clothing" but "little tenderness."

The "father of his country" complained about the financial drain inherent in slaveholding. He explained that he owned twice as many "working negroes . . . [as] can be employed to any advantage in the farming system." He owned approximately four hundred slaves but was cash poor, his fortunes having been diminished by long years of service to his country. When he became president he had to borrow £10,000 to pay his expenses. Although he had made $50,000 in four years from crops and the disposition of lands, he bemoaned in 1799 that the money was "scarcely able to keep . . . [him] afloat." It was estimated that only a third of Washington's four hundred slaves were able to do field work. Like other slaveholders, Washington was trapped in an economic system. He wanted to dispose of his slaves but abhorred the act of selling them. He and other slaveholders could not find replacements for their slave labor, hence they did nothing.

*

In the colonial era the degrading treatment of free blacks in the North was a sign that the future of blacks in white America lay in the cotton fields. Blacks were well aware of white hatred, hostility, and condescension, North and South. Free blacks, for the most part, were relegated to the most menial jobs in the large Northern cities—Boston, Philadelphia, and New York. Prince Hall, a former slave from Boston, noted the degradation of that city's blacks. In the 1790s he observed that "daily insults we meet with on the streets of Boston ... were much more [conspicuous] on public days of recreation ... [when] we may truly be said to carry our lives in our hands." Slaves in the West Indies, he said, were not subject to such "molestation." Philadelphia blacks met the same fate when they were attacked during holiday celebrations.

The black minister Richard Allen, another former slave, chafed under the prevailing judgment of black inferiority. He blamed whites for preventing "superior good conduct" among blacks: "[S]uperior good conduct is looked for, from our race, by those who stigmatize us as men whose baseness is incurable ... yet ... [white people] try what ... [they] can to prevent our rising from a state of barbarism. ..." His concise statement of white responsibility was a model of clarity. "Will you because you have reduced us to the unhappy condition ... , plead our incapacity for freedom ... as a sufficient cause for keeping us under the grievous yoke?"

The responses of black leaders make it clear that they recognized the bleak chances of their acceptance in white America. Free blacks chose either to build separate communities or to remove themselves entirely by emigrating elsewhere. Philadelphia's Philip Forten fostered the development of separate black churches, schools, and community organizations there. Richard Allen worked to create black churches in Boston; the Massachusetts governor rejected his offer of black assistance to put down Shays' Rebellion. In 1786 a frustrated Prince Hall petitioned the Massachusetts legislature to aid black repatriation to Africa. He described the "disagreeable and disadvantageous circumstances" of blacks, and he did not think the situation would change "so long as we and our children live in America." Blacks, he said, earnestly want "to return to Africa, our native country ... where we shall live among our equals and be more comfortable and happy, than we can be in our present situation."

By the early years of the republic, free blacks had already realized the futility of assimilation, even when their numbers were few. The moral catastrophe of slavery may have pricked white America's conscience, but there was no consideration of how free blacks might be assimilated into the society. Charity and vague plans for apprenticeships for blacks appear before the close of the eighteenth century, but despite the small number of free blacks, no consideration of political or social equality ever arose during this period. Without the economics of plantation labor, free blacks found themselves unwanted.

American attitudes toward blacks must be fully appreciated before the Constitution and its legacy can be understood. Edmund Morgan has written that the "majority of the convention" knew "they had thrown equality to the winds. But the sacrifice purchased the continuation of the union and made possible a national government. At the moment, those objectives seemed to be worth the price." But in fact equality was never sacrificed because the delegates never contemplated equality for blacks.

William Henry Seward, an anti-slavery unionist who later faced the ultimate test of disunion, considered the Constitution a distinctly commercial document. For Seward, political supremacy followed commercial ascendancy. In 1854 he expounded this approach in a Phi Beta Kappa address at Yale. The original colonies, he thought,

> needed free and mutual commerce among themselves, and some regulations for securing to each equal facilities of commerce among foreign countries. A union was necessary to the attainment of these ends. But citizens of each state were unwilling to surrender [their rights]. . . . So a federal central government was established, which is sovereign only in commerce at home and abroad, and in the necessary communications with other nations. . . .

In 1860, Seward identified the unanticipated cataclysmic events that had led to both astounding growth and the saga of cotton and race: "The circumstances which the [founding] fathers did not clearly foresee were two, namely: the reinvigoration of Slavery consequent on the increased consumption of cotton, and the extension of the national domain across the Mississippi, and these occurred before 1820."

Only later, when cotton had swept through the country, could an abolitionist pronounce the Constitution a "covenant with death." We do not know what would have happened had the convention failed. Most of the important delegates thought the alternative to unity was anarchy and civil war. In any event, with the advent of the cotton phenomenon, the Constitution sealed the fate of blacks in America, and it was bleak. Abraham Lincoln's earnest wish that slavery would "asphyxiate" itself and thus end without a "disruption of the union" drowned under a wave of cotton.

We can say, in short, that at the nation's founding, economics trumped equality. As the historian Joseph Ellis has noted, "No responsible statesman in the revolutionary era had ever contemplated, much less endorsed, a biracial America." All unions require compromises, and in the case of the Founding Fathers, these compromises came in the form of black slaves. One matter the thirteen states could agree on was the need for a flourishing free market. As a result, the founding document of the United States became the soil in which cotton could flourish. With each new cotton bloom, the need for black workers grew apace.

PART TWO

The Engine of American Growth, 1787–1861

But for the increased and constantly increasing importance of cotton to the industry of the world, those of the American States which were fitted by soil and climate to the production of this plant would not have become rooted in the belief that compulsory labor was essential to their prosperity. And had it not been for this belief, and for the discordance of views which grew out of it between the cotton-producing States and the other members of the American Union upon matters, both political and moral, of vital importance, the terrible convulsion which has shaken the Union to its centre could never have occurred. . . . —Frederick A. P. Barnard, Chancellor, University of Mississippi, 1856–1861; President, Columbia College, 1864–1889

CHAPTER TWO

Birth of an Obsession

 SEWARD'S two "circumstances"—cotton and land expansion—linked black America and cotton in a spiral that led to the fulfillment of his prophecy: the "irrepressible conflict" that was the Civil War. The sheer force of cotton's bruising impact altered the dynamic of America's economic, social, and political future. In the process, cotton and race-based slavery connected England, the American North, and the American South. Slave-produced cotton would eventually engulf the country in a Civil War that left 700,000 Americans dead and hundreds of thousands permanently maimed or injured. Without cotton the South, and eventually the Confederacy, would never have been taken seriously by itself, the North, or any foreign power. Without slave-produced cotton, there would have been no Civil War.

Following America's birth as an independent nation, domestic cotton production grew rapidly. In the 1780s a Liverpool merchant's son noted that English customs officials refused to believe that cotton was grown in America. The Liverpool youth later became a cotton importer, and as an eighty-six-year-old man in 1861 he warned his New Orleans agent of the folly of secession by the Southern states. Thus within one man's lifetime, cotton dramatically altered the world that had been inhabited by the delegates at the Constitutional Convention.

Cotton became the economic engine of the antebellum economy. Its story rests on a confluence of events: the revolution in the English textile industry, the invention of the cotton gin, the availability of massive American acreage suitable for cotton cultivation, and the existence and experience of a black slave labor force that could be moved about at will. These elements coalesced in the first decades of the nineteenth century and, along with an aggressive materialism and an intense racial prejudice, enabled cotton's emergence as a dominant force in the development of America.

Nowadays we see cotton mainly in its manufactured products—T-shirts, blue jeans, and towels—and in editorial-page rants about subsidies to cotton farmers. Although long absent from the center stage of business and economics, cotton continues to remind Americans of the stain of slavery and its legacy, and is generally allowed a brief appearance in historical narratives. Among American agricultural and industrial pursuits, only cotton still evokes a sad association. Despite harsh conditions, raising cattle, growing wheat or corn, mining coal, silver, or gold, or building railroads suggests energy, perseverance, and independence. The image of a black worker dragging a cotton sack through rows of cotton conjures up images of slavery or sharecropping. But to overlook cotton is to neglect the power of economics, money, and profit in American history.

Labor shortages—a clinical term—created slavery in colonial America. In order to exist over a long period of time in America, slavery needed an economic rationale. Psychological and social foundations alone could not sustain a slave culture. White-supremacy palaver was a mere rationalization of an economic system, not the basis of slavery. With no profitability or expected profitability, slaves in the North were gradually emancipated or sold south. The noncotton border states, faced with no economic justification for slavery, also began selling slaves to the cotton South. In the nineteenth century, only cotton provided the ideal medium for the growth of a vast slave culture. And so cotton, slavery, and race became intertwined. Responsibility for the system of slavery was pervasive—in the North, the South, and on the American frontier. In the first decades of the nineteenth century, the Western conception of race suited an economic system that subordinated black people to the cotton plant. Practically, pigmentation allowed slavery to exist on a large scale because black slaves could be distinguished from free whites. Without cotton, slavery would most probably have been headed for extinction.

The cotton empire of the nineteenth century became a truly integrated national and international operation, perhaps the first complex global business. Cotton connected the South with the North, the West, and Europe. Finance, politics, business structure, transportation, distribution, and international relations were all parts of the cotton web. A sophisticated business apparatus developed to service cotton production and the cotton textile industry. And because slavery was a crucial part of the cotton business, slaves could be bought and sold at a public market controlled by commercial law; slaves, a tragic form of collateral, could be financed.

The physical substance of cotton shifted as it left the hands of the men and women who weeded and picked it. Once cotton left the plantation, it became sanitized; quotidian balance sheets, receipts, and bills of lading obscured the taint of slavery. The amoral laws of supply and demand and the natural laws of weather, pests, and soil fertility combined to create a new, powerful, but risk-filled reality: the price per pound. The price of cotton, or the optimistic expectations for the price of cotton, in turn became an important determinant of America's destiny, influencing and even overcoming individual will and ethical behavior. When cotton was selling at four cents a pound in the 1840s, the prices of slaves plummeted. When cotton hit ten cents, slavery expanded. At two dollars per pound during the Civil War, the Union army was besieged by cotton-induced corruption. At forty cents after the Civil War, white Union army veterans moved south to grow cotton and implement a new labor system for freedmen. With cotton at eight cents, and faced with battalions of cotton-destroying insects, white Northerners declared their venture a failure and went home.

At the time of the Constitutional Convention, Britain imported no cotton from the United States. Her textile industry received three-quarters of its cotton from colonies owned by Britain, France, Holland, and Portugal. The rest arrived from Smyrna. By 1807, America shipped 171,267 bales of cotton to her former mother country, more than half the cotton that landed at English ports. Between 1787 and 1807, America's share of the British cotton import market went from zero to 60 percent. But America's cotton story—its unassailable monopoly—was just beginning.

*

The social and cultural histories of race and slavery have been written by skillful specialist historians like David Brion Davis and Ira Berlin. Here we concentrate on the role that money played in the development of cotton and the subsequent story of America's development.

America's production revolution paralleled the cotton textile revolution in Britain. Both were sparked and fostered by inventions and technological improvements. Although we may not wish to acknowledge it, the cotton boom was a perfect example of how machines and technology control human destiny. It also showed how the absence of technology—that is, the inability to replace humans for the cotton production tasks of weeding and picking—exacerbated the need for black labor. Over the course of the nineteenth century, human behavior adjusted to these new machines, resulting in a combustible combination of staggering economic growth, material improvement, and human misery.

The cotton business spread from the farm, to the merchant, to the mill, and to the consumer. Cotton influenced national politics and expansion policies, and spawned a vast and diverse network of interconnected relationships. Individuals migrated or were forced to migrate because of cotton. Commercial ties bound the North, South, and West while Europe was brought into the cotton web directly and indirectly through trade, finance, and diplomacy. Cotton demanded envy, fear, and respect.

From 1800 to 1860, cotton production provoked human and territorial expansion at a blistering pace. While it was not the sole factor in America's rise to economic power, the staple export commodity was, according to Douglass North, "the major independent influence on the evolving pattern of interregional trade. . . . In short, cotton was the most important proximate cause of expansion." David Cohn places cotton in an even larger perspective: "Cotton had indeed a phenomenal place in the whole American economy; a dominance never since attained by any single American product of factory and field."

During this period, the lure of cotton and the anticipation of wealth generated a significant internal migration into the new cotton states—Alabama, Mississippi, Louisiana, Arkansas, and Texas. The scope of the slave migration was enormous; the hardship was manifest and the separation of slave families devastating. A smaller but important migration of whites also followed the cotton trail. Some Northerners settled in the coastal cities where they became cotton middlemen. Others became planters, or educators, or entered the commercial world. The migration—black slaves, Southern and Northern whites—all moved predominantly to areas in which cotton could be grown or traded.

Properly run cotton farms were very much businesses, with trappings similar to Northern commercial ventures. The extensive records, journals, and official documents of the cotton business indicate an effort to understand profits and improve results. The detailed books of the larger plantations compared favorably to Northern businesses except for New England textile mills and large-scale transportation companies. Legal documentation of contracts and court proceedings show how the cotton business was conducted. Business infrastructure developed to handle local, regional, national, and international aspects of the cotton trade.

Cotton may have been powerful, but cotton production was risky. The statistics charting cotton's rise do not capture the very real perils that cotton planters faced. Potential failure was everywhere for a planter: price, weather, insects, debt, supply and demand, management, soil depletion, racial strife, and labor shortages.

Cultivation was time-consuming and labor-intensive. A cotton plant matures only if it has somewhere between 180 and 200 days of frost-free weather above approximately 60 degrees Fahrenheit. Before the invention of the cotton gin, production faced three bottlenecks—weeding, picking, and separating the cotton lint from seed—so that it took one slave an entire day to separate one pound of cotton. These slow procedures and the increase in demand led to high prices for cotton. In 1801 it sold for 44 cents per pound. As always, price generates interest and produces solutions.

In the nineteenth century, cotton seeds were planted in the spring, typically in April or May. When the seed sprouted, the young cotton plant had to be protected by hand-chopping the surrounding weeds. There then followed a couple of months when the plant did not need care. It produced flowers that became cotton bolls, which burst into cotton. The cotton was then picked from the boll by hand from late August through the fall. After picking, and before the advent of the cotton gin, the cotton seed had to be separated from the cotton fiber by hand. It was then packed into bales—which eventually became a standard five-hundred-pound unit—before shipment to mills.

As late as 1802 it was wrongly assumed that cotton could be profitably grown in "the Southern counties of New Jersey, and in the Northern counties of Delaware, Maryland and Virginia. . . . The Southern line of Pennsylvania continued eastward seems to be the northern boundary of what may be called the cotton region." Experience proved that the true boundaries were much farther south, a geographical limit imposed by climate. Only South Carolina, Georgia, Florida, Alabama, Tennessee, Mississippi, Arkansas, and Texas offered the needed temperatures for successful cotton growth.

Fertile soil and a certain amount of rainfall at appropriate intervals were also necessary for cotton to survive. The original cotton produced in America was a "black seed," long-staple variety known as Sea Island. Its cultivation was restricted by nature to a small area along the southeast coast. Later the short and hardy variety of "green seed" was developed for enormous tracts of land in the South and Southwest.

Cotton cultivation was highly labor-intensive in the eighteenth and nineteenth centuries. In addition to cultivation of the crop, labor was needed for ancillary functions such as maintenance and food preparation.

Cotton was harvested once a year; thus there were no cash revenues until the fall crop was sold. The planter could hope to pay his creditors just once a year. This payment schedule meant that cotton farming depended, then and now, on credit to finance production. In contrast, cash flow from a manufacturing concern arrives on a regular basis from the sale of product, so financing is more predictable, planning more precise, and financing more routine than in a cotton operation. Cotton wealth was therefore somewhat illusory as planters were constantly in debt and waiting for the next crop to pay off their loans.

*

The American cotton saga usually begins with a Northerner's invention, Eli Whitney's cotton gin. Cotton was grown in inconsequential amounts in America before Whitney constructed his crude contraption in 1793. A consummate Yankee tinkerer, he entered the cotton world accidentally. At age twenty-eight he was the oldest graduate of Yale College in the class of 1792. He did not excel in his studies and was in debt to his father.

Unable to find a job in Connecticut, Whitney sailed south in 1793 to work on a plantation as a tutor. He soon became transfixed by the problem of separating cotton from seed. After he was hired by another transplanted Yale graduate, Phineas Miller, Whitney devoted himself to finding a solution. At Miller's plantation in Georgia, the impecunious tutor turned his curiosity and mechanical aptitude to the enigmatic, reluctant, and beautiful cotton boll. In a now-famous letter to his father dated September 11, 1793, Whitney related the events that led him to his version of the cotton gin.

> I involuntarily happened to be thinking on the subject [of cotton production] and struck out a plan of a Machine [to remove the cotton seed from the fiber]. . . . I conclude to relinquish my school and turn my attention to perfecting the Machine. I made one before I came away which required the labor of one man to turn it and with which one man will clean ten times as much as he can in any other way before known. . . .

Whitney envisioned his future rewards:

> It is generally said by those who know anything about it, that I shall make a Fortune by it. . . . I am now so sure of success that ten thousand dollars, if I saw the money counted out to me, would not tempt me to give up my right and relinquish the object.

Whitney built a model that "will do more than fifty men." A man could now "clean" fifty pounds of cotton per day rather than one pound; yet the cotton gin was remarkably simple. Essentially, wire hooks were attached to a cylinder that pulled cotton through a wire separator. Because the cotton seed could not pass through the screen, the lint was separated from the seed, gathered by a carding device, and then compressed into bales. Although there are disputes over Whitney's claim to be the inventor of the cotton gin, his name has come to be forever linked with the machine that revolutionized cotton production.

Whitney's application for a patent to Secretary of State Thomas Jefferson, submitted in November 1793, was approved by President George Washington on March 14, 1794. With his partner, Phineas Miller, Whitney manufactured the machines in a factory in New Haven, Connecticut. By the summer of 1797, thirty of the Whitney gins were in use in Georgia. Whitney did more than sell the machines; he licensed them for a royalty of one-third of the cleaned cotton.

This fairy tale ended abruptly. Patent infringements and lawsuits plagued Whitney, and the simplicity of his gin made it easy to copy. The invention spread immediately. Daniel Clark from Natchez, Mississippi, who heard of the cotton gin from a Georgian in 1795, sketched a design from the Georgian's description. He then gave the impressionistic rendering to his slave Barclay, a skilled craftsman, who proceeded to build the first cotton gin in Mississippi. Slave mechanics were responsible for many of the advancements in cotton production.

Whitney's factory burned, and his close encounter with bankruptcy left him fearful of debt. He probably never made any money on the cotton gin. His mechanical breakthrough merely caused him anxiety and dashed his hopes of financial reward. In one of many insults, Whitney's application for renewal of his patent in 1812 was denied by the government.

Despite creating the machine that propelled slavery's prospects, Whitney appeared to have no interest in the "peculiar institution." One of his biographers judged, "There is no evidence that Whitney cared a fig about slavery one way or another." This clever inventor, absorbed by work, inventions, and money, turned a blind eye to the people who operated his new machine.

Cotton gins were consistently improved by the addition of "saws" to handle increasing capacity. Between 1794 and 1803 nine patents for improvements to the cotton gin were granted. New Englanders played a significant role in their manufacture. In 1806 a Massachusetts mechanic, Eleazer Carver, traveled to the South and viewed firsthand the cotton gin and cotton production. The next year he began making superior gins in Natchez. He moved his manufacturing operation to Bridgewater, Massachusetts, and by 1860 was producing a thousand cotton gins annually. Another Bridgewater cotton gin manufacturer, Bates, Hyde & Company, was selling similar numbers of gins. Thus abolitionist Massachusetts became a chief supplier of cotton gins to be worked by slaves. The New Hampshire native Daniel Pratt built a cotton gin factory in Prattville, Alabama, in 1833, which by 1858 was producing as many as nine hundred cotton gins a year for sale in Mississippi, Louisiana, and Texas.

*

Almost simultaneous with the birth of Whitney's cotton gin, the astounding growth of Britain's textile industry came to fruition in the early part of the nineteenth century, creating a continuing brisk demand for American cotton. The familiar and remarkable list of improvements and inventions in textile machinery began in the 1730s and amounted to a revolution. Indeed, the Industrial Revolution itself largely began with the textile industry in Britain.

Advances in spinning and weaving transplanted the industry from the cottage to the fully integrated factory or cotton mill. In the process, mill towns and cities arose. John Kay's flying shuttle (1733) made weaving faster. Richard Arkwright's water frame enhanced spinning. James Hargreaves's spinning jenny (1770) powered one hundred spindles at once. Samuel Crompton's "mule" (1790) further advanced spinning. Edmund Cartwright's power loom (1785) balanced spinning and weaving. These advances produced enormous cost savings, especially when combined with water power and James Watt's steam engine (by 1800).

Here was the first example of a modern large-scale industry, one that contributed significantly to England's growth as a dominant nineteenth-century power. The British textile industry was attended by capital formation, labor consequences, economic growth, and political ramifications. It was the first major modern industry to move across the globe in search of lower production costs and larger markets. It also spawned its legendary critics—Karl Marx and his colleague, the cotton magnate Friedrich Engels—who outlined an alternative economic system. Engels worked in his family's cotton business, Ermen and Engels, in Manchester until the age of forty-nine, when he retired with sufficient assets to support himself and Marx.

The numbers are compelling. In the eighteenth century cotton cloth was more expensive than wool, linen, or silk. Before the industrialization of cotton textile production, it required twelve to fourteen man-days to produce one pound of thread versus one to two man-days for wool and six man-days for silk. But by 1861 the price of cotton cloth had fallen to 1 percent of its 1784 price. Europeans quickly switched to cotton clothing. Between 1783 and 1883, once-dominant wool dropped from 77 percent of the European textile market to 20 percent; correspondingly, cotton rose from 6 percent to 73 percent.

This staggering shift was accompanied by a virtually insatiable demand for raw cotton. Valuable and "practically imperishable," it rivaled gold in settling trade imbalances between America and Great Britain. Raw cotton, in fact, according to the historian James Scherer, "possessed more of the attributes of a legal tender than anything produced by human labor except gold."

The spur of England's economic growth was the Industrial Revolution, which was closely linked to cotton textiles. On the eve of the American Civil War, Britain's cotton mills employed 500,000 workers; related industries—"hosiery, cotton-lace, and sewed muslin factories"—employed another 400,000, a total of 900,000 direct "operatives." Peripheral businesses—"warehousemen, stevedores, mechanics, bakers and small tradespeople of the cotton districts"—employed another 150,000. Estimates of three dependents for each employee yield a total of some 4 million people who depended on the cotton industry, or almost one-fifth of England's population of 22 million. Shipping volumes reflected these numbers. Liverpool shipping tonnage, chiefly due to the cotton industry, increased more than tenfold, from 459,719 tons in 1801 to 4,977,272 in 1861.

Cotton was the single most important contributor to Britain's economic power and rise to preeminence as a world empire. "No industry," Eric Hobsbawm writes, "could compare in importance with cotton in this first phase of British industrialization" between 1780 and 1840. Between 1815 and 1840, cotton textiles constituted roughly half of all British exports. In the 1830s, raw cotton accounted for 20 percent of all British imports. Great Britain's trade balances and much of its shipping industry depended on cotton.

In 1860, Britain's vital cotton industry "appeared to underlie the whole industrial and economic system." The dependence was well known to contemporaries and well chronicled during the decade before the Civil War. The cotton business consisted of three parts—textile exports, domestic consumption, and the re-export of raw cotton. In 1859 the cotton figures were £48.2 million of exported goods, £25 million for domestic use, and £4 million in re-exported cotton out of total exports of £130 million. Forty percent of Britain's total exports were derived from cotton. In 1860 cotton sales amounted to £80 million. Of a total export of £164 million, cotton textiles and cotton re-exports amounted to £55 million, with £24 million consumed at home. The overall cotton industry production figures for export and domestic markets have even greater impact when considering the industry's massive employment in a defined region, Lancashire.

Britain's industrial demands required an enormous supply of cotton. Below we can see how, during the decades leading to the Civil War, Britain's cotton needs exploded.

British and American Raw Cotton Trade (Pounds)

	BRITISH COTTON IMPORTS	AMERICAN COTTON EXPORTS TO BRITAIN (with % of total British cotton imports)
1800	56,010,000	16,180,000 (28%)
1830	263,961,000	201,947,000 (77%)
1840	592,488,000	477,521,000 (81%)
1850	663,577,000	474,705,000 (72%)
1860	1,390,939,000	1,230,607,000 (88%)

The numbers reveal an absolute dependency on America for slave-produced raw cotton.

The enormous demand of the mother country, and to a lesser extent France, was the essential element in America's thirst to grow more and more cotton, and in the South's concurrent growth in its sense of importance. Britain tried unsuccessfully to free itself from the combination of American cotton and slavery. The British feared that a slave uprising or civil war might disrupt their cotton pipeline. British businessmen and politicians looked within the empire to India as a possible alternative source—but they did not like what they saw. The Manchester Chamber of Commerce, home of Britain's cotton mills, sent a team to study the potential for Indian cotton cultivation. Parliament had a standing committee to evaluate the use of Indian cotton to displace American imports.

Despite having cultivated cotton for thousands of years, India could not compete with the United States. The dirty Indian cotton, known by its epithet "surat," produced 20 percent less yarn than American cotton. Mill workers found it difficult to spin. Indian peasants who cultivated the cotton were bound to moneylenders and had little incentive to increase production. Transportation costs were high, for India lacked railroads and navigable rivers to facilitate the movement of goods. As a result, cotton had to be transported by pack animals over long distances. To grow inferior Indian cotton, it took five times as much land as in America. The backwardness of the Indian peasant was a major factor. When British government representatives attempted to introduce a modern iron plow to the subcontinent, the primitive, tradition-bound farmers were overcome with reverence. Their wooden agricultural implements paled by comparison. The peasants, "when the [British] agent's back was turned, took . . . [the iron plow], painted it red, set it up on end and worshipped it." It was no surprise that India's cotton exports to Britain barely rose from £50 million in 1800 to £60 million in 1860.

The complicated, fractious, and combustible relationship between America and Britain influenced domestic U.S. decisions about cotton and race. It should be remembered that the "Star-Spangled Banner," the American national anthem, was written in 1812 when America was in a "perilous fight" with the British, who were launching the "rockets" and "bombs" referred to in the song. During the nineteenth century, Britain was America's enemy as well as a major trading partner, a competitor for its Western land, and an occasional ally.

CHAPTER THREE

Land Expansion and White Migration to the Old Southwest

BY THE early nineteenth century, the ingredients for a massive cotton boom—production technology, trading and financing apparatus, high prices, labor, cheap land, and strong demand—were in place. The invention and widespread use of the cotton gin dovetailed neatly with a growing British desire for cotton: supply and demand grew in fortuitous tandem, and the results were quickly evident. Of the original thirteen colonies, only South Carolina and Georgia became significant cotton producers; the real growth came from western Georgia and from newer states—Florida, Tennessee, Alabama, Mississippi, Louisiana, Arkansas, and Texas. Other crops—rice, indigo, and tobacco—remained in cultivation but provided little competition for cotton in terms of expansion.

The response to the high price of cotton was immediate. A functioning cotton gin was operating in Natchez, on the cotton frontier, as early as 1795. In 1805, François Michaux, a French scientific observer, noted that a small family in Tennessee made a significant profit of $212 on a four-acre cotton farm when cotton brought 18 cents per pound. In 1807 a 600-acre plantation generated a net profit of $4,735, or a 22 percent return on a small investment of $21,000 in 30 slaves, land, and a gin. Rich, inexpensive land in Louisiana—one of cotton's many frontiers—selling at $2 to $4 per acre permitted large farms that by 1812 were growing crops valued at $20,000 to $30,000. As early as 1800 it was possible for a Natchez planter to earn ten times as much as a hardworking New England farmer. In a good year his profits might be 30 percent. These individual results and expectations foreshadowed an increase in Georgia's cotton production from 3,138 bales in 1790 to 177,824 bales in 1810. Just as significant, we should not be surprised to learn that during the same period the Georgia slave population grew from 29,000 to 105,000.

Early correspondence reveals how rising cotton prices and the lure of easy money drew settlers to the western reaches of cotton country. John Steele, a Virginia planter, was just such a price-conscious opportunist. In 1798 he moved to Natchez with his personal slave, George, whose family meanwhile remained in Virginia. Steele's paternalism was at first apparent when he urged his brother to provide warm clothing for his slaves back home. He inquired about "my black people," mentioning that "George enjoys good health but was anxious to hear from Milly and his Children." In 1799, Steele noted that cotton was fetching 25 cents per pound, creating an enormous profit for him. He was moved to describe his cotton "like driving snow as it comes from the Gin." Eventually Steele's paternalism succumbed to "cotton fever" as he frantically pressed his brother to sell property in Richmond in exchange for "two Negroes. . . . They would sell here for 1000 or 1,200 . . . [per slave] this year." His personal obligations extended only to George, whose family he felt "bound from humanity to hold together." He was less caring about other slaves he needed in his quest for white gold.

The availability of cheap land with the appropriate temperature, soil, and rainfall was essential for the explosive growth of cotton cultivation and slavery. Proximity to navigable rivers was also necessary to move the crops to market. In the early nineteenth century a huge tract of just this sort of land belonged to France, and it happened that French foreign entanglements proved especially fortuitous for American interests. France owned more than 800,000 square miles west of the Mississippi—a tract twice the size of the original thirteen colonies. The vital commercial port of New Orleans, the source of much trade friction, lay in this "Louisiana Territory."

Thomas Jefferson eagerly wanted New Orleans for its strategic position at the mouth of the Mississippi River, allowing control of commerce from the American hinterlands. Jefferson empowered James Monroe and Robert Livingston to negotiate with Napoleon for the purchase of either New Orleans or Florida for $9,375,000. Aware that the presence of American settlers in the Louisiana Territory would bring pressure to bear, Jefferson gave his delegates "implicit authority to use the threat of forcible expansion."

Napoleon surprisingly offered not only New Orleans but the entire French territory, which he considered "entirely lost." International forces beyond America's control set in motion the famous real estate purchase. The French emperor presciently added that the acquisition "strengthens forever the power of the United States; and I [Napoleon] have just given England a maritime rival that will sooner or later humble her pride."

The final terms included a payment of $11,250,000 to France for the land and the American government's assumption of $3,750,000 of claims by American citizens against France. The total purchase price, $15 million, was financed by the issue of American government bonds with a 6 percent coupon and a maturity of fifteen years—terms that indicate an international acceptance of American credit that would have been unthinkable ten years earlier.

Unwittingly, Alexander Hamilton, who opposed slavery, facilitated its expansion along with cotton. Through his able efforts, the young American nation had established a stable financial system that enabled the country, using credit, to double its size and gain control of the Mississippi River, a prime boulevard for the transport of cotton. By 1803 more than half of U.S. debt and Bank of the United States shares were held in Europe. Those securities were quoted on the London and Amsterdam stock exchanges. Dutch investors bought the Louisiana Purchase bonds from the French, then resold them to the British, Napoleon's enemies. Eventually the British owned $9.25 million in U.S. bonds and the Dutch $1.5 million. Ironies abounded: Thomas Jefferson, who abhorred government debt, a strong central government, and Hamilton's banking plans, used Hamilton's financial system to purchase the Louisiana Territory.

Cotton was the impetus for the stampede to settle the fertile lands that became known as the Old Southwest, a territory that included present-day western Georgia, Alabama, Louisiana, Mississippi, and parts of Arkansas and Texas. Only later would a new group of arid cattle states be referred to as the Southwest. But, with the minor exception of sugar, none of the major staple crops—rice, tobacco, indigo—mattered in the migration to the Old Southwest. Although its coronation was not yet official, cotton was the word on most people's lips. Native Americans who occupied the land stood in the way of America's commercial and territorial empire, but no obstacle, foreign or domestic, could halt the advancing Americans. The Indians were simply removed. Their forced migration, of which much has been written, occurred simultaneously with the cotton-induced migrations of whites and slaves.

In 1820, Indians still controlled two-thirds of Mississippi. Two years before, with cotton selling for thirty-four cents a pound, cotton fever had been particularly virulent. In that year Generals Andrew Jackson and Thomas Hinds, veteran Indian fighters, met at Doak's Stand, Mississippi, with the Indian chiefs Pushmataha (who had raised a regiment to fight for the Americans in the War of 1812), Apuckshunubbee, and Mushulatubbee, and several hundred Choctaws. For three weeks the Americans hosted a grand party. Twenty thousand dollars' worth of beef, corn, and liquor was used to entice the Indians to move. Jackson offered thirteen million acres in Arkansas and Oklahoma in return for five million acres in central and western Mississippi. He tried to coax the Indians with supplies of food, guns, and ammunition. When they proved unwilling, Jackson did not mince words. The Indians, he said, had three choices—voluntary departure, extinction, or "forcible removal." The Indians blinked.

Land-hungry settlers were not satisfied. During Andrew Jackson's presidency, the Mississippi legislature in 1830 passed laws that removed the "autonomous rights" of Indians within the state. This led to the Treaty of Dancing Rabbit Creek, which was negotiated by the young Choctaw chief and slave-owning cotton planter Greenwood Leflore. When the Choctaws and their chiefs met with U.S. officials, Leflore realized the futility of resistance. He ceded all the Choctaw lands in return for the western Indian Territory plus grants to some individuals who wished to stay. The Chickasaws ceded Mississippi land in 1832 via the Treaty of Pontotoc.

After the removal of their Indian inhabitants, immense tracts of land were made available via public auction. These government auctions and the movement of people west were an American, not a Southern, phenomenon. The Southern aspect, however, was particularly driven by cotton. The "land grab" chronicled by A. M. Sakolski in *The Great American Land Bubble* was raucous, crude, and often corrupt. And it embodied an ever-present American trait—speculation. In 1831 the land auctions disposed of 2,777,857 acres for $3,557,024; the numbers ballooned to 20,074,871 acres for $25,167,833 in 1836, before plummeting to 5,601,103 acres for $7,007,523 in 1837.

In 1834 the French observer Michel Chevalier was surprised by the ubiquitous urge of Americans to speculate:

Everybody is speculating and everything has become an object of speculation. From Maine to the Red River, the whole country is an immense [casino]. . . . The American, essentially practical in his views, will never speculate on tulips. . . . The principal objects of speculation are those subjects which chiefly occupy the calculating minds of the Americans, that is to say, cotton, land, city and town lots, banks and railroads.

Nowhere was America's material and speculative nature more evident than in the cotton South. Money poured in from the American North and Europe to purchase land and slaves. Southern planters and outsiders alike were infected with cotton fever. The land auctions, near riots of excess, were fueled by growing amounts of capital chasing inflated cotton prices and the promise of riches. Payment for land was made in paper money dubbed "rag money," issued by unlicensed, unregulated state "wildcat" banks. The expression "doing a land office business" originated during this boisterous process, which witnessed the participation of "veritable mobs." Bribery was common. Collusion was widespread, with bidders agreeing to withhold offers for certain sections.

Between 1835 and 1837, for example, virtually all of northern Mississippi, nearly half the state, was sold by public auction. In the same period major offerings were also taking place in Illinois, Indiana, Michigan, and Wisconsin. But in Mississippi and Alabama, cotton was the impetus for land sales. Northern enterprises purchased half of the 1.5 million acres of the original Chickasaw allotments in northern Mississippi—the American Land Company (210,000 acres); the New York and Mississippi Land Company (206,000 acres); and the Boston and New York Chickasaw Land Company, the Boston and Mississippi Cotton Land Company, and the New York, Mississippi, and Arkansas Land Company (334,000 acres). Philip Hone, a successful merchant and mayor of New York, noted in his diary in April 1835, "Money is plenty, business is brisk, the staple commodity of the country [cotton] has enriched all those through whose hands it has passed, the merchant, the mechanic, and proprietor of land all rejoice in the result of last year's operations." These financial coalitions had no intention of settling the land or farming it; their motive was pure speculation. Their hope was to hold the land for as short a period as possible and sell at a profit. The lure of cotton had grown far beyond the value of the crop itself. It involved places far removed from the endless acres where cotton was cultivated, and people who had nothing to do with the cultivation itself.

The initial fervor, predictably, did not necessarily lead to riches. The Georgia Company Association purchased land for $23,000 and resold it within two years for $50,000. Local Mississippians purchased 49,440 acres through the Pontotoc and Holly Springs Land Company from the New York and Mississippi Land Company after the price had risen from $1.25 an acre to $2.50. They could not sell the land, so it reverted back to the New York and Mississippi Land Company. Millions of acres purchased in this fashion eventually were returned to the federal government. After an initially profitable start, the New York and Mississippi Land Company floundered during and after the Civil War. Its final 5,000 acres were auctioned at public sale in 1888. The returns over the life of the company were estimated by one analyst at a mere 2.4 percent per year. The notorious Boston-based American Land Company, founded by New Yorkers, made 70 percent of its land purchases in "cotton lands in the southwestern states at or near the Government price," in lands "lately occupied by the Chickasaw Indians." Sakolski recorded the demise of the American Land Company, which "went to pieces" in the financial panic of 1837.

The wild orgy of land speculation in the 1830s was massive and national in scope. Eastern men "during this period poured over thirty million dollars into Mississippi alone." From 1833 to 1836, total federal land sales in Mississippi amounted to 8,331,581 acres. The state of Alabama petitioned Congress at one point to stop the federal auctions because of the speculators' fraudulent behavior. In 1834 the U.S. Senate passed five resolutions to investigate frauds in Mississippi and Alabama. Mississippi's Senator Robert J. Walker attempted to pass legislation to restrict land sales. Bemoaning speculation that "drains the east of millions of capital," he noted that in 1836 the government had auctioned land the size of New England.

The influence of cotton was not limited to agricultural lands; the crop's expansion also created cities. Older cities like Charleston, Savannah, and New Orleans were touched indelibly by the surge of cotton commerce. A traveler in 1827 described a scene at Southern ports:

A plague o' this Cotton.

When I took my last walk along the wharves in Charleston, [I] saw them piled up with mountains of Cotton. . . . I returned to the Planters Hotel, where I found four daily newspapers, as well as the conversation of the boarders, teeming with Cotton! Cotton!! Cotton!!! . . . I crossed over to Mobile in a small steam-boat loaded up to the top of the smoke stack with cotton. . . . In the three days that I was there, boarding with about one hundred cotton factors, cotton merchants, and cotton planters, I must have heard the word cotton pronounced 3,000 times.

From Mobile, I went to New Orleans in a schooner and she was stuffed full of cotton.—I don't know how many hundred thousand bales of cotton there were in New Orleans. . . . From New Orleans to the mouth of the Tennessee River, we passed about thirty steam-boats, and more than half of them were laden with cotton—they calculate on 40 or 50,000 bales of cotton going from Nashville this season. After seeing, hearing, and dreaming of nothing but cotton for seventy days and seventy nights, I began to anticipate relief.

The older cities were joined in this commerce by the inland Mississippi River port of Memphis, known as the Child of Cotton. In 1826, before the cotton territory opened, the port of Memphis handled only 300 bales of cotton. Memphis's population grew from 1,799 in 1840 to 22,623 in 1860; taxable wealth increased from $679,200 to $18,297,545. The extraordinary growth can be traced to the rapid expansion of the city's cotton trade from $1.4 million in traded goods to $16 million during the period. By 1860, Memphis was on the move commercially. Now the largest inland cotton port, it shipped 400,000 bales of cotton a year.

Cotton also brought the railroads to the South. Memphis's Mississippi River location made it a water transportation hub for the South and the West, and it looked to augment its status with railroads. The Memphis and Ohio Company was founded in 1842; the Mississippi and Tennessee was chartered in 1852 to connect Memphis with New Orleans; the Memphis and Little Rock was begun in the 1850s; the Memphis and Nashville commenced in the 1850s; the Memphis and Charleston was completed in 1857. Further planned extensions to Cincinnati would have diverted Western agricultural products to the South. Between 1845 and 1860, $60 million was spent on railroad construction in the South.

The Child of Cotton exuded confidence in the prosperous 1850s. Rainey's City Directory captured Memphis's optimism and dynamism: "The steamers on the rivers are grander than the stateliest ships that rode the deep a few years ago. . . . We are arriving at a dizzy height . . . our gaze is over the immensity of the Southwest, which our railroad arms will soon comprehend." Dreams of the future included industry. The *Memphis Commercial Appeal* in 1847 urged the city to become the "Manchester of the South."

Meanwhile, in the newly settled lands, the white emigrants faced enormous obstacles. David Cohn described them:

Men might flame with malaria and die of yellow fever. They might encounter virgin, vine-entangled forests that had to be removed with fire and ax; great swamps and dangerous flooding rivers. Their families might have to live in clearings amid lonely wilderness. They might lack labor and capital; endure where there were few roads and no railroads. It did not matter. Cotton marched on.

The tribulations of these white settlers paled in comparison to the forced march of slaves to labor in the cotton fields.

The seaboard states provided much of the planter emigration to the Old Southwest. Restless and mobile whites from South Carolina and Georgia were eager to head to the new cotton land. After 1800, half the native white residents of South Carolina left the state. Its population grew by 15.5 percent in the 1820s and by only 2 percent in the 1830s. Twenty-five percent of native-born Georgians no longer lived in the state after 1850. By that year Alabama could claim immigrants from South Carolina (48,663), North Carolina (28,521), Virginia (10,387), and Georgia (58,997). A total of 388,000 Virginians and 128,000 Marylanders were living outside their native state. Mississippi during this period had not one political leader born in the state. In 1850 only 12 percent of the farmers in Mississippi had been born in the state.

In one of the more far-flung examples of emigration, the Tait family moved from Great Britain to the Chesapeake region before heading farther south and settling in Georgia. In 1818, Charles Tait, who had been a judge and a U.S. senator, dispatched his son James to Alabama to purchase land at public auction. The father wanted "Fertility, Salubrity & Navigation." The Taits spoke of "land and slaves," but more often they spoke of "cotton and slaves." The Tait family eventually settled in cotton country in 1819, on the banks of the Alabama River. They were a restless lot. Charles's grandson and namesake, Charles W. Tait, and his wife, Louisa, displayed their independence by moving to Texas in the 1840s.

The most ruthless of the Old Southwestern landowners was the wealthy South Carolinian Wade Hampton. From humble beginnings as the son of a small tobacco farmer, by 1799 Hampton had accumulated land that produced cotton worth $90,000. By 1807 his farm yielded 1,500 bales. He was an inveterate land speculator whose grasp eventually reached into Georgia, Florida, Tennessee, Kentucky, Mississippi, and Louisiana. In 1811 he managed to put down a slave rebellion in which 60 of 500 slaves were killed. He "ordered 'strung aloft' on poles" twenty heads of the rebels.

Numerous anecdotes and myths about the creation of cotton wealth in the Old Southwest circulated around the nation. Cheap land in the newly admitted states of Louisiana (1812), Mississippi (1817), and Alabama (1819) tempted the intrepid emigrant. A traveler in Alabama noted that one planter had purchased land for $15,000 that in just two years was worth $60,000. The land allegedly returned an income of $50,000 per year. Talk of 35 percent returns on cotton farms was common, feeding the dreams of aspiring plantation owners.

Both "Alabama fever" and "Mississippi madness" were variations of the cotton wealth virus. A Northern traveler in the South wrote in 1834 of the Southern obsession: "To sell cotton in order to buy negroes—to make more cotton to buy more negroes, 'ad infinitum,' is the aim and direct tendency of all the operations of the thorough going cotton planter; his whole soul is wrapped up in the pursuit." In 1857 the Northerner James Stirling wrote that "Slaves and cotton are the law and the prophets of the men of the South." Even those who did not emigrate were sorely tempted. The planter and South Carolina senator James Henry Hammond observed that "nearly every one of the young men with whom I was brought up" moved to the Old Southwest. He resisted with difficulty: "I have been trying to get over my desire for a western plantation, but every time I see a man who has been there it puts me in a fever. . . . I must go West and plant."

Statements like these were scribbled in innumerable letters and diaries. Cotton's magnetic pull created a peculiarly American cultural phenomenon. The foundational American goal of making money was realized or anticipated by moving south and west into the cotton fields.

The lure of cotton did not discriminate, and before long Northerners joined the white migration. By 1860, 360,000 white Northerners were living in the South. As cotton traders, especially from New York and New England, found their way to the cotton ports, they became "prominent out of all proportion to their numbers." Mobile, which exported cotton worth $18 million and imported goods worth $451,000 in 1850, counted 10 percent of its population from New York and New England.

In the New Orleans of 1850, 9,461 or 25 percent of American-born white residents came from Northern states. The Pennsylvanian James

Robb came to New Orleans in 1837 to seek his fortune. He established a brokerage firm, founded the Robb and Hoge Bank, managed the New Orleans Gas Light and Banking Company, established the Bank of James Robb, and had substantial involvement in the New Orleans, Jackson and Great Northern Railroad. Northerners started three of New Orleans's newspapers, the *Picayune*, the *Crescent*, and the *Commercial Bulletin*. The state banks—the Bank of Louisiana, the Louisiana State Bank, and the City Bank—as well as four of eight local banks were run by Northerners.

CHAPTER FOUR

The Movement of Slaves
to the Cotton States

AS WITH much of American industrial history, the dreams of the cotton obsessed could be realized only through the toil of laborers. Accepted by the delegates of the Constitutional Convention, the system of slavery occupied a curious place in the new republic. The Founding Fathers could not have foreseen how cotton would change everything.

By the 1820s the "peculiar institution" was firmly and forever linked with America's latest infatuation. Slavery expanded only to those areas in which cotton could be grown. Without cotton, slavery was headed for extinction. The historian Frederick Jackson Turner acknowledged that "never in history, perhaps, was an economic force more influential upon the life of a people. This economic transformation resuscitated slavery from a moribund condition to a vigorous and aggressive life." The scholar and future president Woodrow Wilson agreed: "Before this tremendous development of cotton culture had taken place, slavery had hardly more than habit and the perils of emancipation to support it in the South."

As demand for cotton grew, slavery was considered indispensable as a means of maximizing profit for this labor-intensive staple crop. Equally important, as we shall see, slaves could be financed—that is, purchased on credit. In financial parlance this is called leverage. Planters had one objective: increased cotton production. Arguments about the optimum size of a cotton farm are irrelevant because of slavery's financing characteristic. Simply put, the goal was more cotton, which called for financing the purchase of more land and more slaves. Because a mechanical means of solving cotton's production needs did not exist until the mid-twentieth century, cotton demanded an endless supply of black bodies as long as the price of cotton permitted financing.

The Northerner Frederick Law Olmsted, author of *The Cotton Kingdom* (1861), attributed slavery's growth to cotton production that had been unleashed by Eli Whitney's gin. For Olmsted, "Whitney's invention has, to all appearance, strengthened the hold of slavery a thousand times more than all labors directly intended for that purpose." Olmsted added, however, "The subjection of the negroes of the South to the mastership of white [owners] . . . [was] justifiable and necessary." He advocated a form of apprenticeship for slaves that would prepare them for later freedom. He thought that if gold were discovered in Mississippi, free whites would flock there and slavery would "be practically abolished in that State within two years," as people switched from the "cotton culture." For Olmsted, "slavery . . . [was] an unfortunate circumstance for which the people of the South were in no . . . [way] to blame, and the abolition of which was no more immediately practicable than the abrogation of hospitals, penitentiaries, and boarding schools. . . ."

One historian of cotton, W. B. Hammond, thought that

> the expanding geographical distribution of slaves and of cotton cultivation affords the most striking evidence of the close connection of the two institutions that can be had; for the gradual spread of slavery over the map coinciding almost exactly with those suitable for the extension of cotton: as if this plant-king were literally leading the human captives in his train.

But because the importation of slaves to the U.S. had been largely banned by 1808, this "train" of labor had to come from inside U.S. borders. The result was a dramatic internal migration of slaves that mirrored the movement of whites.

Planters in the Eastern slave states that did not produce cotton soon began selling slaves to the Old Southwest. By 1823, Delaware, Maryland, and Virginia were selling between 10,000 and 15,000 slaves per year to the cotton states. In 1836, Virginia, according to one "probably exaggerated" source, sent 120,000 slaves to cotton country. Eighty thousand may have traveled with their owners. Virginia's cotton production, always negligible, had peaked in 1826. By 1850, 74,031 plantations in the United States raised five or more bales of cotton; only 198 of those farms were in Virginia. So it should come as no surprise that Virginia, like other noncotton states, recognized the relative unprofitability of slaves and the corresponding opportunity to sell them to cotton land. George Washington's nephew Bushrod Washington, a justice on the Supreme Court, in 1821 sold 54 of his 90 slaves. In 1832, Professor Thomas Dew noted that "Virginia is, in fact, a negro raising state for other States."

Between 1830 and 1850 the slave population of Maryland declined and that of Virginia remained steady while Louisiana more than doubled, Alabama nearly trebled, and Mississippi quintupled their numbers of slaves. The slave migrations to Alabama, Mississippi, and Louisiana were staggering—155,000 in the 1820s, 288,000 in the 1830s, 189,000 in the 1840s, and 250,000 in the 1850s.

In the short span of time between statehood in 1817 and 1860, Mississippi became the largest cotton-producing state in the nation. Mississippi's population rose in lockstep with burgeoning cotton production. The white population of the state grew from 5,179 in 1800 to 354,000 in 1860; the slave population from 3,500 to 436,631. Slaves outnumbered whites by 55 percent to 45 percent. Cotton production in Mississippi exploded from nothing in 1800 to 535.1 million pounds in 1859. Alabama's development was quite similar and on the eve of the Civil War ranked second with 440.5 million pounds.

By 1860 the slave population of the South had grown to 4 million, comprising a full third of the region's 12 million inhabitants; in 1790 there had been only 700,000 slaves in the United States population of 4 million. Estimates vary of the number of slaves in cotton agriculture. One source calculates that by 1850 three-quarters of the slave population was involved with cotton; another suggests 64 percent. The 1850 census delineated the slave population among agricultural sectors:

cotton farms accounted for 73 percent of the slave population, tobacco 14 percent, sugar 6 percent, rice 5 percent, and hemp 2 percent. These figures need explanation because only 38 percent of slave labor was expended on actual cotton production. The remainder of cotton's slave labor involved ancillary functions such as corn and livestock production, land improvement chores, other crops, and home manufacturing—all tasks that were necessitated by and supported cotton cultivation. Cotton, the money crop, was the raison d'être of these farms. Within a half-century, an insignificant crop had become the driving force behind America's most horrific institution.

As cotton demanded a greater and greater share of America's slaves, the general price of slave men and women increased substantially from 1800 to the eve of the Civil War. Periodically prices declined, but the trend was continually higher. Rising prices sustained this routine but tragic market in human beings. In 1790 the approximate price for a prime slave field hand was $200; by 1850 it was $1,200, and in 1860, $1,800. There were large price swings. In 1810 the price of field hands in New Orleans rose to $900 before collapsing during the War of 1812. Field hands brought $1,700 to $2,000 in New Orleans in 1819 before falling below $700 in 1823. The financial panic of 1837 forced prices down to $500. They remained low until the late 1840s, when an upward trend resumed.

The price of slaves tracked the price of cotton closely over time. The price of a slave was generally thought to be ten thousand times the price of cotton. Thus 10 cents per pound for cotton would yield a slave value of $1,000. In the 1850s, speculative fervor prompted higher slave prices that ignored this ratio. A Georgian noticed the change and predicted a price decline: "The old rule of pricing a negro by the price of cotton by the pound . . . does not seem to be regarded. Negroes are 25 per cent higher now with cotton at ten and a half cents than they were two or three years ago when it was worth fifteen and sixteen cents. . . . A reversal will come soon." The price of a slave in Virginia was lower than that for a slave in New Orleans, reflecting the closeness of the slave to actual cotton production.

Planters evaluating their labor and production used the language of investors or speculators. The terminology, price data, analysis, and legal apparatus surrounding the slave system eerily resembled the nomenclature of ordinary markets in stocks, commodities, and goods. When casually valuing human property in 1818, the young planter Sam Steer discussed investment options with his wealthy uncle. The older man recommended the purchase of shares in the Mississippi State Bank. The advice was not heeded by his nephew, who theorized that the price of cotton meant that slaves were a better investment: "White cotton can command from 2[0] to 30 cts per lb: Negroes will yield a much larger income than any Bank dividends."

According to the financial historian Robert Sobel, during periods of ebullient cotton markets, slaves took on characteristics of a "growth stock"—an equity security that is considered to have a permanent or quasi-permanent upward momentum. Hence it commands a price that bears no relationship to its past earning potential or other benchmarks. As historians and market participants understand, and as we shall see, these periods of unbridled optimism lead to delusion and excess, followed by pessimism and price collapse. But while American economic growth was being served, the practice of treating people as property is yet another example of the critical reliance on the amoral world of economics. As planters, mill owners, and New York merchants saw the possibility of larger and larger dollar returns, cotton and the slaves who cultivated it became almost synonymous. Thus the experience of millions of black men and women became tied to the price of cotton, a suffocating relationship that would shape black life in America long after slavery's end.

The regulation and treatment of slaves in the Old Southwest, in both theory and practice, is well documented. The Mississippi Constitution of 1817 gave the legislature power to forbid slaves from being transported into the state as "merchandise." This did not prevent their importation. An 1819 import tax on slaves was later excused if a certification of "good character" was provided for each imported slave. Rather than a humanitarian concern, this certification was designed to prevent the unloading of "incorrigible and physically debilitated slaves" on Mississippi buyers. The state legislated stiff penalties for violations, but the laws were violated with impunity as slaves poured into newly opened territory. In 1846, Mississippi removed all restrictions on its domestic slave trade.

The large-scale movement of slaves demanded a legal infrastructure for social control. In Mississippi, for example, it became illegal to give reading and writing instruction to slaves; nor could they work in the printing business. Slaves were not allowed to sell anything without the consent of their owner. A slave could not hold a religious service unless conducted in the presence of two approved white observers. A slave could be whipped thirty-nine times for threatening a white man. Slave testimony was not valid against a white man. If a slave was convicted of a felony, the sheriff could burn the slave's hand in the courtroom. The state paid a slaveowner half the value of a slave who was executed for a capital crime. An organized patrol system monitored local territories for fugitives.

Through the nineteenth century the regulation of free blacks became increasingly strict, though the enforcement of laws was arbitrary and not followed literally. Gradually, Mississippi and other states began to restrict the emancipation process in an effort to eliminate the free black population altogether. Initially a slaveowner could free a slave only with legislative approval. In 1857 emancipation was forbidden. By 1860 there were 773 free blacks in the state and 436,000 slaves.

Slaveowners had a vested interest in the health of their valuable slave property. Yet the overseer system and the overwhelming desire to produce more cotton proved to be a temptation that often meant sacrificing the value of the slave to the goal of greater production. A plantation's overseers were often given production incentives that resulted in an emphasis on short-term profits. Overseers were offered pay inducements of one to five dollars for each bale of cotton over an established benchmark. Not surprisingly, slaves were worked harder.

Slaves received set rations, were allotted specific acreage assignments for their own cultivation of corn and grains, and were expected to pick a certain amount of cotton. They were whipped regularly for "minor transgressions"; they frequently ran away and were punished when caught. Most fugitives returned "voluntarily" or were hunted by the dogs of professional slave catchers.

DeBow's Review, part Southern economic journal, part pro-slavery propaganda vehicle (1846–1867), published articles promoting the proper supervision of slaves. In "Management of Negroes upon Southern Estates" (June 1851), an anonymous Mississippi planter set out specific rules for the supervision of slaves that were part of the contract with his overseer. Each slave would tend ten acres of cotton and six acres of corn. The planter supplied a nursery with an "experienced woman" to care for children. He gave five dollars to each head of household on Christmas; he encouraged marriages and "punished with severity, departures from marital obligation"; he paid for a "good fiddler" for Saturday night dances; and he provided a preacher for Sunday worship. *DeBow's Review* offered these rules in an attempt to counter criticism of slavery, influence the treatment of slaves, and add a veneer of sophistication to the "management of slave labor."

The number of slaves in the Old Southwest grew with each decade of the nineteenth century. With that growth, and the importance of cotton, came a gradual shift in the rhetoric of slavery. Nowhere is this more apparent than during the pivotal decade of the 1830s, during the cotton and land boom. Nat Turner's Rebellion in 1831 and the growing anti-slavery movement in the North exacerbated Southern racial and political fears. In 1831 the Mississippi lawyer and politician Seargent S. Prentiss expressed a commonly held belief, "That slavery is a great evil, there can be no doubt—and it is an unfortunate circumstance that it was ever introduced into this or any other country. At present, however, it is a necessary evil, and I do not think admits of a remedy." Just five years later the quotable Prentiss would offer a diametrically opposed view in his recommendation to the state legislature:

> Resolved, that the people of the state of Mississippi look upon the institution of domestic slavery . . . not as curse, but as a blessing, as the legitimate condition of the African race, as authorized both by the laws of God and the dictates of reason and humanity. . . . We will allow no present change, or hope of future alteration in this matter.

Such after-the-fact rationalizations about slavery arose only to justify an existing system. The South also developed polemics about the relative humanity of slavery versus what they termed Northern wage slavery.

The treatment of slaves in the Old Southwest ranged from brutality to condescending paternalism to the anomaly of the paternalistic utopian experiment of Jefferson Davis's brother, Joseph Davis, at Davis Bend, Mississippi, which will be described later. Jefferson Davis himself, the future president of the Confederacy, was a cotton planter who owned 113 slaves. His views on cotton and slavery—like those of so many Americans—were based on business decisions; he held aggressive pro-slavery and land-expansionist opinions; he viewed black people as inferior, except in individual cases. Davis did not agonize over the institution of slavery or the slave trade. He declared without sentiment, "If we had considered the purposes of humanity alone, we should have continued the slave-trade indefinitely." He saw nothing wrong with the presence of slave pens, the holding areas for slaves before auctions, in the nation's capital, Washington, D.C. Just before he became president of the Confederacy, Davis reiterated his sanction of the international slave trade and expressed no "coincidence of opinion with those who prate of the inhumanity and sinfulness of the trade. The interest of Mississippi, not of the African, dictates my conclusion."

Thus Davis opposed the reopening of the international slave trade on strictly economic grounds, because a new supply of slaves would reduce the value of those slaves already owned by planters. "This conclusion, in regard to Mississippi," he said, "is based upon my view of her *present* condition, not upon any *general* theory." His views were conditioned on money, not morality.

Examples of slaves associated with the most powerful executive in the Confederacy indicate the complex personal and business relationships that developed between master and slave. One such instance involved James Pemberton, a slave who managed Davis's plantation. Pemberton accompanied the young Lieutenant Davis during his military postings outside Mississippi. Letters between the Davis brothers reported on the "well-being" of Pemberton's wife and son. When Jefferson Davis fought in the Mexican War, it was Pemberton who made the decision not to accompany him. After Pemberton was left with management responsibilities for the plantation, he remained an overseer until his death in 1850. Varina Davis wrote that her husband and James Pemberton discussed emancipation. Pemberton, she related, indicated that he would take care of her and her husband until they died. After that, he said, he wanted his freedom. There is no other reference to Davis's interest in freeing another slave.

Quite a different path was taken by William Andrew Jackson, a slave who served briefly as Jefferson Davis's footman in Virginia. Jackson escaped to New York, where his symbolic value as the former slave of Jefferson Davis was immediately recognized. He vilified Jefferson Davis as the "greatest enemy of the slave."

By the 1850s, idealistic Northerners like Frederick Law Olmsted thought that free white labor could replace slave labor in the growing of cotton. Olmsted used the example of successful German immigrants who were raising cotton in Texas in the 1850s. He disputed the conventional wisdom that white people were not capable of working in the hot cotton fields. For Olmsted, all that was needed was a good dose of Northern capitalism to provide economies of scale to cotton production. Thus he bemoaned the fact that there was no joint-stock plantation in Mississippi as there were joint-stock cotton mills in Massachusetts. Olmsted's naive analogy disregards the inherent risk factors and once-a-year cash flow that made cotton farming unsuitable for corporate capital structures. Planters used land and slaves to collateralize loans; additional borrowings were predicated on selling crops.

Cotton and race-based slavery were further connected because free whites were deemed more expendable than slaves for dangerous work. The monetary risk of losing slaves in the "malarial swamps" for levee work on the Mississippi River meant that "gangs of husky foreign . . . particularly Irish . . . [and] foreign laborers became a conspicuous feature of the lower Mississippi Valley, where they could be seen, winter and summer, struggling under the hard and grueling task of levee building." Labor contractors met immigrant ships in St. Louis, New Orleans, Cincinnati, and Cairo, Illinois, to recruit workers for levee construction. A planter, Walter Sillers, Sr., described the life of white levee workers in Bolivar County, Mississippi, part of the cotton-dominated Yazoo Mississippi Delta.

> The levee along what is now Lake Beulah—then the Mississippi River—was built by Irish laborers under a Scotch contractor named Bain, before the War Between the States. When paid off every Satur-

day night, the [Irish] workers invariably got drunk and caroused and fought and howled like Bedlam turned loose. Sunday morning found them badly bruised. . . .

Visitors were particularly struck by the substitution of Irish laborers for black slaves. Tyrone Power, an English actor, observed hundreds of Irish immigrants "digging a canal through a swamp to Lake Pontchartrain [Louisiana]" in 1835. The actor explained that "Slave labor cannot be substituted to any extent, being much too expensive; a good slave costs . . . two hundred pounds sterling." When an Irish worker contracted fever and died in the swamps, he was buried; when a slave died, the "contractor" had to pay his owner as much as $900.

Slave ownership was skewed. By any definition there were few planters or large-scale slaveholders. Of 1.6 million Southern families, 384,000 owned slaves. Twenty percent of slaveholders owned only one slave; 99 percent owned fewer than 100. In 1860 only 14 "millionaire" planters held more than 500 slaves. During the Civil War, nonslaveholders in Mississippi fought to preserve slavery but did force slaveholders to pay additional taxes for "wartime defense."

Domestic slave trading during the nineteenth century was directed one way—toward demand, that is, from noncotton states to cotton states, from nonprofitable or marginally profitable areas to potentially lucrative cotton destinations. Slave trading was conducted with all the trappings of ordinary business procedures—public advertising, credit, legal rules and recourse, and open auctions. New Orleans was the largest auction market, but in big cities and small towns across the cotton South, public notices of demand were common:

Cash for negroes for the New Orleans market and will give more than any purchaser that is now or hereafter may come into the market. Richard C. Woolfolk. (*Village Herald* of Princess Anne, Maryland, January 7, 1831)

The scope and profitability of slave trading gave rise to specialty firms. The slave trader was considered odious even by Southern slaveholders, yet slave trading flourished. Franklin & Armfield, the largest of the slave-trading firms, began in 1824. John Armfield purchased slaves at his base in Alexandria, Virginia, and sold them to his partner,

Isaac Franklin, in New Orleans. The firm owned four ships—the *Tribune, United States, Isaac Franklin*, and *Uncas*—that transported slaves and other passengers from Virginia to New Orleans. It encouraged passengers, who were often planters, to inspect the slave quarters and assess the "merchandise."

Public slave auctions were regulated by the same credit and commercial laws that applied to other businesses. Before the Civil War, slave sales constituted "one-sixth of the nearly 11,000 American appellate cases involving slaves." Disputants sought remedies and were generally concerned with "transfer and protection of property rights, not with the establishment of ownership." Southern courts deemed sales to be "contractual rights and responsibilities agreed to by buyers and sellers." Judges encouraged participants to "develop standardized forms of dealing."

The cash generated by the slave-trading process was a powerful incentive even for anti-slavery advocates such as the English actress Frances Anne (Fanny) Kemble. In 1834 she married the profligate South Carolinian Pierce Butler, the second largest slaveholder in the state. After she wrote a powerful anti-slavery tract, *Journal of a Residence on a Georgia Plantation* (1863), the couple divorced. When Butler was forced to sell his slaves, Kemble was comforted that the sale would provide financial security for her daughters. Her biographer reported that she "grieved over the upheaval the Savannah sale would surely visit on the unfortunate Butler slaves, even as she counted on the proceeds to bring an end to her daughters' poverty."

The legal issues that arose over slavery would prove to be a reliable guide to the destiny of blacks both in and out of the cotton fields. These questions consistently challenged the American system of justice. Much of the case material arises out of economic disputes and illustrates the important nexus between economics, slavery, and race, and the contradictions implicit in the institution of slavery. The Dred Scott case (1857) was the most famous legal opinion involving slavery. Scott, a Missouri slave, accompanied his owner to live in the free states of Wisconsin and Illinois for several years. Upon returning to Missouri, Scott sued for his freedom. The U.S. Supreme Court held that a slave "had no rights which the white man was bound to respect." In other words, a slave was not a citizen.

CHAPTER FIVE

The Business of Cotton

THE BUSINESS of cotton, with all its speculative character-istics, grew into a system that was international in scope. The participants were a varied lot. As cotton moved from the farm to British and New England textile mills, it passed directly or indirectly through intermediaries. Someone had to finance the crop; someone had to supply merchandise to the farmer; someone had to buy and sell the crop. These commercial functions overlapped. The slave was largely invisible during these transactions. The following represen-tative individuals illustrate the range of operations.

*

The acknowledged founder of the "cotton triangle," Jeremiah Thomp-son immigrated to New York from Yorkshire. He began as a woolen-goods trader but transferred to the cotton business and in the 1820s be-came the world's largest cotton exporter. He used the "Black Ballers," the innovative, regularly scheduled packet ship lines, or his own vessels. Thompson, a Quaker, formed a company with his Quaker partners and dealt regularly with the Quaker Liverpool cotton firm of Crop-per, Benson & Co. George Marshall, Thompson's partner and another transplanted Yorkshire Quaker, spent several months a year in Georgia on cotton business.

The Quakers, known to be clever businessmen, were often praised for their anti-slavery stand. Jeremiah Thompson was active in the New York Manumission Society while dealing in slave-produced cotton.

The roller-coaster cotton business was risky for participants, and Thompson was no exception. Gyrations in supply and demand wreaked havoc on prices. When Thompson heard from Cropper, Benson at the close of 1824 that a shortage of cotton existed in England, he immediately sent ships to New Orleans to buy cotton in anticipation of a higher price. Alas, he was too late and suffered a loss. Thompson survived. Three years later his luck ran out when Cropper, Benson curtailed credit during his attempt to accumulate cotton in a declining market. Thompson was, in effect, issued a "financial death sentence." Speculation permeated every aspect of the cotton business.

*

The factorage system dominated the cotton business in the antebellum world. Factors could act as cotton purchasing agents, as credit providers, and as merchants for planters. Cotton was the basis of credit, and credit was the basis of the cotton business. For a full year, until the cotton was sold, the planter operated on credit. "The entire credit structure was built on the presumption that cotton, when it finally came to market and was sold, would cancel all debts." The credit structure was complex, sophisticated, and regional, national, and international in scope. Southern factors, who often had unsavory reputations, depended on financial houses in New York and Liverpool, where the power behind cotton lay.

Fortunately the factors kept detailed records of routine business transactions—loans, crop sales, and merchandise. One such merchant, William Bostwick, a Yale graduate and native of New Haven, operated in Augusta, Georgia, from the 1820s to the 1840s. Like many of the New England–born factors, he enjoyed close, indispensable credit connections with New York. Bostwick was both an agent for cotton sales and a merchant for supplying goods. He journeyed to New York once a year, usually in late summer, to purchase goods on credit terms for four to ten months— "sugar, tea, nails, cotton cloth, shirting, buttons, whiskey from Baltimore and Philadelphia, barrels of mackerel, and cheese from New Haven." From 1830 to 1833 he traded goods worth $170,348.

*

The Mississippi cotton planter William Johnson sold his crop through a factor, Washington Jackson and Co. of New Orleans, as revealed in his correspondence of 1844–1845. The factor used its Liverpool branch, Todd Jackson and Co., to sell the cotton in Liverpool to a local agent or a cotton mill. Typically a cotton factor would charge 2.5 percent on the sale. After Johnson shipped his cotton on the Mississippi River to New Orleans, a series of several transactions that involved both U.S. dollars and British pounds sterling took place, with risk involved at each stage. The cotton was exchanged for negotiable receipts or bills backed by cotton. These instruments were traded in New York, Boston, Philadelphia, Liverpool, London, and elsewhere. A decline in the price of cotton during this paper-chain process would leave the holder of the instrument with a loss. By 1861, 101 private banks conducted this type of business in the cotton states. The system, which was complex even by modern standards, evolved to facilitate the ever-increasing international cotton business.

*

Finance, speculation, and enormous growth were accompanied by excess and crises. Concurrent with cotton's coronation, America was plagued by periodic financial and economic debacles during the nineteenth century. Serious crises occurred in 1819, 1837, 1857, 1873, and 1893. The Panic of 1837, in particular, jarred American society and illustrated the central role of cotton.

The decade of the 1830s was central to the ascendancy of the cotton economy, with more than twenty million new acres made available in the cotton-growing states. The expansion was financed by capital from the North and from Europe, and cotton, in turn, became the critical underpinning of America's ability to borrow money. European capital flowed to America because of its financial system, cotton exports, and perceived investment opportunities. From the beginning America had depended on foreign capital and in particular on European banks, which had extended the new republic $130 million in loans to finance American businesses, canals, and railroads. All the Erie Canal bonds were sold to Europeans. By 1850 foreigners still owned half the federal debt and 20 percent of all U.S. securities. The deep involvement of foreign investors gradually became a flashpoint of Northern anxiety and Southern confidence, and one of the factors that pushed the country toward war.

In 1836, Treasury Secretary Levi Woodbury confidently explained the "preeminence" of American cotton in world trade. He believed that America would remain dominant because of "good cotton land enough in the United States and at low prices, easily to grow, not only all the cotton wanted for foreign export . . . , but to supply the increased demand for it, probably for all ages." Despite "great vibrations," the price of cotton would sustain "great profits" for capital invested in cotton production. The crux of his argument was price:

> The single fact, that in no year has the price been but a fraction below 10 cents per pound, or at a rate sufficient to yield a fair profit, while it has, at times, been as high as 29, 34, and even 44, and been on average, over 16 cents per pound since 1802, and over 21 since 1790, is probably without parallel, in showing a large and continued profit.

As Woodbury noted, the price fluctuations had influenced "the sales of public land and our revenue." Indeed, revenues from land sales and tariffs had allowed the government to eliminate the national debt. He further extolled cotton's impact on "the prosperity of the south, on the rise in the value of their slave property, and on the great profits yielded by all . . . [the] capital invested in growing cotton." The picture painted by Woodbury, and many others, was that cotton could do no wrong. It was a prime vehicle for expansion—and, many would say, explosive growth.

The enthusiasm for conquering the wilderness conformed to the gyrations in the price of cotton. (See Appendix 1.)

When the aggregate data is viewed with a clinical eye, the price of cotton seems quite resilient. In reality there were violent price swings, decade-long roller-coaster rides that devastated individual cotton planters and cotton businessmen. Local production variables—floods, droughts, frost, insects, and disease—added further risk. Either the notorious "army worm" or "black rot" destroyed crops in 1804, 1827,

1839, 1846, and 1853. Normal business cycles produced excess demand or overproduction, causing price extremes of 29.8 cents per pound in 1817 and 5.5 cents in 1844. For the entire decade of the 1850s, cotton sold for around 11 cents a pound when the cost of production for some planters was 5 cents.

The South's entire economic system was perched on the price of cotton, and that perch was a precarious one. In the booming 1830s, J. H. Ingraham waxed enthusiastic about cotton planters' prospects. In southwestern Mississippi, he wrote, "annual incomes of twenty thousand dollars were common and . . . several individuals received forty to fifty thousand dollars a year." A planter, he claimed, could pay off mortgages on slaves and land within three years. These returns of "fifteen to thirty per cent" were predicated on the price of cotton at "twelve to fifteen cents a pound." Ingraham, however, was inadvertently describing a bubble, and like all financial bubbles, this one eventually burst. Even successful planters were exposed to risks. "Sheriffs and trustees' sales, adverse balances on the books of New Orleans merchants, and debts to slave-traders were all evidence that cotton plantations were not sure roads to wealth," Charles Sydnor wrote. Cotton plantations could be roads to temporary wealth but not necessarily to the long-term accumulation of wealth and certainly not to stability. Each of the three major periods of cotton booms—the mid-to-late 1810s, the 1830s before the crash, and the 1850s—was followed by falling prices. But the antebellum period provided enough profitability or anticipation of riches for the country and its seemingly inexhaustible supply of eager planters to expand.

The spirit of the era was captured in *The Flush Times of Alabama and Mississippi* (1853) by Joseph Glover Baldwin. This Virginia native journeyed to the Old Southwest with a law book, a great imagination, and a creative pen. From 1835 to 1837 he recorded his days and deeds. He witnessed the land grab and the typically American avalanche of conflicting land claims and fraudulent activity that created a lawyer's bonanza.

Baldwin noted that the purchase of cotton land was facilitated by cheap money, the result of the government's effort to "democratize capital."

Let the public believe that a smutted rag is money, it is money; in other words, it was a sort of financial biology. . . . Money, or what passed for money, was the only cheap thing to be had. . . . Credit was a thing of course. . . . The State banks were issuing their bills by the sheet, like a patent steam printing-press its issues; and no other showing was asked of the applicant for the loan than an authentication of his distress for money.

The euphoria ended with the banking crisis of 1837, an event that began in London when interest rates were raised to stem the outflow of money and gold. Three Anglo-American banks—Wildes, Wiggins, and Wilson, commonly known as the Three Ws—failed. New York felt the impact, with interest rates rising from 7 percent annually to 2 to 3 percent per month. As the value of U.S. securities plummeted, the New York Stock Exchange experienced bedlam. The weakening price of cotton "wrecked whatever remained of public confidence" and left cotton merchants strapped for cash. In March 1837 several New Orleans cotton banks failed as the price of cotton continued to fall.

The collapse of American stock and bond prices caused several states to default, leaving Europeans holding tens of millions of dollars in lost loans and investments. James Rothschild, head of the Rothschild bank in Paris, supposedly excoriated an American treasury official, Duff Green: "You may tell your government that you have seen the man who is at the head of finances of Europe and that he has told you that they cannot borrow a dollar, not a dollar." Financial memory, however, is notoriously short. By the beginning of the Civil War, a little more than twenty years later, Europeans had forgotten about American financial foibles and were lending money and selling arms to the Confederacy. Cotton was the direct or indirect basis of these loans and sales in the 1860s, just as it was in the 1830s.

Although it took a few years for the damage to be revealed, the cotton South was bludgeoned in the aftermath of the Panic of 1837. The tight-money-induced demise of New Orleans financial houses was followed by cotton price "vibrations." Cotton planters did not feel the full impact until the collapse of cotton prices in the winter of 1839–1840. The price per pound dropped from sixteen cents in 1836 to ten cents in 1838, then rose to fourteen cents in 1839. The price broke hard in the winter of 1839 to five cents, without fully recovering until 1850.

These lingering price problems influenced land values and slave prices, shaking the entire foundation of the cotton economy. In the New Orleans slave market the "Price of Young Slave Men, Able-Bodied, but Unskilled" dropped from $1,300 in 1837 to $600 in 1843. By 1856 the price had rebounded to $1,500. On paper, slaves may have accounted for as much as 60 percent of the South's wealth.

The mountain of debt that had been accumulated to purchase land and slaves brought an avalanche of financial failures. Legal notification of default postings kept county sheriffs busy. Debtors, in many cases, left after jotting G.T.T. [Gone to Texas] on the back of their foreclosure notices. A North Carolina man journeyed to the Old Southwest to collect debts and observed the misery.

> Mississippi is ruined. Her rich men are poor, and her poor men are beggars. . . . We have seen hard times in North Carolina, hard times in the East, hard times everywhere; but Mississippi exceeds them all. Some of the finest . . . lands may be had for comparatively nothing. . . . Lands . . . that once commanded thirty to fifty dollars per acre may be bought for three or five dollars . . . while many have been sold at sheriff's sales at fifty cents that were considered worth ten and twenty dollars. . . . There are a great many farms prepared to receive crops and some of them actually planted, and yet deserted, not a human being to be found upon them.

The wealthy and powerful were not spared. Cotton led to the ultimate demise of Philadelphia's Nicholas Biddle, "America's Napoleon of finance." Biddle, head of the Bank of the United States, had lost the status and privilege of acting as America's central bank in his struggle with Andrew Jackson. As president of the Bank, Biddle had become thoroughly conversant with the cotton trade. In 1836 he obtained a Pennsylvania state banking license and embarked on a bold scheme to "corner the cotton market." He purchased enormous sums of cotton through a Liverpool affiliate, Humphrey and Biddle. His aim was to withhold cotton from the English mills and force up prices.

The senior partner in Biddle's Liverpool firm in 1839 expounded the cotton strategy that would later give fame to South Carolina senator James Henry Hammond in 1858, would be attempted by the Confederacy, and would yet again be propounded by Massachusetts politician and Radical Republican politician Benjamin Butler in 1870:

> [I]f the United States wants to "inflict a deadly blow" on Britain, it could not resort to a more summary and effectual process than by withholding, by purchase or otherwise, say one-third or more of any one year's cotton crop, from the European market. The immediate effect would be to force prices up in England to a point that would suspend consumption and thus throw out of employment an immense multitude of the most turbulent population in the world—when insurrection if not revolution might follow. . . . Cotton bags [bales] will be much more effectual in bringing John Bull to terms than all the disciplined troops America could bring into the field.

Thus "cotton bags" became armaments in an economic battle. No Southern politician or planter was involved. But the Southerners George McDuffie and Robert Y. Hayne reacted favorably to Biddle's strategy by calling a Cotton Planters' Convention in an attempt to institutionalize the intervention technique.

Biddle's plan at first appeared to succeed, as cotton prices appeared favorable. His reputation soared. Soon after, Biddle recognized his identification with cotton when he wrote that my "worthy fellow citizens may now sleep in peace, satisfied that I shall buy neither cotton nor men."

But when the price of cotton dropped and English mills forestalled their purchases, Biddle's reputation and his fortunes soon plunged. His loans, collateralized by cotton, failed, and he was held responsible. He was sued by stockholders and charged with "criminal conspiracy" and financial crimes. Biddle was arrested but acquitted. The Bank of the United States did not survive this cotton speculation. The once-powerful institution folded forever on February 4, 1841. Biddle was subsequently plagued by further lawsuits before his death in February 1844. Former president John Tyler, in 1847, noted Biddle's vision: "His bright and accomplished mind did not fail to embrace in its full extent the value and virtual monopoly of the cotton plant . . . a monopoly more potential in the affairs of the world than millions of armed men."

The Biddle episode illustrated the centrality of cotton to American and European politics and economics. Paradoxically, the antagonists, Jackson and Biddle, were connected through cotton. Biddle needed cotton for his financial operation while the cotton planter and slaveholder Jackson opened vast tracts of land for cotton cultivation.

The interconnected forces of international trade and finance, what today we call globalization, were never more in evidence than in the crisis of 1837. Acre upon acre was deserted across the Old Southwest, and thousands of lives were ruined by the effect of a financial panic that had begun thousands of miles away. The boom-and-bust cycle of the speculative cotton world elevated and then dumped the rich and powerful.

The financial web spun from the cotton plant, and the resulting dependency on American slave-grown cotton, had many facets. The South depended on cotton; cotton depended on slavery. New York City depended on the cotton trade. British, French, and New England textile mills depended on American raw cotton. The American West greatly benefited from the intersectional trade generated by cotton—it sold goods to the South and thus enjoyed greater borrowing capacity. The American government relied on tariff revenues generated by the South. American financial markets—their borrowing capacity—were supported by the favorable balance of trade created by slave-produced cotton. The other side of the coin was the lopsided economy of the South, which had to import Northern manufactured goods, agricultural supplies, and capital. Northern shipping, insurance, and financial skills were also required. British, French, and New England textile mill purchases of cotton were essential.

Southerners chafed under Northern commercial dominance and talked endlessly about the road to economic independence. By the 1830s an Alabama state legislative committee reported that New Yorkers collected one-third of all cotton revenues. Southerners estimated that Northerners extracted $3 billion from their region between 1800 and 1860. Southern journals railed against the North's economic "bloodsucking" and in a fit of self-flagellation chastised the region's own backwardness.

> By merely supineness, the people of the South have permitted the Yankees to monopolize the carrying trade, with immense profits. We have yielded to them in the manufacturing business. . . . We have acquiesced in the claims of the North to do all the importing, and most of the exporting business of the whole Union. . . . Meantime, the South remains passive—in a state of torpidity—making cotton bales for the North to manufacture, and constantly exerting ourselves to increase the production as much as possible. (*Vicksburg Daily Whig*, January 18, 1860)

J. D. B. DeBow, editor of *DeBow's Review*, published the first edition of his influential journal in January 1846. Skilled at marshalling statistics, DeBow was responsible for the publication of the 1850 U.S. Census, "the most detailed and informative census that had heretofore been published." Based in New Orleans, *DeBow's Review* chronicled the economic aspirations and growing national awareness of the South. The inscription on the title page was "Commerce Is King." Dispensing advice on trade, economics, and the improvement of business, the journal survived until DeBow's death in 1867. In an 1849 article, *DeBow's* recommended seven transcontinental railroad routes, all in the South. New Orleans, the Crescent City, was the favorite hub, and DeBow considered it the potential base for a Caribbean trading empire. New Orleans, according to the editor, could recapture the mercantile glory of sixteenth-century Venice.

One *DeBow's* contributor, William Gregg of South Carolina, was a practitioner rather than a mere pundit. The textile mill he founded in 1846, the Graniteville Manufacturing Co., was frequently used as a model for Southern self-sufficiency. Gregg's articles usually began with a citation of Northern manufacturing or mercantile profits. In 1850 he was informed by "the proprietor" of a "Boston tailor's establishment" that "his sales for the last year, to Charleston alone amounted to $50,000, and this year he expected would reach $80,000." Gregg's solution was to "resist the northern tariffites, by resolving not to purchase or use their articles of manufacture. This will cure the evil. . . ." For Gregg, the South had to establish its own manufacturers and "clothiers." Gregg observed that "Every article that a negro wears and everything necessary to his comfort can be made in the South." Gregg was referring to "negro cloth," the coarse fabric manufactured in the North from Southern cotton and then sold to Southern plantations for slave clothing. Much of the "negro cloth" was manufactured in Rhode Island.

Dependence on Northern capital was a degrading feature of the cotton economy, which operated on credit held by Northern banks. Planters were invariably in debt despite good but volatile investment returns. Banking statistics show the disparity. From 1845 to 1860 the number of banking institutions in the South barely increased, from 102 with $64 million in capital to 104 with $67 million in capital. Meanwhile Northern banking institutions grew from 301 with $88 million in capital to 567 with $193 million in capital. The cotton states—South Carolina, Georgia, Alabama, Tennessee, Mississippi, and Louisiana— did not reach the North's 1837 level of $105 million in loans outstanding even by 1860. Southern wealth was tied up in slaves and land and had little capital for other purposes. In addition to the fees of Northern businessmen, Southerners knew they paid almost 90 percent of the country's tariffs because of the South's dependence on imported manufactured goods, which were taxed.

The South's frustration vis-à-vis the North over its colonial status was evident at numerous commercial and planters' conventions that began in the 1830s. In 1851 the Cotton Planters' Convention in Macon, Georgia, proposed that South Carolina, Georgia, Alabama, Louisiana, and Florida form the Cotton Planters' Association. The group planned to regulate the price of cotton by setting up a warehouse for storage and establishing a commission business that would market the entire American cotton crop to overseas markets and thereby circumvent the North's role. The association would purchase cotton at an established minimum price, then sell the cotton at a set price plus storage and commission fees. In effect the scheme resembled a classic cartel, made theoretically possible by the dominance of American cotton production. To accomplish this the Cotton Planters' Association estimated it needed to raise $20 million to support its activities. But it could not raise the capital and so remained at the mercy of the market and Northern commercial involvement.

Another theoretical means of avoiding Northern control was allegedly simple: diversify away from cotton. Journals and conventions urged the development of railroads, financial institutions, manufacturing capacity, and production of foodstuffs. Hinton Rowan Helper ridiculed his fellow Southerners' obsession with cotton in his book *The Impending Crisis of the South: How to Meet It* (1857):

> The truth is that the cotton crop is of little value to the South. New England and Old England, by their superior enterprise and sagacity, turn it chiefly to their advantage. It is carried in their ships, spun in their factories, woven in their looms, insured in their offices, returned again in their own vessels, and, with double freight and cost of a manufacture added, purchased by the South at a high premium.

Southerners may have recognized their plight, but conventions and critics had little substantive impact other than to congeal Southern resentment.

The fact remained that Southern energy was disproportionately focused on cotton production, even though cotton dominance inhibited balanced growth. Immediate or projected financial gains were irresistible, the momentum was in place, and the cotton craze was fueled by generations of eager planters. And beyond the cotton states, intricate, intersecting relationships between the South, the North, and Europe conformed to the world of slave-produced cotton.

After the cotton prosperity of the 1850s, the "peculiar institution" gained in economic stature. Despite debt financing, cotton farming appeared to be profitable on large, well-managed plantations. The soil depletion that accompanied cotton production was mitigated as the Cotton Kingdom moved west to unexploited land. Within Mississippi, production locations shifted away from depleted soil and toward better opportunities. The Yankee traveler Joseph Ingraham, in the 1830s, observed the soil depletion caused by cotton cultivation near Natchez.

He anticipated the correlation between the obsession with cotton and soil depletion.

> Cotton and negroes are the constant theme—the ever harped upon, never worn out subject of conversation among all classes. . . . Not till every acre is purchased and cultivated—not till Mississippi becomes one vast cotton field, will this mania, this mania which has entered into the marrow, bone and sinew of a Mississippian's system, pass away. And not then, till the lands become exhausted and wholly unfit for farther [sic] cultivation. The south-west portion of this state must within a century become waste, barren, and wild.

Degradation of the land was not a concern of entrepreneurial cotton planters. Antebellum cotton cultivation practices would continue until there was no more cheap land, the price of cotton plummeted, slavery was abolished, or a more attractive cash option appeared.

The economic world is dynamic. Only one of the top five cotton-producing counties in Mississippi in 1839 was on the same list in 1859. A shift occurred from the older river counties of the southwestern section to the Yazoo and central section. Both before and after the Civil War, depleted soil provoked a movement of blacks to new cotton lands. In the cotton-intensive Yazoo region, slaves accounted for 90 percent of the population.

America's relentless westward expansion involved two separate issues with respect to the extension of slavery. The slave states wanted each new state to be admitted as a slave state in order to ensure political parity in the Senate. The economic question was whether a large-scale slave population could develop in the absence of cotton production. If not, the political question would be moot as free states would eventually be realized by default. The political confrontation over slavery in the West had been given a reprieve by the Missouri Compromise of 1820, which temporarily established a territory for slavery: it could not exist north of the southern boundary of Missouri, with Missouri admitted as a slave state.

A New Yorker of Jacksonian Democratic persuasion, John L. O'Sullivan articulated America's preordained fate in the *United States*

Magazine and Democratic Review. Referring to the extraction of Oregon from England, O'Sullivan wrote in 1845 of America's "right of ... manifest destiny to overspread and to possess the whole of the Continent which providence has given us for the development of the great experiment of liberty and federated self-government entrusted to us." His sonnet lyrically captured his dream:

> We cannot help the matter if we would:
> The race must have expansion—we must grow . . .
> We must obey our destiny and blood. . . .

Because the United States claimed the continent as its "manifest destiny," migration or anticipated migration touched off new squabbles. America was forced to define its identity, in terms not only of slavery but of race and Northern or Southern political control. An America that could envision no place for free blacks would eventually assign them to the cotton fields. And in this struggle for self-definition, morality took a back seat to brutally aggressive territorial acquisition. Native Americans, Mexicans, and British who stood in the way were defeated, either on the battlefield or at the negotiating table.

O'Sullivan suggested that if Texas were annexed it would function as a drain for the dispersal of slaves. In this he agreed with the expansionist Mississippi senator Robert J. Walker. In an influential pamphlet, *Letter on Texas Annexation,* Walker strongly endorsed the addition of Texas to the Union. Under his scenario, slaves would gravitate toward Mexico or Central America, resulting in the "ultimate disappearance of the negro race." Abraham Lincoln flirted with the concept of diffusion before espousing the view that the North could, of its own accord, reject free blacks. Walker was well aware that the North's small black population was ostracized and for the most part denied the right to vote, and that the Old Northwest had passed black exclusion laws.

Cotton production had brought slavery and political unrest to Texas while it was still part of Mexico. The U.S. government was leery of the close connection of Texas and Europe, apparently with good reason: Britain encouraged Mexico to recognize the independent Texas Republic in an attempt to prevent its annexation by the United

States. Senators Daniel Webster and Henry Clay both encouraged Nicholas Biddle to make a loan to the Republic of Texas in 1838, after Texas had withdrawn her application for American statehood. The major reason for fostering a financial tie was cotton. Webster and Clay were both pleased with the Texas decision to withdraw, for statehood would have upset the precarious balance between free and slave states. At the same time Webster still feared "Any close connection with a European power, so close as to make [Texas] dependent . . . or to identify her interests with the interests of such State." The anxiety was based on cotton:

> It is easy to foresee the evils [of a connection] . . . between Texas & one of the great sovereignties of Europe, [that is] . . . likely to have a direct bearing on our commerce, a connection on the great staple of our southern production. Texas is destined, doubtless, to become a great cotton producing country.

Webster did not wish to see Texas form an alliance with Great Britain that might "threaten" the U.S. cotton monopoly and receive "exclusive favors & privileges, from the hands of a European Government."

The American advance westward eventually brought Texas into the Union on December 29, 1845, with the support of President James K. Polk, who owned slaves and a cotton plantation. Between 1850 and 1860 the slave population of Texas grew from 58,161 to 182,566—from 27 percent of its total population to 30 percent. During that decade, cotton production jumped from 23 million pounds to 193 million pounds. Northern dreams of white Texas cotton farmers who would displace slaves never materialized.

*

While opposing the extension of slavery, white anti-slavery Northerners were also vehemently anti-black. The attitude of white Northerners toward race, not just slavery, helped ensure that blacks would remain in bondage to cotton after emancipation. It was illustrated in the misunderstood Wilmot Proviso of 1846. A little-known Democratic congressman, David Wilmot, forever secured his place in American history by introducing the amendment to a $2 million appropriations bill for the Mexican War:

> Provided, that, as an express and fundamental condition of the acquisition of any territory from New Mexico . . . neither slavery nor involuntary servitude shall ever exist in any part of said territory, except for crime, whereof the party shall first be duly convicted.

Wilmot had favored the annexation of Texas, supported the Mexican War, and wanted to buy New Mexico and California. His amendment passed by nineteen votes in the House but was defeated in the Senate. He referred to it as the "White Man's Proviso" and offered it again in 1847. For Wilmot, the issues were slavery and race.

> When territory presents itself for annexation where slavery is already established, I stand ready to take it, if national considerations require it, as they did in the case of Texas; I will not seek to change its institutions. I make not war upon the South nor upon slavery in the South. I will not first ask the abolition of slavery. I have no squeamish sensitivity upon the subject of slavery, nor morbid sympathy for the slave. I plead the cause of the rights of white freemen. I would preserve for free white labor a fair country, a rich inheritance, where the sons of toil, of my own race and own color, can live without the disgrace which association with negro slavery brings upon free labor.

Wilmot was quoted as remarking, "By God, sir, men born and nursed of white women are not going to be ruled by men who were brought up on the milk of some damn negro wench!" After he switched to the Republican party and ran for governor of Pennsylvania in 1857, he made it clear that "It is not true that the defenders of the rights of free labor seek the elevation of the black race to an equality with the white. . . ." Wilmot wanted blacks, slave or free, excluded from the annexed territories. The "White Man's Proviso" was defeated in 1847, this time by both the Senate and the House.

The American West, which required an enormous flow of new labor, did not want black labor, either slave or free. In a period when millions of white European immigrants were enticed to come to America and settle in the West, black labor was specifically excluded. Wilmot's racial antipathy was historically based in the North and would reverberate through the Civil War and beyond, with dire consequences for African Americans.

The Compromise of 1850 arose from the next heated battleground over slave expansion. The settlement included California's admission as a free state; a popular vote to determine slave policy in the two sections of the Mexican Cession, Utah and New Mexico; a stringent new fugitive slave law; and the abolition of slave trading in the District of Columbia.

But more important for our purposes is how the bill was discussed in terms of cotton and slavery. When Daniel Webster, the anti-slavery Massachusetts senator, delivered his famous Seventh-of-March (1850) speech on the Compromise, he observed that there had been a "general concurrence of sentiment" against slavery in America, but that a change had occurred: "This I suppose . . . is owing to the rapid growth and sudden extension of the COTTON plantations of the South. . . . It was the COTTON interest that gave a new desire to promote slavery, to spread it, and to use its labor."

Cotton, Webster declared, had caused "the South to . . . [become] connected more or less with the extension of slavery" in the West. He continued:

> The age of cotton became the golden age of our Southern brethren. It gratified their desire for improvement and accumulation at the same time that it excited it. . . . There soon came to be an eagerness for other territory, a new area . . . for the cultivation of the cotton crop. . . .

As for the territories of California and New Mexico, cotton could not be grown there, so slavery would not sprout. Hence there was no need to ban the "peculiar institution."

> I hold slavery to be excluded from those territories by a law even superior to that which admits and sanctions it in Texas. . . . I mean the law of nature, of physical geography. . . . Slavery cannot exist in California or New Mexico. . . . I mean slavery as we regard it; the slavery of the colored race as it exists in the Southern States. What is there in New Mexico that could possibly induce anybody to go there with slaves?

. . . And who expects to see a hundred black men cultivating tobacco, corn, cotton, rice or anything else on lands in New Mexico, made fertile only by irrigation? I look upon it, therefore, as a fixed fact . . . that both California and New Mexico are destined to be free, free by the arrangement of things ordained by the Power above us.

The anti-slavery Webster thus disappointed many Northerners who opposed slavery. He would not "put any prohibition" on slavery in New Mexico if he voted on a territorial bill. He thought it useless "to reaffirm an ordinance of nature." His logic was that slavery could only follow cotton, as it had in the past. Despite his reasoning, slavery-related political conflicts, not slavery itself, arose over California, Kansas, Oregon, and the New Mexico territory.

In the mid-nineteenth century the linkage between cotton and the extension of large-scale, race-based slavery could only be challenged theoretically. Outside of cotton, no other crop or industry provided a viable example of the large-scale use of race-based slavery. Wheat, which was slave-grown and profitable in Virginia in the 1850s, is sometimes offered as a possible alternative. The question of the large-scale application of slave labor to wheat farming in the West, while hypothetically intriguing, is highly speculative. The economic historian Gavin Wright acknowledges that the "slave economy ultimately came to resemble the geography of natural cotton-growing areas." The establishment of slave-based agriculture or industry in a noncotton region in 1800 or afterward would have been difficult without a cotton-based, gold-rush mentality. Cotton made slaves too expensive for other pursuits, as we shall see in the use of slaves in industry.

Sentiment against slavery was pronounced even by the end of the eighteenth century. Settlers in an area in which an overwhelmingly large white population was either migrating rapidly or was entrenched had a predisposition to prohibit slavery—but also free blacks. White immigration resolved the labor shortage. A staple crop with a huge profit potential became the only inducement to maintain a large slave population.

Controversy nevertheless moved to the territories where there were no slaves and no potential for cotton production. Each new state meant two new senators and a change in the balance of power between slave and free states. "Bleeding Kansas" was the testing ground. Again, the struggle was over morality and politics, not the economics of slavery; Kansas had no place for blacks, either slave or free. The site of a bloody struggle over slave expansion, the state was home to 625 "free colored" in a population of 107,000. From the opening of the territory to slavery in 1854, two slaves had been introduced to Kansas, and 15 had been brought into Nebraska by 1860. The New Mexico territory, another political battleground, included 24 slaves (12 of whom were servants of military officers) in a population of 94,000. By 1860 there were none. One can be certain that if slaveowners had seen real profit potential, a large-scale slave migration would have ensued. The fight over political power was real; the economic basis of slave expansion was only theoretical because slavery was ill-suited to gain a foothold without the possibility of cotton cultivation.

The union of cotton and slavery was never successfully challenged by other enterprises. Southern manufacturing and mining enterprises could not compete with cotton for slave labor. Efforts to use slave labor in industry in the early part of the nineteenth century succumbed to the price of cotton, as the upward surge of cotton prices—from ten cents a pound in 1811 to thirty-four cents in 1817, and from nine cents in 1830 to fifteen cents in 1838—drove slave values higher. Slaves were more valuable in the cotton fields than elsewhere.

As a result, the instances of small-scale industrial slavery were limited and generally unsuccessful. Although it was theoretically possible for industrial activities to absorb more slave labor, it would be highly speculative to think that slave labor could have been used on a large scale in urban industrial ventures over a long period of time in the United States. The real question is whether a significant number of slaves could have been absorbed in enterprises other than cotton production. Ultimately the answer was no.

The example most often cited as supporting the large-scale adaptability of slave labor to industry is the Tredegar Iron Works of Richmond, Virginia. But on close examination the Tredegar experience illustrates the impracticality and cumbersome nature of slave labor. The Tredegar Iron Works was chartered in Virginia in 1837 and from 1841 was directed by Joseph R. Anderson, a West Point graduate who had no interest in military service. In order to cut costs he advocated employing slaves "in highly skilled industrial positions." In 1846 he put his theory into practice at a related entity, the Armory Iron Company. By then Tredegar had already purchased a few slaves.

The employment terms provided that slaves would have specific jobs that required ten hours of work each day. Leased from owners, they could earn money based on overtime or piecework in excess of quotas. When slaves began to work in skilled positions, white workers at both Armory and Tredegar went on strike to "prohibit the employment of colored people in the said Works." Anderson responded by hiring still more slaves—the number increased from 41 in 1847 to 117 in 1848. In 1850, 100 of the 250 workers were slaves. Twenty-eight slaves were owned personally by Anderson. On the eve of the Civil War in 1860, 80 of 800 workers were slaves, at a time when the slave population of the South was 4 million.

The slave experience at Tredegar was not successful. Tredegar's prices were never competitive with Northern or English iron producers. Both labor and raw material costs combined to create a competitive disadvantage. In order to compensate, Tredegar appealed to Southern pride and the need for self-sufficiency. It sometimes accepted "promissory notes" and the bonds of Southern railroads as payment. This form of credit proved to be of dubious quality, and by the end of 1860 Tredegar was in dire financial straits.

Tredegar's role in supplying iron and armaments to the South during the Civil War required the additional use of slaves, for the exigencies of war created abnormal labor shortages. But this increased reliance on slave labor during the war is of little value in determining the feasibility of large-scale use of slave labor in peacetime. Issues of profit and control were absent. In 1864 the Confederacy reported that 4,301 Negroes and 2,518 whites were working in government-controlled mills. In the same year at Tredegar's main facility, 200 of the 600 workers were slaves; 500 to 600 slaves worked at Tredegar's other operations. The total slave usage was fewer than 1,000 but at one point amounted to more than half the workers at Tredegar. Peak employment for Tredegar was 2,500, which included slaves and free men.

Optimism about the large-scale use of slave labor is contradicted by the Tredegar experience. The lack of substantial profitability, the small number of slaves involved, and the hybrid wage concept combined to derail Tredegar. Slavery could never survive in a climate of marginal profitability. The large-scale use of slaves in an urban or industrial labor force was never a part of the antebellum South.

Examples abound of failed private and public attempts in the South to deploy slave labor in jobs other than staple crop production. All conform to a pattern of small numbers and precarious financial situations. The Brandon Bank in Mississippi spent $159,000 on slaves in 1839 for the Mississippi and Alabama Railroad; the venture went bust. Georgia purchased 190 slaves for railroad and river tasks in the 1820s; the state later sold them and did not repeat the experiment in similar projects in the 1840s and 1850s. Louisiana sold 100 slaves who had worked on "river improvements" in 1860. The Hillman Iron Works in Tennessee lost several slaves to cholera, forcing the removal of the remainder of their valuable slaves until the epidemic subsided. The Nesbitt Manufacturing Co. in South Carolina owned 194 slaves before its bankruptcy in 1845. The Saluda Factory in South Carolina hired 150 slaves before it was declared insolvent in 1852. Slaves were costly, and problems of illness, theft, working conditions, and capital requirements were large barriers to acceptable profitability. And any alternative slave occupations in the industrial sector had to compete with cotton.

*

Cotton dominated the American export market from 1803 to 1937 and played the leading role in the dynamic economic growth of the antebellum period. As the business historian George David Smith wrote,

> Never before, and certainly not since, has the demand for any one crop fired economic growth to the degree that cotton did in the United States during the five decades before the Civil War. Without cotton, that growth would have been far less dramatic.

The South's slave-produced cotton exports were the backbone of its power and sense of nationhood. It was easy to see why the South thought that the American North and Great Britain depended on cotton. In 1858 the South produced 66 percent of all U.S. exports. In 1859 the Northern exports were $45 million compared to $193 million from the South, of which cotton accounted for $161 million.

Cotton revenues allowed America to develop her nascent industries and provide a basis for monetary affairs. In 1860 the Northern cotton textile industry led America's other manufacturing sectors. Northern cotton mills manufactured goods valued at $115 million, "against $73 million for wool, and an almost equal amount for forged, rolled, wrought, and cast iron taken together." Southern slave-grown cotton was responsible for the cheap raw material that fueled the Northern mills. Cotton yielded the revenue to enable the South to buy goods from Northern merchants.

Cotton was unique; it maintained a clout that slave-produced sugar never commanded. The British anti-slavery organization, the Society of Friends, had employed a boycott of sugar in its assault on slave-grown West Indian sugar. In the 1790s an estimated 400,000 British boycotted this sugar, and sugar imports from India increased. But the gesture had a negligible impact on the sugar plantations. Even a symbolic boycott or attack on American slave-produced cotton was impossible. American cotton was far more difficult to replace than sugar grown by slaves thousands of miles from Britain.

Britain, aware of its precarious dependency on American slave-grown cotton, was not concerned about American slavery; it feared a civil war or crop failure in America, which might be devastating. In 1858 the Lancashire mills established the Cotton Supply Association, with the specific purpose of diversifying sources for cotton to India, Egypt, and Brazil. The most ambitious plan emanated from Dr. David Livingstone, the Scottish missionary turned explorer. Livingstone wanted to replace American cotton with African cotton produced by free labor in Batoka. His "bold messianic vision linked together not only commerce, civilization and Christianity but also free trade and free labour." Nothing came of these plans to displace American cotton.

The English press grew alarmed about this dependence. *Blackwood's Magazine* in 1853 bemoaned the fate of "millions in every manufacturing country in Europe within the power of an oligarchy of planters."

Henry Ashworth sounded the alarm of a potential social revolution to a gathering of the Society of Arts in London:

> [Cotton] . . . constitutes the structural weakness, the "feet of clay" of our otherwise gigantic commercial power. . . . The entire failure of a cotton crop . . . should it ever occur would utterly destroy, and perhaps forever, all manufacturing prosperity which we possess. . . .

The *Times* of London dramatically asserted that "the destiny of the world hangs on a thread—never did so much depend on a mere flock of down."

That "flock of down" was cultivated by millions of black slaves, whose value rose with the price and power of cotton. By 1860 the approximately four million slaves in the United States were estimated to be worth $2 billion to $4 billion. The aggregate value of the slaves was calculated by multiplying the number of slaves by a representative price for each age, gender, or occupation category. But caution should be observed when interpreting slave wealth or capital. Except for periods of excess, the price of a slave was vulnerably suspended over the price of cotton. And if a sizable number of slaves were offered for sale, the price would plummet. The paper calculation of slave wealth was thus a static number in a dynamic environment. Planters could not sell their slaves unless they had an alternative labor source. So the $2 billion-plus figure is not accurate in calculating market value. In the long run the slave was worth only as much as the profit or expected profit that could be produced from his or her labor. After the Civil War, because cotton production still generated revenue, it could still be financed.

In addition to its profits, cotton was king because it helped create Southern bombast and inspired rhetoric about slavery and an expanding slave empire. Jefferson Davis, during discussions about California's entry as a free or slave state, was influenced by the Gold Rush in 1849–1850. He blindly promoted slavery: "I hold that the pursuit of gold-washing and mining is better adapted to slave labor than to any other species of labor recognized among us." Southerners other than Davis spoke and wrote of mining ventures in Mexico, Chile, and the American West. Still others dreamed of dominating a slave-based empire that would include the traditional staple of sugar in Cuba and Mexico.

This "Gulf Coast imperialism" and crackpot filibusters, by their implicit association with Southern cotton-based economic strength, received undue national attention. In reality these romantic, grandiose ventures were colorful, sensational fiascoes. Even if the South had won its independence in the Civil War, Great Britain and the American North would never have allowed the Confederacy to conquer Cuba or other Caribbean nations.

CHAPTER SIX

The Roots of War

 BECAUSE cotton was a global business, the ties across the Atlantic played an essential role in the hopes and fears that led to the Civil War. Just as important, cotton created a profound reliance among different regions of the United States. When the Founding Fathers severed ties with England and took stock of their tattered collection of newly declared "states," they longed for a means of creating a unified nation. None of them could have imagined that cotton would become one of the main ingredients in its development. But by the late 1850s, dependence on cotton money gave enormous clout to Southern secessionists, and contributed to the coming of war.

The cotton linkages—between North and South, South and West, and the United States and Europe—can be seen clearly through the prism of New York City. Although geographically a Northern metropolis, New York was the nineteenth-century hub for much of America's commerce, and cotton was no exception. A look at New York's role in the cotton trade reveals fascinating alliances and deep bonds between North and South, built on profit and personal relations. Southerners claimed, with a certain chagrin, that 40 percent of all cotton revenues landed in New York. The mundane commercial aspects of the cotton business were available for all to witness; the players—the financier, the shipper, the insurer, the factor, the broker, the mill owner, the mill worker, the merchant—were exempt from the taint of slavery. New

York City's overwhelming anti-black attitude reinforced its rewarding Southern orientation.

In 1817 the commercial environment allowed New York to develop auction procedures and regular shipping schedules to foster trade, which in turn encouraged what became known as the cotton triangle. The points of the triangle were New York, Liverpool, and ports in the South, including Charleston, Mobile, and New Orleans. The Southern ports transported their cotton to New York, where it was simply moved from one dock in New York to another before it was loaded onto vessels bound for Liverpool, Le Havre, or New England.

The power of the cotton triangle quickly and consistently led to innovations, since each player wanted more direct access to the enormous sums of money to be had. In the 1830s the cotton ports began to deal directly with Europe. Cotton was shipped via rivers to the bustling port cities, which then sent their valuable cargoes to textile mills. In 1834, New Orleans became the leading port in the value of its cotton exports.

Many New Yorkers, then and now, like to see themselves as purely Northern and cosmopolitan, indebted to the global whims of finance, certainly not to anything as banal as agriculture. But an alternate though less popular truth cannot be denied: it was cotton that propelled New York to commercial dominance. By the 1820s cotton had "extended New York's sphere of commercial influence," before the heralded advent of trade from the Erie Canal in 1825. In 1822 cotton accounted for 40 percent of New York's exports. Textile imports, mainly from Britain, to New York by 1860 amounted to $101 million of a U.S. total of $120 million. The "Southern" trade, the sale of manufactured goods and attendant services to the South, has been estimated at $200 million per year. Until the Civil War, according to Philip Foner, "New York dominated every single phase of the cotton trade from plantation to market."

Even when the actual shipment of cotton through New York declined, trade revenues did not diminish because of the multitude of attendant financial services the city provided. In 1825, New York received 174,465 bales and exported 153,757, but domestic consumption and direct shipment by Southern ports reduced New York's export role. Mobile and New Orleans shipments to New York were reduced from 94,000 bales in 1853 to 28,800 bales in 1859. New York began to receive merely samples of cotton for classification, which could be used for trading and financial purposes. Yet New York continued to benefit because the major part of cotton was carried in New York or New England ships; New York ship brokers received commissions; New York marine insurance companies were paid fees.

In the 1850s the young Abram Dittenhoefer, a Columbia College student from the South, seemed surprised by New York's relationship with the region of his birth.

> The city of New York, as I discovered upon reaching the age of observation, was virtually an annex of the South, the New York merchants having extensive and very profitable business relations with the merchants south of the Mason and Dixon line. The South was the best customer of New York.

As anti-slavery advocates noted, New York was "the prolongation of the South . . . [where] ten thousand cords of interests are linked with the Southern Slaveholder." By the 1850s, New York commanded the lion's share of the "Southern" trade. In the summer, New York's hotels—the Astor, St. Nicholas, Fifth Avenue, St. Denis, Clarendon, and Metropolitan—were jammed with Southern merchants and planters who had come to purchase goods for consumption or for resale. Some of the city's firms even advertised that they catered only to the "Southern" trade. Southerners sought financing in New York for their railroads, mines, and other expensive projects. One Southern railroad was organized in New York with a $4 million capitalization. When Southern planters defaulted, New York financial backers had to take possession of slave collateral. Many New York merchants had branches in New Orleans, Memphis, and Charleston.

Northerners were well aware of the dynamics of these sectional ties. The *New York Times*, on December 7, 1860, pointed out that the city controlled the South's business because of its leadership "position, skill, industry and wealth." A Philadelphia journal, as early as 1837, noted that "The growth of the cotton states may be almost entirely traced to eastern capital. Everyone knows that the planter receives goods on credit in anticipation of the next year's crop," and "it is equally well known" that Northern merchants supplied the credit. The North provided commerce; the South provided cotton. The *New York Post* in 1860 summarized the city's position: "New York belongs almost as much to the South as to the North."

While New York regarded the "Southern" trade as a "business necessity," slavery put the business community on the defensive. As early as 1835, one firm, Bailey, Keeler & Remsen, reassured its Southern clients in a notice published in newspapers and signed by numerous other merchants:

> Having learnt that some insinuations have been made [probably with the design to injure us] that our firm is in favor of the cause of Abolition, we hereby declare that such accusations are utterly false and unfounded; and we pledge ourselves that all the members of our house are opposed in principle to the views of the abolitionists, regarding the agitation of the slave question, and the interference with the rights of southern slave-holders as inexpedient, unjust, and pregnant with evils.

The pro-Southern views of New York's flamboyant mayor, Fernando Wood, were well known. In 1859, Wood spoke of the South as a good customer:

> As commercial people it is to our interest to cherish and to keep so good a customer. A strong movement was developing in the South to "do without us.". . . Let us, therefore, do nothing to estrange the South. Not only let us avoid making war upon her own peculiar system of labor but let us become even stronger defenders of the system than the South itself.

On the eve of the Civil War, New York's mayor was not only pro-Southern but pro-slavery.

New England shared in the trade. The amount of raw cotton sent to New England mills grew steadily until the Civil War. This cheap source of raw material benefited the region, which had earlier accumulated money through shipping and the slave trade. The importance of cotton gave rise to the term "Cotton Whigs," a class of New Englanders whose cotton interests caused them to sympathize with Southern slavery. New Englanders, ever resourceful, thus moved from the slave trade to the "merchandise" trade. In 1860 the *Boston Post* reported the "aggregate value of Boston merchandise sold to the South annually we estimate at some $60,000,000." This included $20 million for shoes, $3 million for fish, $1 million for furniture, and an undetermined amount for shipbuilding. Goods sold to the South and West were largely protected by tariffs.

The native Southerner Thomas Kettell sought to explain how the North derived its prosperity from slavery in his 1860 book *Southern Wealth and Northern Profits*. Kettell succinctly noted the South's commercial disadvantages: "If the South produces this vast wealth, she does little of her own transportation, banking, insuring, brokering, but pays liberally on those accounts to the Northern capital employed in those occupations."

As the United States grew in complexity, and as its economic relationships grew accordingly, no one region could dominate all aspects of commerce. Thus the natural resources of the South reluctantly came to rely on the financial strengths of the North—and vice versa. The glistening white cotton boll, though far more visible across the hills and bottoms of the South, became essential to the prosperity of the North. Cotton helped unify the country, for better and for worse.

Just as New York was intimately engaged in the movement of slave-produced cotton, so too were New Yorkers involved in the slave trade. In the 1850s the sustained demand for slaves and the surging price for slaves in Cuba and Brazil caused profit-minded New Yorkers to enthuse over profits from the international slave trade. New Yorkers' obsession with making money and their general disdain for the plight of black people combined in the 1850s to exploit the profits of the trade in human cargo. Although the city was not directly connected with cotton and American slavery, New York's wholehearted embrace of this despicable commerce revealed its priority of money over morals. The international slave trade had been outlawed in 1808; no slave could be imported into the United States. Nevertheless New Yorkers indulged in the buying and selling of slaves until they were forced by the Civil War to stop.

New Yorkers financed and organized slaving expeditions that sailed from the port of New York. Slave traders often used the leading admiralty law firm of Beebe, Dean, and Donohue, with offices at 76 Wall Street. Essentially slaves were purchased in Africa, then taken to Brazil and afterward to Cuba for resale. Large vessels, especially those powered by steam, could carry twelve hundred African captives to slavery. For example, approximately one hundred slaving ships left New York between January 1859 and August 1860. The money was irresistible. A single voyage could yield a profit of $175,000.

Individual stories of slave-trading profits circulated freely in New York, including this matter-of-fact description of one episode: "I know of two ladies, now attracting adoration at a fashionable watering place, who invested in a little venture of this kind not so long ago, and as a result have augmented their banking accounts—one to the extent of $23,000 and the other $16,000."

Slave traders openly discussed their business—documents, financing, and bribes—while dining at their favorite restaurant, Sweet's, on Fulton Street. Trade transactions were arranged near Trinity Church in lower Manhattan. One slaver, the *Wanderer*, sailed under the flag of the New York Yacht Club.

The facts were quite clear to observers and the press. In 1860 the *Times* of London called New York "the greatest slave-trading mart in the world." W. E. B. Du Bois later described New York's role, noting that "The fitting of slavers became a flourishing business in the United States, and centered at New York City." He added, "New York has been until late [1862] the principal port of the world for this infamous commerce; although the cities of Portland [Maine] and Boston are only second to her in that distinction. Slave dealers added largely to the wealth of our commercial metropolis."

New York's slave trading seeped into elite circles, as is evidenced by John Jay's attempt to protest the "infamous commerce" at the Diocesan Convention of the Episcopal Church in 1859. Jay presented a petition that acknowledged that the slave trade "hath reopened and is now prosecuted from the port of New York within the jurisdiction of this diocese." He noted that the slave trade was accepted by the community, and the "legalizing of said traffic is openly advocated, and laws denouncing it as piracy are trampled on with impunity." His petition recommended that the convention "encourage a sound Christian sentiment on this subject to the intent that the City of New York may be purged of its participation in this stupendous crime." Jay's address was bitterly received and was punctuated "frequently by interruptions" and "disorderly behavior," which required appeals by officials to "maintain silence." The audience responded "with [the] sound of suppressed laughter and a slight attempt at hissing." The august Episcopalians rejected the "resolution . . . by a very decided majority, and only the sacredness of the place kept the applause from breaking forth at this result."

In 1858, New York senator William Seward was opposed by New York businessmen when he introduced legislation to control the slave trade. Seward did not mince words in his reaction:

> The root of the evil is in the great commercial cities and I frankly admit, in the City of New York. I say also that the objection I found to the bill, came not so much from the slave States as from the commercial interests in New York.

New Yorkers were removed from the repugnant physical aspects of slave trading. Their involvement was confined to financing, fitting out ships, and supplying crews. Thus their sanitized perspective of the slave trade dovetailed with New York's commercial talents, as did the financing and trading of slave-produced cotton. A commercial country like America, and a city like New York, are eminently capable of adjusting to profit incentives, even in this extreme case of slave trading.

The election of the anti-slavery Republican Abraham Lincoln set in motion the secession of the Southern states and brought commercial anxiety to Northern, and especially New York, business interests. Although Lincoln promised not to interfere with slavery where it existed and was constitutionally protected, the North recognized that the Union faced an immediate threat of disintegration with catastrophic commercial implications.

In the decade before the Civil War, New York City's businessmen convulsed over the prospect of a conflagration and the resulting "Cotton Terror"—the fear that the cotton trade would be jeopardized. Merchants were concerned about their Southern business. Southerners readily acknowledged that if Lincoln were elected and war ensued, "the Northern merchants will suffer for the Southern ones won't pay one cent of their Northern liabilities." To counter the Republicans, New York's pro-Southern men also fanned racial fears. One predicted that a Republican victory would "find negroes among us thicker than blackberries."

Lincoln and the Republicans lost New York City by thirty thousand votes to the Union party. (Lincoln also failed to win New York City in 1864.) The merchants carried the city, but upstate New York gave the state and presidential election to Lincoln. The most important issues to voters across New York and the North were slavery, slave expansion, and union, not black equality.

Although it is easy to accuse the South of racial hatred, we now know that this affliction was just as rampant in the North. Most New Yorkers, like most Northerners, were not only opposed to racial assimilation and black equality, they vehemently and passionately loathed the mere presence of black people in their midst. An increase in the black population was feared. Indeed, in 1860, New York voters overwhelmingly defeated, by 337,934 to 197,505, an amendment to the state constitution that would have removed the $250 property requirement demanded of black, but not of white, voters. New York's free black population, which numbered around 1 percent, was effectively denied the right to vote.

The treacherous, emotionally charged period following Lincoln's election, when Southern states began to secede from the Union, revealed New York's overweening fears of business loss. On January 29, 1861, thirty New York businessmen traveled to Washington for "Businessmen's Week" to recommend a peaceful solution to the secession crisis. They delivered a petition signed by forty thousand of their city's businessmen. Opponents, again and again, referred to New York businessmen as "cotton-loving merchants and manufacturers."

New York businessmen even threatened to withhold vital war funding from the federal government. With secession and a war looming, the federal government faced financial difficulties. New Yorkers knew the power of money—as one merchant put it, "If New York gives the money, we shall have an internal war. If she withholds it, there must be peace." New York could "close the purse strings." The reasoning was seductive until New York businessmen realized what a separate Southern nation would mean for commercial survival.

Although war might be unavoidable, doing away with slavery was another matter. The *New York Times*, a staunch supporter of Lincoln, advocated the reform of slavery rather than abolition:

> We do not believe that it is either just or wise to introduce into discussions of the day any schemes for the abolition of Slavery. It must be distinctly understood that we of the North have nothing to do with that subject, that we propose no Congressional action upon it, but that we regard it as exclusively under the jurisdiction and control of the Slaveholding States. . . . We have admitted the impossibility and the folly of immediate abolition of Slavery, and pointed out the ruin certain to flow from the sudden release of four millions of ignorant slaves from the dependence and control of masters, to whose care they have been accustomed for generations to look for the means of subsistence. . . . The great need of the South is a modification and amelioration of her system of Slavery.

The *Times*' list of slavery reforms included legalization of marriage, criminalization of the separation of husband and wife, Sunday instruction "subject to efficient police regulation," ownership of property, and encouragement of savings. Slaves should be allowed to purchase their freedom if condoned by their state of residence. If a state did not want an emancipated slave to remain "on its soil," the state could require that freedom be conditional on emigration to Liberia. The federal government could encourage these practices by offering to pay $25 per slave to each slaveholding state for an "Education and Reform Fund." The *Times* would allow slaves to be bought and sold as long as families remained intact, but slaves would still be subject to "compulsory labor." The *Times* concluded: "Slavery thus modified and ameliorated would become a very tolerable system, and would deserve the title of *patriarchal* which its friends claim for it."

Horace Greeley's *New York Tribune*, also a Lincoln supporter, and with an eye to commerce, on February 23, 1861, approved of secession if done peacefully. The *Tribune* did regard the South's activities— "robbing arsenals, seizing forts and armories, stealing the contents of mints and sub-treasuries, and firing on vessels bearing the flag and doing the work of the Union"—as treason. In order to be legitimate, the "Cotton States" must submit the "question of Union or Disunion to a direct vote of the People," who the *Tribune* predicted would choose Union.

The reality of secession and the loss of the cotton business made the economic issues clear. An announcement by the Lord and Taylor retailers presaged the loss of the South as a mercantile customer:

> Lord and Taylor would inform their customers and purchasers that they have had Large Quantities of Dry Goods returned to them from Various Sections of the South from firms who have been unfortunate owing to the present Political and Financial Panic. . . .

Northerners fretted over Southern threats to withhold payment on loans. New Yorkers felt the debt issue acutely for they were owed an estimated $200 million in Southern debt.

Amidst the turmoil of early 1861, money and commerce led a few New Yorkers to fantasize about a separate path. There was talk of the city becoming a free port, an independent Republic of New York. On January 7, New York's pro-Southern Mayor Wood proposed the secession of New York City, along with the counties of Westchester, Kings, Queens, and Suffolk, from the state and the Union. According to Wood, New York would be a "free city" with revenue from import tariffs. Such an arrangement would have the "united support of the Southern States." New York merchants and the press generally did not take Wood's proposal seriously. Despite frustrations over the potential loss of the Southern trade and debt repudiation, New Yorkers realized their fate was tied to the Union. The commercial disaster bound to accompany the establishment of an independent "cottonocracy" was overriding. Mayor Wood, who would later serve as a New York congressman, recanted when he was forced to face the grim prospects of disunion.

But the full realization of Southern secession, and its trade implications, smacked New Yorkers and Northerners as they learned that the newly formed Confederate government would impose low duties on all goods imported into the Confederacy after March 1, 1861. Low Southern tariffs meant a loss of federal revenue and import business, as foreign goods would be shipped to Southern ports rather than to New York. The next step was assumed to be Confederate elimination of all tariff agreements with foreign countries, especially Great Britain. The *New York Evening Post* wrote cogently about the extreme consequences of the secession of South Carolina and the possibility of a competitive Southern trade zone:

> That either the revenue from duties must be collected in the port of the rebel states, or the port must be closed to importations from abroad, is generally admitted. If neither of these things be done, our revenue laws are substantially repealed; the sources which supply our treasury will be dried up; we shall have no money to carry on the government; the nation will become bankrupt before the next crop of corn is ripe.

At the same time the U.S. Congress passed the Morrill Tariff, which took effect on April 1, 1861. It was the highest in American history. A Southern nation with no tariffs would have nullified the Morrill Tariff and wreaked havoc on American government revenues. The legislation was foreshadowed in the Republican party platform of 1860 and actually signed by Democratic president James Buchanan. Southerners, who would have opposed the bill, had already left the Senate. The Morrill Tariff raised iron rates to more than 50 percent, and boosted rates on clothing to 25 percent. Goods imported through New York would be subject to tariffs twice as high as in New Orleans. New Orleans and Southern ports would easily supply St. Louis and Cincinnati with "cheaper" goods than New York.

The New York business community had no choice but war. March and April 1861 brought a profound change in merchant sentiment, but this shift was based on economics, not patriotism or higher principles. The drastic implications of trade moving unimpeded through Southern ports to the South and West would have spelled economic disaster for the North. On April 8 the *New York Times* now warned against secession: "No sane man" would think that Illinois would trade with New York when New Orleans imports were cheaper. The paper's economic editor shouted through his column: "At once shut down every Southern port, destroy its commerce and prosperity." The North at last realized the significance of the words of Henry J. Raymond, founder of the *Times*, who had written on January 26 that "no class of men in this country have so large a stake in sustaining the Government, whose prosperity depends so completely upon its being upheld against all its enemies, and who have so much to lose by its overthrow as the merchants of this city." Raymond was specifically referring to New York merchants who were selling arms to the Southerners. On March 29 the *Times* recognized that Southern actions were not mere swagger: "We shall not only cease to see marble palaces rising along Broadway . . . but reduced from a national to a merely financial metropolis, our shipping will rot at the wharves, and grass will grow in the streets."

No less than commercial survival was at stake. The tariff conflict and trade concerns were a corollary of the slave-produced cotton juggernaut. As war loomed, Northerners were forced to acknowledge the South's real power. It is misleading to single out the tariff war as the trigger of the Civil War, but it did provoke Northern businessmen into support for the Union. The conventional narrative of American history so often gives utmost importance to either slavery or states' rights as the driving force behind the war; but we must acknowledge the simultaneous panic and fury of the North's business interests and their influential role in the fight to come.

New York City, America's commercial and financial epicenter, was forced to confront the consequences of the South as a separate economic entity. As Philip Foner wrote,

> The swift change in the attitude of New York businessmen must have had a significant influence upon the administration in Washington. There is no doubt that Lincoln was determined to preserve the Union regardless of what views Wall Street had on this issue. Nevertheless, it would hardly have been wise for him to take any steps until he was certain of support in the business and financial center of the nation.

Immediately before and after the firing on Fort Sumter by Southern forces, New York threw its commercial and financial weight to the Union. In April 1861 bankers solidly backed loans for the federal government. When the Confederacy's president, Jefferson Davis, solicited "privateers" to raid Northern commerce, New York's merchants raised $8 million for defense.

*

On the eve of the Civil War, cotton breathed life into the institution of slavery and made the South a sustainable economic entity, independent from its Northern brethren. The South could hope to go it alone not because it produced enough agricultural or manufactured products but because slave-produced cotton revenues could procure those items, including armaments, from England, the North, or the West.

Still, even with cotton production, the South would have faced economic, political, and moral obstacles and contradictions, especially in its desire to promote industry. In the mid-nineteenth century the removal of tariff burdens seemed to be a rational short-term policy for the South. The resulting aid to the development of Southern industrial capacity would have eased the need to import. But it would also have raised conflicts with slave-produced cotton, because the dreaded tariff would be needed to protect the new Southern manufactures—just as in the North. In fact the issue had already been raised in 1827, when the owners of a new textile mill close to Athens, Georgia, supported high tariffs, a policy in direct opposition to the needs of cotton producers who wished to sell cotton and purchase tariff-free manufactured goods from abroad. A Georgia newspaper reprimanded the textile mill owners.

The South had no formidable economic existence without slave-produced cotton, which is ultimately what allowed the region to consider war. The South would quickly turn to cotton as a threat and a mechanism to finance its war effort. In February 1861, when the fledgling government of the Confederacy considered its options, it cast aside the South's ideological opposition to taxes on exports expressed at the Constitutional Convention of 1787 and imposed an export tax on cotton to fund its fledgling government.

*

Throughout the nineteenth century the South was stigmatized for its stunted growth, its economic backwardness, and its failure to innovate. Its increasing infatuation with cotton, to the detriment of other crops, was understandable because of cotton's power. It became the indispensable product. But the South's single-mindedness brought with it a host of problems. To begin with, slavery as a labor system has long been attacked as the source of the South's economic weakness: "Bondage forced the Negro to give his labor grudgingly and badly," Eugene Genovese notes, "and his poor work habits retarded social and economic advances that could have raised the general level of productivity." Similarly the cotton South is faulted for its woeful lack of patent grants compared to the North. Actually the South had made continual improvements in the cotton gin. But production problems, though they persisted, were not inherent to the South. They were inherent in the nature of cotton production with its bottlenecks of weeding and picking. Neither could be technologically solved until the mid-twentieth century.

Despite the faults of the Southern system, it created an explosive surge in cotton production, and the rest of the world could not get enough of it. The demand for cotton from the textile mills of England and the North grew at an astounding average of 5 percent annually for sixty years before the Civil War. The South, as an entity, realized the aggregate power of cotton as a global economic phenomenon, even as the lives of countless individuals—from white farmers to black slaves, and from plantation owners to mill workers—were subject to its whims. Few planters sold land or slaves when the price of cotton was high because they would be out of business. But at the opposite end of the spectrum, few planters responded to market downturns by changing businesses. Cotton farming, in the words of the historian Ulrich B. Phillips, was "less a business than a life; it made fewer fortunes than it made men."

In the 1850s, cotton seemed like a sure bet. The Panic of 1837 was easily forgotten, and even the dismal 1840s were fading from memory. The price of cotton remained stable in the decade before the Civil War, thus muting the ever-present financial risks inherent in the speculation-heavy and financing-dependent business of cotton. The stability of these years was a prerequisite for the push toward secession and the establishment of the Confederacy.

By the mid-1850s the South had embraced a sense of economic invincibility that led to rash political acts. No account of Southern nationalism would be complete without Senator James Henry Hammond's famous "Cotton is King" speech in the U.S. Senate on March 4, 1858. The supply of cotton was so important, Hammond declared, that "No power on earth dare make war upon it." Despite his "oratorical deficiencies," Hammond was thrust into "national prominence with his provocative speech." But he was not the first to express cotton's definitive power, nor was he the first to use it as proof of the South's economic exceptionalism. Hammond's speech was merely delivered in the right place at the right time.

The origins of Hammond's ideas, as well as one of the South's most enduring phrases, may be found in an 1855 pamphlet, *Cotton Is King: or Slavery in the Light of Political Economy*. The author was a pro-slavery Cincinnatian, David Christy, who wrote what many had been thinking about the dependence of England and the world on Southern cotton. With the publication of Christy's tract, "King Cotton" entered the public domain as a staple expression of politicians, journalists, and economists.

Hammond, a provincial South Carolinian, warned the North about the importance of the cotton trade. He calculated that the South accounted for $220 million of "surplus production," which included both foreign exports and products sent to the North. Hammond's "surplus figure" for the North was $95 million. The senator summarized what would become just a few years later the South's cotton strategy at the beginning of the Civil War:

> [W]ould any sane nation make war on cotton?. . . What would happen if no cotton was furnished for three years?. . . this is certain: England would topple headlong and carry the whole civilized world with her, save the South. No, you do not dare make war on cotton. No power on earth dares to make war upon it. Cotton is King.

The Confederate States of America would indeed place an embargo on cotton. The Southern strategy was simple: once deprived of cotton,

England and France would recognize the South as an independent nation and intervene in its behalf in the conflict with the North. This tactic was flawed, as we shall see. Nevertheless this bold stance of Confederate self-confidence reminds us once again of the huge influence of economic strength on the fate of a nation. Even after the Civil War, the Massachusetts Radical Republican Benjamin Butler would advocate the King Cotton scheme to force England to pay reparations.

It was the lived experience of generations of black Americans that powered the South and made possible both the cotton economy and Southern braggadocio. On the eve of the Civil War, slavery was prospering only in the cotton states of South Carolina, Georgia, Florida, Alabama, Mississippi, western Tennessee, Arkansas, Louisiana, and Texas. Over this entire region, the average price of a slave, as already noted, had reached an astounding $1,800 "per prime field hand." Part and parcel with the value of a slave was a continuing increase in demand for cotton. But slavery in the noncotton border states was moribund. Between 1850 and 1860, Maryland and Delaware experienced declines in their slave population. Virginia and Kentucky had only a small increase. Missouri's white population growth was outstripping the growth of its slave population. Kentucky, despite a slight increase in slaves, and Missouri were slave-selling states.

Nevertheless the years before the Civil War saw a conspicuous though insubstantial effort to reopen the international slave trade. It became an issue at noisy but ineffective Southern commercial conventions. The Vicksburg convention in 1859 actually approved the reopening of the slave trade, but the action had little meaning as Virginia, Maryland, and North Carolina had sent no delegates. The meetings were co-opted by hardcore advocates of slave trading. More important, individual states did not act to reopen the slave trade. In 1858 the Louisiana Senate rejected a plan to bring 2,500 "apprentices" from Africa into the state. Georgia allowed the ban to remain in its constitution. Alabama also voted down a proposal to reopen the international slave trade.

When the Confederacy was formed, it might have seemed logical for the South to provide for the renewal of the international slave trade in its constitution. Yet the dictates of the business of slavery overrode arrogant Southern rhetoric. While the Confederacy did provide substantial legal protection for slaveholders, the Constitution of the Confederate States of America, unanimously approved on March 11, 1861, expressly prohibited the reopening of the slave trade. The legal status of slavery was made explicit in Article I, Section 9, of the Confederate constitution:

> 4. No bill of attainder, or ex post facto law, or law denying or impairing the right of property in negro slaves, shall be passed.

The same section forbids the importation of slaves from foreign countries and from states outside the Confederacy.

> 1. The importation of negroes of the African race, from any foreign country, other than the slaveholding States or territories of the United States, is hereby forbidden, and Congress is required to pass such laws as shall effectively prevent the same.
>
> 2. Congress shall also have power to prohibit the introduction of slaves from any State not a member of, or Territory not belonging to this Confederacy.

Slaveowners simply did not favor an increase in the supply of slaves, which would have reduced the value of their existing workforce.

The voices of the more determined advocates of the international slave trade seemed to fade by the time the Confederacy was established, and the limits placed on the trade were never challenged. Alexander Stephens, who served as a U.S. senator and as vice president of the Confederacy, declared that Southerners were "as much opposed to [reopening the international slave trade] as they are in the North." Delegates to Mississippi's secession convention voted 84 to 15 for secession and 66 to 13 against reopening the slave trade. Mississippi's H. S. Foote appealed directly to the logic of money:

> If the price of slaves comes down, then the permanency of the institution comes down. . . . Would you be willing to shoulder your musket in vindication of slaveholding rights . . . if your slaves were only worth five dollars apiece? Why, every man sees that that is an absurdity. Therefore, the permanence of the system depends on keeping prices high.

Southern slaveowners did not wish to disrupt the fragile equilibrium between the demand for cotton, the price of cotton, and the price of slaves.

While there may have been no economic threats to slavery in the 1850s, moral and political attacks grew. Anti-slavery movements and abolitionists in the North gained momentum in their assault upon the "peculiar institution." Anti-slavery advocates, on the fringe in the 1830s, had become part of mainstream American politics, as expressed in the Republican party's support of limiting slavery to its existing territory. William Lloyd Garrison and a coterie of white and black activists had persevered in their quest to make the North aware of the evils of slavery. The South had retreated to rationalizing slavery as a positive good and attempting to censor debate over the institution.

In this atmosphere of increased tension, the South's vulnerability to slave insurrections and fugitive slaves became a pervasive concern. Uprisings led by Denmark Vesey (1822) and Nat Turner (1831) haunted Southerners, who tried to block anti-slavery literature from entering slave regions. When the Civil War intervened, a version of insurrection occurred. In the Revolutionary War the British had promised freedom to slaves who joined their army; in the Civil War the North emulated the British theme, inducting freed slaves or "contraband" into the Union army. Almost 200,000 African Americans—most of them former Southern slaves—served the Union. James Madison in 1796 had warned America about the possibility of a foreign army enlisting slaves in an invasion of America. Sixty-six years later the South discovered that the foreign army was made up of Union troops.

*

On the eve of the Civil War, cotton and race-based slavery were inextricably bound in America, which had split into two countries. Each country, North and South, had developed an independent but interrelated economy. The defining characteristic of these opposing social systems was more than simply free labor versus slave labor. Race was a crucial factor. The ultimate divide was free white labor versus black slavery or free black labor.

Because of the powerful economic engine created by slave-produced cotton, the South was as much of a threat to the North as the
North was to the South. But the much-touted power of the slaveocracy
to control national politics was exaggerated, for the South could not
prevent the passage and implementation of economically punishing
tariffs in the antebellum period. The Republican party's victory in the
1860 presidential election, with the attendant threat to slavery, was
the specific catalyst in the South's pursuit of formal nationhood. But
the South would not have dared rend the country in two without the
enormous—if erratic—power of slave-produced cotton.

The South's weaknesses were well known: the moral and economic
vulnerability of slavery, a nondiversified economy, lack of manufacturing capacity, and a divisive states' rights orientation. The South had
little time to organize itself as a nation before initiating a war with
the North, whose population was greater and whose industrial strength
was second only to Great Britain's. Despite these disadvantages, cotton
forced Europe and the North to take the Confederacy seriously and
caused the South to take itself seriously. As the stakes mounted, the
North had no alternative in preserving the Union but to meet the challenge of war and hope that Lincoln could build a nation out of a dual
confederacy.

In 1860 and 1861, as each of the Southern states met to discuss
secession, slavery was uppermost in their minds. Some even mentioned
the explicit cotton connection. Judge Alexander Hamilton Hardy, a native Marylander who had settled in Mississippi, remarked that "Without slavery, 'the beautiful cotton fields' would become 'barren wastes.'"
Georgia's Henry L. Benning feared that slavery would be forced to
retreat to the "Cotton States" before ultimately being abolished. Slavery via cotton, or cotton via slavery, was at the fore of the secessionist
thrust.

William Seward was one of many who pointed out the ties between
cotton, slavery, and land expansion, a bond that he argued made a collision between slaveholding and free states inevitable. Seward hated
slavery. On March 11, 1850, he appealed to a "higher law" than that of
the Constitution for ending slavery. In Rochester, New York, on Octo-

ber, 25, 1858, Seward famously and correctly forecast an "irrepressible conflict":

> Shall I tell you what this collision means? . . . It is an irrepressible conflict between opposing forces, and it means that the United States must and will, sooner or later, become either entirely a slave-holding nation, or entirely a free-labor nation.

But the duality of Seward's and America's attitude—anti-slavery and anti-black—condemned the former slaves to remain in the cotton field after emancipation. Seward's America in February 1860 did not envision black equality:

> [W]hat our system of labor works out . . . is the equality of the white man. The laborer in the free States, no matter how humble his occupation, is a white man, and he is politically the equal of his employer. . . . The European immigrant . . . avoids the African as if his skin exhaled contagion. . . . Did Washington, Jefferson, and Henry . . . propose to sink you down to the level of the African, or was it their desire to exalt all white men to a common political elevation?

PART THREE

The North: For Whites Only, 1800–1865

The North has nothing to do with the negroes. I have no more concern for them than I have for the Hottentots. They are God's poor; they always have been and always will be so everywhere.... The laws of political economy will determine their position and the relations of the two races. Congress can not contravene those.—William H. Seward, Secretary of State, 1866

Oregon is a land for the white man; refusing the toleration of negroes in our midst as slaves, we rightly and for yet stronger reasons, prohibit them from coming among us as free negro vagabonds.—Oregon Weekly Times, 1857

Everywhere and at all seasons the coloured people form a separate community.... As a rule, the blacks you meet in the Free States are shabbily, if not squalidly, dressed; and as far as I could learn, the instances of black men having made money by trade in the North are very few in number.... In every Northern city, the poorest, the most thriftless, and perhaps the most troublesome part of the population are free negroes.—Edward Dicey, English commentator, 1862

CHAPTER SEVEN

Being Free and Black in the North

 THE CASE for Northern white complicity in the cementing of cotton and race may be proved beyond a reasonable doubt. In order to understand why freed slaves lacked mobility after the Civil War and were virtually chained to the cotton fields, it is necessary first to look thoroughly at antebellum racial animosity in the North. There whites simply did not want blacks in their society. White Northern racial attitudes are generally dismissed with a cursory reference to racism and prejudice. In reality the blatant racial bigotry of the North played a vital role in consigning blacks to a life in the cotton fields by impeding and even curtailing their physical and economic mobility, thus furthering the entrapment of most blacks in the South after the Civil War. To observe Northern attitudes before the Civil War is to apprehend not only the sad plight of black people but also the vital role of economics in the course of American history.

White America's true racial attitudes and its hypocrisy were fully on display in the North. The roots of pervasive racial animosity there were historically deep, with profound economic consequences for the post–Civil War period. The actual living conditions and the political and social status of blacks in the antebellum North thus deserve important attention; they complete our vision of the devastating difficulties of being black in America before the Civil War, and they foreshadow

the postwar period in which blacks were emancipated but cotton remained king.

For all the differences between the white North and the white
South, they shared a fundamental sense that the black population
was an unwanted source of trouble. And the root of this shared racial
animosity was simple: money triumphed. The relationship of economics and race in America was driven by profit. Blacks were brought to
America as slaves to make money for their owners. When there was no
money to be made, they were sold south to be used as laborers in staple
agriculture—the only real alternative. Before black slaves were used
on a large scale, there had to be at least the expectation of an urgent
economic need. Race-based slavery was suitable for plantation work, as
we have seen, because of the pigmentation distinction, the financing
characteristics of cotton farming, and the assumption of cultural inferiority. A white nation might discriminate against and exploit white
immigrants, but it would not enslave them.

When it had no more slaves, the North wished to rid itself of its
remaining free black population. There was no compelling economic
need for free blacks in the North because of the influx of millions of
white immigrants. White Northern workers could easily say that they
did not want black workers competing for jobs and thereby lowering
wage scales. This racial reasoning existed in tandem with a firmly
held white Northern conviction that blacks were lazy, profligate, shiftless, and immoral—a conviction that, ironically, would have rendered
blacks uncompetitive. This contradiction was never fully tested because
of the lack of economic necessity. When a temporary but immediate
economic urgency occurred, as in the case of a white labor strike, white
Northern employers quickly reacted by hiring racially detested blacks.
Only when white immigration was curtailed during World War I was
the North forced to "import" millions of black laborers. This is economics, with a racial twist.

All too often our simplified vision of American history goes something like this: the North, led by Abraham Lincoln, fought the Civil
War first to preserve the Union and later to end slavery. Because of
the virtually complete association of slavery and race as an exclusively
Southern problem, we assume that Northern whites at least tolerated

black people. But the truth is far more hopeless. We forget that anti-slavery for the most part also meant anti-black. White Americans have decoupled the horrors of slavery from the condition of free blacks. In a fit of national self-congratulation, Americans have applauded emancipation and relapsed into historical amnesia with respect to the condition of blacks in the North.

Following the Constitutional Convention, most Northern states abolished existing slavery within the next three decades. But after slavery was banned, these states and new ones too instituted a wide range of "black laws" aimed to suppress and limit the roles of blacks. These ranged from denial of the right to vote to outright exclusion from the community. In the nineteenth century, even where few free blacks lived in the North, they were largely detested and subject to discrimination. In the new territories of the West, where there were small numbers of slaves or free blacks, whites enacted exclusion laws and harsh "black codes." In both the old North and the new West, whites were enormously fearful of a black migratory invasion; they passed legislation favoring impractical colonization schemes and were outspoken about keeping free blacks, as well as slaves, out of the new territories. During and after the Civil War, white Northerners created a "containment policy" which effectively condemned blacks to the cotton fields of the South.

The racial proclivity of the antebellum white North provides the clue as to why 90 percent of all blacks in America lived in the South on the eve of World War I, despite oppressive conditions, and why there was no mass movement of free blacks to the North after emancipation. Blacks constituted only 2 percent of the North's population. We need to look no further than Boston, the hotbed of abolitionism, for an appropriate example. In 1850, Boston had a free black population of 1.3 percent of its total; by 1930, as David Cohn has noted, the entire state of Massachusetts had 52,000 blacks (1.3 percent) in a population of 4,000,000 while cotton-dominated Bolivar County, Mississippi, alone had 52,000 blacks. The answer lies in the connection between cotton and race that was fully underwritten and supported by the white North. A North hospitable to free blacks would have drained the South's labor force, with dire implications for the cotton world.

America in 1860 consisted of approximately half a million free
blacks, 27 million whites, and 4 million slaves. The free black population
was equally distributed between North and South. A quarter-million free
blacks lived among 22 million Northern whites (including Delaware,
Maryland, Kentucky, and Missouri). The North's pervasive discrimina-
tory and exclusionary activity is startling considering the small numbers of free blacks in the North relative to the white population. State
legislatures spent a wholly disproportionate amount of time and energy
on a miniscule part of their population. And federal, state, and local officials alike, once they had condemned slavery, had enormous difficulties
in considering the tiny black populations in their midst or the massive
numbers of emancipated Southern blacks. The white North's fear of a
large-scale black migration was tantamount to an obsession.

We begin by surveying conditions in two of the original states in
the North, and then several Western states in the decades before the
Civil War. New York and Connecticut provide examples of the black
experience in established settlements. A brief glance at Northern urban
cities, Boston and Philadelphia, offers no respite from racial hatred.
The new states of Ohio, Indiana, and Illinois offer cogent examples of
the extent of racial antipathy in fast-growing areas. Glimpses of other
Western states reinforce the racial story as white immigrants poured
into new settlements.

CHAPTER EIGHT

The Colonial North

NEW YORK, with a relatively significant slave population in the eighteenth century, had to deal with both emancipation and the status of free blacks. By the mid-eighteenth century, blacks, either slave or free, constituted 20 percent of the population of New York County. By 1790 the figure had dropped to 7 percent. By 1860, New York County contained 801,095 whites and 12,574 free blacks (1.57 percent of the population). During the Civil War the black population fell to 9,945. Correspondingly, New York State's black population dropped from 6.27 percent in 1790 to 1.26 percent in 1860. (See Appendix 1.)

Slavery in New York, as elsewhere, had been a response to labor shortages during the period of European settlement. The vast North American continent required labor for survival and for the production of wealth to the shareholders of the colonies. After the Dutch colony of New Amsterdam became New York in 1664, under English rule, black slavery became even more significant because of the powerful shareholders of the Royal African Company, a slave-trading corporation. The Duke of York, the proprietary ruler of the colony, was a shareholder. The crown's instructions were explicit: "And whereas we are willing to recommend . . . that the said province [New York] may have a constant and sufficient supply of mercantable negroes [slaves] at moderate rates, in money or commodities . . ."

The high percentage of slaves to the total population in New York fell because of insufficient profits and growing Southern demand for enslaved agricultural laborers. Still, during this period the presence of black slaves created fears within the white community. Two eighteenth-century slave insurrections, in 1712 and 1741, reinforced the need for social control, were brutally repressed, and became a prelude to racial violence in America.

In 1785 a bill providing for gradual emancipation was introduced in New York's legislature and eventually foundered. Gradual emancipation finally became law on July 4, 1799. A controversy was avoided because the "civil status" of black people was deliberately removed from the debate. The new law provided that slaves born after that date would serve apprenticeships such that all would be free by March 31, 1827. In New York by 1800, the slave population had dropped to 3.4 percent. An enormous increase in the white population further undermined the economics of slavery. The New York governor assumed that slaves would be worthless as property by 1827, so no hardship would befall slaveowners.

In 1821, New York passed legislation that eliminated the property requirement for white voters while increasing the qualification fee for blacks from $100 to a prohibitive $250. Article 2, section 1 of the New York constitution stated that ". . . no man of colour . . . unless . . . possessed of a freehold estate of the value of two hundred and fifty dollars . . . shall be entitled to vote." Thus only 16 blacks voted in New York in 1826; even in 1861 approximately 300 blacks out of a New York City black population of 12,000 could vote. The black voting restrictions were upheld in 1846 by a vote of 224,336 to 85,406. In 1860 and 1869 state constitutional conventions a majority again defeated black enfranchisement. In each case, black inferiority became a talking point, and delegates overwhelmingly voted to deny blacks suffrage in a period of relative decline of the black population. Racial antennae were highly sensitive, even in places with miniscule black populations.

*

As white immigrants arrived in New York en masse during the eighteenth century, skilled black laborers were displaced and relegated to menial positions. Free blacks were left with jobs whites did not want. Some blacks remained as sailors, but most became domestics in "private homes, hotels and boarding houses," or worked as chimney sweeps, washerwomen, and "tubmen" (cleaners of privies). The gritty job of crawling down a chimney to remove soot was performed by black children between the ages of four and ten. These jobs, rather than stepping-stones to advancement, were forced steps backward. Examples of race-based economic conflict illustrate the fragility of the black's status. An historian, citing the memoirs of a black New Yorker, described their wretched plight:

> Everywhere Negroes were shunned, cut off from free society, and excluded from most of the skilled occupations. Life held no promise for the Negro, for he was caught in a vise designed to crush and degrade him. . . . Great numbers of Negroes sank to the level of pariahs condemned to a bitter existence on the fringe of free society. . . . The Negroes were in a very real sense, a population in quarantine, trapped in a system of racial bondage.

The number of New York black males who had occupations that required an education—2 percent—compared poorly to the figures for the South's slave capital, New Orleans, where 10 percent of free blacks had vocations that required an education. Only 10 percent of free black males in New Orleans were categorized as unskilled. New York's appallingly low numbers have been attributed to racial animosity for any person with a "strain of negro blood."

Along with economic degradation, blacks had also to contend with violence in the 1830s. White abolitionists and blacks in New York City were attacked in July 1834, in riots based on white apprehension of blacks. Whites were particularly concerned about amalgamation, interracial sex, and interracial marriage. Lydia Maria Child, a prominent abolitionist, made it clear that she did not wish to violate the "distinctions of society by forcing the rude and illiterate [blacks] into the presence of the learned and refined [whites]."

Anti-black sentiment in New York erupted into the most violent civil disturbance in American history during the Civil War. The stage was set in the spring of 1863 when the war was going poorly for the North. The well-chronicled Draft Riots began on July 12. New York's

Anti-black sentiment in New York City erupted in 1863 during the Draft
Riots, producing the most violent civil disturbance in American history and
the lynching of African Americans. *(New York Historical Society)*

working-class whites rampaged through the city's streets, lynching
innocent blacks, roughing up white businessmen, and burning the
Orphan Asylum on the west side of Fifth Avenue between Forty-third
and Forty-fourth Streets. Predominantly Democratic white workers,
who were anti-black, were protesting a deliberate Republican party
policy of recruiting a disproportionate number of draftees from heavily Democratic districts. At least a hundred people were killed and a
thousand wounded in the melee. New York was fortunate in that six
thousand Union soldiers returned from their victory at Gettysburg on
July 4 to help quell the insurrection that reduced the city to chaos.

*

Despite overwhelmingly anti-black attitudes, white charity on behalf
of the black community is a recurring theme in American history.
Inspired by humanitarian concerns, such benevolence was often so paternalistic that it led black groups to seek control of their own destiny.

The New York City riots of 1863 provoked the burning of the Colored Orphan Asylum on Fifth Avenue. *(New York Historical Society)*

Whites hoped to create an uplifting process by which blacks would be "civilized," mainly in the areas of education, jobs, and morality. One such endeavor, the African Free Schools, was founded in 1785 by the New York Manumission Society, whose members were heavily involved in the New York City Colonization Society, which began in 1817, and in the state organization that followed in 1829. Both organizations encouraged sending blacks to Liberia. The Manumission Society also recommended Texas for black colonization because it was a less expensive solution than Liberia and because it was closest to "those states which are overcharged with the descendants of Africa."

In 1859 the historian Thomas De Voe lamented the plight of New York's black population. Freedom had boundaries, he observed, as blacks were "poor, squalid, dirty, half-dressed, ill-fed and bred and some no doubt with a strong inclination to be thievish." In fact blacks were convicted of crimes at a rate three and half times that of whites. De Voe blamed black poverty on the severe limits imposed by whites.

In their own communities, blacks formed cohesive social organizations, established schools and churches, chafed under white control, and aired their grievances publicly. In 1840 the New York State Convention of Colored Citizens petitioned the "People of New York" to repeal the property requirement clause for black voters. The petition fell on deaf ears. Further, the delegates described their situation:

> We find ourselves crippled and crushed in soul and ability . . . we were translated into the partial enjoyment and limited possession of freedom. . . . The prejudice against us in the community, has been more potent than the dictates of Christian equality.

Blacks for the most part rejected colonization. The frustrated black minister Henry Highland Garnet, however, did encourage emigration to the West Indies and Africa in 1858, when he organized the African Civilization Society. In a symbolic but futile exercise, Garnet also promoted the Free Produce movement, which advocated boycotting slave-produced sugar and cotton.

Through laws and customs, whites pushed the black population toward a separate, subordinate society. Segregation was observed in virtually every aspect of life except in working-class taverns. Housing in New York City was segregated, with 86 percent of New York's African Americans living below Fourteenth Street; fully 75 percent of the city's streets were exclusively white. When Seneca Village, the only area of significant black land ownership, was taken over by the city in 1857 as part of Central Park, its residents were poorly compensated and were not able to purchase land elsewhere.

*

Most New Yorkers experienced no conversion to racial enlightenment during and after the Civil War. When the issue of black suffrage emerged again, in 1867, New York's Tammany mayor and later governor, John Hoffman, rejected black political equality on racial grounds: "The people of the North are not willing . . . that there should be negro judges, negro magistrates, negro jurors, negro legislatures, negro Congressmen." Fear of intermarriage and "Negro supremacy" was used to deny black suffrage and as a form of intimidation. Samuel J. Tilden, the future governor who nearly became president in the disputed 1876 election, condemned black suffrage as a threat to white freedom: "It is not the white race of the South which is to be borne down [by black enfranchisement]. . . . It is ourselves also. . . . It is, therefore, for our own emancipation that we strike today." In 1868, Tilden had recommended that "our position must be condemnation and reversal of negro supremacy":

> On no other issue can we be so unanimous among ourselves. On no other question can we draw so much from the other side and from the doubtful. It appeals . . . to the adopted citizens—whether Irish or Germans; to all the workingmen; to the young men just becoming voters.

The Democratic candidate for president in 1868, Horatio Seymour, also campaigned against black equality. Seymour drew a picture of Louisiana's racially mixed legislature to frighten voters. While losing the presidential election, Seymour won 70 percent of Manhattan's vote. John Hoffman became governor with a determination to defeat the Fifteenth Amendment that conferred suffrage on black males. Black political equality was defeated in the New York referendum on the amendment in 1869—Manhattan voted 65,189 to 27,390 against black suffrage. The majority of New Yorkers had spoken.

*

Perhaps the most important New York politician of the mid-nineteenth century was William Henry Seward, who served as governor of New York, U.S. senator from New York, and secretary of state for eight years under Presidents Abraham Lincoln and Andrew Johnson (1861–1869). Seward's prominence made him the initial favorite for the Republican presidential nomination in 1860 before the emergence of the relatively unknown but formidable Abraham Lincoln. Seward made his mark on history with his anti-slavery stand, his opposition to slave expansion, his aggressive promotion of territorial expansion, his bold stance against British intervention in the Civil War, and his purchase of Alaska.

His oratory is best remembered for his phrases—the "higher law," which appealed to morality taking precedence over the Constitution with respect to slavery, and the "irrepressible conflict," which predicted the Civil War. Stripped of his hatred of slavery, however, Seward aided and abetted the continuation of the unholy union of cotton and race.

His predominantly commercial obsession can be traced, without interruption, throughout a long political career. Other issues were subordinate; slavery was an obstacle that had to be dealt with. Seward desperately wanted California, for example, so much so that he was willing to admit it "even as a slave state." "The westward trend of empire," he said, "was a 'higher law, a law of Providence.'" While he abhorred slavery, he deferred to trade.

Like most other anti-slavery politicians, Seward held blacks, either free or enslaved, in low esteem. For him, slavery constituted "the only element of discord among the American people." In 1860 he spoke in Detroit of black inferiority and the impossibility of black equality:

> The great fact is now fully realized that the African race here is a foreign and feeble element . . . incapable of assimilation . . . a pitiful exotic unnecessarily transplanted into our fields, and which it is unprofitable to cultivate at the cost of the desolation of the native vineyard.

He strongly adhered to the plan—Lincoln's and then Andrew Johnson's—for a swift and lenient integration of the Confederate states into the Union. After the war he wanted no further interruptions. He asked rhetorically, "Who will advocate the employment of force merely to hinder and delay, through prolonged anarchy, a reconciliation which is feasible and perfectly consistent with the Constitution?" Seward granted pardons to Confederate soldiers. When he invited a former prisoner of war, the Virginian R. M. T. Hunter, to dinner, the Confederate found a pardon under his plate. Seward also helped obtain a pardon for the vice president of the Confederacy, Alexander H. Stephens.

Seward held that the states should determine regulations for black suffrage. His views hardened over time. In 1846 he declared that suffrage was the right of "every man, learned or unlearned, bond or free." By 1865, in a cabinet meeting, he voted against black enfranchisement. He also advocated vetoing the bill that would have renewed and strengthened the Freedmen's Bureau, the agency set up to oversee the welfare of freed slaves. In April 1866, Seward reiterated his views on a prompt reconciliation without concern for blacks, and advocated no federal intervention on their behalf:

William H. Seward, New York governor and senator, and Lincoln's secretary of state, championed the anti-slavery clause but, like most Northerners, spoke condescendingly of African Americans, whom he had "no more concern for than Hottentots. They are God's poor, they always have been and always will be so everywhere." (Lincoln Museum)

I am ready to leave the interests of the most intelligent white man to the guardianship of his state, and where I leave the interests of the white I am willing to trust the civil rights of the black. The South must take care of its own negroes as the North did and does. . . . The North must get over this notion of interference with the affairs of the South. . . . The South longs to come home. . . .

Seward supported black suffrage in New York State where "their numbers were negligible," but in 1867 he opposed a bill that enfranchised blacks in the city of Washington because of the size of the potential black vote there. Black control, for him, was unthinkable. In time he thought that black enfranchisement would be appropriate. But he also thought that the civil rights legislation of 1866 was "unconstitutional on technical grounds."

Like Alexander Hamilton, Seward made commerce his priority. The Civil War was a distraction, but a necessary one, from his real goal—American global commercial hegemony, with New York City replacing London as the world's financial center. As early as 1837 he forecast that New York would be "the true and proper seat of commerce and empire." California was vital because California and the Pacific were keys to Seward's orientation toward Asia. Alaska was not "just another piece of real estate," it was "an entrepot in the Northwest for the trade of the Pacific and Asia." In a speech in 1870 he declared that America would "[assume] the leadership . . . in the regeneration of civilization in the East." In these aspirations Seward, who did not even believe in black equality, had no trouble sacrificing freedmen for what he considered higher goals.

Seward's overriding commercialism exemplified the driving force of American democratic society, and the cotton world was part of this commercial preoccupation. Black America did not figure in this equation, except in the cotton fields. During aberrations like the Civil War or depressions, the nation's materialistic impulses might be unavoidably restrained, only to reassert themselves quickly. The 1830s, 1840s, and 1850s were no different from the 1870s, 1880s, and 1890s in terms of America's fervor for making money. Even during the Civil War, Seward's New York—America's business capital—found a way to create an economic boom by supplying goods and munitions to the combatants.

*

At first glance Connecticut would seem an unlikely setting in which to find roots of the Northern antipathy toward African Americans. Certainly Connecticut mills needed cotton, but their needs could not compare to the demand and dependency of Great Britain. Nor are slavery and racial tensions ordinarily associated with Connecticut. Its black population, either slave or free, was statistically irrelevant. But cotton and race were an indelible part of the New England experience, as we shall see, and the Connecticut Survey of 1800 was an important and underappreciated document in American history.

As a colony of Great Britain, Connecticut residents purchased slaves to ameliorate a labor shortage. British imperialism fostered slavery as a means of supplying labor to its colonies. In the seventeenth century the first black slaves appeared in Connecticut, chiefly concentrated in maritime or small farming communities. An eighteenth-century Connecticut slaveholder might typically own one to three slaves who lived in close proximity to the family. According to the historian Peter Hinks, "Slaves . . . commonly took their meals with the [slaveowners] . . . received religious instruction and prayed with them, slept in a corner of the house, relaxed with the family around the hearth in the evening." This arrangement has been called "familial and gently paternalistic."

Slavery was hardly an economic bonanza in Connecticut and was simply not profitable enough to expand. In 1784 the state put an end to slavery with gradual emancipation legislation, by which all slaves born after 1784 would be freed at age 25; females were to be freed at age 21. In 1775 the state had more than 5,100 black slaves, about 3 percent of the population. In 1800 the number of free blacks in Connecticut was 5,330 (2.1 percent) of a population of 244,721; by 1860, 8,627 (1.9 percent) of a population of 451,520 people were black.

After the state's gradual emancipation process, we should not be surprised that Connecticut businessmen displayed no inhibitions about trading with or providing credit to a slave economy. Connecticut traders shipped livestock and dairy products from New Haven and New London to the West Indies and brought back sugar and molasses to New York. New York became a magnet for aggressive New England youths who aspired to wealth as merchants. George Griswold of Old Lyme moved to New York to trade flour with the West Indies for sugar and rum. His ships bore the family initials "N.L. & G.G.," which were dubbed "No Loss and Great Gain." His son Charles Griswold moved to Savannah as a cotton buyer. Anson G. Phelps, from Simsbury, traded cotton for metals and formed Phelps, Dodge & Co. with his son-in-law, William E. Dodge. The direct cotton trade with the South grew throughout the first half of the nineteenth century as the number of textile mills grew from 67 to 136. No onus attached to conducting business with the slave-related economy.

Connecticut has left an extraordinary record of white attitudes toward free blacks in the antebellum North. In 1800 the Connecticut Academy of the Arts and Sciences conducted an ambitious survey of more than one hundred Connecticut towns. The major sponsors were Timothy Dwight, the president of Yale College, and Noah Webster. The survey sought information about thirty-two "Articles," the twenty-seventh of which dealt with race. It specifically asked about

> Free blacks; their number, vices and modes of life, their industry and success in acquiring property; whether those born free are more ingenious, industrious and virtuous, than those who were emancipated after arriving to adult years.

This inquiry, possibly inserted by Webster, embodied the viewpoint that blacks had been degraded by slavery and, once freed, would undergo a transition to "proper" morality and productive citizenship. In Connecticut a brief period between gradual emancipation and the first decades of the nineteenth century were marked by this sort of white idealism and a hope that the ill effects of slavery could be whitewashed from black character. During a defined apprenticeship phase, according to this theory, blacks would depend on white tutelage and charity. The goal was an acceptance of white norms by black residents who would become productive citizens in a white society. If this transition could not work in Connecticut, so the thinking went, what would the fate of blacks be in the rest of America?

The survey responses from officials in Connecticut towns, which trickled in over a number of years, were devastating. The few towns that did report gave a damaging picture of blacks as lazy and immoral. No distinction could be seen between the character of emancipated and freeborn blacks. Even in these early years of the nineteenth century, blacks in Connecticut were viewed as an intractable problem. A sample of the reports revealed the racial sentiments of the white town leaders:

[New Haven] The . . . vices [of black people] are of all the kinds, usually intended by the phrase "low vice." Uneducated to principles of morality, or to habits of industry and economy, they labour only to acquire the means of expense, and expend only to gratify gross and vulgar appetite. Accordingly, many of them are thieves, liars, profane, drunkards, Sabbath breakers, quarrelsome, idle, and prodigal, the last in the extreme. Their ruling passion seems very generally to be a desire of being fashionable. . . . There are, however exceptions to this character. . . . (150 blacks, Timothy Dwight, President of Yale College, 1811)

[Sharon] There is little in the condition of these people to gratify the benevolent wishes of the inhabitants. . . . Not one is possessed of any real property and few indeed obtain even a decent support. Indolent and thoughtless, they make no calculation for the future, and are too regardless of the means by which present enjoyment is secured, nor does there seem any essential difference in the habits of those manu-mitted and those born free. (40 blacks, 1807)

[Farmington] We have said they have but Little Industry. Their Inge-nuity we have not had a Specimen of & their Virtues if any they have are a talent hid in the Earth. (30 blacks, 1802–1812)

[Cornwall] They are rather of a desultory disposition, some drink too much for their good, and are not very oeconomical in general, and sometimes it is thought when a gang meets for a high set, the Neigh-boring Poultry is not perfectly secure. (11 blacks, 1800, 1801)

There were few positive comments like this one from New London.

Their vices are fewer than those of the whites in the same grades of society. . . . Their industry is equal to that of the whites—their success in acquiring property seems to fall short. (103 blacks, 1812)

This important document is a firm indication of white Connecti-cut's attitudes toward its tiny free black population. The reports were more than pessimistic about the likelihood of black advancement and assimilation.

Yale's president Timothy Dwight, one of the leading intellectuals of his day, offered a scathing appraisal of free blacks' prospects. This prominent abolitionist believed blacks to be thoroughly dependent on white charity. In 1810, in his sermon "The Charitable Blessed," Dwight did not mince words in describing the plight of blacks.

> [T]hese people . . . are, generally, neither able, nor inclined to make their freedom a blessing to themselves. When they first become free, they are turned out into the world, in circumstances, fitted to make them only nuisances to society. They have no property; nor any skill to acquire it. Nor have they . . . generally any industry. They have indeed been used to labor; but it was under the control, and for the benefit of others. The hatred of labor, in this situation becomes habit; not the labor itself. They have no economy; and waste, of course, much of what they earn. They have little knowledge either of morals or religion. They are left, therefore, as miserable victims to sloth, prodigality, poverty, ignorance, and vice.

After Dwight died in 1817, the attitude toward free blacks continued to worsen. The Reverend Leonard Bacon succeeded Dwight as pastor of New Haven's most prominent Congregationalist church. In 1823, Bacon forcefully articulated the hopelessness of New Haven blacks: "In short, are they not, in the estimation of the community and in their own consciousness, aliens and outcasts in the midst of the people?" Bacon eliminated all possibility of uplift for free blacks in Connecticut. He regarded free blacks as "dangerous to the community" and wished his state rid of them.

Connecticut's white intelligentsia took the next step by advocating the removal of blacks by colonization to Africa. Blacks, of course, were not consulted. But colonization proved to be merely an impractical white fantasy. Blacks considered themselves Americans, and for the most part abhorred the thought of relocating to Africa. As one black resident of Middletown explained, "Why should we leave this land, so dearly bought by the blood, groans and tears of our fathers? Truly, this is our home, here let us live and here let us die."

The Connecticut Academy of Arts and Sciences moved from a prospect of black adjustment to the drastic conclusion that blacks must be eliminated altogether. The change of direction was dramatic. The state's abolition society and the Academy became enthusiastic supporters of the American Colonization Society, which they both formally endorsed in 1820. The Society's founder, Robert Finley of New Jersey, in 1816 had no doubt that blacks were "an idle, worthless, and thievish race" who could never assimilate with white America. Simeon Baldwin, a founding member of the Connecticut Academy, became president of the New Haven colonization organization in 1820. The same Simeon Baldwin in 1792 had been the staunch abolitionist who had advocated white stewardship of the free blacks' transition to "proper" conduct. By 1820, however, he had conceded that former slaves could not become productive citizens.

Connecticut's views on the unfitness of blacks for citizenship led in 1814 to state legislation that disfranchised its black residents. One wonders why the state would even be concerned about the voting rights of 2 percent of its population—until one considers the Connecticut Academy's survey. The law was included in the 1818 state constitution and was passed over several challenges. In 1857, in a state referendum held to challenge black disfranchisement, the law was upheld by a vote of 19,148 to 5,553. Even after the Civil War in 1865, Connecticut voters retained the disfranchisement. Suffrage came to blacks only with the ratification of the Fifteenth Amendment.

Connecticut experienced several episodes that provide insight into the complexity of racial issues in America. In 1831 the Reverend Simeon S. Jocelyn of New Haven proposed that "a Collegiate school [for teaching] a manual labor system" for blacks be established in New Haven. The proposed school was designed to help blacks "cultivate habits of industry" and "obtain a useful *Mechanical* or *Agricultural* profession." Reverend Jocelyn had impeccable credentials as a friend of African Americans. He helped found the anti-slavery society of New Haven in 1833; he was pastor of New Haven's Temple Street Church, which had a black congregation; and he was actively involved in charities for blacks.

New Haven was hardly a land of opportunity for blacks. Despite the town's anti-slavery trappings, its citizens had voted heavily against black suffrage in 1857. In the years before the Civil War many blacks in New Haven lived in poverty, typically working as domestic servants or manual laborers. The successful black barbers in New Haven were an exception.

In a hastily convened town council meeting, the "air ran hot and foul" as New Haven condemned Reverend Jocelyn's proposed school on racial grounds. A resolution passed by the mayor, aldermen, and the Common Council was clear:

> Yale College, the institutions for the education of females, and the other schools [in New Haven] . . . are important . . . and the establishment of a College in the same place to educate the Colored population is incompatible with their prosperity, if not the existence of the present institutions of learning, and will be destructive of the best interests of the city. . . . We will resist the establishment of the proposed College in this place, by every lawful means.

New Haven did not wish to encourage blacks to come to New Haven.

The fear of black migration helped derail another Connecticut school founded in Canterbury. The well-documented efforts of Prudence Crandall to educate young black girls in 1831 met with staunch resistance by Canterbury's citizens. Connecticut had instituted "black laws" in 1833 to prevent out-of-state blacks from coming into the state for an education. Crandall was accused of violating these laws and was acquitted on a technicality. Afterward her school was subject to attempted arson and vandalism as the citizens of Canterbury descended on the school and destroyed all its windows. Eventually Crandall abandoned Connecticut for Illinois, an even worse environment of racial intolerance.

*

Three noteworthy nineteenth-century figures with Connecticut roots—Eli Whitney, Frederick A. P. Barnard, and Harriet Beecher Stowe—offer insights into Northern conduct in the saga of cotton and race. All were successful innovators, possessed of intellectual creativity and physical mobility. All were native New Englanders who lived in and wrote about the cotton South. Eli Whitney we have already met. The life of Frederick A. P. Barnard, a distinguished scientist and educator, allows a useful glimpse into the cosmopolitan world of cotton, race, and education. Barnard is tied to Connecticut through his family and Yale.

Frederick Augustus Porter Barnard was born May 5, 1809, in Sheffield, Massachusetts, a few miles from the Connecticut border. Unlike Eli Whitney, who was the oldest member of his Yale class, the brilliant Barnard was the youngest student in Yale's Class of 1828. Like many of his New England contemporaries, he was enticed south in 1838 by the booming cotton kingdom of Alabama. The University of Alabama's president, Dr. Basil Manly, a Baptist minister and scientist, invited Barnard as he sought to rebuild the school using Yale and Harvard as models. In 1854, Barnard moved to the University of Mississippi, in the most dynamic cotton-producing state in America. By 1856 he had become the university's chancellor. In this role he successfully promoted both the expansion and the quality of the university and grew fond of life in the Deep South. He was extremely popular with the students, who wrote of his "genius of the most versatile talents."

Even so, Barnard's tenure was marked by great political controversy. He won every battle with the support of the school's board of trustees. Meanwhile the *Jackson Mississippian* and the Sumter *True Southron* praised Barnard for building the "literary Gibraltar of the South." In 1861 he was elected president of the American Association for the Advancement of Science.

Barnard was challenged by his political adversaries in what became known as the "Branham affair," a reference to his arch enemy, Dr. Henry B. Branham. Barnard returned home on May 17, 1859, to discover that his female slave Jane had been beaten and probably raped. She identified a student, Samuel Humphreys, as her attacker. Six days later Humphreys was tried by the faculty. Relying on Jane's testimony, Barnard voted guilty while most of the faculty found the student "morally convicted" but "legally" innocent. Nonetheless Barnard expelled Humphreys, whereupon Branham raised the issue of Barnard's support of slavery and states' rights—because under Mississippi law "negro testimony" was not admissible in court. Barnard argued that since this was not a legal proceeding, he could use the testimony of his slave.

Barnard then requested a hearing of the university's board of trustees to dispel any rumor that he was opposed to slavery. On March

2, 1860, when the board met to decide Barnard's fate, he expressed his position on the peculiar institution:

> I was born in the North. I cannot help that. I was not consulted in the matter. I am a slaveholder, and if I know myself, I am sound on the slavery question.

He was exonerated by the faculty and received a supportive letter from the head of the board of trustees, Jacob Thompson, who was also U.S. secretary of the interior.

A Unionist, Barnard viewed slavery as "an unwelcome fact" but held that it was protected by the Constitution. He was clearly uncomfortable with the institution and would eventually reject it. Barnard inclined toward the colonization of blacks. He disliked extremists on both sides, North and South. As early as 1837 he declared himself to be "a warm supporter of Southern institutions." Barnard knew that the slavery issue could not be negotiated. He did not wish to spend his energy on it when science and education beckoned.

When the war came in 1861, Barnard resigned from the University of Mississippi after the entire student body, with the exception of twelve students, left to join the Confederate army. On June 13, 1861, Barnard's last sermon in Mississippi reflected his sadness. He prayed that "this painful struggle, . . . may soon end in peace and brotherly love, and lead not only to the safety, honor and welfare of our Confederate States, but to the good of all."

The talented professor journeyed north to New York, where in 1864 he became president of Columbia University. He presided over a dynamic growth, expanding the student body from 150 students to 1,863 in 1888. Schools of law, mines, medicine, political science, and library science were added. Barnard lobbied for coeducation, but the board of trustees, in 1889, acquiesced only to the founding of a separate college for women. The result, Barnard College, was named in his honor. His funeral service on May 2, 1889, was attended by the presidents of Harvard, Yale, Princeton, and a host of others. All paid tribute to this respected educator.

The connection of the Civil War with cotton was no mystery to the erudite and mobile scholar who had lived in Mississippi. Barnard

Harriet Beecher Stowe in the late 1870s. A seminal figure in the anti-slavery campaign, she later succumbed to the lure of cotton riches, moved to the South, and rented a cotton farm for her son. When it failed, she returned to New England. *(Stowe-Day Foundation)*

attributed the "terrible convulsion" to "the increased and constantly increasing importance of cotton," with its attendant reliance on "compulsory labor."

Abraham Lincoln supposedly remarked that Harriet Beecher Stowe was the "little woman who wrote the book that started this great war!" Stowe captured the horrors of slavery in her monumental novel, *Uncle Tom's Cabin*, which appeared in 1852. Despite her difficulty in finding a publisher, copies of the book literally flew off the press: 10,000 copies sold in the first week, 300,000 in the first year. The background for her story was actually observed and conceived while Stowe was living in Cincinnati.

Stowe's enlightenment had limits. Like many of her fellow abolitionists, she was vehemently anti-Semitic. The most vile slave catcher
in her novel is the Jew Mr. Marks, a stereotypical caricature with pur-
ported Semitic features and values. The "amoral, anti-black" Marks is
the only slave catcher who is completely "untouched" by the fate of the
black heroine and her son. Even his fellow slave catcher says of Marks,
"Was there ever such a sneaking varmint?" He is also a "coward" and
thoroughly "mercenary."

We know what Harriet Beecher Stowe thought about slavery. What
did she think about black people and cotton? She had done considerable
homework. In *Uncle Tom's Cabin*, slaves were sold "down the river."
The river, of course, was the Mississippi, and slaves were sold to satisfy
the labor demands of cotton farms. Stowe realized that the price of cotton controlled the price of slaves. One of her characters explicitly states
that if "something should bring down the price of cotton once and
forever, . . . [it would] make the whole slave property a . . . [burden] in
the market." Who financed cotton and slavery? For Stowe it is the "fine
Christian firm of B. & Co. in New York." The loathsome Simon Legree
owns a cotton plantation on the Red River.

The reader of *Uncle Tom's Cabin* may easily overlook the book's
compelling denouement—the fate of its heroes and heroines. Stowe
dispatched them to Africa. She speaks through George Harris, the former slave. After gaining his freedom, he articulates his future plans to
settle in Liberia:

> I might mingle in the circle of whites, in [America], my shade of color
> is so slight, and that of my wife and family scarce perceptible. . . . But
> to tell you the truth, I have no wish to. . . . I have no wish to pass for
> an American, or to identify myself with them. . . .

> We have more than the rights of common men;—we have the claim
> of an injured race for reparation. But, then, I do not want it; I want a
> country, a nation, of my own.

> As a Christian patriot, as a teacher of Christianity, I go to my
> country,—my chosen my glorious Africa. I go to Liberia, not as to an
> Elysium of romance, but as a field of work.

Harriet Beecher Stowe sent her characters George, Eliza, their family, and Topsy to Liberia as missionaries to "civilize and proselytize." The most powerful anti-slavery tract ever written in America prompted colonization while denouncing reparations. In response to Stowe's colonization solution, the black leader Frederick Douglass brimmed with indignation: "The truth is, dear madam, we are *here*, & and we are likely to remain."

Stowe's rejection of the proposal of funds for black education brought forth a condescending indictment of blacks. The reasoning for her peevish rejection was contained in a letter to the abolitionist Wendell Phillips:

> Of all vague unbased fabrics this floating idea of a colored industrial school is the most illusive. If they [black people] want one why don't they have one—many men among the colored people are richer than I am & better able to help such an object—Will they *ever* learn to walk?

After the Civil War, Stowe provided $10,000 for her son, Frederick, and two of his Connecticut army friends to rent a cotton plantation in Florida, near the St. John's River. She stayed with him in 1866 and described the work ethic of blacks in a book of sketches called *Palmetto Leaves*: "As a class they are more obedient, better natured, more joyous, and easily satisfied [than whites]."

At the time, conventional white American opinion held that blacks were better suited than whites to manual labor in hot climates. Stowe agreed:

> The thermometer, for these three days past, has risen over ninety every day. No white man that we know of dares stay in the fields later than ten o'clock. . . . Yet the black laborers whom we leave in the field pursue their toil, if anything more actively, more cheerfully, than during the cooler months. The sun awakes all their vigor and all their boundless jollity. . . . A gang of negroes, great brawny, muscular fellows, seemed to make perfect frolic of this job which, under such a sun, would have threatened sunstroke to any white man.

She also emphasized the emotional nature of blacks—"animal content" and the "impressible nervous system" are the terms she used to describe it. She referred to one black woman as an "amusing and picturesque specimen of a human being" but useless in domestic tasks.

For Stowe, education during this transition from slavery to freedom resembled the much-criticized practical and apolitical philosophy later espoused by Booker T. Washington. Here is the education she envisioned for black children:

> The teaching in the common schools ought to be largely industrial, and do what it can to prepare the children to get a living by doing something well. Practical sewing, cutting and fitting, for girls, and the general principles of agriculture for boys, might be taught with advantage.

Harriet Beecher Stowe's foray into cotton farming, like those of other Northern soldiers, met a disastrous fate. Her son's friends, the two Union army captains she financed, were joined by a third New Englander with farm experience. All, including Stowe, dreamed of making a "fortune" in cotton, which she described as the "one thing *sure* always to be wanted in the world." She took trips around her thousands of acres to identify "selected spots where we would build our houses when our ship of gold came in." She was dazzled by projections from observers that the cotton would yield a $10,000 profit, which she dreamed could be "reinvested for larger harvests."

Unfortunately cotton was easier for her to write about than to grow. The army worm, an insect capable of devastating a cotton field, intervened. Her brave Union captains who had won many military battles were "defeated and routed" by the worms within two days. Only two bales of cotton were harvested. She lost her entire $10,000 investment, and her cotton partnership was dissolved. A chastened Stowe returned to the North. Her commitment to black uplift in the South dissipated once there was no "golden fortune" in the cotton fields. Such was the fickle nature of Northern reformers after a brush with reality. The celebrity novelist had identified the free black's destiny with cotton and manual labor and hoped to keep blacks in their place in the Southern cotton fields.

*

The two other major cities in the North, Boston and Philadelphia, shared New York's racial antipathy. Boston, reputed to be the most racially tolerant of American cities at the time, greeted blacks with "incredible obstacles"—residential segregation, separate and inferior schools, exclusion from juries, separation in churches, lecture halls, and places of entertainment, and "condescension and contempt in polite circles." Blacks "held the worst jobs at the lowest pay." Irish immigrants added to the plight of Boston's black community by pushing them out of an already difficult employment situation. Frederick Douglass noted that blacks were displaced from their normal occupations—"house servant, cook, waiter, porter, and laborer"—by the Irish, "whose hunger and whose color [were] thought to give [them] a better title to the place." Thus the two decades before the Civil War were "a time of economic crisis for Boston's blacks." The black population of Boston stagnated, barely growing from 1,988 (3.1 percent) in 1840 to 2,261 (1.3 percent) in 1850 while the white population doubled from 84,400 to 177,800. Most blacks lived in a section called "Nigger Hill." In the ensuing decades, blacks did not flock to Boston and Massachusetts.

The English Quaker visitor Joseph Sturge made a damning observation about Philadelphia in 1841: "There is no city in the known world where dislike, amounting to hatred of the coloured population, prevails more than in the city of brotherly love." Frederick Douglass in 1862 deplored the treatment of free blacks there: "There is not perhaps anywhere to be found a city in which prejudice against color is more rampant than in Philadelphia."

CHAPTER NINE

Race Moves West

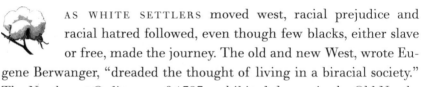 AS WHITE SETTLERS moved west, racial prejudice and racial hatred followed, even though few blacks, either slave or free, made the journey. The old and new West, wrote Eugene Berwanger, "dreaded the thought of living in a biracial society." The Northwest Ordinance of 1787 prohibited slavery in the Old Northwest—Indiana, Ohio, Illinois, Michigan, Wisconsin, and Minnesota— yet the black population never amounted to more than 1 percent of the total population in the region. In general, both pro-slavery and anti-slavery whites thought blacks were inferior, had low morals, exerted a corrupting influence, and should be excluded entirely or denied rights. As in the older states of New England, New York, and the North, whites feared a potential large black migration, either free or enslaved. Laws discouraged any form of black migration. Colonization plans were promoted in states to eliminate even the insignificant numbers of resident blacks. Although colonization was infeasible and ineffective, as we have seen, the persistence of the idea is a gauge of hostile white attitudes. Northerners in both old and new sections of America would eventually advocate a "containment policy" to keep blacks in the South.

Despite the growing momentum of the anti-slavery movement before the Civil War, sentiment against blacks remained strong as white America moved farther west. We can see the virtually complete separation between abolitionism and racial antipathy in the Western states that gained admission. A review of policy and attitudes in Ohio, Indiana, and Illinois confirms the pervasiveness of anti-black attitudes. The views of whites in the first wave of Western states presaged those later in Iowa, Michigan, Minnesota, California, and Oregon. The legal response to the imagined threat of a black invasion was drastic— exclusionary residence laws, segregated schools, denial of suffrage, laws against miscegenation, prohibition of blacks serving on juries or testifying against whites, denial of poor relief, flogging, and exclusion from the militia. These were only the explicit laws; custom further inhibited the freedom and livelihood of blacks. Ninety-four percent of the free black population of the North was completely disfranchised by law; the remaining 6 percent lived in five states with tiny black populations. The social response to blacks was violence, ostracism, repression, and forced isolation. The consequences were black poverty, degradation, and a separate existence.

*

Ohio exemplified the racial antipathy that prevailed in states carved out of the Northwest Territory. In 1810 the state had 1,889 blacks (.8 percent) in a total population of 228,861; by 1860 there were 36,673 blacks (1.5 percent) in a total population of 2,302,838. It did not take long after its admission to the Union in 1803 before Ohio passed "black laws," legislation designed to discriminate against free blacks and generally associated with the South. In 1804, Ohio required blacks or mulattoes to prove they were free before they could enter the state. Despite the measure's mild wording, the intent was clearly exclusionary. In 1807, Ohio law mandated that blacks and mulattoes post a $500 bond to insure "good behavior and self-support." In 1832 an Ohio legislative committee described "free blacks" as without "moral constraint" and "more idle and vicious than slaves." Free blacks were considered a "distinct and degraded class" who "demoralized whites simply by association." Anyone with one-quarter black blood could not join the militia, vote, serve on a jury, or testify against a white person in court.

Cincinnati, the major trading city of the Old Northwest, was a scene of frequent racial strife. The black population grew from 410 in the 1820s to 3,237 (2.8 percent) in 1850, when the total white population was 115,438. Nevertheless black children were not allowed to attend public schools, and only a few white teachers braved the ostracism of working at a "nigger" school. White churches discouraged blacks from joining; those who did sat in the "black pew." Blacks seeking employment were left with "drudgery," only the tasks that whites refused to perform. Trade unions prohibited the use of black labor. An employer could be fined for hiring a black.

In 1829 violence erupted when the trustees of Cincinnati demanded, under the 1807 law, that blacks pay the $500 bond or leave the city within thirty days. When blacks did not comply, a riot ensued. Mobs of whites, who could not be contained for three days, attacked blacks, murdered some, and damaged their homes. Almost a thousand blacks fled for Canada, where they founded the town of Wilberforce. In 1841 yet another racial riot exploded in Cincinnati.

Blacks in Cincinnati found solace in their own communities. Some managed to accumulate property as artisans, workers in the meatpacking industry, and servants on steamboats. The riots provoked them to build their own schools; education, in Cincinnati and other Northern cities, was the "greatest problem" for blacks. By 1856 they were allowed to elect trustees of their own schools. One black school, the Gilmore High School, was used by white planters to educate their mulatto children.

Although the black exclusion clauses were repealed in 1849, the city's "black laws" stood basically unaltered until after the Civil War, when fear of a black migratory invasion subsided. Blacks were then allowed to testify against whites, and education could be provided for black children from the tax on black property.

Despite a few changes, Cincinnati's black population remained in dire straits after the Civil War. Peter Clark, a respected black community member, noted of racial animosity in Cincinnati, "It hampers me in every relation of life, in business, in politics, in religion, as a father or as a husband."

Even anti-slavery Cleveland was a hostile environment for free blacks. The prominent black John Malvin "found every door closed against the colored man . . . excepting only the jails and penitentiaries, the doors of which were thrown wide open to receive him."

Ohio indulged in the "most extensive colonization" rhetoric during the 1840s movement. In 1849, Ohio citizens pledged $11,000 to begin an "Ohio in Africa" resettlement. A bill providing $25 each for up to fifty black people a year to be sent to Liberia was introduced in the Ohio legislature. It failed to pass only when legislators realized there was no way to monitor blacks who might enter Ohio expressly to collect the inducement. The legislature did agree to petition the federal government to establish a black reservation on land recently obtained from Mexico.

If blacks could not be effectively excluded or deported, white Northerners—either Eastern or Western—wanted them to remain in the South or move there. In a twist of logic, Northerners reasoned that blacks would flee Northern racial antipathy by moving to a more congenial physical environment in the South. In this view, there would be no need to worry further about the black migration north. The Ohio Democrat Jacob Brinkerhoff wanted slavery excluded from Western territories, but his motivation was racial not humanitarian: "I have selfishness enough greatly to prefer the welfare of my own race to that of any other and vindictiveness enough to wish . . . to keep [in] the South the burden which they themselves created." The Republicans George Julian (Indiana), Albert G. Riddle (Ohio), and Thaddeus Stevens (Pennsylvania), as well as Salmon P. Chase (Ohio), voiced hope that emancipation would "drain" the tiny Northern black community to the South.

Ohio senator John Sherman, brother of the Union general William Tecumseh Sherman, declared matter-of-factly that Ohioans were both anti-slavery and anti-black. Ohioans, according to Sherman, were "opposed to having many negroes among them," and blacks in general "were spurned and hated all over the country North and South." Sherman supported colonization. In June 1852 he worried that an emancipation bill "would have made Southern Ohio uninhabitable or driven us to the enactment of harsh and cruel [exclusion] laws." He spoke of the impossibility of assimilation as an immutable "law of God. . . . The whites and blacks will always be separate, or where they are brought together, one will be inferior to the other." After emancipation Senator Sherman wrote to his brother, "No one cares about the negro except

[that] as . . . he is the cause of the war he should be made useful in putting an end to it."

Chase, the Ohio senator and secretary of the treasury in Lincoln's cabinet, hoped that blacks would migrate south after emancipation. He gained visibility in Ohio by defending fugitive slaves. As chief justice he admitted the first black lawyer to practice before the U.S. Supreme Court. He had been a strong anti-slavery advocate and supported black suffrage. Yet he also wanted blacks out of the North. In July 1862 he encouraged General Benjamin Butler, commander of the Union forces in the Gulf States, to emancipate the slaves in his territory. His motive was to make the area attractive to Northern blacks. After emancipation, he reasoned, blacks would gravitate toward the more appealing Southern climate.

Senator Benjamin F. Wade, an Ohio Republican, supported black suffrage but personally loathed black people and favored colonization. Wade's political career ended "partly because of his forthright advocacy of allowing black men to vote in Ohio." In a referendum held in Ohio's 1867 general election, black suffrage was trounced, and Wade's defeat marked the end of his political career. In 1851 he had described Washington, D.C., "as a mean God forsaken Nigger ridden place," where the food was "all cooked by niggers until I can smell and taste the nigger." In 1873 he sought to hire a white servant because he was "sick and tired of niggers." He abused a black attorney by calling him "a damned Nigger lawyer." In 1871 he traveled with Frederick Douglass to explore the annexation of Santo Domingo as a home for freed slaves.

Ohio's newspapers were outspokenly anti-black. In 1862 the *Cincinnati Enquirer* vehemently opposed "confiscating," the term used for freeing Southern slaves: "The hundreds of thousands, if not millions of slaves it will emancipate will come North and West, and will either be competitors with our white . . . laborers, degrading them by the competition, or they will have to be supported as paupers and criminals at public expense." The *Columbus Crisis* raised the specter of miscegenation, suggesting that Ohio's "farmers and mechanics were not prepared to mix up four millions of blacks with their sons and daughters. . . ." Ohio's Western Reserve, in the northeastern part of the state, was relatively tolerant; yet a Republican editor there who had opposed black exclusion laws voiced his desire to rid Ohio and the country of blacks: "We have no special affection for negroes. We neither desire their companionship or their society. . . . We would be glad if there was not one in the State or one in the United States."

Ohio's involvement with the Underground Railroad that assisted fugitive slaves in their journey to freedom in Canada has been widely acknowledged. White Ohioans viewed the Underground Railroad as a pneumatic tube: fugitive slaves entered it in Cincinnati and were spewed out in Canada. In 1862 an Ohio farmer waxed proudly about his state to an English visitor, but added, "There is but one thing, sir, that we want here, and that is to get rid of the niggers."

*

Illinois, the home of Abraham Lincoln, treated its tiny black population with disdain, fearing a black invasion that might be unleashed by emancipation. In 1830 there were 2,486 blacks (1.6 percent) in a population of 155,806; by 1860 there were only 7,698 blacks (.4 percent) in a population of 1,704,323. Slavery never took root in Illinois, except for the slaves exempted by the state constitution to work in the Shawneetown salt mines. A referendum that called for a constitutional convention to consider legalizing slavery was defeated in 1824 by a vote of 6,640 to 4,952.

Black laws, however, were quickly enacted. In 1813, Illinois territorial laws provided that justices of the peace force every "incoming free black or mulatto" to exit. If a free black or mulatto did not leave, thirty-nine lashes were to be administered every fifteen days while the person was resident. Free blacks had to register with the local court and purchase documents attesting to their freedom.

By 1818, when Illinois was admitted to the Union, anti-slavery literature stressed the importance of prohibiting slavery in order to avoid the inheritance of free blacks through manumission. One tract asked, ". . . why should we bring among us a class of men . . . whom the prejudices of our educations will always render distinct?" In 1819, Illinois passed a law that required a slaveowner to post a $200 bond for manumission. A black without requisite free papers would be indefinitely apprenticed to a white man. In 1823, Governor Edward Coles, a staunch anti-slavery advocate, declared that slavery corrupted the morality of the white population. His particular concern was miscegenation, "the shameful, the disgraceful, the degrading commerce between white persons of one sex and colored persons of the other sex." By 1829 free blacks had to post a $1,000 bond with proof of freedom in order to enter Illinois. Like Indiana, Iowa, and Michigan, Illinois not only outlawed interracial marriages but nullified any that had already occurred.

Anti-black measures continued into the Civil War years. In 1848, Illinois voters, by a vote of 60,585 to 15,903, passed a black exclusion clause. When a black organization proposed in 1852 that the restriction on black court testimony against whites be removed, the proposal was tabled. In January 1853, "An Act to Prevent the Immigration of Free Negroes into the State" passed the legislature by 45 to 23. Under this law, any person who brought a free black or mulatto into Illinois was subject to a fine of $100 to $500 and a jail sentence of one year. Blacks who entered and stayed in Illinois for ten days were subject to a $50 penalty. If the black could not pay, his services were sold to pay off the fine. Although an exclusion law was already in effect, Illinois citizens in March 1862, by a two-to-one majority, supported exclusion. In August 1862, Illinois voters by a five-to-one majority renewed the prohibition on black suffrage.

As in other nonslave states, Illinois lawmakers almost unanimously wanted black people out of Illinois, even though they comprised less than 1 percent of the population. Republican senator Lyman Trumbull opposed the extension of slavery as well as "giving, Negroes . . . privileges" equal to white citizens. He favored colonization or any plan to get rid of blacks "Godspeed." In 1859 he declared, "We the Republican Party, are the white man's party. . . . We are for the free white man, and for making white labor acceptable and honorable, which can never be when negro slave labor is brought into competition with it." He pondered what to do with blacks: "What will you do with them [slaves]; we do not want them set free to come in among us; we know it is wrong that the rebels should have the benefit of their services to fight us; but what do you propose do with them?"

Other Illinois politicians agreed. Republican congressman Owen Lovejoy, brother of the slain abolitionist editor Elijah Lovejoy, opposed slavery but held that blacks were inferior and that the United States was meant exclusively for white people. General (and future governor) John M. Palmer, a Republican, wrote that freedom was not the issue. For him, "It was the presence of the negro race: a race which the sentiments of our people doom to a condition of racial and political inferiority beyond the reach of all efforts for their elevation." In 1863 the Republican governor, Richard Yates, suggested that competition with white labor would lead blacks in the North to a life of "pauperism and neglect." He believed that the benefits of freedom in the South would rid the North of blacks.

President Abraham Lincoln, a native son of Illinois, was a lifelong opponent of slavery and its extension but an advocate of colonization. Lincoln's strong supporter and hometown paper, the Republican Springfield *Illinois State Journal*, in 1862 offered a whiff of prevailing racial sentiment:

> The truth is, the nigger is an unpopular institution in the free States. Even those who are unwilling to rob them of all the rights of humanity, and are willing to let them have a spot on earth on which to live and to labor and to enjoy the fruits of their toil, do not care to be brought into close contact with them. . . . Now we confess that we have, in common with the nineteen-twentieths of our people, a prejudice against the nigger. . . .

Lincoln's Peoria, Illinois, speech of 1854 staked out his own position on black equality:

> Let it not be said I am contending for . . . political and social equality between blacks and whites. . . . I am . . . arguing against the EXTENSION of a bad thing [slavery], which where it already exists, we must of necessity, manage as we best can. . . . [Should we] make Free [blacks] . . . politically and socially our equals? . . . My own feelings will not admit to this, and if mine would, we well know that those of the great mass of the white people will not.

Lincoln has been pardoned for his racially inspired comments as merely a clever pragmatic approach to winning election. This presupposes an electorate to which racial antipathy appeals. In an attempt to deify

Lincoln, he is further exonerated by interpretations of his evolving enlightened attitude toward blacks. As an example, the historian George
M. Fredrickson euphemistically describes Lincoln as "clearly a white
supremacist, but of a relatively passive or reactive kind. . . ." Lincoln
knew that slavery was the "root cause" of the Civil War; he wanted it
abolished by gradual means, by force if necessary. But he had no plan
for the millions of freed slaves.

Colonization, according to V. Jacque Voegeli, was Lincoln's "favorite
answer to the race problem." In 1862 he posed the question to a black
audience, "Why should the people of your race be colonized?. . . You
and we are different races. . . . You suffer very greatly by living among
us while we suffer from your presence." Lincoln approved a plan to
colonize blacks on the Chiriqui land grant in Central America. His secretary of the interior contracted in September 1862 with the Chiriquis'
sponsor. In August 1862, Lincoln told a group of blacks, "There is an
unwillingness on the part of our people, harsh as it may be, for you free
colored people to remain with us."

Lincoln signed the Emancipation Proclamation on January 1, 1863.
A day earlier he had signed a bill authorizing $500,000 to fund colo-
nization schemes. One such plan presented by the promoter, Bernard
Kock, would remove 5,000 blacks from America to Ile Vache, an island
owned by Haiti, for $250,000. The first 400 colonists indeed left in
1863; the surviving 368 returned in 1864 after the attempt failed. The
man whom America credits for freeing the slaves also wanted them out
of America. Lincoln was not alone in grasping at the colonization solution. Republicans John A. Bingham, Owen Lovejoy, and George Julian
were responsible for $500,000 in federal funds to finance the "removal
of slaves freed in the District of Columbia" and the South.

Lincoln too was concerned about a mass migration of free blacks
to the North. He paid homage to the diffusion principle, by which
"Equally distributed among the whites of the whole country . . . there
would be but one colored to seven whites. . . . Could the one, in any
way disturb the seven?" In the North, Lincoln overlooked the fact
that across the North and throughout the nineteenth century, a ratio
of one black person to one hundred whites already greatly disturbed
whites.

Ultimately Lincoln recognized the impossibility of colonization and seized the only available option: keeping blacks in the South. In December 1862 he argued:

> Heretofore, colored people, to some extent, have fled north from bondage; and now, perhaps, from bondage to destitution. But if gradual emancipation and deportation be adopted, they will have neither to flee from. Their old masters will give them wages . . . till new homes can be found for them in congenial climes, and with people of their own blood and race.

Lincoln was reassuring the North that there would be no black invasion because of the triple solution, favored by so many white Northerners, of "emancipation, colonization, and exclusion."

Illinois newspapers generally succumbed to various forms of racial hostility. The *Chicago Tribune*—Republican, radical, adamantly anti-slavery, and pro-emancipation—pleaded for justice for blacks and a repeal of the "black laws." Yet in 1864 the sympathetic *Tribune* wrote of the "white and superior race." The paper condescendingly characterized the black person as childlike, his "kindly and affectionate" demeanor "rarely agitated by the profound passions which belong to his superiors." It opposed miscegenation, supported separation, and favored colonization in Haiti. The *Tribune* defined the Republican attitude, which was

> [t]o let the African race alone; neither marry or cohabit with them; to give them freedom, treat them as human beings; pay them for their work; separate the whites from adulterous communication with them; and preserve the purity of the Caucasian blood from African admixture.

For the *Tribune*, the answer to the racial problem was to keep blacks in the South. As the paper noted in 1861,

> The greatest ally of slaveholders in this country is the apprehension in the Northern mind that if the slaves were liberated, they would become roaming, vicious vagrants; that they would overrun the North, and subsist by mendicancy and vagrancy; and that from the day [they] were made free they would cease to work.

The *Tribune* hoped to allay the fears of Northerners by predicting that Northern blacks would prefer to live in a South without slavery. Their departure from the North, according to the *Tribune,* would eliminate the Northern racial problem. After emancipation, "every fugacious chattel will shape his bearings and route by the Southern Cross instead of the North Star." In 1864 the paper suggested that blacks be used "in their homeland," the South. This plan would not only decide "the question of deportation, but evades the prejudices of Northern communities, and also contributes a valuable contribution to the resources of the country."

The *Tribune*'s opinions paled in comparison to the caustic Democratic *Chicago Times*, which observed that the "great masses of white people have a natural and proper loathing of the Negro which forbids contact with him as a leper. . . . The negro, with his wooly hair, thick lips and idiotic countenance, grins upon us . . . with the same half-human, half-beastly leer which characterizes him now."

*

Indiana, admitted to the Union in 1816, had a record on race perhaps even harsher than that of Ohio and Illinois. In 1830 there were 3,629 blacks (1 percent) in a population of 339,399; by 1860 there were only 11,428 blacks (.8 percent) in a population of 1,339,000. In 1813 a petition from Gibson County to the territorial legislature requested that free blacks and slaves be prohibited from settling in the area. Citizens in Harrison County became alarmed when 47 freed slaves arrived. They formally "opposed the introduction of Slaves or free negroes in any shape" because their "wives and daughters may and no doubt will be insulted and abused by those Africans."

Indiana territorial legislation was explicit. In 1803 a law prohibited free blacks from testifying against whites; by 1807 they were banned from militia service. In 1810 they were denied suffrage. Later an annual three-dollar tax was levied on all "adult Negro and mulatto males." In 1815 a slave who came into Vincennes without his master was subject to fines and flogging. Both intermarriage and interracial sexual relations were made illegal. By 1831 any black person who entered Indiana had to show proof of freedom and post a $500 bond or face expulsion. Governor James B. Ray sought "to regulate for the future . . . [the immigration of blacks] . . . and the continuance of known paupers, thrown upon us from any quarter."

Even though blacks did not enter Indiana in great numbers, fear persisted. In 1845 the town of Cambridge passed its own exclusion law in addition to existing state legislation. Nearby newspaper editors warned that "we shall soon be overrun with all the worthless, idle and dissolute negroes in the surrounding counties." Article 13 of Indiana's 1851 constitution provided that "no Negro or mulatto could settle or enter the state." All contracts with Negroes were void, and persons hiring or encouraging Negroes to settle in Indiana were subject to a $500 fine. An Indiana supreme court judge in 1829 cautioned about the "low, ignorant, degraded multitude of free blacks" who would soon flood the state in the absence of a colonization plan.

Article 13 spelled out Indiana's colonization plan, which was designed to rid the state of its black population. In 1851 the document was adopted by an overwhelming margin, 113,628 to 21,873. But the scheme failed: only 47 free blacks emigrated in 1853 and 1854.

The Indiana Radical Republican George Julian recognized the depth of racial hatred in his state and the nation at large. In the 1850s he spoke of the "superficial and sickly" support of anti-slavery positions from Indiana citizens who have a "perfect, if not supreme hatred of blacks." The congressman favored black suffrage and expected that the free black populations of the North and Canada would migrate south after emancipation. He was a strong supporter of land reform— that is, confiscating Southern land and turning it over to farmers both black and white. He thought the freed slave would be "excluded from the northern States . . . by their uncongenial climate, by his birthplace attachment [to the South] and by Anglo-Saxon domination and enterprise." He voted to appropriate funds to deport freed slaves from Washington, D.C., to Africa. Julian was repulsed by the "prospect of miscegenation." In the North "no such intimate relations" existed, but in the South "slave mothers and slave masters . . . are brought on to the level of social equality in the most loathsome forms."

Another Indiana Republican congressman, Albert S. White, supported both emancipation and colonization. His belief in black inferiority rested on "irreconcilable differences between the two races which separate them, as with a wall of fire. . . . [The] Anglo-American never will give his consent that the negro, no matter how free, shall be elevated to such equality."

The well-intentioned, idealistic, but naive Robert Dale Owen had a long association with anti-slavery activities and issues relating to the status of blacks in Indiana and America at large. Owen was a spiritualist, a dreamer, and a theoretician. His practical attempts at reform ended in failure. He was involved with his father's failed utopian community in New Harmony, Indiana, and backed the Nashoba fiasco in Tennessee in the 1820s. He served in the Indiana House of Representatives in the 1830s and as a U.S. congressman from 1843 to 1848. As a delegate to the Indiana constitutional convention of 1850 he advocated black suffrage, yet he also supported exclusion and colonization. Since racial animosity was so "deep-seated," the free black, according to Owen, would be better off out of the country.

In 1863, Owen was appointed by Secretary of War Edwin Stanton to chair the "American Freedmen's Inquiry Commission." The man who thirteen years earlier had written the exclusion clause of the Indiana constitution would now compose the plan for the transition of slaves from bondage to freedom. His 1864 report recommended that a federal organization be established to protect and nurture freed slaves in an apprenticeship for freedom. This document, a "Radical Blueprint for Reconstruction," endorsed a form of political and civil equality. Owen was adamant about enfranchising freed slaves. The "guardianship" idea he and others propounded was the basis of the Freedmen's Bureau. Owen's commission advised that the federal role should be temporary; blacks were to be speedily weaned from government protection.

Still, the commission report, written by this white reformer, betrayed the attitudes of condescending paternalism and black inferiority:

The Anglo-Saxon race, with great force of character, much mental activity, and unfailing spirit of enterprise, has a certain hardness, a stubborn will [and] moderate geniality . . . its intellectual powers are stronger than its social instincts. . . . It is a race . . . better fitted to do than enjoy.

As for the traits of black people:

Genial, lively, docile, emotional, the affections rule. . . . It is a knowing rather than a thinking race. . . . It is little given to stirring enterprise, but rather to quiet accumulation. It is not a race that will ever take a lead in material improvement of the world. . . . [They have] Christian graces of meekness and long suffering. . . .

The report condemned the "amalgamation of these two races" as likely to lead to "degeneration." Blacks were not prepared for a "progressive, materialistic society."

Owen's philosophical support of black political equality did not include an appreciation of how to achieve it, given American racial attitudes. Like so many others, he confidently prophesied and hoped that blacks would remain in the South after emancipation and that more than half of Northern blacks would move to the South because of climate and Northern "racial animosity." Emancipation would solve the amalgamation problem because blacks in the South would form separate communities. This typically unquestioning acknowledgment of the nation's racial divide foretold doom for abstract notions of black rights. Who would enforce the precepts of equality? Northern whites were merely relieved by the expectation that blacks would be contained in the South.

Such marginalization apparently did not distress the important abolitionist minister Lyman Abbott of Terre Haute, Indiana. He hoped that emancipation would coax blacks to the South. He excluded them from political rights: "It is not true that the ignorant and the degraded should be invited to participate in Government. . . . I would confine . . . Government always to the moral and intelligent. For generations it is probable that the African must be governed."

*

Wisconsin, where blacks numbered 1,171 (.1 percent) in a total population of 777,710 in 1860, had denied black suffrage by a vote of 40,106 to 27,550 in 1857. The state had been admitted to the Union in 1848. The Wisconsin State Colonization Society was established in 1855 for the purpose of sending its blacks to Africa. Strapped for money, the Society managed only to pass an ineffectual resolution. The intent was nonetheless clear: Wisconsin wanted no blacks. Wisconsin Republican newspapers cited fears that emancipation would produce a "Negro in-festation." Wisconsin Democrats raised the specter of miscegenation. If blacks could vote, they asserted, black men would "marry our sisters and daughters and smutty wenches . . . [would marry] our brothers and sons." Republican senator James R. Doolittle favored colonization in order to "keep our Anglo-Saxon institutions as well as our Anglo-Saxon blood pure and uncontaminated." Doolittle wanted blacks colonized in Florida.

In 1863 the Wisconsin Assembly determined that the most effective way of keeping blacks out was to ensure that they had "freedom, homes and employment" in the South. Northern blacks, according to this plan, would be coaxed into the South. Blacks, the Wisconsin lawmakers con-tinued, could not compete in the North because the Northern boss was "an exacting taskmaster" while the Southern manager "has less repug-nance to the black man's shiftless ways. They understand each other better . . . and while the black man keeps the place assigned to him he would be treated with more consideration in the South."

Even as Wisconsin and states in the North were excluding or dis-couraging black settlement, the West was attempting to augment its sparse population by actively promoting white European immigration. Wisconsin formalized its white immigration policy in a law that in 1852 set up an immigration commissioner in New York. Iowa passed a similar law in 1860. The commissioner's office was a conduit for infor-mation about Wisconsin to white European immigrants, and worked with a Dr. Hildbrant, a Wisconsin native, who represented America in Bremen, Germany. The office disseminated thirty thousand German-language brochures, half of which went to Europe. Wisconsin continued to publish these brochures through the nineteenth century. Thousands of immigrants sought information at Wisconsin's New York office. The orchestrated effort involved contact with foreign consuls and railroad and steamship companies. Immigration to the state surged. In 1853, Wisconsin received the following white European immigrants: sixteen to eighteen thousand Germans, four to five thousand Irish, three to four thousand Norwegians, and two to three thousand others. The recruit-ment efforts succeeded: by 1900, 710,000 (34 percent) of Wisconsin's 2 million population were of German lineage.

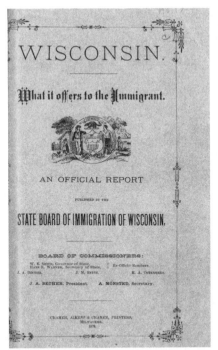

Immigration recruiting pamphlets from Wisconsin, English-language version 1879, German-language version 1881. In the second half of the nineteenth century, Northern states, like Wisconsin, used such pamphlets to attract white Europeans while deliberately ignoring potential black settlers. In 1879, Kansas closed its doors after several thousand black "Exodusters" from the South tried to emigrate, even as Midwestern states were eagerly accepting white immigrants. *(Wisconsin State Historical Society)*

*

Michigan, admitted as a state in 1837, took the same anti-black, anti-slavery stance as its neighbors. By 1860 there were 6,799 black residents (.9 percent) in a total population of 742,314. In 1827 the state passed its exclusion legislation, which required blacks to post a $500 bond when entering the territory. Michigan formally prohibited black suffrage in 1836 with the comments:

> [T]he negro belonged to a degraded caste of mankind. . . . Nature had marked the distinction [and] Society had recognized and sanctioned it. . . . If blacks are to be admitted to all rights of citizens, they will

be encouraged to come and fix their residence in the new State. And
. . . the consequence will be dangerous to say the least. . . . A state of
society would be produced, by no means desirable.

A miscegenation law followed in 1846. Michigan again voted 32,000
to 13,000 to prohibit black suffrage in 1850 when blacks constituted .6
percent of the population.

The Radical Republican senator Jacob M. Howard yelped when
confronted in 1862 with the possible relocation of 123,000 freed slaves
to Michigan. He responded that "Canada is very near us, and affords
a fine market for wool." After it became apparent in 1865 that blacks
would be contained in the South, Senator Howard voiced his opinion
that freed slaves "ought to be created as equals before the law."

*

In Iowa, where the black population was a truly inconsequential 1,059
(.2 percent) in a total of 673,844 residents in 1860, exclusion laws appeared as early as 1827. Iowa demanded a $500 bond and proof of
freedom; intermarriage was made illegal; blacks could not serve in the
militia; jury service was prohibited. At the constitutional convention of
1840, six years before statehood, a transplanted New Yorker declared
that he would "never consent to open the doors of our beautiful state"
to blacks. As late as 1857, Iowans voted 49,511 to 8,489 against black
suffrage. As elsewhere, a colonization effort materialized. Iowa's colonization society encouraged formal recognition of Liberia so that the
state's black residents would be tempted to move there. A speaker at a
colonization meeting declared that "As long as [blacks] are here, they
must be treated as outcasts and inferiors." With the threat of black immigration removed, Iowa removed its exclusion laws in 1864.

*

In the 1850s, Kansas was best known as a battleground between pro-
slavery and anti-slavery advocates. By 1860, a year before statehood,
there were 625 free blacks and two slaves among the 106,579 residents
of Kansas. Yet Kansas too feared a black migration, disdained free
blacks, and wanted white settlers. Slavery was thought to be the precursor of a surging black population that would also include free blacks.

The issues were complex and often local. Pro-slavery supporters backed the Lecompton Constitution, which contained a clause excluding free blacks. The failure of the Lecompton Constitution in 1857 saw the number of slaves in Kansas fall from 55 to two.

The anti-slavery Topeka Movement was a diverse collection of "abolitionists, antislavery Southerners, Democrats, former Whigs, Republicans and members of the Know-Nothing Party." Not surprisingly, this motley group could agree on little but preventing the extension of slavery. Most did not wish to tamper with slavery where it already existed. A black exclusion clause was adopted at the Topeka Constitutional Convention of 1855. Typically, blacks were prohibited from "suffrage, office holding and militia service." By contrast, Native American males who chose to leave their tribes and assimilate were allowed the same rights as white males. The *New York Times* reported that the people of Kansas "are terribly frightened at the idea of being overrun by negroes. They hold to the idea that the negroes are dangerous to the State and a nuisance." Anti-slavery men at the state referendum voted 1,287 to 453 to exclude blacks.

Ultimately the anti-slavery Wyandotte Constitution (1859) became the basis for Kansas statehood, which was granted in 1861. The Wyandotte Constitution included bans on black suffrage and a provision for separate black schools. Black exclusion was not included over concern that such a measure would delay statehood approval. In 1859 the editor of the *Kansas Herald* did not want Kansas to become a "sort of Botany Bay [for] all the lazy, worthless, vagabond Free negroes of the other States."

*

The California Constitution of 1849, a year before statehood, contained the familiar prohibitions on black suffrage and militia service. The California Gold Rush had attracted free blacks, and by 1860 California had 4,086 blacks (1.1 percent) in a total population of 361,353. In 1857 the California legislature considered, but failed to pass, an exclusion law. In 1858 the house did pass an exclusion bill, but it died in the senate because of technicalities.

White Californians were as inhospitable to free black settlers as other Americans. By 1851 the state did not allow blacks to vote or serve on juries, and black children were not allowed to attend public schools. "We desire only a white population for California," declared the editor of the *Californian* in 1849. The sponsor of the exclusion bill asserted that "no population on the globe [was] more repugnant to the feelings of the people than idle, thriftless Negroes thrown into the state." The first two California governors were "decidedly anti-Negro." Governor Peter Burnett warned against "the evils . . . of mixed races" as he strongly supported an exclusion clause. Governor John McDougall thought that blacks, in general, were "degraded and conspicuous for their drunkenness and improvidence." In 1857, James Estell, head of the state penal system, shipped black prisoners to New Orleans where they were auctioned as slaves. When the usual miscegenation alarm sounded, California categorized blacks as those with "one-sixth African blood." Protests of discrimination at three California Colored Conventions—in 1855, 1856, and 1857—produced no change.

*

The curious case of Oregon illustrates how a miniscule number of blacks could inspire white hostility. By 1860, a year after being admitted to the Union, Oregon had 128 black people (.2 percent) in a total population of 52,337. The provisional government of Oregon in 1844 told free blacks and mulattoes to leave within two years. "Most settlers had little sympathy with slavery," according to Eugene Berwanger, "but [many] had a greater aversion against free Negroes." In 1848 the Oregon territorial legislature followed other Western states in passing "black laws."

The Oregon constitution of 1857 contained an exclusion clause that passed by a vote of 8,640 to 1,081, a greater margin than the vote to prohibit slavery. Oregon was admitted to the Union as the "only free state with a Negro exclusion provision in its original constitution." The anti-slavery senator Lyman Trumbull of Illinois justified his approval vote by stating that he could be against slavery without putting blacks "on an equal footing in the states with white citizens." In the year of the constitution, the *Oregon Weekly Times* did not mince words: "Oregon is a land for the white man; refusing the toleration of negroes in our midst as slaves, we rightly and for yet stronger reasons, prohibit them from coming among us free negro vagabonds." Oregon's exclusion law was finally repealed in 1927. The expulsion, exclusion, and denial of rights to a group that barely existed would amount to satire if it were not part of the tragic American racial saga.

CHAPTER TEN

Tocqueville on Slavery, Race, and Money in America

 IN THE 1830s, Alexis de Tocqueville, the preeminent nineteenth-century European observer of American life, turned his attention to race and commerce in the fledgling republic. For the most part, slavery's "black victims faded rapidly from European attention" after their emancipation, but not for Tocqueville. The implications of his keen observations would become apparent in the saga of cotton and race over the succeeding decades.

Tocqueville famously wrote that racial animosity was greater in the free states than in the slave states. He noted that "prejudice" derived from "manners," by which he meant custom.

> Thus it is in the United States that the prejudice which repels the Negroes seems to increase in proportion as they are emancipated, and inequality is sanctioned by the manners while it is effaced from the laws of the land.

As we have seen, Tocqueville placed heavy importance on American materialism and identified "love of wealth" as the motivating influence in America.

> I know of no country, indeed, where the love of money has taken stronger hold on the affections of men. . . . The love of wealth is

therefore to be traced, either as a principal or an accessory motive, at the bottom of all Americans do.

Tocqueville saw that white America had retained race-based slavery only where it was profitable over a long period of time.

Tocqueville believed that the "presence of the black population" constituted the greatest threat to the Union. Even after an American slave had been freed, he would, according to Tocqueville, still be regarded as inferior. Laws would be subordinate to custom; "the abstract and transient fact of slavery . . . [was] fatally united with the physical and permanent fact of color . . . the eternal mark of . . . ignominy."

Tocqueville's conclusion was pessimistic and unalterable. He noted that free blacks in the North "remain half civilized and deprived of rights in the midst of a population that is superior to them in wealth and knowledge, where they are exposed to the tyranny of the laws and the intolerance of the people." Many Northern blacks, he reported, "perish miserably, and the rest congregate in the great towns, where they perform the meanest offices and lead a wretched and precarious existence." Even if laws allowed marriage between the races, "public opinion would stigmatize as infamous a man who should connect himself with a Negress." Mortality rates between 1820 and 1831 hinted of the black race's oppressed status: "one out of forty-two individuals of the white population died in free Philadelphia, but one out of twenty-one of the black population died in the same time." The size of the Southern slave population made gradual emancipation impossible because it meant replacing a labor system and raised the unimaginable issue of assimilation.

Tocqueville envisioned two scenarios: "the Negroes and the whites must either be wholly apart or wholly mingle." He reiterated his conviction that "the white and black races will [never] . . . be upon an equal footing." Tocqueville does allow that an "isolated [black] individual may surmount the prejudices . . . of his race . . . but a whole people cannot rise above itself." The exceptional individual would have little impact on the whole of society.

He assumed that if the South abolished slavery, there would be an "increase [in] the repugnance of the white population for the blacks." The prospect of the "danger of a conflict" between whites and blacks

in the South seemed "inevitable." He observed that such a conflagration "perpetually haunt[ed] the imagination of the Americans like a
painful dream."

> In the North, everything facilitated the emancipation of slaves, and
> slavery was abolished without rendering the free Negroes formidable,
> since their number was too small for them ever to claim their rights.
> But such is not the case in the South.

In a sense, Tocqueville forecast a white Northern containment policy, a
post-emancipation "conflagration," and a triumph of white American
materialism which by inference left former slaves subdued in the cotton field.

Later, because of French colonial emancipation, Tocqueville was
forced to consider the transition of French slaves to freedom. His solution, as expressed in 1843, was harsh. The former slaves should be
prohibited from acquiring cheap land. The freed slave would undergo
a ten-year "apprenticeship" without wages. During this period, former
slaves could not leave their colony; former masters would not "let the
freed slaves remain idle, nor . . . work for themselves"; wages would be
set by the French government. Former slaves would be granted certain
rights to further their "progress in morality or civilization." Marriage
and education would be encouraged. After the initial ten-year period,
Tocqueville suggested a continuation of "rigorously enforcing existing
vagrancy laws . . . and prohibiting the purchase or occupation of land
for a certain number of years." The former French slave would be
chained to sugar production.

*

Despite the presence of small numbers of free blacks, the white North
was virtually unanimous in its disdain for its black population. Anti-
slavery governance in the West often coexisted with anti-black feelings;
anti-black attitudes underpinned even anti-slavery actions. In the East
the existing small communities of blacks were ostracized, despised, and
denied basic political and social rights to such an extent that blacks
sought refuge in separate communities. Few anti-slavery advocates supported equal rights for blacks. In the West, 80 percent of the voters of

Illinois, Indiana, Oregon, and Kansas approved legislation to exclude blacks, either slave or free, out of racial animosity.

The Northern white attitude toward blacks, slave or free, was attributed to fear of economic competition. Blacks, it was assumed, would work for lower wages and undercut the status of white laborers— though clearly this fear could not apply to farmers. And blacks could be and were used to break labor strikes in various cities. In fact black workers were allowed to compete with white workers only where there was an urgency resulting from a labor shortage, such as a strike or a wartime halt to immigration. Where white workers could take over jobs held by free black laborers without a major labor cost increase, blacks were simply pushed aside. This was race-tinged economics. Race determined who could be enslaved, but it could not determine the survival of slavery; only economics could make that determination. Slavery was just the sort of uncommon economic situation in which (1) black slaves, who had been organized for plantation production, could be financed in an ever-expanding Cotton Kingdom; and (2) whites could not be enslaved. Without profit or the expectation of profit, slavery could not have existed; nor could it have existed if there had been a viable and financeable alternative to cotton production.

Race-influenced economics can be seen at work in nineteenth-century America, where whites accepted millions of white immigrants but reviled black emigrants. The West was critically dependent on immigrants to fill its farmlands. The vast territory to be settled could have easily accommodated black and white farmers, but black laborers remained in the South instead.

The condescending white stereotypes of blacks could hardly have inspired competitive fear. White prose was laced with harsh denunciations of blacks as "lazy, shiftless, vicious and biologically peculiar." Blacks were held to be "untrustworthy, lacking in moral restraint and ignorant." Whites worried about the "wretched [black] population" that would become a burden on the community. Interracial marriage was held in contempt socially and legally.

White Northerners explored several solutions to get rid of their unwanted black population. Before and during the Civil War, emancipation was viewed as a means of enticing or draining blacks to the South.

Even Senator Charles Sumner and Governor John A. Andrew, abolitionists from Massachusetts, hoped that emancipation would create a
black "exodus" from the North. Impractical colonization schemes were
a mere recognition of white contempt for blacks. Exclusion provided
the ultimate expression of white racial hatred. The question remained:
where do free blacks belong in America? As we shall see, the answer
was a containment policy to keep freed slaves in the South.

Northern treatment of free blacks reinforced white Southern attitudes and actions. In 1821, Charles Pinckney, the South Carolinian who
had participated in the Constitutional Convention of 1787, condemned
Northern hypocrisy. He accused the North of trying to eliminate its
black population "by treating them on every occasion with the most
marked contempt" in addition to denying "political privileges." Seargent Prentiss of Mississippi argued that "the free negroes, who infest
the Northern cities," were worse off than slaves. In 1864, Frederick
Douglass did not mince words about the impact of Northern racial
animosity on the South: "the national prejudice and hatred toward the
colored people of the country, . . . has done more to encourage the hopes
of Rebels than all other powers besides."

White Northern soldiers who fought to preserve the Union held
similar anti-black opinions. As an historian of Civil War soldiers wrote,
"It seems doubtful that one [Union] soldier in ten at any time during
the conflict had any real interest in emancipation per se." In June 1862,
Illinois soldiers voted three to one for black exclusion and black disfranchisement. Rarely did Union soldiers mention *Uncle Tom's Cabin*
in their correspondence. Most opposed emancipation because it might
extend the war. Others believed that slaves' ignorance and irresponsibility would create problems. Many did not want freedmen to move
North on "terms of equality." Most succumbed to "an unreasoning
hatred of people with black skins."

As the war progressed, many white Union soldiers were converted
to the idea of emancipation as long as freed slaves stayed in the South.
The historian James McPherson has written that perhaps three in ten
supported emancipation for the first eighteen months of the war, but
that the Emancipation Proclamation prompted a majority to view
emancipation as a goal. Many viewed emancipation as an expedient

tactic to weaken the South. After the Civil War, Northern whites returned to their white units and segregated reunions in the North. These
soldiers, back in their towns and states with 1 percent black populations, were content to have the freed slaves remain in the South. In
fact the white North and its soldiers did not become advocates of black
political, civil, and social rights, as blacks remained a subordinate caste;
otherwise, during Reconstruction, the white Northern population and
its soldiers would have been more forthright and determined in their
support of the former slaves. Northern Republicans supported black
rights in the South after it became clear there would be no black migration north. Their brief foray into black rights was for the most part
derived from expediency, not out of a real concern for black equality—
after all, black votes for Republicans would ensure a Republican majority and a Republican presidency. A defeated white South could hardly
have imposed its racial solutions on the nation without the complicity
of the victorious white North.

The participation of approximately 186,000 black soldiers in the
Union army had won a measure of respect from white soldiers. The
experience also fostered black self-esteem and "lessons in self-reliance
and in the exercise of authority, choice and discretion." Black troops
served under white officers, and their struggle for equal pay finally
bore fruit. They were expediently used by the white power structure to
rectify manpower shortages and weaken the Confederacy, but within a
decade after the Civil War the white power structure forgot about black
veterans and the freed slaves, except as critical components of cotton
production

White racial attitudes remained entrenched. The evidence indi-
cates that they were not ambivalent or ambiguous about the status of
free blacks in American society. Some white Northerners did advocate
black suffrage or a limited form of it, and some did acknowledge black
humanity. For the most part, though, the North wanted blacks out of
their communities. The reality of day-to-day treatment of blacks in
the North demolishes the racially enlightened rhetoric of a few politicians and ministers. Even dedicated white abolitionists were scolded
by blacks. The black abolitionist minister Samuel R. Ward wrote that
many abolitionists "best love the colored man at a distance." Certainly

some relics of Northern discrimination were removed after the war, but the North did not become a magnet for freed slaves.

By denying blacks mobility, white Northern racial antipathy became largely responsible for the destiny of former slaves and their return to the cotton fields. As the historian C. Vann Woodward cogently wrote, ". . . when the chips were down, the overwhelmingly preponderant views of the North on [black equality] were in no important respect different from those of the South—and never had been." But the key difference between North and South was that 4 million black people lived in the South before the Civil War, compared to only 250,000 in the North; and unlike the North, the South depended on black labor for cotton production.

PART FOUR

King Cotton Buys a War

If slavery was the cornerstone of the Confederacy, cotton was its foundation. At home its social and economic institutions rested upon cotton; abroad its diplomacy centered around the well-known dependency of Europe, especially England and France, upon the uninterrupted supply of cotton from the southern states.—Frank L. Owsley

CHAPTER ELEVEN

Cultivating a Crop,
Cultivating a Strategy

 COTTON provided the South with the determined mind-set, the financial credit, and the fearsome gravitas needed to initiate the conflagration that was the American Civil War. Simply put, no one would have taken the South seriously without cotton. And fundamentally embedded in cotton power was race-based slavery. The consequences of the cotton-and-race connection were profound. Any discussion of cotton's ability to generate revenue and credit, buy arms, or influence politics is directly and unambiguously linked to race.

The South's only economic resource was slave-produced cotton. The other slave-produced staples—tobacco, sugar, and rice—were simply not relevant. Without cotton, Southern leaders had nothing to back up their increasingly fiery secessionist rhetoric. In the long war years, cotton would provide credibility for the government, arms for the military, a basis for tax revenue, and a diplomatic strategy for the fledgling Confederate nation.

The North, too, had to confront the power of cotton, and had to grapple with the crop's black labor force both during and after the Civil War. Even before the bloody conflict had ended, the North had formulated a policy that would retain former slaves in the cotton fields. Northern politicians and military officials would accept no other solution for the millions of black men and women across the South. While the story of cotton's role in the Civil War lacks the human drama of the battlefield or the Emancipation Proclamation, the economic, financial, and strategic importance of cotton was very much a part of the war's tragic saga.

From the beginning of the war, cotton formed the basis of the South's overarching strategy to force Great Britain into open recognition of the Confederacy. Although we think of the Civil War as being confined to bloody battlefields, the struggle's foreign policy ramifications loomed large, including American, Canadian, British, and French priorities. Cotton was of course vital to Britain, but her attitudes toward slavery, race, commerce, Canadian security, and American aggressiveness also became factors. Britain's support of the Confederacy lengthened the war considerably; her own imperial and economic interests reduced humanitarian feelings about slavery to relative insignificance. Canada, much praised as a haven for fugitive slaves, proved to be just as exclusionary for free blacks as the American West. British and Canadian racial policies before, during, and after the war further reinforced the entrenched racial antipathy of white America. Moreover Britain's failure to reconstruct its slave colonies foreshadowed America's relegation of its former slaves to the Southern cotton fields.

Clues to the continuing link between cotton and race may easily be discerned during the Civil War. Cotton's brute commercial influence and irrepressible attractiveness were highly in evidence throughout the war. Although Britain technically remained neutral, its bald need for cotton shaped an involved and mutually advantageous relationship with the Confederacy. And though white Northerners and white Southerners might have been pitted against each other in battle, the two sides continued to trade cotton. King Cotton was not toppled by the Civil War. Afterward, the indispensable product would demand a free but subservient black population dedicated to its cultivation.

*

The future president of the Confederacy, Jefferson Davis—a Mississippi cotton planter, graduate of West Point, veteran of the Mexican War, and former secretary of war—occupied a position of power and status within the South and the nation. On January 21, 1861, he resigned his post in the U.S. Senate just a few days after the secession convention in his home state voted 84 to 15 to leave the Union. Davis, who had been called the "Cicero of the Senate" by the *New York Times* and "one of those born to command" by *Harper's Weekly*, referred to the day of his departure from the Senate as the "saddest day of my life." But his allegiance to states' rights prompted his secessionist interpretation of the Constitution; in his actions, Davis believed he was being true to the founders of the Republic. Secession, according to Davis, resulted "not in hostility to others, not even for our pecuniary benefit; but from the high and solemn motive of defending and protecting the rights we inherited, and which it is our duty to transmit unshorn to our children." The most important of these "rights," of course, was the right to own slaves. After a fifteen-minute speech to his Senate colleagues, Davis was greeted with a "general and very cordial shaking of hands" by both Republicans and Democrats. Indeed he cherished the Union, but he held a higher allegiance to his section.

Davis was joined in resignation by most of his Southern colleagues, and events moved with alacrity after this painful Southern exodus from Washington, D.C. On February 4 delegates from six Southern states met in Montgomery, Alabama, to form the Confederate government. On February 18, Jefferson Davis was inaugurated as president of the Confederate States of America. One of the new government's first tasks, not surprisingly, was to raise money.

The Confederacy's first ledger sheet showed revenues of $718,294 resulting from the takeover of federal customs houses and mints in New Orleans and Charlotte. Clearly this was not enough to fund a government. On February 28 the Confederate Congress therefore authorized Christopher Memminger, secretary of the treasury, to raise $15 million. The money was to come via loans to be paid for by the first tax created by the Confederacy, an export duty of one-eighth of 1 percent upon all cotton exported after August 1, 1861. As noted earlier, the South had vigorously opposed any export tax at the Constitutional Convention of 1787, but this earlier goal of avoiding a burden was now superseded by financial necessity.

On the morning of March 11 the constitution of the Confederate States of America was ratified in Montgomery. A month later, on April 12, the Confederacy fired upon Fort Sumter, South Carolina, at 4:30

in the morning and in effect declared war on the North. Within a few months 360,000 men had volunteered for Confederate military service. The Confederacy had initiated the American Civil War.

In the north the financial stakes were also high. Tactically, Lincoln had to respond immediately to the Confederacy's belligerent actions with force because the Confederacy had captured U.S. customs houses, the source of tariff revenues, an indication of a policy designed to damage U.S. funding. The *Philadelphia Press* logically inferred that the South would establish customs houses along its coastline and that inland rivers would be "subject to Southern tolls." This not only would fill Southern coffers but would cut into the revenues the federal government had come to rely upon. Furthermore an export tax on cotton would hurt Northern mills while Britain would be able to import American cotton without a tariff. New York merchants, who were clamoring for peace at the beginning of 1861, visited Lincoln at the end of March and now wanted action. Wall Street reversed course in response to the shifting political tides. On March 12 the market rallied on reports that Lincoln had decided to abandon Fort Sumter; the financial world, it seemed, was eager to avoid conflict. But on April 7, Lincoln's order to support Fort Sumter created an ebullient stock market—New York's financial power had capitulated to the coming war.

The next four years witnessed unprecedented destruction in which more than 600,000 soldiers were killed and another 600,000 injured. The human loss across the country was staggering; the physical damage to the South was catastrophic. And the financial costs were truly astronomical: in a mere four years, the North amassed a $3 billion debt and the South spent more than $2 billion. By any measure, the war was closely contested; the victory of the North was in doubt until Sherman's conquest of Atlanta in September 1864.

None of this devastation would have occurred if not for cotton. Indeed, the crop formed the basis for the South's two basic war strategies, the first of which used cotton as a political bargaining tool, and the second of which relied on cotton as an economic weapon.

The South's first grand strategy has been called "King Cotton diplomacy." Other plans based on cotton were possible, but the South's tactic was to coerce England and secondarily France into formally

This portrayal of cotton as a scorpion conveys the sense of fear and destructive potential of cotton's power. (*Leslie's Illustrated Newspaper*)

recognizing the Confederacy by withholding and threatening to curtail their vital supply of slave-produced Southern cotton, the essential raw material for their industrial textile juggernauts. The Confederacy's existence was a huge bet placed on this tactical ploy. If England could be brought into conflict with the American North via cotton, Confederate independence would be a foregone conclusion.

The origins of this strategy may be traced to the North, as early as 1839, when Nicholas Biddle's bank in Philadelphia realized that cotton could be used as a negotiating tool with foreign powers. In the ensuing years Ohio's David Christy (in 1855), South Carolina's James Henry Hammond (in 1858), and Massachusetts' Ben Butler (in 1870) all articulated similar plans to coerce concessions from Britain by withholding cotton. The reappearance of such schemes over four decades is evidence of cotton's ever-present position in the American psyche and of Britain's utter dependence on the American crop. J. B. DeBow captured the spirit of cotton as the sine qua non of Southern strength and noted the interconnectedness of cotton and slavery:

> To the slave-holding states [cotton] is the great source of their power and their wealth, and the security for their peculiar institution. Let us

teach our children to hold the cotton plant in one hand and a sword in the other, ever ready to defend it as the source of commercial power abroad and through independence at home.

Even before they seceded, the South and its leaders were well aware of the compelling trade and labor statistics that related to cotton. Jefferson Davis was an immediate disciple of King Cotton diplomacy. Davis's literary wife, Varina, described her husband's belief that cotton would "compel recognition" by England. Charles Francis Adams, Jr., son of the American ambassador to Great Britain during the Civil War, wrote of Davis's "over-weening faith in the practical world mastery enjoyed by . . . the South—through its exclusive control of cotton." In 1861, South Carolina's Edmund Rhett told the London *Times* correspondent William Howard Russell that "you British must recognize us before the end of October" because of cotton requirements. Russell, in turn, noted the arrogance of Southerners who believed they were "masters of the destiny of the world. Cotton is King—not alone king, but czar."

King Cotton diplomacy must be distinguished from cotton power that could actually be mobilized as financial muscle. Early on Confederate leaders were aware of another and ultimately more productive use of cotton—as a means of obtaining credit to purchase arms. During early cabinet meetings the vice president of the Confederacy, Alexander H. Stephens, and the secretary of state, Robert Toombs, advocated the shipment of cotton to Europe, "where it could be stored with greater safety and provide funds to finance the war." The Confederacy's attorney general, Judah P. Benjamin, though a proponent of King Cotton diplomacy, nonetheless recommended in the first Confederate cabinet meeting, in March 1861, that 100,000 bales of cotton be shipped immediately to England. Part of the proceeds would be used to purchase 150,000 "small arms, and guns and munitions"; the "residue of the cotton was to be held as a basis for credit." Benjamin cautioned his cabinet members that "we are entering a contest that must be long and costly."

The South's infatuation with King Cotton diplomacy quickly buried the credit possibilities of cotton. As one cabinet member, Leroy P. Walker, later admitted, "All the rest of us fairly ridiculed the idea of a serious war." Benjamin's suggestion was dropped. Cotton as a means for credit was ignored until the fall of 1862. Cotton-backed credit could have obviated the immediate need for gold or a sophisticated financial system, two problems that would soon come to haunt the Confederacy. The South would return to cotton as credit only when its diplomatic efforts failed.

*

Almost as soon as shots were fired at Fort Sumter, both the North and the South enacted policies that impacted cotton. In April 1861, President Lincoln ordered a blockade on all Southern ports, intended to strangle the Confederacy by interrupting the flow of cotton to Europe and thus preventing arms shipments to the South. This was a daunting task that required the small Union navy to patrol 3,500 miles of coastline, a dozen major ports, and 200 minor harbors.

Almost simultaneously the South instituted an informal embargo on cotton exports. The result was an odd juxtaposition of policies by adversaries, both of which were designed to stop cotton from leaving the South. Both presidents wanted to be sure their point of view was clear; but for Davis the duplicate rulings served another purpose. He did not want an official Confederate embargo for fear of antagonizing England and France. Instead the Confederate Congress entertained resolutions and discussions rather than a bill for a complete embargo. Davis preferred to hold "a threat of an embargo . . . over Europe." According to one of his biographers, the Confederate president "welcomed the [Northern] blockade and vaunted it as a blessing in disguise."

Meanwhile in England, the Queen signed a formal nonintervention policy on May 13, 1861, declaring "our Royal determination to maintain a strict and impartial neutrality in the contest between the said contending parties." This policy would soon be all but ignored as the war continued and as the lure of money influenced North, South, and Britain alike. Only threats of Northern military reprisal reined in British support of the Confederacy.

The Confederate Congress relied on its states to implement the informal embargo, encouraging them to pass individual laws that would impede both the production and the shipping of cotton. To achieve these aims, states curtailed the growth of the crop, prevented transference of cotton to Confederate ports, and forbade trading with the North. Produce loans also allowed Confederate states and the Confederate government to purchase cotton that might have been shipped overseas. South Carolina, for example, in the spring of 1862 resolved to forbid "the exportation of cotton" from its ports. Louisiana governor Thomas Moore signed a proclamation that made it illegal to bring cotton into New Orleans after October 10, 1861. When Judah P. Benjamin challenged the legal grounds for his proclamation, Governor Moore responded that his actions were based on state public opinion rather than on legality. As the Confederacy discovered, Governor Moore's actions were but one example of states' rights ideology run amok. Governor John Milton of Florida was a fervent proponent of the embargo. Both Mississippi and Louisiana provided for the purchase of cotton to help planters and support the embargo. Arkansas placed a limit on cotton production to "two acres per field hand"; Georgia taxed all cotton above 2,500 pounds per farm at ten cents per pound. In September 1861 the governor of North Carolina would not allow six British ships laden with cotton to leave the port of Wilmington. A local citizens' organization, the Committee of Public Safety, monitored the informal embargo and caused consternation among British consuls who were stationed in Southern ports.

After a planters' convention was held in Memphis in February 1861 to discuss a prohibition on planting cotton, a Memphis newspaper editorialized: "Keep every bale of cotton on the plantation. Don't send a thread to Orleans or Memphis till England and France have recognized the Confederacy—not one thread." The embargo was popular with an "almost complete unanimity in the public press and among the articulate southern population."

The secessionists, however, were not satisfied with merely preventing the movement of cotton. In 1862, Southerners witnessed what must have been a bizarre sight: the burning of hundreds of thousands of bales of cotton at Southern ports. As Union forces captured Southern territory, the Confederate Congress on March 17, 1862, authorized the burning of cotton "when in the slightest danger" of being confiscated. The *Charleston Courier* reported that "At eleven o'clock last night the heavens towards the southwest were brilliantly illuminated with the

The ill-fated Confederate strategy of coaxing England's formal recognition by limiting cotton flows to Liverpool was furthered by burning cotton at ports such as Memphis. *(University of Memphis Libraries)*

patriotic flames ascending from burning cotton. As the spectators witnessed it they involuntarily burst forth with cheer after cheer."

The Confederacy's propaganda arm exploited the curtailment of cotton exports in the pro-Southern journal the *Index*. A Confederate supply agent in England, Henry Holtz, a twenty-seven-year-old Swiss-born Southern sympathizer and editor of the *Index*, supplied information to the British public about the cotton burning—"ten million dollars" worth in New Orleans, "ten thousand bales destroyed near Franklin, Tennessee," "fifty thousand bales" near Montgomery, "one hundred thousand bales" at Memphis, and "between half a million and a million on the Mississippi" River.

The embargo was a quick success in curtailing both cotton production and exports. In the first half of 1861 the South shipped 1.5 million bales of cotton to Britain; in the first half of 1862, Britain was able to import only 11,500 bales. Along with plunging exports, the production of cotton plummeted from more than 4.5 million bales in 1862 to 449,000 in 1863, and then to 299,000 in 1864. This shocking decline—nearly 90 percent in both production and exportation within a single year—testifies to the early unity of the Southern states on this issue. It has been estimated that between 1861 and 1865, 2.5 million bales of cotton were deliberately burned.

By the summer of 1862 the embargo was wreaking havoc in British textile mills. Production diminished, unemployment exploded, and the aptly named "cotton famine" arrived in Lancashire. But this desperate and potentially revolutionary situation, which the Confederacy had hoped for, occurred later than many expected because of the huge American cotton crops of 1859 and 1860. Europeans were able to purchase more than 3.5 million bales in 1859 and more than 3 million bales in 1860. Thus in June 1861, as the Civil War unfolded, England held an inventory of more than 1 million bales, which was far greater than normal. If England had not received one bale of cotton from the South, it would still have had more than 700,000 bales in early 1862. Britain's mills experienced no shortage of cotton until that summer. Before this there was no immediate economic leverage for the South. This bizarre and pivotal miscalculation by the Confederacy seriously, if not fatally, damaged the King Cotton grand strategy.

In addition, mill owners had an incentive to restrain their support for the Confederacy. According to Frank Owsley, the "twenty six members of Parliament from Lancashire and eight or ten from Lanarkshire, Derbyshire, and Leicestershire—the cotton districts—and especially from Liverpool" sat "silently . . . apparently bored with questions of intervention" during the legislative session of 1861–1862. They held a huge inventory of raw cotton at a cost of fourteen cents a pound, and a glut of cotton textile goods could not be sold even at cost. Overproduction had filled warehouses in China and India with tons of merchandise. English merchants held 300 million pounds of surplus textiles. The Civil War soon changed this dismal commercial outlook, as cotton moved to 60 cents a pound. The burdensome inventory of cotton textiles was sold at a profit of "not less than 200 million dollars." As the war progressed, the conflict in America became a boon to English business.

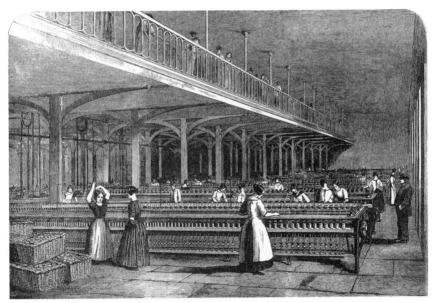

A doubling room in an English textile mill, where two strands of yarn were combined into one. The English displayed the Victorian textile mill as a symbol of their economic power and progress. *(Illustrated London News)*

While mill owners thrived, however, textile workers faced devastating unemployment. By the summer of 1862 the shortage of cotton had closed half of Lancashire's spindles. The *Saturday Review* summarized the appalling conditions:

> The cotton famine is the saddest thing that has befallen this country in many a year. . . . In the worst of our calamities there has seldom been so pitiable a sight as the manufacturing districts present at this time.

The London *Times* reported from a decimated textile town, Blackburn:

> Every family had passed through the last winter without wages and were entirely dependent on relief. . . . Some of them were lying four and five in a bed. . . .

The small mills that had borne the brunt of overproduction now faced high cotton prices and shortages. Employment figures revealed the severity. By December 6, 1862, more than 500,000 workers were unemployed. This led to a "total destitute population" of almost two million people who received assistance from "relief committees." The unemployed sold their family possessions—pictures, beds, blankets, china, and so on—before resorting to charity.

The American North capitalized on the propaganda value of charity. In March 1863 two Union ships, the *George Griswold* and the *Achilles*, landed in Liverpool with gifts of flour, meat, and rice for destitute workers. The North also contributed $2.6 million to English charities.

In the fall of 1862, Lord Palmerston, the British prime minister, Foreign Secretary Lord Russell, and Chancellor of the Exchequer William Gladstone were seriously concerned that a rebellion among textile workers might pressure England to "intervene in her own interest" on behalf of the Confederacy. The pain was particularly intense because of the geographical concentration of the problem. But the delay of the "cotton famine," owing to surplus cotton, shortened the period of the worst distress and allowed England to survive the crisis without domestic unrest. As cotton flowed into England and France from India and other sources after 1862, conditions began to improve. By January 1864, England's "total destitute population" fell to 811,000, and by December 1864 the number declined to 478,000.

With the notable exception of the mill workers who suffered through mass unemployment, Britain had a good war. The American conflict stimulated business and employment in various sectors of the economy—in linen and wool, for example, and in shipbuilding, munitions production, and transportation-related industries. Great amounts of armaments—pistols, rifles, powder, and artillery—flowed to both the North and the South. British shipyards supplied two cruisers, six ironclads, and more than twelve hundred blockade runners to the Confederacy. These responses to demand neutralized the damage of the cotton embargo. Total British imports increased from £210 million in 1860 to £269 million in 1864; exports rose from £164 million in 1860 to £240 million in 1864. These figures do not capture the windfall for the merchant marine. The vacuum that was created by the South's utter destruction of the North's merchant marine vessels was filled by the British, with higher profits and a major impact on the demand for labor.

Prosperity was evident to the London *Times*, which thereby demeaned the power of cotton in 1864:

> [O]utside of Lancashire it would not be known that anything had occurred to injure the national trade. . . . An industry which we conceived to be essential for our commercial greatness has been utterly prostrated, without affecting the greatness in any perceptible degree. We are as busy, as rich, and as fortunate in our trade as if the American war had never broken out and our trade with the states had never been disturbed. Cotton was no king. . . .

The North hoped that American wheat might also undermine King Cotton diplomacy. British wheat crop shortfalls in 1861–1863 created a large appetite for greater imports from America. This demand coincided neatly with the North's need for British armaments. Both Lincoln and Seward promoted the idea of a potential wheat-induced famine if Britain recognized the Confederacy. But the London *Times* attributed British grain purchases from America to "matters of convenience of transportation and slightly cheaper purchase price, not of necessity." Britain resumed importing grain from Eastern Europe, ceased purchasing American wheat, and the North developed its own capacity to manufacture arms. Frank Owsley judged that "wheat had little if anything to do with preventing English intervention in the American Civil War."

Another economic consequence of the South's cotton embargo was the soaring demand for Indian cotton, a fiber of inferior quality. This deficiency was somewhat alleviated by the Macartney gin that appeared in India in the 1860s and did a better job of cleaning the cotton. During the Civil War, England did import 600 million pounds of Indian cotton, sparking the growth of cotton production in India. As a temporary solution Indian cotton was partially effective, but it did not displace American cotton. Britain was still bemoaning its dependency on American cotton in the early twentieth century, when her mills began to decline in significance.

The South's cotton embargo did not work as diplomatic strategy. In practical terms the embargo died a natural death in 1862. By February of that year, Governor A. B. Moore of Alabama recognized the increasing ineffectiveness of the embargo when he implored Jefferson Davis to strengthen the prohibition on cotton export. The contradiction of the South's embargo policy was apparent. The South's need for cotton exports to finance the war flew in the face of the stated policy of preventing their shipment. Thus the embargo gave way and "slowly relaxed" after the spring of 1862, until finally it was no more.

CHAPTER TWELVE

Great Britain and the Civil War

 HISTORIANS have long argued that Britain withheld formal intervention in the American Civil War because of moral considerations over slavery. It is appealing to attribute resistance to King Cotton diplomacy to idealism, but the essence of British formal nonintervention policy was based on a complex set of economic and diplomatic factors. Here the force of cotton can be seen; the British attitude toward slavery was subordinate to real money and military might, and concern for the rights of free blacks was absent. Britain's dependence on American cotton would reappear immediately after the war. British anti-slavery societies would accordingly go out of business and exert no pressure on behalf of freed American slaves.

Britain knew that recognition of the Confederacy held considerable risk. Such intervention almost surely would provoke an invasion of British North America, Canada, by the North, and war. Attacks on British merchant marine vessels would follow. Britain greatly favored a divided America, which would present a less formidable competitor. Beyond these considerations, Britain believed the Confederacy would win the war—or at least force mediation—without foreign support. The *Economist* prophesied that the war would be fought "for a year at least, perhaps two years more, till the Presidential election," by which time "the substantial independence of the South" would be an accepted fact. Ultimately the military battlefields determined Britain's policy toward the combatants. There is no doubt that Britain enjoyed the tangible mercantile profits created by the war as well as the thought of a divided America. One historian described the British sentiment toward America: "The average member of Parliament, the average merchant, banker, shipper, and newspaperman, and the average man on the streets, hated America and wished her disruption."

Contemporary Southerners knew quite well that Britain subordinated morality to commerce. Florida governor John Milton reasoned by analogy:

> I know of no reason why, if England and France were willing to engage in war with China to secure commerce in opium with the Chinese people against their will and the decree of their government, England and France would not . . . [violate] a blockade for commerce in cotton, tobacco, etc. with the Southern States, while their people desire and their Government proposed the commercial intercourse.

Both the North and the South competed vigorously through the press, meetings, lectures, and bribes to influence the British public and its officials. It is generally thought that the British upper class and particularly the cotton textile barons supported the South for social, political, or economic reasons. British aristocrats also feared the spread of an aggressive form of democracy associated with the American North. The working classes, even in the cotton districts, were thought to be aligned with abolition.

While it is useful to examine the thrusts and parries of the propaganda wars for the hearts and minds of the British, the real struggle for Britain was waged by the North and the South on the military and financial battlefields. Slavery did not enter into the exchanges among British senior officials when they considered the possibility of a Southern victory or a stalemate. Gladstone, speaking for himself, famously concluded on October 7, 1862, that

> Jefferson Davis and other leaders of the South have made an army; they are making . . . a navy; and they have . . . made a nation. We may anticipate with certainty the success of the Southern states so far as regards their separation from the North. . . .

In September 1862, British prime minister Palmerston, during the dark days of the North's precarious defense of territory near the nation's capital, "suggested that in case Washington or Baltimore were captured, England might intervene on the basis of separation." In a joyous mood, Palmerston wrote to Lord Russell, the British foreign secretary:

> [T]he detailed accounts . . . of the battles of August 29 and 30 between the Confederates and the Federals show that the latter got a very complete smashing, and it seems not altogether unlikely that still greater disasters await them, and that even Washington or Baltimore may fall into the hands of the Confederates. If this should happen would it not be time for us to consider whether in such a state of things England and France might not address the contending parties and recommend an arrangement upon the basis of separation?

This was the same Palmerston who twenty years earlier had rebuked American attempts to interfere with the British mission to end the international slave trade. Then, the irate Palmerston had said that returning captured slaves "would be so entirely at variance with every principle of the British Constitution" that neither Parliament nor British troops could "be expected to carry it out." He also condemned the American government for sheltering the slave trade, "which the laws of the Union stigmatize as piracy and punish with death." Yet in September 1862 he was ready seriously to consider recognizing a slave nation. Lord Russell, on September 13, 1862, thought the battlefield victories of the Confederate Stonewall Jackson "seemed about to end the war." He replied to Palmerston:

> Whether the Federal army is destroyed or not, it is clear that it is driven back to Washington and has made no progress in subduing the insurgent states. Such being the case, I agree with you that the time is come for offering mediation to the United States Government with a view to the recognition of the independence of the Confederates. I agree further that, in case of failure, we ought to recognize the Southern States as an independent state. . . .

British deliberations on recognition of the Confederacy were resolved not on moral grounds but on the grounds of a battlefield, with a
Union victory at Antietam. This is the same Britain that had no ethical
problem in purchasing slave-produced cotton before the Civil War.

*

Britain took an adversarial position toward the Union. In fact the
anti-slavery North had no allies except perhaps for the despotic Russia.
Tensions between the Union and the British arose on many occasions,
beginning with the North's irate reaction to British neutrality as set
forth in the Queen's proclamation of 1861.

The well-known *Trent* Affair, the most serious of the confronta-
tions, illustrated the precariousness of peace between Britain and the
North. On November 7, 1861, James M. Mason and John Slidell, two
Confederate envoys on their way to England, ran the blockade from
Charleston, boarded the British vessel *Trent* in Havana, then embarked
for London. The "hotheaded and often erratic" Union captain Charles
Wilkes intercepted the *Trent*, "forcibly removed" Mason and Slidell,
held them captive, and allowed the *Trent* to continue to England. The
British were furious at this brazen violation of international law. The
hostages were released, but Union diplomacy in the wake of the *Trent*
Affair narrowly prevented a war with Britain.

The British feared a war with America. They recognized that this
aggressive, expansionist nation might swallow up Canada. As early as
July 1861, Britain sent 2,144 officers and men equipped with the recently developed Armstrong rifle to reinforce the 4,300 regular British
troops in Canada. After the *Trent* Affair, Britain sent 11,000 additional
troops to defend Canada from a possible American invasion.

The cotton-financed armaments and ships built by the British for
the Confederacy were a constant source of friction between Washington and London. After two British-built ships, the *Alabama* and the
Florida, wreaked havoc on the U.S. merchant marine, the Union again
seriously threatened Britain. When it was discovered that two deadly
ironclads were being built for the Confederacy in British shipyards, the
North was furious over British complicity. Palmerston reacted to what
he termed "Yankee bullying" by suggesting that the Americans be told,

"You be damned." America made it clear through the communiqué of Charles Francis Adams, the American ambassador to Great Britain, that the ships, the Laird rams, were intended to "carry . . . on war against the United States. It would be superfluous in me to point out to your lordship that this is war." Palmerston capitulated when faced with the ever-present American threat to invade Canada and declare war against Britain. War with America would mean that British commercial vessels would be preyed upon by American raiders. Lord Russell had already understood the gravity of the situation and had ordered the ironclads to remain in Liverpool.

*

Canada stood at the intersection of race and diplomacy before, during, and after the Civil War. Rather than an enlightened and benign Northern neighbor, Canada was fully complicit in the continuing entrapment of free blacks in Southern cotton fields. Canada has been credited with offering a sanctuary of freedom for fugitive slaves, a "promised land" for blacks. It has been praised as a "stronghold of freedom for the Negro in an alien North American environment," and a provider of "pro-Northern moral support against the slaveocracy." The historian Robin Winks has judged both these observations "seriously overemphasized." Again, reality displaces idealism. The bulk of Canada's involvement with abolitionism resulted from its "proximity [to America] rather than ideological affinity." Enslaved blacks were running away from America; Canada was no more than another place. Its harsh racial attitudes were no different from those of Massachusetts or Ohio. Winks notes that fugitive slaves may have been free in Canada, but they were scarcely equal. The Canadians were never seriously interested in the Anti-Slavery Society or in black fugitives. After the Civil War began, the ineffectual Canadian arm of the American Missionary Association closed, and "most Canadians appear[ed] to close their pocketbooks, their schools, and their churches to the [black] fugitives in their midst." They assumed correctly that most of the fugitives would return to America.

Because of its refuge for fugitive slaves and the myth of Canadian racial tolerance, Canada's support of the Confederacy may come as a

surprise. Even "Canadian abolitionists proved to be anti-Northern, opposed to a war fought to preserve the Union, in fact rather inclined to
the Southern position once they saw that Lincoln was not . . . fighting to
end slavery." The outcome of the Civil War was not viewed as a victory
by Canadian abolitionists, for they shared the general Canadian postwar fear that the federal triumph intensified the dangers of annexation
by an avaricious republic bent on continentalism. The unwillingness of
Canadians to back the North angered American abolitionists. The peripatetic pro-Northern English journalist William H. Russell recorded
the Canadian opinion that the North would try to "keep their armies
in good humor by trying to annex Canada." News of the Confederate
victory at Bull Run was welcomed by Liberal-Conservative politicians
with champagne and a "three cheers" salute to the Confederate states
in the Canadian Legislative Assembly.

Canada's anti-Northern leanings appeared in various concrete
ways. Halifax, Nova Scotia, became a major port for serving Confederate blockade-runners and commerce. The *Halifax Sun* described the
city as a "hot southern town." Halifax had a good war: it "was prosperous as never before in her boom and bust history. The city was glutted
with money." Although coal for Confederate steamers and gypsum
flowed through Halifax, cotton was the real money maker. With cotton
at sixty cents a pound in 1863, blockade-runners would take any risk to
make a fortune. The Confederate captain John Wilkinson, a successful
blockade-runner, found Halifax so hospitable that he settled there after
the war. The dashing naval commander was treated "as a celebrity by
the local gentry."

Any pretense served to fan the fires of American expansionism.
The *Chicago Tribune* and the *New York Herald* persistently "advocated
annexing all of Britain's possessions on the continent up to the Hudson
Bay." Postmaster General Montgomery Blair suggested that America
invade British America when the Civil War ended. In a direct reference
to Canada at the 1864 Republican Convention, Henry Raymond, editor
of the *New York Times*, recommended that "all monarchical governments should be driven from the proximity of the United States."

By adding another chapter to the restriction of free black mobility,
Canada reinforced the ties between cotton and race. In the late nine-

teenth century, thousands of American blacks from all-black towns in Oklahoma and Kansas sought to emigrate to western Canada. The specter of a black invasion prompted fears in Canada, just as it had in the American North before the containment policy confirmed by the Civil War. The secretary of the Edmonton Board of Trade sought to prohibit the entry of blacks. An Alberta official demanded that a tax be applied to all blacks. The Winnipeg Board of Trade passed a resolution declaring that blacks had "not proved themselves satisfactory as farmers, thrifty as settlers, or desirable [as] neighbors." The commissioner of immigration for Western Canada paid medical inspectors a fee for each black they rejected in Emerson, Manitoba. In 1911 the Great Northern Railway advised its employees not to sell tickets to blacks who wished to travel to Canada because they would not be allowed to enter. In the same year, Sir Wilfrid Laurier, Canadian prime minister and a former anti-slavery advocate, addressed black immigration before the House of Commons:

> For a period of one year from and after the date hereof, the landing in Canada shall be . . . prohibited of any immigrants belonging to the Negro race, which race is deemed unsuitable to the climate and requirements of Canada.

British and Canadian attitudes toward cotton, slavery, and the American Civil War must be viewed in the context of economic self-interest, diplomacy, racial attitudes, and the possibility of military conflict.

CHAPTER THIRTEEN

Cotton and Confederate Finance

 FOR THE CONFEDERACY, just like the South since 1820, all financial roads led to the cotton fields. Slave-produced cotton gave the young Confederacy financial credibility. Although Confederate financial policy was riddled with blunders, cotton as a potential revenue source was always present as a lifesaver. In the end, the South's fateful error, which perhaps caused its defeat, was its failure to deploy cotton early enough as a substantial financing device.

The South's defeat is sometimes attributed to logistical difficulties based on an inadequate rail system, an inability to manufacture weapons or other basic goods to fight a war, and a shortage of manpower in comparison to the North. The new nation also confronted a combination of economic hurdles: financial backwardness, a small banking system, and financial dependency on the North. The seceding states faced the daunting task of creating a constitution, forming a government, and initiating a war with the second-largest industrial power in the world. This was accomplished within two months. The South had no armaments industry, no army, no navy, no diplomatic corps, no money, and, perhaps most important, no credit.

The Confederacy's shortcomings were glaring when contrasted to the North's manufacturing and financial strengths. The North had a well-developed banking system centered in New York. As noted, New York banks reluctantly provided loans to the federal government at the outbreak of the war when the existence of the Union—and thus the banks' commercial future—was at stake. The huge amount of financing needed to conduct the war spawned the upstart financier Jay Cooke, who pioneered the mass marketing of government bonds to individuals. Treasury Secretary Chase, who did not wish to rely solely on Wall Street, welcomed Jay Cooke's sales prowess. At one point Cooke had 2,500 agents selling government bonds. In November 1861 he boasted of the success of another of his innovative techniques, the payroll deduction. One thousand employees out of fifteen hundred who worked in the transportation department of the Philadelphia and Reading Railroad had allowed money to be deducted from their paychecks to purchase bonds. In 1863 one of Cooke's agents sold bonds to 6,000 people in an Ohio district. Cooke managed to sell bonds worth $500 million during the war.

Despite this financial strength, the North was not immune to the perils of war. War-related borrowings raised the indebtedness of the United States from $65 million to $2.75 billion during the war. The North's fund-raising efforts did not go smoothly. Each battlefield loss sent the gold value of the dollar plummeting. Gold was the standard by which currencies were measured, so a drop in the price of the dollar versus gold meant higher borrowing costs. Correspondingly, each victory brought a rise in the value of the dollar. These kinds of risks made it impossible for the North to borrow money in Europe until victory seemed likely.

Yet the South's predicament was more grave. Considering the economic obstacles faced by Jefferson Davis's new government, it is a wonder—and a testament to the arrogance of King Cotton thinking— that the South ever voted to secede at all. Only in a very short war could the cotton embargo have worked. The Confederacy had little to rely on other than its expectation of a cotton-generated revenue stream. The fledgling Confederacy had no functioning tax system, no borrowing mechanism, and no tariff collection agency. The federal government's revenues, except for land sales, came mainly from tariff duties on imported items. The South was an exporting region, so its import revenue collection was minimal. In 1860, Southern ports accounted for $27 million in imports, Northern ports $327 million. The South sent $182.5 million in exports abroad, the North $151.5

million. Moreover the Confederacy contemplated a low-tariff or no-tariff policy that would have kept import revenues low. So how was the Confederacy to be financed? For the most part, approaches to the revenue problem proceeded haphazardly.

The South was forced to turn immediately to its foundational crop, establishing an export tax. But the South's potential to raise money was short-circuited by the Confederacy's ill-fated ban on the export of cotton. Other than taxing its population, the only other option was to use cotton. That meant allowing the shipment of cotton to Europe in exchange for arms and establishing a credit system based on cotton. This fledging, squabbling collection of states nonetheless managed to borrow a great deal of money. By October 1, 1864, the South had spent $2.3 billion, of which only $122.5 million was raised by taxes. The Confederacy raised the vast majority of its funds through bonds, call certificates, notes, and bank loans. Although well-documented mistakes—including rampant inflation—permeated the South's financial apparatus and policymaking, it did obtain the armaments to fight a closely contested war. A more judicious handling of Confederate financing might have had a major impact on the war's outcome.

The South's task of financing the war was hampered by mundane details, such as the shortage of bank-note paper that delayed the printing of financial instruments. The South did not even have the capacity to print treasury notes, money, or postage stamps. Thus the Confederate government embarked on a program to purchase cotton with notes it could not produce. C. C. Memminger, Confederate secretary of the treasury, admitted "there was not to be found in the whole of the Confederacy a sheet of bank-notepaper on which to print a note. . . . How, then, was cotton to be paid for?" The printing problem was solved by English imports of paper and craftsmen. This pedestrian difficulty illustrates the sheer volume of fundamental challenges faced by the upstart nation.

Borrowing needs were critical from the start. In rapid succession a number of loan offerings appeared. At the end of February 1861, a mere twenty-four days after the Confederate states convened, the Confederate Congress approved the issuance of a government loan for $15 million with a ten-year maturity and an 8 percent semiannual coupon. This was to be backed by a cotton export duty of one-eighth of 1 percent upon the resumption of cotton exports—clearly a contradictory policy in light of the embargo on cotton. Another small note was approved by the Congress in March. Then, on May 16, 1861, a $50 million issue with 8 percent interest was announced. In August a $100 million twenty-year issue was used to purchase "agricultural produce." On April 14, 1862, the Confederacy announced another produce loan that enabled the government to purchase more than 400,000 bales of cotton from Southern farmers. But by mid-1862 the South was in dire financial straits. Interest on obligations was paid with additional bonds, which generated inflation.

The shifting tides of the Southern military campaign created a concurrent shift in the Confederacy's ability to borrow. With battlefield victories—at Bull Run, Springfield, Belmont, Bowling Green, and Ball's Bluff—Southern creditworthiness was deemed acceptable by loan purchasers. But when the Confederacy suffered losses at New Orleans and in Kentucky, Arkansas, and Tennessee, Southern borrowing capacity plummeted.

With the failure of the King Cotton strategy of forcing England into the war, the Confederacy turned to cotton and to Europe for financing. But Europe was concerned about the credit of the Southern government. In April 1861 the London *Times* reported that Southern debt "has nothing to recommend it to European consideration." Gladstone, Britain's pro-Southern chancellor of the exchequer, was concerned about the Confederacy's ability "to levy taxes and the disposition of the people to pay them." Therefore Europe required that Confederate loans be guaranteed by cotton or gold. The English opposition was based not on moral values but on creditworthiness.

Belatedly the Confederacy's financial strategy evolved into a more effective plan. As finances worsened into the spring of 1862, the South was forced to rely on its only asset, cotton. Cotton warrants, or obligations to purchase cotton at a specific price, were proposed in July 1862 by the secretary of the navy, Stephen Mallory, who was desperate for funds to pay for ships. When Mallory sent his agent, George T. Sinclair, to England to purchase ships, he had to resort to cotton-warrant bonds, which allowed the holder of the bonds to convert them into cotton at a fixed price. There was sufficient incentive in the warrant price of 8 cents per pound when cotton was trading at 30 cents per pound. The holder could theoretically make a profit of at least 22 cents per pound if prices held. A small amount of cotton, £60,000 worth, was sold via the English firm Lindsay and Co. to two or three private buyers. Lindsay recommended that an additional £500,000 could be raised—but only with this attractive option to purchase cotton.

The South moved farther along the path of cotton credit with legislation on April 30, 1863, that authorized the sale of $100 million in twenty-year bonds with a 6 percent coupon and, in an important innovation, "with interest and principal payable at the pleasure of the government, either in specie or in cotton." This meant that the purchaser of the bonds might receive his interest payments in cotton or in foreign currencies—French francs or British sterling. The "cotton option" provided that cotton bales would be available at Southern ports. The cotton price was stipulated at 6 pence when the market price was 23 pence. It was theoretically possible for the buyer of such a bond to make a huge profit because the price of the bond was related to the price of cotton. The South could no longer borrow without promising this added incentive of cotton. Only $9 million of these bonds were sold as military events placed the Confederacy's very existence in danger.

The epitome of cotton-backed financing was the deservedly famous Erlanger cotton bond of March 1863. This bond paid large commissions, raised only a limited amount of money, and failed to hold its value, but the concept behind it remains prescient and brilliant. The Erlanger bond was the most imaginative financing instrument of the Civil War and has remained relevant as a sophisticated international security designed to trade on multiple European exchanges. The bond underscored the importance of cotton and the interconnectedness of the cotton world. Indeed, President Lincoln took an active interest in its development.

After being authorized on January 29, 1863, in a secret meeting of the Confederate Congress, the bonds were offered simultaneously by Erlanger & Cie. and its London agent, J. Henry Schroeder & Co., for sale on March 19 on exchanges in London, Liverpool, Paris, Frankfurt, and Amsterdam. The transaction was initiated by Emile Erlanger, whose

A forerunner of modern finance, the innovative, sophisticated Erlanger bond, issued by the Confederacy, demonstrated cotton's power and international appeal.

firm in 1862 was the first to suggest a cotton-backed loan. He knew that with the proceeds the Confederate navy would be able to purchase cruisers and rams that would be a menace to the North.

The terms of the Erlanger bond reflected its novelty as well as its simultaneous use of political, military, and credit risk. The amount of the offering was £3 million (or 75 million francs). No other public bond in the history of finance had incorporated all the sophisticated features of the Erlanger bond—convertibility into either of two currencies, or into a commodity, cotton, which commanded the respect of the financiers. The twenty-year bond paid a 7 percent (semiannual) coupon, and the bondholder had the option of payment in pounds sterling or French francs. The bonds could be redeemed upon maturity at 100 percent when the offering price was 90 percent. Erlanger's cost was 77 percent, with additional commission fees. The response was overwhelming. There were bids for £16 million, or five times the amount offered. By one estimate the South raised $8.6 million, less interest, principal, and expenses, from the transaction. The bond price rose briefly to 95 percent, which gave bondholders an immediate profit. They could either receive cash or convert the bonds for cotton at a fixed price of 6 pence per pound when the real price of cotton was 24 pence. Accordingly a £1,000 bond was theoretically worth £4,000 in terms of cotton. There was strong incentive to purchase the bonds based on the underlying value of cotton. The proceeds paid for armaments. In addition, Confederate agents used unsold bonds to pay creditors such as S. Isaac Campbell and Co., a procurer of armaments, and as collateral for other transactions.

The risks were clear. A bondholder could redeem bonds for cotton, but the cotton had to be picked up at a designated Southern port. This meant that the bondholder had to arrange for his cotton to run the Union blockade—successfully. If the Union navy captured the cotton, the bondholder would lose his entire investment. If the South lost the war, in all likelihood the victorious North would not honor Confederate debt.

Erlanger bonds were also conspicuous because of the importance of their holders. The British elite were especially optimistic about the South and became eager investors. A partial list of the bondholders included William Gladstone; Evelyn Ashley, private secretary to Lord Palmerston; John Thaddeus Delane, editor of the London *Times*; M. B. Sampson, city editor of the *Times*; W. J. Rideout, proprietor of the *London Morning Post*; Lord Robert Cecil, M.P. and future prime minister; and J. S. Gilliad, a director of the Bank of England. On March 21, 1863, the *Economist* observed, "It may appear somewhat startling that the Confederates should be able to borrow money in Europe while the Federal Government has been unable to obtain a shilling from that usually liberal and enterprising quarter!"

As the South established credit via the Erlanger bond, other European firms began to make offers. Lafitte and Co. (Paris) suggested a £4 million, 7 percent coupon bond with a cotton option at 6 pence. Boucarue and Gentil (Paris) and Deveaux (London) made a proposal in June 1863. Erlanger himself wanted to do another transaction for £5 million with an 8 percent coupon.

The ultimate solvency of the bonds depended on the South's military success. Between April 7 and 24, 1863, the price of the bonds fluctuated between 87 and 92 percent. Then, Southern defeats at both Vicksburg and Gettysburg on July 4 sent the bonds into a downward spiral. Any scheme for bond financing to purchase more arms died on the battlefields of Mississippi and Pennsylvania. By December the bonds had sunk to 34 percent. As hope for an armistice developed, the bonds jumped to 80 percent in September 1864. Atlanta's capitulation at the hands of General Sherman removed any hope for the Confederacy, Confederate debt, or the presidential peace candidate, General George McClellan.

*

The South's haphazard and flawed financial apparatus was to be expected from such a hastily improvised government, founded virtually in the midst of war. Historians often excoriate the Confederacy for its financial bungling, but the real failure lay with its grand strategy of King Cotton diplomacy. Certainly there was sufficient cotton to implement a credit strategy that would have handily financed a government and a war. Frank Owsley estimates that more than two million bales of cotton could have been shipped to England during the early part of the war. After the war, even Jefferson Davis is reported to have repudiated his reliance on the cotton embargo in favor of a cotton credit system. He is said to have acknowledged that a sale or transport of three million bales of cotton early in the war, before the North's blockade, would have yielded a billion dollars in gold. Davis is quoted as determining that

> Such a sum . . . would have sufficed . . . for a war of twice the actual duration; and this evidence of a southern prosperity and ability could not but have acted powerfully upon the minds and securities and avarice of the New England rulers of the North. . . .

It would indeed have been feasible to ship a large amount of cotton to Europe in the spring and summer of 1861, either for immediate sale, for storage and later sale, or for use as collateral to finance loans for the Confederacy in Europe. Instead the South chose to stop the shipment of cotton and even burn it in order to implement its embargo.

If money had not been a hindrance to the Confederacy, the potential for greater bloodshed would have been inevitable. The military struggle was close; the South was sufficiently well armed. The tide-turning losses at Antietam and Gettysburg were not foreordained. Before the capitulation of Atlanta, the combination of Southern resistance and Northern war weariness gave the peace candidate, George McClellan, a likely victory in the presidential election of 1864. A better-financed and better-equipped Confederacy could have been a far more formidable combatant.

Historians mistakenly malign the power of cotton because of the failure of the South's cotton embargo strategy. Cotton was surely misused in the Confederacy's diplomatic strategy. But this was not a question of cotton's irrelevance. If Jefferson Davis had used the crop to buy credit, it could have been highly effective. Cotton remained the economic and political underpinning of the Confederacy and the only reliable source—however misused—of financing for arms.

CHAPTER FOURTEEN

Procuring Arms

 EVEN BEFORE the end of the official embargo on cotton, the Confederate government by necessity had allowed a trade with England in which cotton was bartered for arms. Slave-produced cotton allowed the South to take advantage of Britain's manufacturing capability. Britain was more than happy to supply the South (and the North) with weapons, ships, boots, and clothing. The South's sole source of revenue or anticipated revenue for the purchase of these imported goods, as we have seen, was cotton. Without Britain, the Confederacy could never have mustered a sustained military effort against the North. Lieutenant Colonel J. W. Mallet, a Confederate ordnance officer, extolled the armaments supplied through the blockade with "cotton in payment" as "being of incalculable value all through 1862, '63 and '64."

The dramatic story of the Southern importation of materials through the Union blockade is legendary. The well-established Southern shipping links and personal ties with England, many based on the decades-old British love for cotton, were converted during the war to the procurement of arms. The Confederacy appointed the established Charleston cotton firm of John Fraser & Co. to act as agent for overseas shipping and finance. Fraser, established in 1803, operated closely with its two affiliates, the New York–based Trenholm Brothers and Fraser, Trenholm & Co. in Liverpool. The head of both firms, George Alfred

Trenholm, in July 1863 became the Confederate secretary of the treasury. The agents were empowered to handle cash, deposits, letters of credit, drafts, and cotton transactions, and for their services received a 1.5 percent commission. The antebellum South has been much maligned for provinciality, but when we look deeper we see that the international presence of cotton provided a network and familiarity with global trade, especially trade with Britain.

Cotton spawned a bustling war trade. The shipments of both arms and luxury goods from Britain usually went first to the British colonies of Bermuda or Nassau, before the fall of New Orleans in 1862 shifted the trade chiefly to Bermuda. In the colonial ports were official Confederate agents, Louis C. Heyliger in Nassau and Major Norman S. Walker, a West Point graduate, in Bermuda, to facilitate the trade.

British goods were offloaded onto ships called blockade-runners, which were designed to "run" past the Union blockade and into Southern ports. The ships were modified into shallow-draft, speedy vessels which eluded Union forces with a considerable degree of success. Some had engines that could help the ship reach a speed of eighteen knots, which was faster than most of the interceptor vessels used by the U.S. Navy. Blockade-runners were built, repaired, and retrofitted in England and manned by British crews. After delivering their cargo, they were loaded with cotton for a return journey to Nassau or Bermuda.

The blockade was difficult for the Union to enforce. Owsley colorfully describes the "Herculean task of blockading the 3,549 statute miles of Confederate coast from Alexandria, Virginia, on the Potomac to the Rio Grande River with its 189 rivers, numerous bays, inlets and harbors," which the Union in 1861 had to do with 90 vessels. By 1863 the Union navy had 588 blockade vessels. Nevertheless the main Confederate blockade-running port, Wilmington, remained active until its capture in January 1865. The growing presence of the Union navy simply prompted better-built blockade-runners as shipbuilders adapted with faster and faster ships. Southern supply was impacted by the Union army's victories on land and the capture of Southern ports, not by the blockade.

The crew and the backers of blockade-runners were motivated primarily by the enticing potential for profit generated from the difference in the price of cotton between the Confederacy and England.

There were of course examples of patriotism, and the quest for adventure and fame was also a factor. But once the British supply of American cotton dried up, the war-induced cotton shortage produced a price explosion that promised astounding profits. In 1863 cotton traded at $1.00 a pound in New York; before the war's end it would trade at $1.80 a pound. Remember that in 1863 cotton could be purchased for 8 to 10 cents a pound. The logic of money and its stepchild, profit, was an irresistible inducement. By one account, blockade-runners could expect a return of 300 to 500 percent per expedition, based on what their cotton would sell for in Britain. According to the generally accepted wisdom within the blockade-running fraternity, "a shipowner could shrug off the loss of his vessel after two safe round trips through the blockade."

Risks of injury, loss of life, or loss of cargo were no deterrent. Confederate folklore described ship captains "who possessed . . . the cunning of a fox, the patience of Job and the bravery of a Spartan warrior." A common toast summarized the logic:

> Here's to the Southern planters who grow the cotton; to the Limeys who buy the cotton; to the Yankees that maintain the blockade and keep up the price of cotton. So, three cheers for a long continuance of the war, and success to the blockade-runners.

Initially the South relied on private citizens to run the blockade. Later it was necessary to create a combination of private and government approaches and an exclusively government-managed effort. The first official government-owned blockade-runner was the *Fingal*, a British ship purchased by James Dunwoody Bulloch, head agent for Confederate naval procurement. The experienced, knowledgeable, and resourceful Bulloch became a thorn in the side of Union officials stationed in Britain.

The *Fingal* saga illustrates the intrigue that accompanied Confederate procurement activities. In the summer of 1861, Bulloch ordered a steamer, falsely named the *Oreto* and described as a transaction for an Italian purchaser. The Union could not prevent the *Oreto*, which was in reality the *Fingal*, from leaving the Scottish port of Greenock on October 10. Union agents in Scotland sent a complete list of the munitions cargo on board to the Union blockading fleet stationed on the other side of the Atlantic. Bulloch boarded the vessel at Holyhead in Wales with a British crew, and sailed it to Bermuda. The British sailors who were used extensively on blockade-runners carried false papers. If caught, they knew they would eventually be released, whereupon they would find employment on other blockade-runners.

Once the ship reached Bermuda, the British again rebuffed Union efforts to intercept the *Fingal*. Bulloch then picked up a Savannah, Georgia, pilot and proceeded. On November 12, 1861, the *Fingal* landed in Savannah with its essential munitions cargo. The payload for the Confederate military was enormous. According to one source, the sailors unloaded "15,000 [mostly] Enfield rifles, more than 2 million cartridges, 24,000 pounds of powder, 2 million percussion caps, 230 swords and 3,000 cavalry sabers, 500 revolvers with ammunition, 2 Blakely guns, 2 smaller cannon, 7 tons of artillery shells, 400 barrels of gunpowder, as well as blankets, medical supplies, and army and navy uniforms and uniform cloth." A significant portion of the *Fingal*'s cargo was immediately shipped to General Albert S. Johnston's army in Tennessee, where it was used in the bloody battle of Shiloh.

The pattern of British-produced arms, cotton payments, and blockade-running became a critical part of the Confederate war machine. The *Fingal*'s successful voyage was only a typical episode. Despite remaining "neutral" throughout the war, the British supplied four hundred steamers and eight hundred sailing ships as blockade-runners. The well-known British shipbuilder John Brown and Co. is alone credited with providing 111 blockade-runners. The master engine maker Fawcett, Preston was responsible for most of the engines.

The *Banshee*, built in Liverpool in early 1863, was representative. This pioneer in ironclad commercial shipping was 214 feet long and 20 feet wide, and light enough that it sat in only eight feet of water. After nine successful runs, the *Banshee* was captured by the Union navy in November 1863. Despite its brief life, the *Banshee* made a 700 percent profit for its English owners. *Banshee No. 2* had already been built in England when the first *Banshee* was seized. We can only speculate on how much money was earned by other blockade-runners like the *Robert E. Lee*, which made 21 successful runs, or the *Hattie*, with a shocking 60 successful runs.

Owsley's conclusion that the Union blockade was a "leaky and ramshackle affair" has been confirmed by many other historians. He reasoned that only one in ten ships was captured in 1861, and even after a major increase in the size of the Union navy, in 1864 only one in four. Estimates range from 4,500 to more than 8,000 successful runs to Southern ports during the war. Of 2,054 runs along the Carolina coasts during the war, 1,735 (84 percent) made it through the blockade. Thus an average of one and a half ships per day docked in Southern ports. Even in 1864, 723 attempts yielded 521 (72 percent) successful deliveries.

Surely the cotton-based rewards of 300 to 500 percent per expedition guaranteed that blockade-runners would not be deterred by the risks. Wartime trade soared. The intermediate ports, Nassau and St. George's in Bermuda, became boom towns. The rise in the price of cotton during the war compensated for reduced volume. Owsley surmised that after the spring of 1862 between 1 million and 1.25 million bales of cotton evaded the blockade. Stanley Lebergott calculates that 500,000 bales evaded the coastal blockade while 900,000 additional bales were smuggled overland to the North. With cotton selling at ten to almost 20 times the prewar price, the payload was substantial. Cotton valued at $65 million was said to have been exported through Wilmington. Concurrently the value of goods shipped by Britain to the Confederate states totaled an impressive $200 million. Neither anti-slavery attitudes nor morality influenced the Northern and British purchasers of cotton.

Eventually the South attained "preferred purchaser" status with the British while the North developed domestic manufacturing capability. The British exported a wide array of arms and equipment to the South—"large cannon . . . railway artillery, incendiary bombs . . . machine guns . . . Armstrong rifles . . . the Enfield rifle . . . the Whitfield rifle [which could hit a target at 2,000 yards], the Brunswick rifle . . . the Vandenburg Volley Gun," and so on. The London Armoury Co. sold 150,000 Enfield rifles to the Confederacy. In 1864, "46,254 rifles, pistols and carbines were imported" by the South. Only 20,485 were manufactured in the South during this period. In total, 600,000 "pieces of equipment" and 550,000 pairs of boots were shipped by Britain to the South. From October 1864 through January 1865 extensive supplies arrived at Wilmington—1,507,000 pounds of lead, 1,933,000 pounds of saltpeter, 546,000 pairs of shoes, 516,000 pairs of blankets, 500,000 pounds of coffee, and 69,000 rifles. Confederate uniform jackets, "a shortened version of standard British army jackets," were manufactured by the Irish company of Peter Tait & Co.

"Bermuda bacon," the meat imported by the Confederacy, was an essential cargo. Meat purchased in Boston or New York would be sent to Canada, then to Bermuda or Nassau, before being shipped to Southern ports. Northerners also shipped meat to Liverpool, where it was unloaded and reshipped to the intermediary ports. In the year ending January 1865 the Confederacy obtained 8,632,000 pounds of meat through Wilmington. This was extremely good business for Northern farmers whose sons were dying on Southern battlefields.

General Ulysses S. Grant, the victorious Union commander, was well aware of the effects of British-supplied armaments. In describing the surrender of Vicksburg, Grant acknowledged the superiority of the sixty thousand Enfield rifles he captured. He proceeded to replace his own rifles with Southern arms:

> At Vicksburg 31,600 prisoners were surrendered, together with 172 cannon, about 60,000 muskets with a large amount of ammunition. The small-arms of the enemy were far superior to ours. . . . The enemy had generally new arms which had run the blockade and were of uniform caliber. After the surrender I authorized all colonels whose regiments were armed with inferior muskets, to place them in the stack of captured arms and replace them with the latter.

The South proved that an international trading system based on the logic of money and experience in the cotton trade could overcome its lack of manufacturing capacity. The incentive of cotton profits produced a blockade-running effort that effectively defeated the Union's blockade strategy.

*

Beyond the import of innumerable weapons and basic goods, cotton allowed the Confederacy to purchase the deadly raiding vessels that plagued the U.S. merchant marine and the U.S. Navy, struck fear in American seaport populations, and led to a bitter, almost violent dispute between America and Britain over wartime damages inflicted on American shippers.

At the onset of the Civil War, Northern shipping and commercial prowess had built a successful Atlantic trade. In 1860 two-thirds of New York's trade was carried in American ships, but by 1863 foreign ships were responsible for three-fourths of New York's commerce. The U.S. merchant marine was decimated by Confederate raiders, notably the *Alabama*, the *Florida*, and the *Shenandoah*—all purchased through cotton credit. All were built in England with full knowledge of the British government, by British employees of British companies, with British materials and manned primarily by British seamen. The legendary *Alabama*, under the command of Raphael Semmes, terrified and terrorized American commercial vessels from its launching in July 1862 until its sinking off Cherbourg, France, in June 1864 by the *USS Kearsage*, under the command of the North Carolinian John A. Winslow. As the *Alabama* sank, Semmes was rescued by a British yacht, *Deerhound*, taken to England, treated as a celebrity, and returned to serve the Confederate army. Captain Winslow was duly outraged by the British aid in Semmes's escape.

The estimates of actual destruction by the raiders vary. The *Alabama* is acknowledged to have taken between 66 and 69 prizes, the *Shenandoah* 48, and the *Florida* 36. Confederate cruisers and privateers sank more than 200 Union ships with a value of $30 million. These successes caused insurance rates for American commercial vessels to rise substantially. Foreign vessels paid 1 to 2 percent of cargo value for insurance while Americans were charged 5 to 6 percent. This and the risk of capture prompted 385 American ships to be "reflagged to foreign ownership." Most of the premier fleet of trapped "Yankee clippers" were sold at auction, mainly to British competitors. The British purchased $42 million worth of vessels out of a total sale of $64 million. The only remaining part of the once-formidable U.S. merchant marine consisted of "obsolete and coasting vessels." Britain had destroyed her "only rival . . . for an indefinite span of years," merely by constructing ships for the Confederacy in return for cotton credit.

After the Civil War the U.S. government initiated a testy dialogue with Britain over compensation for the direct and indirect losses of U.S.

vessels due to British construction of warships for the Confederacy. An acrimonious dispute led to an international tribunal convened in Geneva, Switzerland. Secretary of State Seward, always aggressive in his pursuit of territory, wanted Canada as compensation. At one point he indicated he would settle for Nassau. Senator Charles Sumner spoke of British responsibility in prolonging the war. He speculated that Britain owed the United States $2.5 billion for lengthening the conflict. Sumner too suggested that Canada be part of the settlement. He was supported by Michigan senator Zachariah Chandler. The erstwhile Massachusetts politician Ben Butler in 1870 demanded that Britain "instantly cede Canada, pay the claims or face a declaration of non-intercourse." Butler resurrected King Cotton diplomacy by declaring that Britain "shall have none of our cotton or breadstuffs" until compensation was settled. He echoed the earlier thoughts of Southerners in advising that "Such deprivation [of our cotton] to Manchester, Birmingham and Bradford might work a revolution in her government in six months."

Capital requirements tempered the belligerent rhetoric and extravagant claims of U.S. officials. America's need for "more foreign investment" demanded "good relations with Europe, especially England." The national debt was a major concern. In May 1872 the financier Jay Cooke, who was encountering difficulties in selling shares of the Northern Pacific Railroad, pleaded with Senator Carl Schurz to "secure ... an amicable adjustment of the *Alabama* question." European bankers, especially the Rothschilds, had rebuffed the attempts of Treasury Secretary George Boutwell to raise money because of the unsettled *Alabama* claims. Finally, on September 2, 1872, reality dictated a settlement. Arbitrators agreed on an indemnity of $15.5 million as British reparations for damages inflicted by the *Alabama* and her sister ships.

The penalty imposed on Britain was a pittance when compared to her wartime business gains and the dismantling of the merchant marine of her closest commercial rival. Cotton, profits, and *realpolitik*, not morality, had determined British actions. The British retained Canada and quickly implemented the British North America Act of 1867, which established the union of Canadian provinces, in order to preempt American annexation. In effect the American Civil War gave birth to two countries, the United States and Canada, as Robin Winks has noted.

CHAPTER FIFTEEN

Cotton Trading in the United States

 THE FRENZY of cotton trading during the Civil War strongly reaffirmed the attraction and force of King Cotton. Such a valuable commodity was of major interest to the North, just as it was to the British. Profit, as we have seen, knows no geographical boundaries. Even one's enemy in war can look like a brother in trade. As the pent-up demand for cotton drove prices higher, opportunities for profit and corruption on both Union and Confederate sides abounded.

Northern regulations for dealing with cotton appeared by necessity. Early in the war the Treasury Department was given authority to regulate the cotton trade and specifically to forbid trading with the South. An act of May 20, 1862, for example, prohibited officers of the Union army and navy from engaging in the "sale or purchase of cotton or any other merchandise." But, as we shall see, this prohibition was violated by Union soldiers with impunity. Treasury Secretary Chase described the interest in cotton as "vast and complicated" and noted that "the appetite for trade is eager and exacting." He was empowered to appoint special agents to purchase and sell cotton, but profits proved too tempting for these officials to function honestly. The problem of the cotton agents was compounded by Chase's poor judgment in making appointments. Henry Halleck, Lincoln's chief of staff, implored General Grant to "See that all possible facilities are afforded for getting out cotton. It is deemed important to get as much as we can into market." On August 2, 1862, Halleck approved the use of gold as payment for cotton.

Beginning in 1862 with the Union capture of important Confederate port cities, the illicit internal cotton trade mushroomed. New Orleans fell in May 1862, Memphis in June, and Vicksburg in July 1863. The federal government needed cotton for its own use and desperately wished to prevent Confederate cotton from being shipped to Britain. There ensued a muddled policy as corrupt Northern licensees traded "salt, bacon, powder, firearms, percussion caps, etc." to Southerners for cotton. The supplies found their way to the Confederate army, much to the consternation of Generals Grant and Sherman. In August 1862 communications among Halleck, Chase, Grant, and Sherman were filled with complaints about the important aid being given to the Confederacy in the cotton-for-goods trading. Cotton, the "bait," was traded for gold, which in turn purchased the "salt, powder, and lead" in St. Louis and Cincinnati that ended up with the Confederate army. On October 9, 1862, Sherman wrote to Grant that "The great profit [from the cotton-for-goods] trade . . . is converting everybody into rascals and it makes me ashamed of my countrymen." On June 15, 1864, Sherman was still stewing over the illicit trade: "I never knew a cotton dealer, male or female, but what would falsify." General N. J. T. Dana, stationed in Natchez, complained in July 1864 that "the enemy have been freely supplied through our lines on the Mississippi River." Such a lucrative trade could not be regulated or contained.

During the war, as Union forces captured Southern cotton lands, cotton trading became extensive. Cotton owned by Confederates was deemed subject to confiscation without pay, but cotton owned by loyalists had to be purchased. The federal government and the Union army faced the problem of whether to trade with the enemy—if they could determine who was the enemy. It was nearly impossible to distinguish "enemy" cotton from "loyal" cotton. So Union treasury agents and troops capitulated to the vast profits that could be made by purchasing cotton. And while the Confederate government ordered the burning of all cotton on land held by Union forces or about to be captured, there were powerful incentives for not obeying this edict.

Union troops, as they moved into cotton territory, often pretended to act as agents for the federal government in confiscating cotton. Rather than relinquish the cotton to the government, the soldiers collected tidy profits for themselves by selling to cotton speculators. Thus they essentially provisioned their enemies. A Union officer in Holly Springs, Mississippi, Colonel A. S. Norton, in December 1862 vented his frustration about the illegal but unstoppable cotton trade: "War and commerce with the enemy! What a Utopian dream!"

The mathematics of the trade were simple. In 1864 the price of cotton rose from 81 cents a pound to $1.90. At any given time, cotton could be purchased for eight to 20 cents a pound in the South. Thus a shipment of only one bale could reap a potential profit of more than $900, less small transport costs.

Federal government mechanisms for regulating cotton trading were riddled with fraud and corruption. The government issued "permits" to private citizens to buy and sell cotton, which naturally led to bribery for the much coveted permits. They could be bought and sold freely in New York. Treasury agents, military personnel, and private citizens were caught in the web of the cotton market. Both federal and Confederate laws were violated in the scramble to buy and sell cotton.

As president it was impossible for Lincoln to avoid cotton. In 1863, at the height of the war, he and Treasury Secretary Chase embarked on a scheme to purchase cotton from Southern planters who would take an oath of allegiance to the Union. The planters would then be entitled to sell cotton to government agents and receive 25 percent of the proceeds. The balance of 75 percent would be paid by the federal government after the war. Both Chase and Lincoln also used the valuable cotton licenses needed to purchase and sell cotton, to pay off friends and political debts. And Lincoln allowed goods that were sent to Confederate territory to be exchanged for cotton. The president's purchasing plan may have enabled the federal government to buy cotton, but it also encouraged army officers and troops, agents, and Southern planters to collude in the profitable venture. The realist Lincoln knew of the corruption, but he also recognized the power of cotton. In December 1864 he wrote that it "is immensely important to get the cotton away" from the South. He wanted cotton to stay in the United States by means of a blockade, and would even tolerate a corrupt federally sponsored domestic cotton trade. If greed allowed domestic traders to buy cotton, Lincoln was "thankful that so much good can be got out of pecuniary greed." Lincoln's actions are startling proof that the lure of cotton rose to the top of American politics.

Lincoln's policy proved to be a nightmare for General Grant, who had to deal with corruption as well as trade with the enemy. Grant described his dilemma:

> Among other embarrassments . . . was the fact that the government wanted to get out all cotton possible from the South and directed me to give every facility toward that end. Pay in gold was authorized, and stations on the Mississippi River and on the railroad in our possession had to be designated where cotton could be received. This opened to the enemy not only the valuable means of converting cotton into money, which had a value all over the world and which they needed, but it afforded them means of obtaining accurate and intelligent information with regard to our position and strength. It was demoralizing to the troops. Citizens obtained permits from the treasury department and had to be protected within our lines and given facilities to get out cotton by which they realized enormous profits.

Grant would have preferred that no trading occur. That was of course impossible because of the importance of cotton. The crop was so crucial that at the start of the war Lincoln's policy provided the cash-strapped South with money.

The extent of the illicit trade was apparent. Senator Zachariah Chandler lamented that by mid-1864 $20 million to $30 million in goods and supplies had been shipped to the Confederacy through Memphis alone. General Daniel E. Sickles wrote to Lincoln in May 1864 that "goods and to the amount of half a million a week went through our lines, [and were] sold" in Memphis. Northern soldiers and private citizens were more than eager to buy cotton and sell goods to the Confederacy.

Cotton provided a lucrative opportunity for New York, the financial and commercial center of America. Thurlow Weed, the influential New York Republican, obtained one of the lucrative cotton-trading

At the onset of the war, President Lincoln ordered a naval blockade to disrupt the South's cotton trade with Europe. He knew that the Confederacy could procure armaments and financing in exchange for Southern cotton. He even condoned corruption that diverted cotton from Confederate use. *(Brady Collection)*

permits. Hundreds of thousands of bales that originated in Memphis, Vicksburg, and New Orleans were transported to New York, much of the commerce illegal. As Edwin Burrows and Mike Wallace have noted, "Trading with the enemy, an old New York staple, again became big business." Cotton was the staple; the cotton states were the enemy. New York's and the North's single-minded commitment to commerce and cotton would have ominous long-term implications for postwar Reconstruction. New York wanted nothing more than a return to normal business activity, which in this case meant a resumption of the cotton trade, with blacks in the cotton fields.

The fall of Memphis in June 1862 was followed by an orgy of cotton trading. The Union army was reportedly "paralyzed by hordes of speculators who followed on its heels to reap the harvest that awaited in its wake." As early as the fall of 1862 the English merchant W. C. Corsan observed that "large fortunes" were being made from cotton commerce in New Orleans. Merchants would send agents to purchase cotton for eight to ten cents a pound from plantations in the interior when cotton could be sold for sixty-seven cents in New York. As cotton reached an unprecedented one dollar a pound in early 1863, the New York journalist Charles Dana formed a partnership with Roscoe Conkling to trade cotton in Memphis, from where he sent reports to Secretary of War Edwin Stanton:

> The mania for sudden fortunes in cotton, raging in a vast population of Jews and Yankees scattered throughout this whole country and town [Memphis] almost exceeding the number of regular residents, has to an alarming extent corrupted and demoralized the army. Every colonel, captain, or quartermaster is in secret partnership with some operator in cotton; every soldier dreams of adding a bale of cotton to his monthly pay. I had no conception of the extent of this evil until I came and saw for myself. . . . The resources of the rebels are inordinately increased from this source. . . . No private purchase of cotton should be allowed in any part of the occupied region.

Union officers participated at every level of the illicit trade. President Lincoln was fully aware of

> the fierceness with which . . . profits are sought. The temptation is so great that nearly everybody wishes to be in it; . . . the question of profit controls all, regardless of whether the cotton seller is loyal or rebel. . . . The officers of the army, in numerous instances, are believed to connive and share the profits, and thus the army itself is diverted from fighting rebels to speculating in cotton.

The Union army's General Canby was furious at the cotton speculators who "follow in the track of the army, and barter the cause for which it is fighting with all the baseness of Judas Iscariot, but without his remorse."

But the trade could not be stopped. Federal permits and restrictions led only to clever circumvention. General Sherman discovered funeral coffins leaving Memphis with cargoes of medicine—secured through the cotton trade—for Confederate troops in Mississippi. Dead animals were found with "bellies full of gold." Senator Jacob Collamer sarcastically suggested that the army should be replaced by "Yankee peddlers . . . to go down there and trade them out." Thomas Knox, who leased a plantation in Mississippi, wrote in 1865 that New Orleans merchants "found themselves crowded aside by the ubiquitous Yankees."

> In '63 and '64, New Orleans could boast of more cotton factors than cotton. The principal business was in the hands of merchants from the North, who had established themselves in the city soon after its occupation by National forces. Nearly all cotton sent to the market was from plantations leased by Northern men, or from purchases made of planters by Northern speculators.

Sherman asserted that Memphis, because of cotton trading, was more valuable to the Confederate army after it capitulated. Both he and Grant identified the perennial financial scapegoats, the Jews, as culprits. Sherman summarized the unbridled competition for cotton in his characteristically unvarnished prose. He wrote to Secretary Chase on August 11, 1862:

> But, the commercial enterprise of the Jews soon discovered that ten cents would buy a pound of cotton; that four cents would take it to Boston, where they would receive thirty cents in gold. The bait was tempting, and it spread like fire, when here, they discovered that salt, bacon, powder, fire-arms, percussion caps, etc. were worth as much as gold; and strange to say this traffic was not only permitted, but encouraged. Before, we in the interior could know it, hundreds, yea thousands of barrels of salt and millions of dollars had been distributed to [Confederate troops in Tupelo and Vicksburg].

The irate General Grant did more than blame the Jews. On December 17, 1862, he issued General Order 11, which expelled all Jews from the military district in western Tennessee. They were given forty-eight hours to leave. One historian has termed General Order 11 a "logical culmination of the history of anti-Semitism in Grant's army and his own intensifying bigotry." The band of speculators in fact consisted of a motley crew of "Yankees, Confederates, treasury agents, army officers and vagabonds," including Northern and Southern Jews. They were merely part of the entourage, but their "manners, accents, and surnames invited special attention." Jewish protests moved President Lincoln to rescind Order 11, but the intent nevertheless survived with General Henry W. Halleck, who instructed Grant on January 21, 1863, that "the President has no objection to you expelling traitors and Jew peddlers."

Despite protests and orders to regulate it, the cotton trade between North and South flourished. Perhaps 900,000 bales made their way from the South to the Northeast. The cotton trade through the Bahamas and Bermuda was thus joined by a domestic trade. Even though the Union would eventually win victory on the battlefield, the willingness—and eagerness—of Northerners to trade with their enemy was also a victory for commerce. Despite the failures of King Cotton diplomacy and the belated introduction of cotton credit, the South was reminded yet again of the enormous influence of a bale of cotton.

CHAPTER SIXTEEN

Cotton and the Freedmen

 THE WARTIME machinations of cotton involved a simultaneous shadow history: the experience of African Americans
during the Civil War. As the Union army marched through
the South, tens of thousands of enslaved blacks were freed and thousands of plantations abandoned. The federal government had no policy
with regard to the destitute thousands whom they set free. Plans
evolved by necessity in different areas of the South, each policy subject
to interpretation, violation, and different degrees of enforcement.

A "containment policy," a form of domestic colonization in the
South, evolved as the white North faced its day of racial reckoning.
Thousands of freed slaves, known as contraband, appeared behind the
lines of the Union army in Virginia. The question of what to do with
freed slaves in Confederate territory was no longer abstract. The pre-
cipitating event occurred in September 1862 when General John Dix,
an anti-slavery Union commander in Virginia, requested that the governors of Massachusetts, Rhode Island, and Maine accept two thousand
needy former slaves. Massachusetts governor John Andrew rejected
the plea. He had optimistically expected that free blacks in the North
would gravitate south, where their "pecularities of physical constitution" were better suited.

> For the . . . [former slave refugees] to come here for encampment or
> asylum would be to come as paupers and sufferers into a strange land

and a climate trying even to its habitués . . . to a busy community where they would be incapable of self-help—a course certain to demoralize themselves and endanger others. Such an event would be a handle to all traitors and to all persons evilly disposed.

Western governors warmly supported Andrew's policy of keeping black refugees in the South.

In February 1864, however, Governor Andrew changed his tune. He wrote to President Lincoln complaining that Union commanders in Virginia refused to allow contraband to immigrate to Massachusetts where there was a labor shortage. The governor's real agenda—using blacks to fill Massachusetts' military quotas—was transparent, and a furious Lincoln replied with undisguised sarcasm.

If I were to judge from the letter, without external knowledge . . . I would suppose that all the colored people of Washington were struggling to get to Massachusetts; that Massachusetts was anxious to receive them as permanent citizens; and that the United States Government here was interposing and preventing this. But I suppose these are neither the facts, nor meant to be asserted as true by you. . . . If, however, it be true that Massachusetts wishes to afford permanent home within her borders, for all, or even a large number of colored persons who will come to her . . . I would not for a moment hinder [them] from going. . . .

The conscription of Northern troops, as we have seen in New York, was a combustible burden. Driven by expediency, Andrew had initiated a meeting of governors at Altoona, Pennsylvania, to demand the recruitment of black troops. Iowa's governor, Samuel Kirkwood, did not mince words when he insisted on some "dead niggers" in addition to dead white men on the battlefield. When blacks began to be conscripted into the Union army they were actually seized as substitutes for draftees who wished to avoid serving.

The West had to face a similar situation. When the accumulation of black refugees in the lower Mississippi Valley—Tennessee, Mississippi, Louisiana, and Arkansas—prompted federal action, in September 1862 the Union army began sending freed slaves north. Many were sent to Cairo, Illinois, by Union commanders. Secretary of War Stanton validated this policy by requiring the Union general in Cairo to care for the blacks. In one of America's extreme racial ironies, Illinois still had a black exclusion law. More important, Stanton was turning a blind eye to racial animosity in the state. As the railroad began carrying trainloads of black refugees daily to Illinois, white reaction was instantaneous and predictable. Pike County citizens attacked Secretary Stanton for resettling a "worthless negro population" in their midst. At Olney, Illinois, black refugees were halted and forced to return to Cairo. The mayor of Chicago refused to set up a committee to help resettle the freed slaves. Backed by the city council, the mayor cited Illinois black laws. The *Chicago Tribune* reported that "The Republicans will generally have nothing to do with the [black refugees]." The Republican governor, Richard Yates, declared that the "scattering of those black throngs should not be allowed if [it] can be avoided. . . . The mingling of blacks among [us will mean that] we shall always have trouble."

On October 13, 1862, Stanton countermanded his order, halting the shipment of black refugees to Cairo. Stanton's brief foray into the racial background of the white North has been described as a tactical "blunder." In fact the secretary of war had inadvertently exposed America's racial nerve. Lincoln and Stanton learned a hard lesson about Northern white hostility in Illinois, the "land of Lincoln," and in Massachusetts, the land of Charles Sumner, William Lloyd Garrison, and John Andrew.

In the wake of this experience in Illinois and Massachusetts, the federal government settled on a "containment policy" of keeping freed slaves in the cotton fields of the South. The new policy was enunciated publicly by Adjutant General Lorenzo Thomas of the Mississippi Valley. He outlined his plan, which was prompted by Northern racial animosity and the need for cotton and military laborers, on April 1, 1863, to Secretary Stanton, leaving no doubt as to why it was necessary:

It will not do to send [the black refugees] in numbers into the free states, for the prejudices of the people of those states are against such a measure and some of the States have enacted laws against the reception of free negroes.

The solution, for General Thomas, appeared straightforward: "[The black refugees]. . . must, in great measure, continue in the Southern states now in rebellion . . . and they should be put in positions to make their own living." The men should be "employed as military laborers," encouraged to join the Union army, "or conscripted if necessary . . . and the others with the women and children placed on abandoned plantations to till the soil." The 186,000 black men who were Union soldiers consisted of 134,000 from the slave states, of which 17,800 were from Mississippi. Most of Mississippi's former slave population of more than 400,000 remained in the cotton fields. On April 9, General Thomas elaborated:

> What is best done with this unfortunate race? They are coming in upon us in such numbers that some provision must be made for them. You cannot send them North. You all know the prejudices of the Northern people against receiving large numbers of the colored race. . . . Look upon the river and see the multitude of deserted plantations upon its banks. These are the places for those freedmen where they can be self-sustaining and self-supporting. . . . They are to be encouraged to come to us. They are to be received . . . fed and clothed; they are to be armed.

For white America, all roads for blacks led back to cotton. The current war, and the need to arm black men, was to be an interruption in the far longer and more important national narrative of growth. That growth came in the form of cotton production, which in 1863 represented the past, present, and future role of black America. Secretary Stanton ordered Grant to use freed slaves "in the military service and put them to work picking cotton for the government." Freed slaves were no longer given passes to travel north. The white North breathed a collective sigh of relief.

Influential voices from across the North were pleased with the containment policy. The *Chicago Tribune* had urged the government to employ freed slaves in the South. Illinois Republican senator Lyman Trumbull had recommended that Southern cotton land be confiscated and sold to Union supporters or white Northerners who would then employ freed slaves. The *New York Tribune* urged that land be given to freed slaves to prevent a massive black migration to the North. An Iowa editor enthusiastically endorsed a plan to retain the freed slaves in the "Cotton States" with "work and just compensation." He concluded hopefully that by these means the Northern free black "will thus withdraw from our population."

The containment policy has been called by V. Jaques Voegeli a "brilliant fusion of common sense, military exigency, and political expediency." With these considerations, the fate of newly emancipated slaves was placed in the unreliable and uncommitted hands of a racially intolerant and segregated white North. It was abundantly clear that the freed slaves would reside in the cotton South.

The question of residence settled, the federal government next had to address the status and prospects of a newly freed black population in the cotton South. The area along the Mississippi River became an important incubator of policies toward free blacks. When throngs of freedpeople poured into Union-occupied Vicksburg, Mississippi, the army there was faced with the problem of establishing order. Union colonel Samuel Thomas attempted to control the flow of free blacks by officially requiring a "letter of employment" to enter the city, but this failed. General C. C. Washburn even issued a command that the "large number of . . . Colored people of the city and vicinity, that were living in idleness and vagrancy . . . be removed."

The federal government wanted free black labor in the cotton fields so that they would learn self-reliance and harvest the valuable commodity. The first arrangement around Vicksburg in 1862, on the earliest Southern lands captured by the Union army, provided that the freed slaves receive one cent for each pound of cotton they picked. The government would receive half the cotton and the lessee the other half. In June 1863 tax department officials were given the authority to lease land around Vicksburg on these terms. The federal government intended to "line the banks of the Mississippi River with a loyal population . . . and give employment to freed negroes." White Northerners "swarmed" into the area to lease cotton land. "The desire of gain alone prompts them," wrote the journalist Thomas Knox, "and they care not whether they make it out of the blood of those they employ or from the land." For the lessees, "God is a bale of cotton." The freedmen were forced to work on these leased plantations:

> In many cases, the newly freed slaves had little or no choice but to work for those with whom cotton arrangements were made, for the provost marshal at "every military post" was charged with seeing that "every negro within the jurisdiction of the military authority is employed by some white person, or is sent to the camps provided for freed people."

Knox noted that

> The majority of the lessees were unprincipled men, who undertook the enterprise solely as speculation. They had as little regard for the rights of the negro as the most brutal slaveholder had ever shown. Very few of them paid the negroes for their labor, except in furnishing them small quantities of goods, for which they charged five times the value. One man, who realized a profit of eighty thousand dollars, never paid his negroes a penny.

An ex-slave later recalled the experience: "De Yankees come 'roun'. . . and tol' us we's free an' we shouted an' sang, and had a big celebration fer a few days. Den we got to wonderin' bout what good it did us."

After the Union army advance, 136 plantations were abandoned near Vicksburg in 1863. Northern whites leased 113 of them, and freedmen leased 23. An additional 29 were contracted to plantation owners who had remained. Labor guidelines called for a ten-hour work day in the summer and nine hours a day in the winter for "respectful, honest, faithful labor." Once a laborer made an agreement with an employer, he was obligated to that employer for one year. If a freedman was deemed to be not in accordance with the rules, he was sent to work on public projects without pay. "First class hands" were to be paid eight dollars a month. If a laborer missed two hours of work, he lost half of his day's pay. He was not allowed to leave the plantation without a pass from his supervisor, or to grow cotton in his garden, only vegetables. The rules stipulated that "labor is a public duty, and idleness and vagrancy a crime."

The lessees were driven by cotton money. The Northerners were rough, as one former overseer observed in 1865:

> I'm hiring now a Northern man who gives me three thousand. A Northern man will want more out of the niggers than we do. Mine said to me last night, "I want you to get every last drop of sweat out of my niggers."

Ironically a War Department survey concluded that the "'old planters' of this country, so far as dealing fairly with the freedmen is concerned . . . have paid them more promptly, more justly and apparently with more willingness than have the new lessees from other parts of the country." General Oliver O. Howard, head of the Freedmen's Bureau, acknowledged that the program benefited the lessees more than the laborers. And because cotton planters were paid only when their crop was sold, laborers generally could not receive their monthly stipends. A form of credit was instituted, and this gave rise to abuses as lessees kept various sets of books to defraud the laborers. Colonel Thomas thought "that nearly two-thirds of the freedmen . . . had been defrauded of their wages in 1864."

The freedmen who leased abandoned plantation land met with mixed results. Thomas Knox discovered several profitable freedmen ventures in 1863 on small plots of land. One family of four raised twelve bales, which they sold for $200 a bale. The price per pound was 40 cents, a prewar bonanza. Another six freedmen raised 20 bales on leased land. In 1864, Knox reported that two freedmen who leased 40 acres in Helena, Arkansas, cleared $6,800. At Miliken's Bend he reported freedmen were "not as successful" because of the army worm invasion.

In 1866 the experiment of leasing cotton land to freedmen at Davis Bend, the land owned by Joseph and Jefferson Davis, was terminated. Ulysses Grant had hoped to create a "Negro paradise" for former slaves on the plantation of the Confederate president. With high cotton prices and an accommodating planting season, the freedmen had made money in 1865. But the precarious nature of cotton farming makes one-year results irrelevant. Experience over time would yield a more appropriate generalization about the success of a farming venture. Joseph Davis's land was restored to him when he received a pardon in March 1866. The freedmen were allowed to continue their leases in 1866 before the land reverted to Davis. Their 1866 crop was plagued by drought.

Fraud was not limited to the payment of black laborers. On leased land, corruption abounded. Congress established a Commission on Corrupt Practices in the South to investigate widespread allegations of wrongdoing. The commission found that in New Orleans, Colonel Harrai Robinson had commandeered 336 bales of cotton because they exceeded what the attached permit allowed. He released these after receiving a bribe of $5,000. Bribes of $1,500 were routinely paid to Treasury officials to facilitate the transport of cotton.

In the Mississippi Valley, the period between 1863 and the end of the war has been described as "uninterrupted confusion both within the Treasury Department, which ostensibly controlled trade, and between it and the War Department, which was supposed to look after the freedmen's interests." Just as important, the experiments in the Mississippi Valley foreshadowed the postwar preservation of the plantation system. The regulatory apparatus of the contract system indicated the federal government's preference for black labor's attachment to land owned and supervised by whites.

As the war moved toward a Confederate surrender, the federal government had developed no specific policy about the disposition of former slaves. Throughout the war, just as in the decades preceding it, blacks had been used by both North and South as expediency demanded. The North embarked on a recruitment program of blacks when its own draft proved inadequate. Southerners discussed enlisting slaves as soldiers in return for a promise of freedom. In December 1864, in the waning and desperate days of the Confederacy, Jefferson Davis and Judah Benjamin sent an envoy to England to offer emancipation in return for British recognition of the Confederacy. Lord Palmerston refused. Blacks were always problems to be pushed away, political pawns at best, nuisances at worst.

The experience in the area around Vicksburg offered clues to the postwar landscape and the eventual course of Reconstruction. A Washington-based general directive would be administered locally by individuals with different backgrounds and differing goals. The number of federal officials would be decidedly small for the task to be undertaken. The racial attitudes of whites, both public officials and private citizens, would cripple the possibilities for blacks in America.

While we typically see the Civil War as a struggle to preserve the Union and ultimately to end slavery, and a force that fundamentally changed the nation, we must also acknowledge that the war did not alter two foundational aspects of American history: the subordinate status of African Americans and the pivotal position of cotton. As the historian Harold Woodman wrote, "If the war had proved that King Cotton's power was far from absolute, it did not topple him from his throne, and many found it advantageous to serve him."

In the years to come, those who had fought in the Civil War, white and black, Northern and Southern alike, would have to adjust to new relationships to the still indispensable commodity, cotton. The guideposts for the future—an ever-increasing demand for cotton, the reluctant need for a black labor force, the abhorrence of white Northerners for blacks living in their midst, and America's relentless commercial priorities—would in many ways look much like the guideposts of the past.

PART FIVE

The Racial Divide and Cotton Labor, 1865–1930

White ingenuity and enterprise ought to direct black labor. Northern capital should flow into these rich cotton-lands on the borders of the Atlantic and Gulf. . . . The negro race . . . would exist side by side with the white for centuries being constantly elevated by it, individuals of it rising to an equality with the superior race. . . . [Cotton production requires] the white brain employing the black labor. . . .—New York Times, February 26, 1865

We cannot produce cotton enough for the wants of the world. We should be in the position of South Africa . . . but for the faithful, placable, peaceful, industrious, lovable colored man; for industrious and peaceful he is compared with any other body of colored men in the world—not up to the standard of the [white person] in the colder North. . . . It is certain we must grow more cotton to meet the demands of that indispensable product. We cannot afford to lose the Negro. We have urgent need of all and more [to produce cotton]. . . .—Andrew Carnegie, 1903

CHAPTER SEVENTEEN

New Era, Old Problems

 W. E. B. DU BOIS may have called Reconstruction a "splen-
did failure," but it was a failure nevertheless. The former
slave gained mobility to move from cotton farm to cotton
farm in the South, but not to move to the industrial North until the
exigencies of World War I. The white North experienced no conversion
to racial tolerance during the war; indeed it was relieved that blacks
would remain in the South rather than move north. Despite emancipation and a brief phase of political enfranchisement, America's pattern
of racial animosity remained constant.

Now that the Union had not been sundered by the Civil War, now
that the country had been saved from the brink of self-destruction, the
question must have been asked in many ways, What happens next? For
the newly freed slaves, the question must have been all the more poignant. They faced a world without human bondage, a world they had
literally never before known. Who would assist the freedmen to end
their bondage in the cotton fields? Would their committed, long-term
ally be Congress, the president, the Supreme Court, the Republican
party, the white soldiers of the Union army, the white Northern business community, white Northern philanthropists, or Northern state
governments? As white Southern resistance to black equality immediately sought to create a racial caste system, we shall see how each of
the white Northern groups continued to view the black population as

inferior and as second-class citizens, undeserving of the rights taken for granted by white Americans. Each group, in effect, helped create a subordinate role for black Americans in the cotton fields. In addition, Americans were preoccupied with new commercial goals that excluded black America. Former slaves were therefore virtually entrapped in the cotton South after the Civil War.

The underlying, and often underappreciated, assumption of Reconstruction was that blacks would remain in the South and cultivate cotton. In the years leading up to the Civil War, more than 90 percent of African Americans lived in the South. Fifty years later, nothing had changed: 90 percent of all black Americans still lived in the South. If conditions were so deplorable in the South, why was there so little movement north of a growing black population? Now that they were free, why didn't blacks flee the lands to which they had been chained for generations? Why didn't they flock to Detroit, New York, and Chicago?

The story is terribly simple. Although they were no longer bound to a plantation, they were stuck between a white North that didn't want them and a white South that desperately needed them. African Americans were contained in the South by a web of forces that included the amoral economic imperatives of cotton, white Northern racial antipathy, and the process of reconciliation between North and South.

While political turmoil over Reconstruction found Radical Republicans, moderate Republicans, and Democrats at loggerheads in 1865, the real economic adjustment was occurring on countless Southern farms and plantations even before the war ended. Cotton seeds were planted in the soil of a newly surrendered South. As it had for several generations, the surviving large plantation system required black labor. A series of attempts were made to adjust to a new financial environment. Experiments begun during the war in the Sea Islands, Georgia, and in Davis Bend, Mississippi, succumbed to the fierce postwar desire to return to normal. And on the cotton fields, normalcy was simple: a return of private property to Southern owners, and to the belief that whites could best manage cotton production (and the lives of African Americans). White Northerners during and after the war flocked to the South, hoping to share in the most basic of American pursuits: growing rich. As the Freedmen's Bureau sought to monitor and manage the relationship between black labor and white plantation owners, a new caste labor system evolved to accommodate the peculiarities of cotton and the dictates of finance. After the Civil War, the economic fate of African Americans remained irrevocably intertwined with cotton. The former slaves, now called freedmen, had no choice.

As the war ended, demand for cotton was high and so was its price. Indian and Egyptian crops may have been given a boost by the Civil War, but they had not displaced the preeminence of American cotton. Much of America, from Wall Street bankers to poor farmers, was still ruled by that seemingly timeless calculation, the price per pound of cotton. Cotton at forty cents a pound in 1865 was a multiple of the ten to eleven cents a pound before the war. This amount—both a simple reflection of the laws of supply and demand and a complex determinant of American history—led multitudes of white Northerners to undertake cotton cultivation.

The federal government knew that the crop would play a vital role in getting the nation back on its financial feet and in deciding what to do about the surrendered South. The North's only means of economic retribution against the former Confederacy—in the absence of any Southern manufacturing capacity or other profitable endeavor—was a tax on cotton.

Eastern financiers coldly calculated the importance of the restoration of cotton production. Their goals were two: repayment of the war debt and buttressing of the financial system. These same businessmen also enthusiastically organized and invested in rail links between Northern cities and Southern cotton-producing areas. Private property was sacrosanct to white Northerners, so it was natural for plantations to be restored to their prewar owners. It was also conventional wisdom that the newly freed slaves needed to be supervised by white men. The white North endorsed free labor as a replacement for slavery but left white control firmly in place.

But simultaneous to American's eager return to cotton production, another American tradition had abruptly come to an end. Slavery was over. Following the South's capitulation, the system that most of the Founding Fathers had hoped would "wither away" was now officially dead. What was to be done with the former slaves? Frederick Douglass rhetorically posed the question, "What shall we do with the Negro?" His answer, "Do nothing. . . . Give him a chance to stand on his own legs! Leave him alone!" Douglass feared that state intervention might raise the specter of blacks as "wards of the state." He thought that ensuring suffrage, civil rights, general property rights, and the end of discrimination was sufficient protection. Radical Republicans, who wanted a drastic reformation of the South to protect the freedmen, sought a deep government involvement, even land redistribution.

As early as January 1863 the *New York Times* asked, "If the [Emancipation Proclamation] makes the slaves actually free . . . there will come the further task of making them work. . . . All this . . . opens a vast and most difficult subject." Almost all Northern and Southern whites considered blacks an inferior race; at best they might improve under the guardianship of whites. But neither the federal government nor ordinary Americans had come to any consensus on how to treat the seceding states or the freedmen. The nation pondered how they might become part of the free-labor system. There was no model to emulate. Would the plantation system be replaced by smaller agricultural units? Would the freedmen be given land? Would these men and women work as wage laborers, or would a new system emerge? What political and civil rights would they be given? Despite the confusion, two things were clear: whatever system evolved, freedmen would remain in the South, and they would cultivate cotton.

The containment policy of keeping freed slaves in the South during the Civil War had relieved the anxiety of white Northerners. Superficial attempts to move freedmen north had foundered. Legislation designed to encourage dispersal of freed blacks in the North was met with disapproval. In April 1864, Kentucky senator Garrett Davis proposed that Congress redistribute blacks to Northern states in "proportion to their white population"; the Senate "scorned" his plan. In June 1864 a "milder form" of dispersal was presented by West Virginia senator Waitman T. Willey and met with an equally negative response. Willey wanted to give the Freedmen's Bureau permission to contact Northern governors and city leaders about sending freedmen north. This, Senator Willey thought, would relieve labor shortages and provide guidance for the freedmen. Radical Republican Charles Sumner thought the dispersal was "entirely untenable." His Massachusetts colleague Senator Henry Wilson thought the inclusion of the idea as an amendment to the Freedmen's Bureau bill would "have a bad influence in the country." Radical Republicans recognized that the white North wanted no blacks, despite a labor shortage.

The Republican party had managed a requisite degree of unity in conducting a war over the survival of the Union, but the complicated challenge of readmitting the seceding states and dealing with freedmen created enormous strains within the party. Expediency proved to be a powerful force in party machinations. The issue of black suffrage was tempting to political opportunists who could portray themselves as idealists. The black vote in the South, Republicans thought, could be instrumental in perpetuating Republican ascendancy. Well-chronicled disagreements between President Lincoln and the Radical Republicans, between Lincoln's executive-directed Reconstruction and the Radicals' congressional-orchestrated Reconstruction, between Radical and moderate Republicans, and between Republicans and Democrats created rough political terrain for the task of reconstructing the nation.

In theory the white North could have dictated terms and conditions to the utterly defeated South, which it occupied. In just four years of fighting the white South lost 265,000 men; 25 percent of its white men "of productive age were dead or incapacitated." In Mississippi alone, of the 78,000 soldiers and officers that the state provided for the Confederacy, 35 percent perished; 12,000 died in battle and 15,000 succumbed to disease. Transportation and infrastructure throughout the South were disrupted as the war destroyed towns and cities, roads, railroads, and bridges. Farms were in disrepair. Large numbers of freedmen were destitute. One tiny but poignant statistic of devastation may be found in the Mississippi budget: in 1866, 20 percent of all state revenues were spent on artificial limbs for Confederate veterans.

Despite the North's dominant position, no firm plan for Reconstruction existed—nor could one have existed. Parts of the makeshift contract labor system that began in the Mississippi Valley offered guidance in terms of cotton workers. Otherwise the U.S. government found itself in uncharted territory. No unifying strategy presented itself to a white America that had a long history of oppressing free blacks. A series of reactions and experiments followed.

Reconstruction witnessed the passage of an impressive amount of legislation that supported the rights of freedmen. With these laws the federal government (still dominated by white Northerners) attempted to impose rules and values that its own constituencies—even with their tiny black communities—had not accepted. The legislation had to be tested locally, not in Washington. It had to be interpreted through the judicial process; the new laws would require enforcement. Abstract concepts of freedom and citizenship, embedded in Reconstruction legislation, were crushed when applied to the real world of nineteenth-century America. In the end, the North had not and would not shed white blood in order to accomplish black equality.

Within this environment the standard story of the postwar years is as follows: The South convinced the North that the Reconstruction governments were corrupt and needed to be forcibly removed. Moreover the South successfully created the myth of the "lost cause," which fostered nostalgia and white reconciliation. Was the North really this gullible? After all, the North had held the intellectual attributes of white Southerners in low esteem, the Southern white ruling class having been described as honor bound, violent, emotional, indolent, and devoid of commercial skills. It is difficult to imagine that the stereotypical white Southerner could dupe the North. Yet historians claim that white Southerners, a discredited group that had been trounced in war, were a few short years later able to influence the minds of the North.

For a more plausible explanation we must return to an economic perspective: the North wished to get on with business; the reconciliation of white America was seen as a far better alternative than Reconstruction, which had become a nuisance. Similarly the Reconstruction government could be negotiated, but the need for cotton wealth could not be negotiated. America's aggressive materialism remained the most important determinant in post–Civil War America. Reconstruction has even been called a "Yankee euphemism for capitalist expansion." Areas of agreement, especially cotton-based commercialism, were much stronger than areas of disagreement. And so the "lost cause" was re-ified, and Reconstruction failed.

*

From the beginning of the war's end, the stage was set for a confusing but ultimately firm reunion of white America. When General Robert E. Lee surrendered his army at the Appomattox Courthouse on April 9, 1865, the conquering general, Ulysses S. Grant, offered lenient conditions. The Confederates were required to take an oath to give up their arms and not continue the rebellion. Confederate officers were allowed to keep their pistols. Confederate cavalry could take their horses back to their homes. Lee himself was paroled. Grant wrote that his "own feelings . . . were sad and depressed":

> I felt like anything rather than rejoicing at the downfall of a foe who had fought so long and so valiantly. . . . [Lee and I] . . . soon fell into a pleasant conversation about old army times . . . our conversation grew so pleasant that I almost forgot the object of our meeting.

On the courthouse grounds, as Union and Confederate leaders communed, the officers of both armies presented gifts to one another and chatted. On June 13, 1865, Grant submitted a pardon application for Robert E. Lee with his personal "earnest recommendation." Fewer than five years later, the leader of the secessionist army would be hosted in the White House by a magnanimous President Grant.

The federal government did not even prosecute the president of the Confederacy, Jefferson Davis, who was captured just a few weeks after Lee's surrender. Davis was incarcerated at Fort Monroe for two years. President Andrew Johnson then suggested a pardon, but Davis adamantly refused to accept it. The deposed president said, "To ask for a pardon would be a confession of guilt." Davis relished the idea of pleading the justice of his cause in a courtroom with the nation as an audience.

But before his trial for treason could go forward, Davis was released on a $100,000 bail provided by an unlikely group. The newspaper editor Horace Greeley, the abolitionist Gerrit Smith, and Cornelius Vanderbilt each guaranteed $25,000, and ten others guaranteed $2,500 each.

Greeley, who had attempted to shorten the conflict by compromise, now was eager for a peaceful reunion. Davis was freed on a technicality designed by Chief Justice Salmon P. Chase, who declared that the man who had led the insurrection against the United States could not be tried for treason. The honor-bound Davis had outwitted the federal government.

Despite historians' efforts to divine what Lincoln's Reconstruction policy might have been, they shed little light on future events. Lincoln did, however, espouse the very American view that "every man should have the means and opportunity of benefiting his condition." To deprive anyone of the "fruits of their labor" was tyranny. The black man therefore had a "right to eat the bread, without the leave of anybody else, which his own hand earns, [in that regard] he is my equal . . . and the equal of every living man." Lincoln was adamant about the need to work; his philosophy of "Root, hog, or die" applied to blacks as well as whites. But he was noticeably silent on specifics. He expressed no views on land distribution and the famous "forty acres and a mule" concept. In his last public address on April 11, 1865, Lincoln said he "would . . . prefer that [suffrage] were now conferred on the very intelligent and those who serve our cause as soldiers." This endorsement of limited suffrage for freedmen has been given broad and speculative meaning which has had a soothing effect on the conscience of later generations of white Americans.

America had no blueprint for Reconstruction when Lincoln was assassinated on April 14, 1865. His lenient policies toward the South had been opposed by the Radicals and abused by Southerners. He had expressed views of black inferiority, had supported colonization, and generally did not know how free blacks would fit into American society. In the judgment of Frederick Douglass, Lincoln was "the white man's president." Blacks "were only his stepchildren."

Lincoln's sudden removal from American politics left the Republican party divided over the issue of Reconstruction. Into this dispute stepped Andrew Johnson, who assumed the vacant presidency and ushered in an era of bickering and confrontation with the Radical Republicans. Ultimately Johnson was unwilling to compromise. He capitulated to the white South, which wanted strict control of black cotton labor and no political rights for blacks. The all-important struggle for black suffrage would ultimately work to consign blacks to the cotton fields with no political redress.

In the long run, white America's attitudes and priorities, not Lincoln, would determine the course of Reconstruction. In a very real sense, Republicans, even moderate Republicans, came to realize that black suffrage would encourage blacks to stay in the South and would ensure a Republican majority. The version of American history that most of us have learned often disguises this bald reality. Historians have viewed the postwar period as a time of promise for racial equality. The possibilities for black acceptance in these years, between 1865 until the election of Rutherford B. Hayes in 1876, which we refer to as the era of Reconstruction, have been grossly exaggerated in our history. The motivations during this time are far more nefarious than most historians are willing to acknowledge. White Southern resistance would provoke reactions in the white North, but ultimately the underlying forces of materialism and American racial antipathy would supersede the superficial, abstract commitment of white America to black political equality and economic opportunity.

*

As Congress and the president began to spar over the postwar Reconstruction and reconciliation policy, cotton was simultaneously influencing the nation's course. The problem was clear: the government not only had to unite the two sections of the country but also had to extricate the nation from an unfavorable financial situation. At war's end the federal government was deeply in debt. The debt needed to be tackled and the financial house set in order so as to attract much-needed European funds for American railroads and industry. In April 1865 the New York Chamber of Commerce advised that federal debt repayment depended on massive cotton exports, which would bring gold to the United States. Northerners knew that cotton was the obvious means of paying for the war, and cotton meant black laborers.

In 1865 a U.S. Treasury official, Alanson Penfield, envisioned a National Cotton Convention that would encourage the expansion of cotton production to five million bales or $1 billion in value annually. Penfield calculated that "if three fourths of the crop was exported . . . six or seven hundred million" dollars of foreign exchange would be created. The country needed gold, which was mainly accumulated through cotton exports and domestic gold production. The convention, he thought, would provide credit and encourage immigration to the South. It would be given the unrealistic task of expanding cotton production to the cold climes of Kansas, Illinois, and Indiana by finding a way to make cotton "mature one month earlier" than normal. George Opdyke, the former mayor of New York, thought the price of cotton alone would be enough to satisfy "the capital requisite to produce a fair crop."

Of the several schemes advanced to address the war's economic dislocations, several involved cotton. Of these, the "cotton tax" was the most important. Simply put, a tax would be paid by the producer on each pound of cotton sold. The cotton tax was an implicit recognition that cotton production was a prime means for generating revenue. At the same time it penalized the South and fostered U.S. borrowing capacity. Boston businessmen strongly supported a cotton tax while New York's free traders were opposed.

The cotton tax seemed like an obvious and essential solution to some of the country's economic woes, but Congress had to decide on the amount of the tax. In June 1865, David A. Wells, head of the National Revenue Commission, produced a "Report on Cotton" which recommended a tax on cotton of five cents a pound. The Radical Republican Thaddeus Stevens was impressed by the financial power of cotton in his call for a ten-cent tax:

> I think there is very good reason why this one article [cotton] should pay a very large portion of the taxation which we are obliged to raise. If we had a right to lay an export duty, which the constitution at present forbids, we could with an export duty of ten cents per pound, raise $200,000,000 annually, while at the same time protecting our own manufacturers and selling abroad just as much cotton as we do.

The bill that passed Congress placed a tax of 2.5 cents on each pound of cotton, later raised to 3 cents. The tax would be levied on the cotton producer, not on the manufacturer. A bale of cotton worth $67 in 1867 was subject to $12.50 in federal tax. The young French journalist Georges Clemençeau, who would later become prime minister, wrote of the ill-conceived cotton tax that raised American cotton prices, made it less competitive on world markets, inhibited production, and "produced unheard-of wealth for a few men in high places." Protests came fast and furious until the punitive cotton tax was repealed in 1868. In a short and turbulent lifespan it had produced $68 million in revenue.

The federal government received another $30 million through the Captured Property Act, which allowed government officials to seize everything from horses to mules to farm equipment, but most important cotton. The act was subject to widespread personal abuse by officials via "tolling," the practice of imposing multiple taxes, and "plucking," the practice of stealing cotton by taking excessive amounts for sampling. With these techniques, federal agents carried on the tradition of illegal moneymaking schemes inaugurated by Northern soldiers during the war. An adept federal agent who both seized the cotton and collected the cotton tax could thus pocket 25 to 50 percent of the value of the goods. As the historian John Hope Franklin writes, the fee proved to be quite an incentive:

> During the year following the close of the war a horde of Treasury agents made their way through the South. That the federal government would seek to exploit the South's one remaining asset was especially revolting. The fact that many of the agents were corrupt merely added to the contempt in which they were held.

The military struggle was barely concluded when New Yorkers began to clamor for cotton. The *New York Times* endorsed President Johnson's plan to restore Southern lands to their white owners in order to further payment of the national debt. The *Times* reasoned that "if northern capital should flow into those rich cotton lands" and "make them bloom with wealth, intelligence and civilization," some blacks would rise "to an equality with the superior race" and become part of "a great, prosperous, increasingly intelligent peasantry in the southern country." Any chance that blacks had of bettering themselves would evaporate under this patronizing, all-too-convenient formula, requiring them to remain in the cotton fields under white management.

Despite political chaos and economic dislocation, the South could still produce its valuable staple. In 1866, New York's Chamber of Commerce received a report from Colonel T. W. Conway, an ex-Union officer who was planning to raise money in Europe for investment in Southern cotton production. Conway spoke directly: "Cotton is gold anywhere in Europe, and by its extensive production our currency will be more rapidly reduced to a gold basis than in any other manner." In 1865 a key member of the Boston Board of Trade, Edward S. Tobey, outlined the importance of cotton in "The Industry of the South: Its Immediate Organization Indispensable to the Financial Security of the Country":

> [The] balance of trade must be paid in specie [gold], unless paid in cotton, which is to Europe the same as specie; and if the additional amount of specie could be retained at home it would tend greatly to strengthen the paper currency of the government, and probably avoid altogether the much-dreaded financial crisis.

For East Coast financiers, cotton-based financial stability would encourage Europeans to purchase American stocks and bonds. And Europeans did indeed participate. In 1853 foreigners had invested $51.9 million in U.S. railroad securities. By 1869 their holdings rose to $243 million.

Questions about currency, taxes, debt, railroad, tariffs, and land were an integral part of the nation's politics despite their relative absence from history textbooks. Although nearly 150 years after the Civil War the issue of racial injustice may be the most resonant theme of the Reconstruction Era, it is important to note that white America was deeply involved with issues other than black suffrage. America's commercialism was not dormant throughout the Civil War and Reconstruction. Land as always was a foremost consideration in government economic policy. America had plenty of land and would not hesitate to use it for railroad development, settlement, and revenue. The freedmen, however, were not allowed to participate in the land acquisition orchestrated by the federal government. They received a meaningless share during a period of major government land grants. During Lincoln's administration, 74,395,801 acres were given to Western railroads; 34,001,297 acres were handed out to these same interests during

President Johnson's term, and 19,231,121 acres during the Grant years. From 1850 to 1923 the states gave away 37,789,169 acres to railroads and 91,239,389 acres to corporations for railway construction. The freedmen were simply not a part of the American economic equation except as laborers on cotton farms owned chiefly by whites.

The aftermath of the Civil War soon eased into a commercial war that pitted American cities against one another in competition for the cotton trade. The issue of black equality receded. The political-business nexus began in earnest after the Civil War as another chapter in the uninterrupted saga of American materialism. Cotton was very much a part of this activity.

Northern businessmen responded to the postwar "romance" of King Cotton, which "still held the allegiance and imagination of the best political and commercial brains of the Northeast." The avenues for the cotton trade were the railway lines that brought cotton north and goods south. A commentator in 1879 noted that "throughout the entire South, cotton and groceries move through the same channels, but in opposite directions, so that very largely cotton goes where groceries come from."

It wasn't long before the Northern states were joined in the cotton commotion by Midwestern states and Kentucky. Businessmen from Louisville who coveted the Southern cotton trade established the Louisville and Nashville Railroad, which reached its planned destination, in the words of George Woolfolk, with the assistance of some "good Kentucky bourbon" and "millions of bonds placed in the London market." St. Louis also vied for the cotton market with railroad construction and acquisition, which culminated in 1874 in the Missouri Pacific Railroad. Because of the ease of transportion on the Mississippi River, the South in 1861 had been St. Louis's best customer for "produce and provisions." New rail traffic allowed St. Louis to organize a "Cotton Association" and develop a "great commercial empire and second packing and inland cotton market in the nation." The surge in cotton receipts prompted the construction of storage facilities to accommodate the purchasers, speculators, and traders from the East and Europe. Trade with the "new cotton territory" contributed $100 million annually to the St. Louis economy.

Cincinnati built its connection to the South through Chattanooga, Tennessee, a city fondly remembered by Union soldiers who flocked there after the war. Chattanooga was a rail hub with links through Georgia, Virginia, Alabama, and Mississippi. The cotton trade enhanced Cincinnati's business because mills in Ohio, Indiana, Kentucky, Michigan, and Canada purchased cotton there. The Cincinnati and Southern Railroad Company was finally completed in 1879 as a step toward making Cincinnati the preeminent "cotton market of the interior." The proud merchants of Cincinnati feted their Southern business counterparts at a celebration on March 18, 1880. The well-connected Southern attendees included Governor Alfred H. Colquitt of Georgia; ex-Governor Joseph E. Brown of Georgia; General John T. Wilder of the Roane Iron Works in Chattanooga; Governor Rufus Cobb of Alabama; Ben E. Crane, president of the Atlanta Board of Trade; Leslie Brooks, president of the Board of Trade of Mobile; and a host of lawyers and journalists.

Chicago was the northern terminus of the fabled Illinois Central Railroad, which connected Chicago and New Orleans. This railroad literally bisected America and opened trade relations along the entire line. In the pursuit of profit from beginning to end, Chicago businessmen cultivated a coterie of investors in New York. By the 1870s it was no surprise in the increasingly interconnected postwar economy that New Yorker Edward Harriman was the largest shareholder of the Illinois Central; in 1886 another New Yorker, Stuyvesant Fish, would become its president. Cotton, timber, and land holdings were common pursuits for Chicagoans in the fertile Mississippi Delta, a newly settled frontier stretching from Memphis to Vicksburg that boasted the richest cotton land in the world.

*

New York City's commercial journals were filled with warnings about the freedmen's unwillingness to work and the impact that would have on America's cotton business. One journal lamented the damage to cotton production because the "liberated negroes appear to be absorbed in the celebration of an idle and lawless jubilee." The New York business community's priority was clear: it wanted cotton as a stabilizing factor in foreign trade and as the paramount means to secure foreign capital. Labor disruption would be a detriment to cotton output and a disturbing example for white Northern workers. Secretary of State Seward wanted the freedmen to "'take their level' in the cotton field."

White Northerners may have supported black rights, but their motives were hardly noble. The influential Massachusetts congressman and Radical Republican George S. Boutwell wrote, "Next to the restoration of the Union, and the abolition of slavery, the recognition of universal suffrage is the most important result of the war." But in 1866 he sounded the alarm that black people must be given rights or they would move north. The consequences of that move would be disastrous for white workers:

> I bid the people, the working peoples of the North, the men who are struggling for subsistence, to beware of the day when the southern freedmen shall swarm over the borders in quest of those rights which should be secured to them in their native states. A just policy leaves the black man in the South where he will become prosperous and happy. An unjust policy on our part forces him from home to those states where his rights will be protected, to the injury of the black man and the white man both of the North and the South. Justice and expediency are united in indissoluble bonds, and the men of the North cannot be unjust to the former slaves without suffering the bitter penalty of transgression.

In Boutwell's logic, it would be unjust not to keep the black man in the South. Boutwell's "bitter penalty" was the long-dreaded black invasion. He may have inadvertently acknowledged the intractable racial dilemma by recommending that Georgia, South Carolina, and Florida be given exclusively to the freedmen.

Lee's surrender at Appomattox unleashed a flood of white Northern wealth seekers in pursuit of Southern riches. Confident they could transform white and black Southerners into replicas of the efficient, hardworking laborers they knew in the North, men ventured South to get rich quickly and return home. This brief chapter in the cotton story nonetheless relied on black labor working for white owners or managers. The high price of cotton fueled this interest. Traders came to seize the financial opportunities; Union officers, in droves, headed south or stayed there to become planters, to get rich, and revolutionize the labor system. A Southern visitor to New York in May 1865 cautioned his cotton-farming friends back home, "Cotton fever awful, hold on to your cotton, don't let anyone frighten or swindler [sic] you or your friends out of it." Southerners who visited New York noted that "Money is offered freely by N.Y. or Northern houses." In a frantic search for cotton, Northern-backed buyers scoured the South as 2.25 million bales of cotton traded for $400 million in 1865. The Boston Board of Trade passed resolutions that called for federal funding to "increase the production of [Southern] staples, and especially cotton." Boston, Philadelphia, and New York were vying for Southern trade.

In the fall of 1865 former governor John Andrew of Massachusetts became president of the American Land Company and Agency, an investment company designed to conduct money to cotton producers in the South. The principals of American Land hoped to prove that Northerners could "show the Southern people . . . how to cultivate cotton." Northern business expertise would demonstrate that free labor and practical, efficient white Northerners could outperform Southerners in producing cotton. In the process, Northerners would make a lot of money quickly and transmit the Northern work ethic to freedmen. Profit and moral mission would be joined.

In the winter of 1865–1866 it seemed as if every steamboat and railroad car destined for the South was filled with Northern cotton speculators. The American Land Co. showed that the best elements of the conservative New England business class would also join the cotton parade. John Andrew and New England businessmen in general wished to instill a "respect for honest labor" and "an industrious spirit" in the newly freed slaves and poor Southern whites. White Northerners, he believed, would be the vanguard in establishing "churches, schools, presses and habits of self-government" that would propel the South on a road of sound economic development far superior to that advanced by admirers of King Cotton. The American Land Co. began by raising $35,000 from Boston and New York investors, then proceeded to buy, sell, and broker land for cotton farming.

The white Northern work ethic was widely invoked. Edward Tobey, merchant and influential member of the Boston Board of Trade,
warned that "If . . . [the freedmen] refuse to labor, the Scripture rule
may be applied, If any will not work neither should they eat." The
abolitionist Henry Ward Beecher declared that "The black man is just
like the white, in this—that he should be left, & obliged to take care of
himself & suffer & enjoy, according as he creates the means of either."
White Northerners thought that freedmen would succumb to "idleness"
if left to their own devices, but also believed that these same men and
women would adopt the work habits of white Northerners who treated
them equitably. Andrew and his like prescribed a good dose of "northern paternalism." Always present was the desire to keep the freedmen in
the South. Andrew was explicit about sending Northern blacks south to
a suitable climate; this program would "tend to confine [the freedmen]
to a portion of the country which he, alone, can properly develop."

Edward Atkinson, one of Andrew's most influential colleagues,
qualified these grand assistance plans. Atkinson held the firm conviction that "negroes must come into the possession of land by working
for it and purchasing it." He thought that leniency would "do the
freedmen more harm than good." Early on, in 1861, he offered a harsh,
uncompromising attitude:

> [W]e must admit that we must have cotton, and that the emancipated
> slave will be idle and utterly worthless;—we may leave out of sight
> the fact that even in our Southern climate, labor or starvation would
> be his only choice, and that labor upon the cotton field would be
> the easiest and most profitable in which he would engage;—let him
> starve and exterminate himself if he will, and so remove the negro
> question,—still we must raise cotton; who will cultivate it?

The American Land Co. suffered serious setbacks within six months
after it began operating and finally closed its books in February 1867.
The 1866 cotton crop—plagued by floods, poor weather, and insects—
took its toll on lessees who could not pay fees to American Land. Barely
a year after the country's reunification, the experience was a stark reminder that nature could thwart man's most determined plans.

At the close of the war the abolitionist Major Henry Lee Higginson, like many others, was faced with the challenge of earning a living. For this Bostonian, the South seemed like a "carpet-bagger's paradise": "Making money there is a simple question of being able to make the darkies work." Again, "free labor, Northern capital, and Northern energy," it was thought, would reform the inefficient Southern labor system. Like others, Higginson succumbed to "a sort of after-the-armistice intoxication."

His financial and moral adventure began with the collaboration of two army and Harvard friends, Channing Clapp and Charles Morse. In 1865 they quickly spent $30,000 to buy a five-thousand-acre Georgia plantation called "Cottonham." The newly minted cotton farmers equipped their plantation with six mules and an army ambulance. Higginson's acquaintance with cotton plantations was based on his reading of three books: Frederick Law Olmsted's *Sea Board Slave States*, Fanny Kemble's *Journal of a Residence on a Georgia Plantation in 1838–1839*, and, of course, *Uncle Tom's Cabin*. Confidently Higginson predicted, "If cotton is going to advance even more, we shall do well."

On November 15, 1865, Higginson outlined his rosy income projections and supposedly conservative assumptions in a letter to his father. The calculations were simple. Cotton production from 400 acres would yield between 80 and 120 pounds per acre. At the low end of 80 pounds per acre, 32,000 pounds of cotton could be harvested. At Higginson's estimate of $1 a pound, he and his friends would realize an annual income of $32,000. Labor costs of $12,000 and incidental expenses would leave a $17,000 profit or $5,633 for each of the three partners.

The freedmen, according to Higginson, would submit because only "work or starvation was before them." He dismissed the idea of a possible federal government grant of forty acres to each freedman as "chimerical." Instead his plan was to offer a wage of $370 per year for a man and a woman and the prospect of a school for the freedmen's children.

On the plantation, Higginson was careful to set an example. He whitewashed the buildings himself and took personal responsibility for managing the details of his labor force of freedmen. He wanted to contrast his behavior with the habits of the Southern planter. He believed that "Bye and bye, when [the freedmen] . . . see us plough and chop and hoe, and drive mules and clean horses . . . , they will feel still more

An anti-slavery New Englander, Henry Lee Higginson, one of many Union officers seduced by the temptations of cotton wealth and the calling to help the freedmen, purchased a cotton farm in the South after the Civil War. He and most others quickly lost their investment, abandoned their interest in revolutionizing black labor, and retreated north. (Bliss Perry, *Life and Letters of Henry Lee Higginson* [Boston, 1921])

persuaded to do their duty." The freedmen would begin to understand that they would not be cheated.

Higginson's idealism was tested immediately. In January 1866 the freedmen called a strike for higher wages. Mrs. Higginson described the strike in her diary:

The darkies have been coming round about the strike, now that they find they cannot stay unless they work, and no credit is given them in the store unless they are earning wages. . . . They still do not understand the value of work and wages.

Higginson was clearly frustrated. He declared that he would not "give [the freedmen] things for various reasons: they had better work for everything now." In a letter to his father, Higginson expressed his bewilderment: "As for the blacks . . . their future is a mystery as dark as their skins. . . . They learn quickly, comprehend easily, both as regards work and in school. But their moral perceptions are deficient, either from nature or from habit or from ignorance. They know that it is wrong to steal and lie, but they do it continually."

The entrepreneur's spirit was lifted as the prospects for a bountiful cotton crop brightened. Then, in July, a drought and insects spreading through the region tempered Higginson's enthusiasm. His new projections called for 25,000 pounds of cotton at 80 cents a pound. His new income estimate was $12,000, which would cover only the year's wages. By September, Higginson thought his cotton crop was "in fair condition," but then the rains, which he had desperately needed in the summer, came instead during cotton-picking season. The rains, he told his father, had "cut off all our profit." By November he confessed that "we have lost a good deal of money." In the end the plantation produced 12,000 pounds of cotton. Higginson's costs were $16,500, but his income was only $9,000 to $10,000. Undaunted, he reminded his wife that "one great reason for our coming here was the work of great importance to be done for these blacks. Money is less valuable than time and thought and labor."

By Christmas 1866, Ida Higginson wrote in her diary of "these imperturbable darks. . . . The more I see of them, the more inscrutable do they become, and the less do I like them." By spring, Higginson was particularly annoyed about thefts: "The house-servants stole. Supplies were stolen." In the spring a discouraged Higginson wrote that "The black population . . . will listen, but not heed much from a white man." Things deteriorated further. It turned out that Mr. Rogers, the old man who had sold the trio "Cottonham," had title to only half the land that was purchased by the young Northerners. By May, Mrs. Higginson, who had contracted malaria, was utterly defeated:

It is discouraging to see how utterly wanting in character and conscience these people [the freedmen] seem to be, and how much more hopeful they appear at a distance than near to. . . . I am sorry, for I shall leave this place with a sense of utter failure.

The final financial accounting was dreadful. An insect invasion destroyed the 1867 cotton crop. In two growing seasons the three Union officers had lost $65,000. They sold the plantation for $5,000 and "were glad to be rid of it." Channing Clapp summed up the experience: "What a d——d piece of business the whole thing was."

Other groups of prominent white Northerners ventured to the South for profit. Soon after the war, Bellefontaine Cotton Co. of Ohio raised $150,000 to lease up to five thousand acres; Kenosha, Wisconsin, boasted of two cotton companies; the Ann Arbor (Michigan) Cotton Co. was the brainchild of University of Michigan science professor Alexander Winchell. The university board of regents approved Winchell's leave of absence to move south to farm cotton. One regent and substantial citizens of Ann Arbor bought shares in the cotton company, and the president of the university, Erastus O. Haven, not only invested in it but became its secretary. In 1864 the Michigan company leased two thousand acres in Louisiana. Professor Winchell's plans went awry, however. Guerrillas, some of whom were deserters from both armies, created havoc with their plundering raids. To add insult to injury, Union officials had colluded with the guerrillas. Winchell was forced to cede control to the guerrillas in return for half the proceeds of the cotton plantation as his dream of cotton-generated financial security evaporated.

These attempts by white Northerners to grow cotton during and after the Civil War illustrate the powerful attraction of cotton and its promise of quick money. It influenced white Northerners to venture into a brand-new landscape—which just months before had been enemy territory—and radically alter their lives. The high price of cotton had made the novices oblivious to the risks—price, weather, insects, the uncertain labor pool in a new environment, the hostility of white Southerners, and fraud. The adventurers came to make money and leave. The freed slave was seen as a source of labor, often a baffling one. Henry Lee Higginson, Harriet Beecher Stowe, the Ann Arbor Cotton Co., and the American Land Co. were among thousands—private citizens and governments—who were lured by cotton wealth. The disreputable among the newly arrived cotton farmers were pilloried by the black editor of the *New Orleans Tribune*, who condemned these "avaricious adventurers from the North, whose sole desire was to exploit the services of the freedmen, and make out of their labor as much money as possible. The slaves were made serfs and chained to the soil. . . . Such was the boasted freedom acquired by the colored man at the hands of the Yankees." By 1867 the "avaricious adventurers" had all departed, and thus ended the white Northern attempt to grow cotton while proselytizing the freedmen in Northern ways and morals. The freedmen and white Southerners were left to grow cotton.

CHAPTER EIGHTEEN

Ruling the Freedmen
in the Cotton Fields

BY THE END of the Civil War the federal government faced the daunting task of dealing with four million former slaves. During the war, government and private experiments in organizing the freedmen had been ad hoc. As we have seen, the freedmen at Port Royal, South Carolina, in 1862 were employed as wage earners for Northern lessees. In the Mississippi Valley the government had supervised the transition of blacks by using written labor contracts.

On January 16, 1865, General Sherman instituted what would become the most misunderstood freedmen project during the war years. For the sake of expediency, he authorized the distribution of a swath of land south of Charleston—to each ex-slave family a plot of "not more than forty acres of tillable land"—and he agreed to "furnish . . . subject to the approval of the President of the United States, a possessory title in writing." Sherman's Special Field Order No. 15 became the basis of the oft-discussed claim of forty acres and a mule. The order derived from Sherman's desire to rid himself of black refugees whom he viewed as a nuisance and "an irritating distraction from winning the war." The general would later disavow any intention of giving land title to the freedmen. Within a few months, 40,000 freedmen had occupied 400,000 acres of land in the area specified by Sherman, land that white farmers were forced to leave. The freedmen were "furnished" with work animals that were unfit for military use. The order conveyed no title and was subject to government approval. The land was soon restored to its former owners.

But these isolated experiments were clearly not enough to deal with a massive problem. On March 3, 1865, after two years of debate, and as the war's conclusion became apparent, Congress created the Bureau of Refugees, Freedmen and Abandoned Lands, otherwise known as the Freedmen's Bureau. President Lincoln had not given "much attention to the Freedmen's Bureau." This nascent federal organization would act as guardian for the newly liberated by providing government assistance in education, relief, and protection in earning a livelihood. It would act as referee between planters and the freedmen. In essence the Freedmen's Bureau was established to further an orderly transition to a free society and, just as important, reestablish cotton production. The agency was expressly designed to be temporary; no funding was appropriated. Operating expenses were to be drawn from the general budget for the War Department. The language of the act establishing the Freedmen's Bureau was wrapped in ambitious ideals: it "would safeguard [the freedmen] . . . from abuse, would foil the selfish designs of northern speculators, and would transform the South from a plantation economy to an economy of small, family-owned farms." These ideals quickly faced a less tolerant reality.

The harsh management of most Northern lessees, the strict control of Southerners, the chaotic conditions of growing cotton, and basic survival requirements all combined to quash the immediate euphoria of the freedmen. Prior experience in Vicksburg indicated the use of strict labor contracts with stipulated wages and stiff penalties for absenteeism. The latter was a forerunner of the notorious vagrancy laws. The high prices of cotton would succumb to increased supply and the removal of artificial wartime shortages. The attendant risks of cotton farming were in full force.

The national need to reestablish cotton production, its priority among white Northerners and Southerners, and the unambiguous preference to cultivate a cash crop meant that cotton would continue to be paramount. It would defeat any attempts toward self-sufficient diversification in the agricultural South. Farmers would grow cotton to make money while they neglected food crops; private credit would be available only for cotton production, thus reinforcing the singular obsession with cotton cultivation.

The freedmen's future remained bound to cotton and to working on land they did not own. When a debate arose about what to do with Southern land, the boldest proposal came from a segment of Republicans who advocated the confiscation of Confederate-owned land and its redistribution to freedmen. Some of these politicians wanted retribution, some had the interests of the freedmen genuinely in mind, some wanted a black Republican political base in the South that would ensure Republican ascendancy. In September 1865, Thaddeus Stevens, leader of the Radical Republicans, stated bluntly that Southern plantations "must be broken up and relaid, or all our blood and treasure have been spent in vain." But the question of land ownership was settled quickly. Once title was ascertained, the laws of private property were sacred, as the freedmen would discover. In one small example of the failure of redistribution, by the end of 1867 all eighty thousand acres administered by the Freedmen's Bureau were returned to their former owners. The Southern Homestead Act of June 21, 1866, set aside three million acres in the South for settlement by freedmen who were obligated to pay five dollars an acre. The land was decidedly poor in quality. By 1869 only four thousand freedmen had obtained land through the act. It was repealed in 1876.

The freedmen were bound to the South; they were not eligible for land under the original Homestead Act that distributed government land to white settlers in the West. A Delaware senator taunted his Northern colleagues by suggesting that freedmen be eligible for Western homesteads, which would entail payment for transporting them west. The Senate successfully blocked attempts to settle blacks in the West.

Despite rhetoric about confiscation, no enabling legislation was passed in Congress. In addition, in May 1865, President Johnson granted pardons to a broad range of Confederates. The recipients were entitled to the return of all their property that had not been disposed of through legal process. Although wealthy and high-ranking Confederate officials were not included in the amnesty, many of them soon received individual pardons, granted on the basis of favors, past friendships, or money.

General Oliver Otis Howard was appointed commissioner of the Freedmen's Bureau and placed in charge of its nine hundred agents. The fervently religious, battle-tested veteran told a black audience in New Orleans, "You must begin at the bottom of the ladder and climb up." He wanted blacks to "return to plantation labor, but under conditions that allowed them the opportunity to work their way out of the wage-earning class." Howard was echoing white fears that the freed slave would be idle and would not work within a free system unless coerced. The "Christian general" assured the audience that the Freedmen's Bureau would assist in the short transitory period during which freedmen "would soon be contentedly working as wage laborers for their old masters."

General Howard initially allowed his agents to lease lands and speculate in cotton. Howard wanted cotton cultivated by Northern men, "to afford promptly as many examples as possible of the successful employment of negroes under a free labor system." This led to flagrant abuses. One of the most egregious examples of misconduct featured Eliphat Whittlesey, a Yale graduate from Connecticut. Whittlesey, assistant commissioner of the Freedmen's Bureau in North Carolina, believed that the freedmen were inferior and could achieve equality with the Anglo-Saxon only through the experience of "hardship." On May 15, 1866, Whittlesey and nine other bureau officials were charged with various offenses including theft and the "torturing" of freedmen. The crimes occurred at New Bern, on plantations in which Whittlesey held a partial interest. The "deaths and mistreatment" of freedmen forced his removal and caused considerable embarrassment for the bureau. General Howard thereupon forbade agents to invest in plantations under their supervision.

While the Freedmen's Bureau served as a buffer in labor relations between planters and the freedmen, its ultimate aim was to make "the freedmen agree to work for their former masters." In some cases "the Bureau literally forced the Negroes to work for the planters." In 1866 the journalist Whitelaw Reid reported of a case in Mississippi in which freedmen went on strike in protest of an alleged contract violation. The bureau agent immediately ruled that the contract was in force, and the striking freedmen returned to work. The goal, we should not be surprised, was to get the freedmen back into the cotton fields.

After it was apparent that freedmen were not about to receive "forty acres and a mule," the former slaves were left to become wage earners. The Freedmen's Bureau established rules for contracts that stipulated wages, hours, and fair arbitration proceedings. Disputes were settled in a bureau court which generally consisted of three people—a representative from the bureau, the planter, and a freedman. Samuel Thomas, assistant commissioner in Mississippi and an advocate of land ownership by blacks, warned the freedmen in 1866 that failure to sign a contract would lead to their arrest.

The paltry number of bureau agents made their task still more difficult. In April 1866 there were only twenty-five agents in Mississippi, of which twenty-two were still in the occupying Union army. The remaining three were veterans whose salaries, as Thomas wrote, "were paid by those planters anxious to retain an officer of the Bureau for their influence among the Freedmen." Planters even asked Thomas for more agents with similar offers of compensation, because the agents were instrumental in "keeping the Freedmen quietly at work." The bureau's temporary mandate was made clear during the fractious encounter between Andrew Johnson and the Radical Republican Congress. When Johnson vetoed the extension of the Freedmen's Bureau Act in 1866, Congress overrode the veto but extended the life of the bureau only until 1868.

In the absence of clear standards for the labor contracts, white Southerners often took the initiative in recommending rules. William King of Savannah outlined a comprehensive labor code in a letter to General Howard on May 30, 1865. King's proposal contained eighteen clauses, including the following:

2. All capable labor shall at once make engagements to labor in the country or agriculture. . . .

5. Should any Freedmen not find permanent employment for a year, before the first of January of each year, then the local superintendent shall bind such person out to labor . . . to such party as he may think proper. . . .

7. In all such engagements made for labor on plantations . . . the laborers shall be required to perform properly and faithfully . . . not to exceed in labor over time from sun rise to setting of the sun, allowing two hours from 1st April to 1st October and one hour from 1st October to 1st April during the day for meals. . . .

8. All freedmen without visible means of support for himself and family who shall neglect or refuse to make a contract for one year, before the first of January or refuse to make a contract for one year, before the first of January of each year shall be arrested. . . .

11. No Freedmen to be allowed to trespass on the property of others, nor to make visits on the plantations or farms on which they are not employed without first obtaining the consent of the owners, thereof for such trespass the trespasser shall be arrested and punished by the local superintendent. . . .

Mere weeks after General Lee's surrender, white Southerners had already formulated a repressive plan for a wage-earning black labor force. And the details bore a resemblance to slavery. It was only a short step from King's proposals to the Black Codes that, as we shall see, were soon enacted by the reconstituted governments of the Southern states.

The Freedmen's Bureau in effect operated as a white paternalistic caretaker whose primary goals were national stability, black self-reliance, and economic reconstruction. It was also a relief organization and a sponsor of education. But the bureau was clearly more concerned with the work ethic of the freedmen and the need to reestablish cotton production than it was with the dangers of exploitation by planters. In 1901, W. E. B. Du Bois identified two obstacles that had confronted the bureau:

[T]he tyrant and the idler: the slaveholder, who believed slavery was right, and was determined to perpetuate it under another name; and the freedmen who regarded freedom as perpetual rest. These were the Devil and the Deep Sea.

The bureau did somewhat ameliorate the work regulations that could have been imposed upon the freedmen. Howard himself thought he had done a superb job in not allowing the agency to become a "pauperizing agency," for he regarded charity as "abnormal to our system of government." The federal government's creation of the Freedmen's Savings and Trust Bank to encourage thrift among the newly freed slaves met an ignominious death in bankruptcy while losing the savings of thousands of freedmen.

*

The eventual status of former slaves in the cotton fields would be determined by the North's opposition to white Southern plans during Reconstruction. Events in the chaotic aftermath of the Civil War gave every indication that the South intended to relegate freedmen to an inferior economic, social, and political position. So what would the North do? The victorious and powerful North would be severely tested in terms of its commitment to the newly liberated slave. Would the North give freedmen rights? More important, if former slaves were given rights, would the North enforce those rights and protect the four million former slaves who were consigned to the South?

Racial violence soon ended any notion of a smooth transition from war to peace. And the Northern reaction to racial violence in the South was short-lived. This kind of violence had been a consistent feature of the American social landscape; after the Civil War, racial animosity was directed against the freedmen, whose labor in the cotton fields was "the great desideratum."

Racial violence should have come as no surprise to the North. Even before the war ended, Union forces themselves initiated racial clashes that were numerous and well documented by the press and congressional investigations. White Union troops under the command of General Hancock clashed with blacks in Washington after the "Grand Review" celebrating the emancipation of black slaves. In 1865 white New Yorkers in the Zouave regiment brawled with black Union soldiers of the Third South Carolina. The Southern contribution involved black school and church burnings, clashes, and shooting incidents.

In 1865 the Union chaplain, Colonel John B. Eaton, noted the racial hostility of Union soldiers even during the war. He described the "hordes" of black refugees who approached Union soldiers occupying the South: "Unlettered reason or the inarticulate decision of instinct brought them to us. Often the slaves met prejudice against their color more bitter than they left behind." Eaton wrote to President Lincoln that the "interests" and "old prejudices" of Northern officers and enlisted men toward blacks was similar to that of slave masters. The Union soldiers condoned the "exploitation of freedmen by civilians . . . [and] proceeded to 'use' the 'slave' or practice . . . economic bondage, by ignoring minimum wage standards" and by refusing to pay former slaves.

During the spring and summer of 1866, racial conflagrations between Southern whites and blacks occurred in Norfolk, Vicksburg, Nashville, Charleston, Memphis, and New Orleans. The Memphis race riots broke out in earnest on May 1. The commanding Union general, George Stoneman, initially declined to interfere, claiming that "he had not many troops and that he had a large amount of public property to guard; that a considerable part of the troops he had were not reliable; that they hated Negroes too." The gruesome casualty total listed 46 blacks and two whites dead, and 285 blacks injured. A congressional investigation ensued, though the committee was intent mainly on publicizing the violence for political advantage. Indeed, one historian concluded, the Northern "reaction to these and other atrocities helped the Radical Republicans sweep Congressional elections later that year."

The New Orleans race riot erupted within three months of the Memphis bloodbath. The circumstances were different, but the underlying racial animosity was similar. New Orleans, like Memphis, had been captured in 1862, early in the war. The ensuing occupation was fraught with problems. After the war a special convention met on July 30, 1866, at the Mechanics Institute building to promote a law providing for black suffrage. Despite warnings of violence, Secretary Stanton, in highly uncharacteristic fashion, did not reply to a telegraph requesting additional troops to prevent disorder. The violent confrontation between white civilians and their allies, the police, and the black supporters of the convention and its delegates left approximately forty-eight men dead, most of them black, and some two hundred injured. General Philip H. Sheridan, who had expressed "no sympathy for the purposes of the convention," famously remarked that the confrontation was "an absolute massacre."

The New Orleans race riot captured the attention of the nation. Whites in both New Orleans and Memphis had attacked virtually defenseless blacks. Another congressional investigation revealed the gory details of the event. The Radical Republicans, who sought to empower blacks with political rights, were now able fully to exploit the violent encounters for political purposes.

*

When not hosting riots, Southern states were enacting highly restrictive legislation to ensure social control of the newly freed slaves and a regulated labor force in the cotton fields. These laws, first passed in Mississippi in late November 1865, became known as the Black Codes. The governor of Mississippi, Benjamin G. Humphreys, who had been a Confederate general, spoke immediately before the first meeting of the postwar legislature. He was explicit in his remarks, which were intended for Northerners as well as Mississippians. White Mississippians, he declared, understood that they had been defeated, but they would make the rules for freedmen in the new environment.

> Several hundred thousand of the negro race, unfitted for political equality with the white race, have been turned loose upon society; and in the guardianship [white men] . . . assume over this race, she must deal justly with them and protect them in all their rights of person and property.

The Mississippi legislature proceeded to pass laws to regulate the freedman. He was allowed to own property, but only in "incorporated towns." He could seek judicial remedy only in a case that involved another freedman. He could serve as a witness only in cases in which a freedman was involved; he could not give testimony in a case involving a white person. He was required to sign a labor "contract before the second Monday of January, 1866 and annually thereafter." The absence of a contract and nonperformance were grounds for a freedman's arrest as a vagrant. Vagrancy was defined broadly—as "idle, disorderly" conduct, and included even freedmen who "misspend what they earn." The services of those apprehended could be sold to other employers. Orphans of freedmen or freedmen under eighteen were subject to apprenticeships with "competent and suitable" employers, with the former owner having the right of first refusal. The penal statutes for slaves were declared to be "in full force and effect, against freedmen, free negroes and mulattoes, except [those] changed or altered by law." Control of labor was deemed essential. Any person, white or black, who enticed a freedman to break a contract would be subject to a $500 fine.

Mississippi's model proved to be an enticing example, and other Southern states followed suit by adopting their own versions of the Black Codes. In an interesting nod to cotton, South Carolina required all freedmen to pay a fee for engaging in a vocation other than farming. The North correctly saw the Black Codes as an attempt to recreate a structure resembling the slave system.

CHAPTER NINETEEN

Reconstruction Meets Reality

HOW DID the freedmen end up on the bottom rung of a racial caste system after the brief period of Reconstruction? Why was the former slave abandoned by the North? Or was it perfectly natural that the North collude with the white South to place the newly liberated slave in a subordinate position, without rights, to perform his indispensable role in cotton production?

America's postwar calculus was based on fundamental needs: national reunification and a resumption of normal business activity. In this equation the freedmen would fit effectively in the cotton fields. Their political role became an issue only when the Republicans realized how fragile their ascendancy was following the elections of 1864. Hence black suffrage became a political imperative that jibed nicely with moralistic rhetoric. By allowing the freedmen political rights, the Republicans could achieve two goals: political supremacy, and containment of blacks in the South, where their labor was essential to plantation cotton production. No serious discussion of land redistribution or confiscation took place in Washington. Southern violence (tantamount to insurrection), harsh Black Codes, and the unpopularity of a stubborn, irritable, Southern-leaning Democratic president played into the hands of the Republicans, who rode to victory in the 1866 elections with a theoretically veto-proof majority of almost three to one in Congress. Rifts among the Republicans would eventually divide the party

over the treatment of blacks, but the jostling for control over Reconstruction between the president and congress was over. Yet to view this
time as a period of enormous possibilities for racial justice ignores the
realities of racial animosity in America.

This was, after all, the America that had restricted black suffrage.
After the Civil War, all Northern states that held elections to determine
black suffrage voted to deny (or effectively deny) suffrage to blacks
except for Minnesota and Iowa, which had virtually no black residents.
Ohio defeated a black suffrage amendment. New Jersey remained
"white" in its suffrage laws. On November 2, 1869, a referendum was
held in New York to determine whether the onerous property requirement that effectively eliminated black suffrage would be removed.
New York, where blacks comprised about 1 percent of the population,
voted against enfranchising blacks.

In the North, blacks were faced with different but nonetheless
formidable obstacles. According to Eric Foner, they were "trapped in
urban poverty and confined to inferior housing and menial and unskilled jobs (even here their foothold, challenged by the continuing
influx of European immigrants and discrimination by employers and
unions alike, became increasingly precarious)." Throughout the country, blacks had no "viable strategy" and a tiny business class to serve
as an example of economic uplift. Other than the far-fetched dream
of "forty acres and a mule," blacks had little economic strategy. The
sliver of hope held by blacks to acquire Southern land after the war was
dashed in a white America.

Over the next few years, legislation provided a form of citizenship to
the black population but made no pretense about creating social equality. Rhetorical gestures and some laws paid homage to political and civic
equality, especially in the important area of black suffrage, but the critical testing ground of reality made a mockery of legislative language.
Some Northern politicians were genuinely concerned about extending
rights to black people. Others feared that Southern treatment of blacks
would provoke the dreaded Northern invasion. Legal protection for
Southern blacks was viewed by apprehensive Northerners as a way to
appease the freedmen, who would thus remain in the South. Northern
politicians, in general, wanted a Republican base in the South.

From this more realistic perspective we can see that the Reconstruction interlude was rife with Northern hypocrisy. Republican (and sometime Democratic) congressman Samuel W. Moulton of Illinois supported civil rights legislation to contain freedmen in the South. He was quite explicit:

> Whenever the colored man is completely and fully protected in the southern states he will never visit Illinois, and he will never visit Indiana, and every northern State will be depopulated of colored people as will be Canada.

In 1866, Roscoe Conkling, a New York senator and an author of civil rights legislation, clearly pointed to the need to keep blacks in the South:

> Four years ago, mobs were raised, passions were roused, votes were given, upon the idea that emancipated negroes were to burst upon the North. We then said, give them liberty and rights at the South, and they will stay there and never come into a cold climate to die. We say so still, and we want them let alone.

The expedient support of white Northerners for black equality could hardly be expected to withstand sustained Southern resistance.

A variety of federal legislation attempted to outline the civil and political rights of freedmen during the Radical Republican ascendancy. In the period from 1866 to 1875, the Republicans, moderate and Radical, held a large majority in both the Senate and the House of Representatives. Civil rights legislation was preceded in 1865 by the Thirteenth Amendment, which abolished slavery, and the Civil Rights Act, which passed over President Johnson's veto. The bill acknowledged the duty of the federal government to protect civil rights, but it did not grant political rights or suffrage specifically to the freedmen. This protection was added with the ratification of the Fourteenth Amendment in 1868. The first section of that amendment contained the familiar "due process" language. A state was prohibited from passing laws that "shall abridge the privileges or immunities of citizens of the United States; nor shall any state deprive any person of life, liberty, or property, without due process of law; nor deny to any person within its jurisdiction the equal protection of the laws."

The Fifteenth Amendment, guaranteeing the right to vote, was adopted in 1870. It stated that "The right of [male] citizens of the United States to vote shall not be denied or abridged by the United States or by any State on account of race, color, or previous condition of servitude." The amendment provided for federal protection of all citizens' voting rights. Yet the narrow basis of the protection "race, color, or previous condition of servitude" opened other possibilities for exclusion. In the coming years a variety of roadblocks—notably literary tests, poll taxes, and subjective evaluation of an understanding of state constitutions— would be employed to stop blacks from reaching the ballot box.

Meanwhile the Reconstruction Acts provided for military and federal government control of the South. In 1866, Congress divided the former Confederate states into five military districts, each commanded by an appointed military official. The commanding officers were empowered to supervise elections and monitor constitutional conventions. Under the Reconstruction Act of 1867, a state could be readmitted to the Union when a majority of its qualified electorate ratified a constitution acceptable to Congress.

Southerners quickly read between the lines of the 1867 act. They were well aware of election results in the North and knew that the Radical Republicans had prompted the legislation. They knew too that black male suffrage was advanced not out of desire for racial justice but in order to bolster the party's Southern prominence. They also recognized that there was "no direct mention of the Negro" in the Republican platform of 1868. Not surprisingly, the white South was bound to resist. The Ku Klux Klan and other white organizations would violently challenge the federal government's commitment to blacks.

Senator Charles Sumner, the prime mover behind the passage of the Civil Rights Act of 1875, died before a part of his dream was realized. The bill provided that "all persons within the jurisdiction of the United States shall be entitled to the full and equal enjoyment of the accommodations" in hotels, theaters, restaurants, ships, and railroads. It prevented the exclusion of citizens for jury duty "on account of race, color, or previous condition of servitude." Penalties of $500 to $1,000 and prison sentences of up to one year could be imposed for violations. The Civil Rights Act was hurried through the legislature before the

Democrats resumed power in the House of Representatives. The act, however, was never enforced and finally declared unconstitutional.

After Grant's election to the presidency in 1868, a new leader entered the growing maelstrom of Southern antagonism. For the next two terms Grant oversaw the final years of Reconstruction. The former commander-in-chief of the victorious army was a former slaveholder and a recent convert to black rights. He had presided over an army that had lost hundreds of thousands of soldiers to combat and disease; he was not afraid to risk the lives of thousands of men in the cause of preserving the Union.

Grant's rhetorical and legislative advocacy of black issues was solid. He applied pressure to secure passage of the Fifteenth Amendment and was ebullient in his "message from the President," a departure from "the social custom" in announcing ratification:

> A measure which makes at once 4,000,000 people voters who were heretofore declared by the highest tribunal in the land not citizens of the United States . . . is indeed a measure of grander importance than any of the kind from the foundation of our free Government to the present day.

Later, as with other events, Grant would express second thoughts about the Fifteenth Amendment. At the end of his frustrating second term, he announced to his Cabinet that the Fifteenth Amendment "had done the Negro no good, and had been a hindrance to the South, and by no means a political advantage to the North."

During Grant's presidency the federal government confronted repeated acts of violence and intimidation directed against freedmen in the South. Congressional hearings on the activities of the Ku Klux Klan and other white-supremacy organizations led to the Enforcement Acts, which gave the president power to intervene militarily on behalf of the freedmen. Grant occasionally authorized military force to curtail "lawlessness, turbulence, and bloodshed," but he failed to intervene in the pivotal 1875 Mississippi election that effectively ended Reconstruction in the state. Another act, in 1871, gave the federal government enormous scope to thwart the Klan and protect freedmen's voting rights, providing the attorney general with $50,000 in discretionary funds for the monitoring of elections by the Secret Service. But Grant gave the freedmen no foundation for future security. Most federal expenditures under the Enforcement Acts were spent in the North, not in the South. In effect the Republican party used federal money to gain political advantage in the Democratic cities of the North.

In order to combat the Ku Klux Klan in South Carolina, Grant issued a proclamation "asking the insurgents to disperse within twenty days." He warned the South that he would "not hesitate to exhaust the powers vested in the executive whenever it should be necessary to do so" to protect the rights of citizens. In 1871 he suspended habeas corpus in nine counties in South Carolina, sent in troops, and made hundreds of arrests. Some of the suspects were convicted and fined. In North Carolina and Mississippi there were also hundred of arrests but no convictions. In 1872, Grant ordered troops in New Orleans to protect the Republican regime; in 1873 he ordered troops to Louisiana in response to the massacre of 280 blacks in Colfax.

Oddly, during this period of military occupation, the army was being reduced to a mere shadow of the fighting machine that had won the Civil War. Clearly the Republicans, the Northern population, and President Grant were aware of the widespread violence in the South, and that troops had to cover a vast area in the enforcement of newly enacted laws. Yet the Radical Republicans presided over the dismantling of the Union army, which was reduced from 1 million men on May 1, 1865, to 152,000 by the end of the year. There were 200,000 troops in the South in July 1865, 20,000 for the 1868 elections, 8,000 in 1871, and 6,000 at the close of 1876. Other than a few aggregations in cities, the troops were dispersed in small units. In 1869 there were only 716 Union soldiers in Mississippi; Texas had 4,612, of which more than 3,000 were occupied with Indian problems.

Federal troops did take part in a great many operations, but their efforts in suppressing resistance were ineffective. Despite the army's presence, Southerners persisted in vigorously challenging federal authority and reestablishing white rule. The white South was not deterred. In a nod to priorities, the federal government actually expended vastly more time, money, and men in subduing and placing Indians in

the West on reservations than it did in enforcing laws to protect freedmen in the South. The white North was not prepared to shed white
blood to enforce black rights. The actions of white America, rather
than the words of a few Republicans, demonstrated that black equality was not a priority in a country obsessed with land expansion and
railroads, rife with racial animosity, and devastated by financial panic
and depression in 1873.

In 1942 the Mississippi Delta planter William Alexander Percy
made no apologies for wresting power from blacks to stop what he
termed Reconstruction's "orgy of graft, lawlessness, and terrorism." He
matter-of-factly described his uncle, a leader of the whites:

> His life work became the re-establishment of white supremacy. That
> work required courage, tact, intelligence, patience; it also required
> vote-buying, stuffing of ballot-boxes, chicanery, intimidation. Heart-
> breaking business and degrading, but in the end successful.

According to John R. Lynch, the black congressman from Mississippi, Grant admitted that political expediency had controlled his
actions. Congressman Lynch, during an audience with Grant in November 1875, asked the president why he had not intervened in the
recent Mississippi election, a "sanguinary struggle" that was "practically an insurrection against the state government." Lynch suggested
that prominent Ohio Republicans had warned that any federal action
on behalf of the Republicans in Mississippi would jeopardize their
own prospects in October elections. The Ohio delegation next informed
Grant that Mississippi would be lost to the Republicans with or without
federal assistance. Grant confessed that he had succumbed to political
expediency. The bold general, in this instance, had become a political
hack.

In a broad sense, Grant was not at all sure what to do about the
freedmen. He thought the annexation of Santo Domingo would provide a safe haven for blacks who wished to leave the country and might
provide leverage for their better treatment in America. In essence it was
Grant's admission that America could not absorb four million freedmen.
He wanted to "secure a retreat for the portion of the laboring classes of

our former slave states, who find themselves under unbelievable pressure." He continued:

> The present difficulty in bringing all parts of the United States into a happy unity and love of country grows out of the prejudice to color. . . . The colored man cannot be spared until his place is supplied, but with a refuge like Santo Domingo his worth here would be soon discovered and he would soon receive such recognition as to induce him to stay: or if Providence designed that the two races should not live together, he would find a home in . . . [Santo Domingo].

Grant's scheme had a tortured existence before it died at the hands of the Senate.

In his final message to Congress on December 5, 1876, Grant maintained his support of the Santo Domingo annexation plan. Santo Domingo promised to be a "congenial home" for the freedmen, Grant believed, "where their civil rights would not be disputed and where their labor would be so much sought after that the poorest among them would find a means to go." Racial separation was Grant's preference; his plan was yet another variation of schemes to remove or resettle black people.

The extent of legislation that was enacted to establish the political citizenship of the freedmen and to protect their rights was indeed impressive. An ascendant Republican majority was in power; the South was being occupied by federal troops. The preservation of the Union and the emancipation of the slaves, however, were no longer issues that could preserve the fragile unity of the Republican party and the limited common ground that briefly cast Radicals and moderates together. The 1875 elections returned the Democrats to power in the House of Representatives.

Reconstruction officially ended with the compromise that followed the disputed presidential election of 1876, in which the Republican candidate, Rutherford B. Hayes, agreed to withdraw remaining federal troops from Southern states. The Democratic and anti-black candidate, Samuel J. Tilden, had won popular election by 4,300,000 votes to Hayes's 4,036,000 votes, but the electoral votes of Florida, South Carolina, and Louisiana remained in doubt. Hayes's bargain allegedly called for the removal of troops from the South and government support for a transcontinental railroad through the South in return for the contested electoral votes.

*

Given the treatment of blacks by white America and the importance of black labor in the production of cotton, the demise of Reconstruction was inevitable. Legislative attempts to secure black political and civil rights simply faced too many obstacles. Some place the blame entirely on the South. But during these years white Northerners underwent no moral transformation with respect to race. The Union soldier who witnessed the courage of the black soldier during the war did not return to his white enclave and demand black equality or encourage blacks to resettle in the North. After President Johnson had been neutered in 1866, congressional rule could have instituted a permanent program to assist blacks if white America had been so inclined. The picture of Reconstruction as a window of opportunity for racial equality that was foiled by the white South gives a false impression. This alleged "interlude of virtue," "when Americans renounced their racism and rededicated themselves to the ideals of equality," is a myth conjured up by a guilt-ridden white America.

Black equality is often wrongly thought to be part of the same struggles as nineteenth-century support for abolition, the prevention of slavery's westward extension, and preservation of the Union. But black equality, as we have seen, was scarcely a goal of these campaigns. The fervency of abolitionism ended with emancipation. As the abolitionist Henry Ward Beecher so tellingly put it, once they were freed African Americans had to learn to "Root, hog, or die." William Lloyd Garrison and others would press for black equality from afar, but the issues of civil, political, economic, and social rights did not command the attention of a white America that thought blacks were inferior and should be confined to a separate status and place. Despite impressive rhetoric, the level of commitment and moral fervor that the North attached to Reconstruction was superficial at best.

Reconstruction could best be described as a knee-jerk political reaction reflecting the anxieties of a post–Civil War North; the efforts of

Republicans indicated not the desire for racial equality but a concern over well-publicized violence in the South and the imposition of the Black Codes, and a fear that the South was again capable of insurrection. Reconstruction was led by a small group of Radical Republicans who were often at odds with members of their own party, not to mention the whole gamut of Democrats. With internal divisions and broad dissent from Northerners and Southerners alike, the bold rhetoric of the Radicals was tested immediately. The result was that few of their policies had any lasting effect.

Substantive efforts like land redistribution had no chance. The white Northerner knew that the freedmen wanted land. As one freedman poignantly put it, "We wants land—dis bery land dat is rich wid de sweat of we face and de blood ob we back." Southern legislatures, even under freedmen, scalawag, and carpetbagger influence, gave little attention to land distribution. The attempts to help the freedmen economically were confined to writing wage contracts for planters, a process that left freedmen some bargaining room.

Through the 1870s, the North's commercial interests remained while government intervention in the South became increasingly unpopular. Fear of a Southern insurrection subsided; news of dishonest, inept rule by freedmen and carpetbaggers provoked sympathy for the white South; and the federal government's own rampantly corrupt activities won attention. All contributed to the shift away from Reconstruction policies. The propaganda tide was given a boost in favor of the white South by James S. Pike, an anti-slavery journalist with strong anti-black opinions. *The Prostrate State*, a searing account of carpetbagger corruption first published in 1872, found a willing audience in the pliant white Northern public. With their well-developed views on black inferiority and their proclivity for racial antagonism and racial separatism, Northerners were predisposed to accept Pike's account. Pike was not alone in attacking Southern governments. Senator George Hoar of Massachusetts, a consistent advocate of black suffrage, used less inflammatory language than Pike's, but his meaning paralleled that of the anti-black journalist:

> I incline to think that a large number of the men who got political office in the South, when the men who had taken part in the Rebellion

were still disfranchised, and the Republicans were still in power, were of a character that would not have been tolerated in public office in the North.

Horace Greeley, the eclectic anti-slavery editor of the *New York Tribune* and presidential aspirant, while condemning Southern violence also attacked the freedmen, as an "easy, worthless race, taking no thought for tomorrow." After an 1873 visit to Louisiana, Wisconsin senator Matt Carpenter, an initial supporter of Radical Republican policies, recommended that his party "turn their attention from politics to trade and business." His Wisconsin colleague, Senator Timothy Howe, enthused after the passage of the Reconstruction Act of 1867, "we have cut loose from the whole dead past and have cast our anchor out a hundred years." A disillusioned and chastened Senator Howe would write in 1875, not a decade later, that the Civil War was not "fought for the 'nigger,'" and the black person was not "the end and aim of all our effort."

The racial attitudes of Rutherford B. Hayes, the anti-slavery Ohio congressman, governor, and U.S. president from 1876 to 1880, vividly illustrate the transition from Reconstruction to reconciliation. Expediency was an integral part of Hayes's actions. His support for the Fourteenth Amendment was based not on equal protection but on the clause that denied representation where black voting was restricted. Like other Republicans, Hayes understood that a black vote was a Republican vote. When Cincinnati blacks voted for the first time, he gleefully announced, "They vote Republican almost solid."

Despite his bargain that secured the presidency in 1876, Hayes had made his decision about troop withdrawal and reconciliation well before the election and certainly before any deal was made. By 1876 he had moved away from Radical Reconstruction. In 1875 he had replied to a Kenyon College classmate, "As to Southern affairs 'the let alone' policy seems to be the true course. . . . The future depends largely on [the] moderation and good sense of [white] Southern men." Hayes was aware that a removal of federal troops would leave freedmen at the mercy of white Southerners. Nevertheless, after he received the Republican nomination for president in 1876, Hayes informed his friend Guy Bryan, "You will be almost if not quite satisfied with my letter of acceptance—especially on the Southern question." In early February 1877, Hayes supported an end to the North's "injudicious meddling." As for the use of federal troops in the South, the candidate wrote unequivocally to Carl Schurz that "There is to be an end of all of that." On his September 1877 Southern trip, the president spoke to a Georgia group that included blacks:

> And now my colored friends, who have thought, or who have been told that I was turning my back upon the men whom I fought for, now listen. After thinking it over, I believe your rights and interests would be safer if this great mass of intelligent white men were left alone by the general government.

In 1880, Hayes anticipated Booker T. Washington's famous comparison at the Atlanta Exposition of 1895. The occasion was the twelfth anniversary of the founding of the all-black Hampton Institute. Hayes, now the former president, spoke:

> We would not undertake to violate the laws of nature, we do not wish to change the purpose of God in making these differences of nature. We are willing to have these elements of our population separate as the fingers are, but we require to see them united for every good work, for national defense, one, as the hand.

To his nineteenth-century audience, the meaning of Hayes's remarks was unmistakable. At an 1890 commencement address at Johns Hopkins University, Hayes condescendingly remarked that "hitherto [blacks'] . . . chief and almost only gift has been that of oratory."

*

The most significant of the initial Southern acts of reconciliation featured Congressman L. Q. C. Lamar's eulogy for Charles Sumner. After Sumner died on March 11, 1874, the Massachusetts congressional delegation asked Lamar to "deliver a memorial address." Lamar's oration resonated within the Senate and across the North. The Mississippian praised Sumner, a man universally disliked in the South. Lamar had genuine respect for Sumner and used the opportunity to promote reconciliation. As he finished, his tribute gave way to a deafening silence and then to thunderous ovation. "Democrats and Republicans alike, melted in tears." One bystander noted, "Those who listened sometimes forgot to respect Sumner in respecting Lamar." The secessionist supporter of slavery had become the reconciliatory and rhetorical supporter of black suffrage. The Northern press was rapturous.

Lamar would continue to garner honors and praise from the North. His career advanced without pause. He was elected to the Senate in 1876, appointed secretary of the interior in 1885, and served as associate justice of the Supreme Court from 1888 until his death in 1893.

In his memoir, George Hoar, who sparred aggressively with Lamar over Reconstruction policy and the protection of black citizens, wrote glowingly of Lamar:

> He was a far-sighted man. . . . Mr. Lamar was made an Associate Justice of the Supreme Court. . . . I voted against him—in which I made a mistake. . . . He was a delightful man in ordinary conversation. He had an infinite wit and great sense of humor.

Massachusetts had joined with Mississippi in reconciliation.

The Northern press wrote the obituaries for Reconstruction. The anti-slavery *New York Tribune* expressed disappointment in the freedmen: "After ample opportunity to develop their own latent capacities, . . . [freedmen had only proved that] as a race they are idle, ignorant and vicious." *The Nation* gave a benediction in 1877: "The Negro will disappear from the field of national politics. Henceforth, the nation, as a nation, will have nothing to do with him."

Even the black soldier who had won praise for his courage was treated as an alien in America. By the 1880s and 1890s almost all Grand Army of the Republic posts were segregated. Blacks, as was usual in the North, formed their own posts.

CHAPTER TWENTY

The Black Hand
on the Cotton Boll

 WITHIN a few years after the official end of Reconstruction, the North's tolerance for a growing black presence in its midst would be tested. The result: blacks would continue to be confined in Southern cotton country. In 1879 a combination of oppression, destitution, and a depressed cotton market sparked a black-initiated exodus. These black migrants, called "Exodusters," left the cotton South for the "promised land" of Kansas. Most conventional discussions of the Exodusters focus on the dismal conditions and subjugation that prompted a mass movement, but it is also important to note the alacrity with which white Kansans blocked the migration. Black mobility was once again squelched, and cotton production continued to control black destiny.

Kansas prided itself on being anti-slavery before the war and as the home of John Brown's stand against the peculiar institution. Kansas wore the antebellum label "Bleeding Kansas" with honor. But Kansas had few free blacks, and anti-black sentiment there was as strong as anti-slavery feeling. In 1867, Kansans voted two to one against black suffrage. The state did ratify, with "strong opposition," the Fourteenth and Fifteenth Amendments. Interestingly, Kansas retained the word "white" in its constitutional suffrage requirement until 1884. In 1870, Kansas's population had grown to almost one million and continued to expand by 50 percent in the next decade. Meanwhile the number of blacks in Kansas grew from 625 in 1860, to 17,108 in 1870, and to 49,710 by 1880. At no time did blacks account for more than 5 percent of the total population of Kansas.

In the spring of 1879 large numbers of Southern blacks, the Exodusters, seemingly spontaneously decided to make a new home in Kansas. Possibly five thousand freedmen traveled to St. Louis on their way to Kansas, and during the ensuing two-year duration of the exodus, perhaps fifteen thousand to twenty thousand embarked "in search of Canaan." Soon promoters were falsely promising free transportation, free land, and a hospitable reception in Kansas. Most of the impoverished migrants were starving, and many were seriously ill. The white South, anticipating a labor shortage, responded by talking about ameliorating the conditions of the freedmen. What blacks did not reckon with was the resistance they would encounter in Kansas.

White city and state officials in Kansas sought to dispose of the Exodusters as quickly as possible. St. Louis officials were terrified as the numbers of migrants overwhelmed any charitable effort that arose to minister to them. St. Louis wanted the migrants to move on quickly to Kansas, where the cities of Topeka, Kansas City, Wichita, Lawrence, Wyandotte, and Pittsburg were equally deluged and wanted no part of the impoverished hordes. Lawrence city council members, after their "conscience [was] purged by statements of racial equality and good will toward all men," raised money "to send these undesirables to some other city." Humanitarian efforts stalled.

The results of the exodus were predictable. Going to Kansas may eventually have resulted in a better life for some freedmen, but it was no "promised land." Even though Kansas was encouraging white immigrants by the tens of thousands to settle there, the state and the nation would do nothing to promote black migration. The Exodusters moved to the black enclaves of the cities or settled in the countryside, mainly as subsistence farmers. Although their situation was for the most part desperate, few of them moved back to the South. One of the leaders of the black exodus explained that "we would rather sufer [sic] and be free."

Black leaders had varying responses to the Exodusters. In May 1879, Frederick Douglass famously recommended to a black group that freedmen stay in the South. He viewed Kansas as yet another false Canaan along with Haiti and Liberia. He cautioned that the "dumping" of thousands of impoverished blacks would reinforce the image of "that detestable class from whom we are not so free—tramps." Douglass predicted the growth of black urban ghettos occasioned by a black migration to the North. The result, he wrote, would leave blacks "crowded into lanes and alleys, cellars and garrets, poorly provided with the necessities of life. . . ." Douglass again turned to his themes of self-help, hard work, and patience.

Kansas could be a "land of milk and honey for white farmers" but "a veritable hell for blacks." While the slavery-induced political struggles of bleeding Kansas in the 1850s were past, the reality of racial antipathy toward blacks in Kansas was very much alive. The overworked biblical allusion to the exodus would ring hollow except in song.

The absence of blacks outside the cotton fields is the underappreciated aspect of the oft-repeated American immigrant saga. Despite the country's periodic depressions, America has had a chronic demand for immigrants. In the decades following the Civil War, workers were needed to settle on Western farms and work in urban industries, but in one of the most compelling migrations in human history, blacks were consistently bypassed. From 1861 to 1890, 11.3 million white immigrants—primarily from the United Kingdom, Germany, and Scandinavia—arrived in America. Most of them were destined for the North and West, precisely the areas where few blacks lived. Between 1879 and 1881, when a few thousand blacks made their way to Kansas, more than a half-million Germans immigrated to the Midwest. From 1890 to 1920, 18.2 million people arrived from southern and eastern Europe. When white foreign immigrants were available, the North and South did not want blacks. Fewer than 40,000 blacks became homesteaders. Oppression of blacks in the postwar South would have produced a mass refugee exodus if an alternative area had been available. No safety valve existed in America for blacks.

W. E. B. Du Bois easily saw the connection between America's eager acceptance of white immigrants and its rejection of native-born blacks. In a 1906 speech he asked rhetorically, "Cannot a nation that has absorbed ten million foreigners into its political life without catastrophe absorb ten million Negro Americans into that same political life at less cost than their unjust and illegal exclusion will involve?"

*

The Supreme Court further determined the status of former slaves in the cotton fields. While the aggregation of powers by the central government has been a theme of the Court's activity over time, the justices of the post–Civil War era left the political and civil rights of blacks largely in the hands of the states. The former slaves soon found themselves devoid of rights and at the mercy of white Southerners. White Northern Republican-appointed justices decimated national legislation and amendments that were passed during Reconstruction. The civil rights legislation—which was routinely ignored, circumvented, and violated—was no match for reality.

Grant's appointments to the Supreme Court played a key role in nullifying Reconstruction legislation. After the Slaughterhouse Cases (1873) restricted the due process clause of the Fourteenth Amendment, *United States v. Cruikshank* (1876) demolished the Enforcement Acts. Grant's appointee, Chief Justice Morrison Waite, issued the *Cruikshank* opinion. Waite, a strong defender of states' rights and a former Ohio corporate lawyer, consistently voted against black rights in his fourteen years on the bench.

In 1883 the Supreme Court dealt a fatal blow to the Civil Rights Act of 1875, which stated that "all persons within the jurisdiction of the United States shall be entitled to the full and equal enjoyment of the accommodations" in "restaurants, theaters, hotels, and railroads." The act was ignored extensively by white America. Lawsuits alleging that black citizens were denied "equal enjoyment" arose in Kansas (1875), California (1876), Missouri (1877), and Tennessee (1879). These cases, joined as the Civil Rights Cases, reached the Supreme Court in 1883. In the California case, a black man named George M. Tyler was denied entry to Maguire's Theatre after he had purchased a ticket, because he was "of the African or negro race, being what is commonly called a colored man, and not a white man."

Justice Joseph Bradley, a Grant appointee, wrote the opinion in the Civil Rights Cases. Bradley, a railroad lawyer, had arrived on the bench with "a record of hostility toward equal rights for blacks." In his opinion he analogized that to deprive "white people of the right of choosing their own company would be to introduce another form of slavery." The court, 8 to 1, ruled that the black plaintiffs were not protected under the Thirteenth or the Fourteenth Amendment. Justice Bradley's opinion amounted to a lecture to blacks who he said were no longer "to be a special favorite of the law."

The decision nullifying the Civil Rights Act was applauded by the establishment Northern press. *Harper's Weekly* called it "an illustration of the singular wisdom of our constitutional system." The *New York Times* observed that the "The Court has been serving a useful purpose in thus undoing the work of Congress." According to the *Times*, blacks "should be treated on their merits as individuals precisely as other citizens are treated in like circumstances." In the 1890s the *Times* elaborated further, declaring that the Civil Rights Act had been responsible for sustaining "a prejudice against negroes . . . which without it would have gradually died out." The newspaper proposed "self-help and reliance." It suggested that blacks follow the leadership of "eminent leaders of the white race in the South."

Other racial landmark cases continued to flow from the Republican-appointed Supreme Court justices. The year 1896 saw *Plessy v. Ferguson*, which formally enshrined racial segregation. The Court held that a Louisiana law codifying racial segregation in public accommodations could be legally enforced if facilities were separate but equal. The decision was quickly interpreted as applying to all aspects of American life, including schools. The opinion in *Plessy* was written by Judge Henry B. Brown, an appointee of President Benjamin Harrison. Brown wrote that "separation of the two races," in and of itself, did not convey a "badge of inferiority" upon blacks. The states were free to legislate separation.

> If the two races are to meet upon terms of social equality, it must be the result of natural affinities, a mutual appreciation of each other's merits, and a voluntary consent of natural affinities. . . . If one race be inferior to the other socially, the Constitution of the United States cannot put them upon the same plane.

Harrison's administration recommended two pieces of legislation, the Federal Elections Bill and the Blair Education Bill, designed to benefit blacks. The Federal Elections Bill, introduced by Senator Henry Cabot Lodge in 1890, would have provided some measure of federal protection for black voters. The Blair Education Bill sponsored federal aid to education for blacks and whites. The education bill passed the House by a vote of 155 to 149 but died in a Senate committee, as Republicans were "dubious of their ability to pass the bill or enforce it if it were passed." Senator Don Cameron of Pennsylvania spoke out emphatically against the Federal Elections Bill:

> Whatever form it may assume, I am opposed to [the Federal Elections Bill] in principle and in its details. The South is now resuming a quiet condition. Northern capital has been flowing into the South in great quantities, manufacturing establishments have been created and are in full operation, and a community of commercial interests is fast obliterating sectional lines. . . . The election law would disturb this desirable condition, and produce ill-feeling between the North and the South.

The final nail in the coffin for black suffrage, it could be argued, was the 1898 Supreme Court decision in *Williams v. Mississippi*, which upheld Mississippi's 1890 constitution that had effectively disfranchised blacks. The results of the constitution of 1890 were striking. In 1880, 110,113 whites and 130,606 blacks were registered to vote in Mississippi. In 1896, 108,998 whites and 16,234 blacks could vote in the state. The poll tax operated to deter both blacks and whites as only 64,339 voted in the closely contested state elections of 1895. In its consideration of the constitutionality of Mississippi's law, the Court's opinion was written by Justice Joseph McKenna, an appointee of Republican President William McKinley.

*

Black education reinforced the status of former slaves as cotton laborers. Both blacks and sympathetic whites unanimously touted education as the primary avenue for advancement. As political and social equality was not attainable in the South, where more than 90 percent of the black population lived, education was deemed by many as the long-term solution to America's racial dilemma. In terms of numbers, the education of blacks largely meant the education of Southern blacks.

The problem of mass illiteracy among the freedmen immediately confronted postwar America. Even before the end of the Civil War, Northern religious missionaries came south in droves as teachers for black youths and adults. As the zeal of the Northern teachers abated, they left. Their average stay was around two years. The American Missionary Association maintained 157 schools for blacks in 1870, 70 in 1871, and only 13 in 1874.

After the war, the task of educating freedmen and whites was left to the individual states. Reconstruction governments established public schools on a segregated basis. The attempt to supplement state efforts by the federal government never left a Senate committee. As the momentum for black schools was stymied by the loss of black political participation, funding for black schools plummeted in relation to white schools. In Alabama in 1890, black and white schools received almost equal funding, $3.14 million for white schools and $3.1 million for black schools. Twenty years later Alabama spent $10 million for white schools and $2.69 million for black schools. In 1929–1930, Mississippi spent $5.94 per black pupil versus $31.33 for a white student. Gavin Wright has written that this "assault on black schools affected the lives of black Southerners directly for generations."

As Northern teachers departed the South, they were replaced by white Northern philanthropists who poured money into educational efforts for black Southerners. The list of wealthy philanthropists involved in the education of blacks for cotton farming includes John D. Rockefeller, Andrew Carnegie, Julius Rosenwald, John Fox Slater, and Robert Ogden. In obtaining money the most successful black educator was the controversial former slave Booker T. Washington. His Tuskegee Institute, founded in 1881 in Tuskegee, Alabama, and its predecessor, Washington's alma mater, Hampton Normal and Agricultural Institute, inculcated theories of self-help and "industrial" training. This plan echoed Frederick Douglass's ideas of the 1850s. Washington's goals were totally sympathetic with the expectations of white America's political and business leaders for black America. The Tuskegee-Hampton

concept of education emphasized practical training in farming and vocational skills. Students, while receiving some classical education, were
prepared for such jobs as farmers, cooks, and laundresses, stressing habits of efficiency and hard work. The school required students to work
on farms during their stay. Farming, for the most part, was synonymous
with cotton farming. Washington chose to avoid issues of political and
racial equality, believing that blacks could best rise through practical
employment. Black schools on the Tuskegee-Hampton model spread
throughout the South. General George Armstrong, the first head of
Hampton Institute, adhered to an industrial education philosophy that
would place blacks in a "subordinate social role in the emergent New
South."

Washington rose to national prominence because of his perfor-
mance at the Cotton States Exposition in Atlanta on September 18,
1895. Atlanta's leaders eagerly seized on the exposition as an opportunity to showcase the city's progressive attitude and promote national
unity. The white organizers of the exposition picked the respectable but
little-known Washington to address the opening ceremonies. Washington contrasted his strategy with that of blacks after the Civil War who
wished to begin at the "top instead of the bottom." He faulted those
who thought that "a seat in Congress, or the state legislature was more
important than real estate or industrial skill." He knew that blacks
were confined to the South; his literary turn of phrase—"Cast down
your bucket where you are. . . . Cast it down in agriculture, mechanics,
in commerce, in domestic service, and in the professions"—expressed
his recognition of the obvious geographic and vocational restrictions
placed on blacks. According to Washington, "no race can prosper until
it learns that there is as much dignity in tilling a field as in writing a
poem. . . . The opportunity to earn a dollar in a factory just now is worth
more than the opportunity to spend a dollar in an opera-house."

Respect, Washington believed, would come only with economic
success. As he told a rapt crowd at the exposition, "No race that has
anything to contribute to the markets of the world is long in any degree
ostracized." But he acknowledged that a precondition of racial coop-
eration was a just administration of the law. The results would follow.
"[A black laboring class] will buy your surplus land, make blossom the

waste lands of your fields, and run your factories. . . . [Black workers would be] the most patient, faithful, law-abiding, and unresentful people that the world has seen." His most frequently quoted passage dismissed social equality with whites as a goal: "In all things that are purely social we can be as separate as the fingers, yet one as the hand in all things essential to mutual progress."

Washington's practicality was shown in the homage he paid to "Northern philanthropists, who have made their gifts a constant stream of blessing and encouragement." His financially induced praise has been interpreted by some as obsequious. But Washington's ambitious school plans required hundreds of thousands of dollars in donations from white philanthropists. If he hoped to build Tuskegee, Washington had to accommodate and compromise. He worked silently at times to assist those who challenged the system.

White America—educators, politicians, and businessmen— subscribed to the Tuskegee-Hampton idea. President William McKinley lauded Tuskegee for its emphasis on "practical industry" and for wisely "not attempting the unattainable" by offering a classical university curriculum. Theodore Roosevelt, who served Washington as a trustee for nine years, praised the Tuskegee-Hampton approach: "If there is any work which every American must believe in, it is the work . . . at Hampton and Tuskegee." Harvard's president, Charles Eliot, added his accolades. John D. Rockefeller, Jr., felt that the Tuskegee-Hampton model provided "the most important contribution yet found towards the solution of the race problems in this country." The list of prominent white American supporters of the Tuskegee-Hampton model as a solution to the "Negro Problem" is endless and includes Ulysses S. Grant, Rutherford B. Hayes, James Garfield, Woodrow Wilson, Julius Rosenwald, and George Eastman.

Along with praise came Northern money. The General Education Board, founded in 1902 with a $1 million gift from the Rockefellers (who by 1921 expanded their contribution to $129 million), was an influential channel of Northern philanthropy to black education in the South. Wallace Buttrick, executive director of the organization, unabashedly declared, "I recognize the fact that the Negro is an inferior race and that the Anglo-Saxon is the superior race." Robert

Ogden, a wealthy department store owner and a trustee, noted that blacks were "thriftless, careless, shiftless, and idle by disposition" and were characterized by "childlike qualities." He proposed a New York City vocational school that would train blacks to be domestics: "The English, Irish, French, and Swiss are holding domestic service in [New York City] . . . that would naturally belong to the colored people, but for the latter are distanced from competition because of ignorance and easy-going ways." For personal and professional reasons, Ogden and other Northern philanthropists strongly endorsed the role of blacks in the cotton fields. "Our great problem," he said, "is to attach the Negro to the soil and prevent his exodus from the country to the city."

Northern philanthropists made a direct, unambiguous connection between black education and cotton production. George Foster Peabody, financier turned philanthropist, asked President Woodrow Wilson to speak at Hampton's fiftieth anniversary, telling Wilson of the importance of Hampton's contribution to cotton cultivation: "One-ninth of our population is of Negro blood, and the prosperity of the South and the world's supply of cotton are intimately bound up with the development of the Hampton Idea. . . ." Andrew Carnegie was equally clear about the cotton-race relationship. Carnegie's gift of $600,000 to the Tuskegee Institute in 1903 represented the first major contribution to Washington's school. For Carnegie, Tuskegee was a training ground for black cotton farmers. In 1903, in his archaic, obtuse prose, Carnegie spelled out the nexus of cotton, black laborers, and international trade: "It is certain we must grow more cotton. . . . We cannot afford to lose the Negro. We have urgent need of all and more. . . ."

Blacks would contribute 64 percent of the money raised for the expansive Rosenwald Fund program for constructing educational buildings for black schools between 1914 and 1932. The black children who would benefit from these schools were bound to cotton. The black novelist Richard Wright described their plight.

[America] can not let them leave the fields when cotton is waiting to be picked. When the time comes to break sod, the sod must be broken; when the time comes to plant seeds, the seeds must be planted. . . . Hunger is the punishment if we violate the laws of Queen Cotton.

The seasons of the year form the mode that shapes our lives, and who can change the seasons?

*

Post–Civil War America was rife with racial conflict. New York alone witnessed racial violence in 1900, 1905, 1935, and 1943. A countrywide sampling of racial encounters would include those in Philadelphia in the 1830s and 1840s, in Detroit (1863), in Atlanta (1906), in Springfield, Illinois (1908), in East St. Louis (1917), in Chicago and Omaha (1919), in Tulsa (1921), and in Mobile, Los Angeles, and Detroit (1943).

In the South, racial violence in its most egregious form, lynching, was used as the most extreme means of social control. Lynching was most prevalent in the cotton belt. Without legal recourse or protection, black cotton laborers were subject to sporadic attacks by whites. If a viable relocation alternative had been available, blacks would have moved north to avoid the perils of an arbitrary system. But racial violence in the North, despite its few blacks, was much in evidence.

Lynching conjures up the most revolting scenes of the Ku Klux Klan engaging in racial violence. The first chapter of the KKK's history was filled with the intimidation and murder of freedmen. With its white-hooded Klansmen and burning crosses, the KKK enjoyed mythical popularity as a defender of whites in the South.

White America's acceptance of the Klan as a social-control mechanism is graphically illustrated by the reception of the celebrated film *Birth of a Nation*. This movie glorifying the Klan, released in 1915, was seen by 200 million people in the United States and abroad. The movie ran for almost a year in New York, Boston, and Chicago. In New York the film was greeted with "ecstatic" reviews by critics. Protests in Chicago and Boston did not dampen the enthusiasm of moviegoers who paid a two-dollar admission fee when the normal charge was ten to fifteen cents. The film made an astounding $13 million in profits, the "very first movie blockbuster," and set the movie industry on its golden path. Woodrow Wilson said of the movie, "It is like writing history with lightning." Later, after the film "inflamed racial tensions," Wilson referred to *Birth of a Nation* as an "unfortunate production."

The Ku Klux Klan was resurrected in the 1920s by Atlanta hucksters after a dormancy that began in the late nineteenth century. In 1925 the organization's membership grew to 8.9 million Americans. Membership by state showed national acceptance: Michigan, 875,000; New Jersey, 720,000; Texas, 450,000; Kentucky, 441,000; Ohio, 400,000; Florida, 391,000; Nebraska, 352,000; California, 350,000; Illinois, 300,000; New York, 300,000; Pennsylvania, 300,000; Arkansas, 150,000; Mississippi, 93,000; and Louisiana, 50,000.

The Klan met with pockets of white resistance in some areas of the South after the Civil War because planters feared that violence would provoke black laborers to leave. Some critics, like former Mississippi senator and cotton planter Leroy Percy, opposed the Klan in general. In 1922, Percy confronted a Klan recruiting meeting in Greenville, Mississippi, and caused the assembled group to disperse. Senator Percy railed against the Klan and wrote articles condemning it. He viewed the organization as a "public evil" that "good citizens could not ignore." Despite the fact that there was no well-organized Klan in Percy's Washington County, thirteen blacks were lynched there between 1889 and 1945.

The racially inspired brutality of the vigilantes was generally spontaneous, and part of a design to instill fear in the black community. The gory statistics vary. Some estimates indicate that as many as 5,000 blacks were victims—for the most part in the South—of lynch mobs. One study calculates that 2,805 lynchings occurred between 1882 and 1930; 2,462 of the victims were black. Another report found 3,437 lynchings of blacks and 1,293 lynchings of whites between 1882 and 1951. The number of lynchings vary widely from year to year—44 in 1882, 129 in 1892, 62 in 1902, 54 in 1912, 37 in 1922, 13 in 1930.

The only broad conclusion about the frequency of lynchings makes "a reasonably strong association between the dominance of cotton cultivation in the local agricultural economy and the level of racial violence in the county." Cotton production generally indicated that a higher percentage of blacks lived in particular counties; those counties with large black populations were the sites of the most lynchings. The violence was used specifically to deal with people "accused of crimes against the white community" and to provide a symbol of white power.

*

For the most part, the Eastern intelligentsia fully accepted the notion of black inferiority and the relegation of blacks to the Southern cotton fields, which they visited to observe firsthand the racial conditions. The Harvard-educated Theodore Roosevelt excluded blacks from his progressive domestic agenda.

Roosevelt, the man of action, forthright opinions, and aggressive behavior in foreign and domestic policy, became decidedly timid when it came to racial issues. He provided yet another example of a white Northerner whose abstract grasp of black rights withered when exposed to reality. He thought that Reconstruction was a "mistake," that it proved how "federal legislation in itself could not solve the racial dilemma." In a nod to custom, Roosevelt saw the solution in "the constant working of those often unforeseen forces of the national life which are greater than legislation." Roosevelt wanted blacks to lower their expectations and not hope for the impossible or be "led away, as the educated Negro so often is . . . into the pursuit of fantastic visions."

On numerous occasions Roosevelt elaborated on his thoughts about white superiority and black inferiority. He had a detailed correspondence about blacks with his Harvard friend Owen Wister, the author who popularized the Western literary genre with his book *The Virginian*. In 1906, Roosevelt responded to Wister, "I entirely agree with you that as a race, and in the mass, the [blacks] are altogether inferior to the whites." He distinguished between the few blacks whom he held in high regard and the mass of black Americans. He admired Booker T. Washington, whom he hosted at a White House dinner in 1901. No other invitations to blacks were forthcoming.

Roosevelt viewed the black person as a child "unable to stand alone." He expounded, "I do not believe that the average Negro in the United States is as yet in any way fit to take care of himself and others as the average white man, for if he were, there would be no Negro race problem." He thought the black man survived because he was a good "breeder." He abhorred the lynching of blacks (and whites) in the South, but he never made a public anti-lynching pronouncement, nor did he introduce legislation to remedy the situation. He associated rape with black men: "This worst enemy of the colored race is the colored man who commits some hideous wrong, especially if that be the worst of all crimes, rape. . . ." At Tuskegee he warned black students about descending into crime and told them that blacks were a "backward race."

In politics, Teddy Roosevelt's attitude toward blacks and his ear for public opinion determined his actions. He thought most of the black population was unqualified to hold public office, but he wanted the others to be given an opportunity to succeed: "If ninety-five percent of the blacks were unfit to hold office . . . rule those ninety-five out, but not the other five percent simply because of the color of their skin." He was proud of the fact that he had reduced the number of black appointments to federal offices in the South but had upgraded the quality of his selections. He viewed the Republican party in the South with disdain as a "set of black and white scalawags, with few decent men."

Roosevelt was wary of black suffrage.

> . . . All I have been doing is to ask, not that the average negro be allowed to vote, not that ninety-five per cent of the negroes be allowed to vote, not that there be negro domination in any shape or form. . . .

He believed that some sections of the South "would become another Haiti if the ballot was given to blacks without qualification." "Universal suffrage" for blacks he regarded as a crime and a joke:

> I know the negro fairly well. I have seen him at close quarters in the Yazoo Delta, where he formed ninety per cent of the population, and where universal suffrage in his hand is the veriest criminal farce.

Roosevelt's deeds spoke as loudly as his rhetoric. In November 1905 black soldiers stationed in Brownsville, Texas, were accused of killing a white saloon keeper, shooting a white police officer, and running rampant through town. An exhaustive investigation revealed no evidence that the soldiers were guilty. Nevertheless Roosevelt resolved to discharge 167 of the 170 men, many of them decorated combat veterans. He was vindictive because no black soldier had divulged the name of a perpetrator.

Another representative of Eastern intellectual life was the historian Frederic Bancroft, scion of a wealthy family who was educated at

Amherst College and Columbia University. Young Bancroft, the son of
an Illinois abolitionist, revered Charles Sumner, William Lloyd Garrison, and John Brown. In 1885 this diligent scholar published his views
on a trip to Mississippi and South Carolina in a series of articles in the
New York Evening Post that chronicled the effects of Reconstruction.
Bancroft found that white Mississippians were frank about the "mutual
dependency" of the races. This racial reciprocity meant that "the negro
cannot live without our capital and we cannot live without his labor"
in the cotton fields. Bancroft sought to offer a realistic portrait "of the
negro as he is." Mississippi freedmen, he wrote, were inherently childlike, dependent, extravagant, gullible, impulsive, irresponsible and
self-indulgent.

> Slavery gave . . . [the freedman] the only training he received before
> 1865. That gave him no moral code; it bred in him no sense of honor,
> or right as distinguished from wrong except for fear of punishment.
> . . . In the Negro's opinion, it was no serious offence to receive a bribe
> or enrich himself out of the public treasury. . . .

Bancroft was incensed by the freedman's propensity to spend:

> [H]e has no ambition to become rich; he has a desire to spend money
> only because he wants to enjoy the pleasures of spending it extrava-
> gantly. He does not save enough to pay cash for his provisions, so he
> must have credit until his cotton is sold . . . the storekeeper must de-
> pend for his pay entirely on the future crop, it is necessary for him to
> charge credit prices for the articles, and these are from 10 percent to
> 50 percent in advance of the cash prices. If the storekeeper be dishon-
> est, as he frequently is, he gives false weights and makes false charges.
> With credit to the extent of a hundred dollars, a negro feels that he is
> rich, and that his chief duty is to enjoy the present. . . . Some few are
> fortunate enough to escape both the cupidity of the storekeeper and
> their own self-indulgence. . . .

Bancroft lambasted Republican carpetbaggers and scalawags, who
he thought were "responsible for the political excesses of Reconstruction." He thought Republican supporters of freedmen were basically
opportunists. By 1870, Bancroft wrote, "The policy of the [Republican]

. . . leaders was to protect the Negroes in all their rights which were essential to their voting the Republican ticket." In general, Bancroft considered that white Republicans were "as bitter toward negro superiority as the Democrats." Black-controlled governments, Bancroft thought, "were markedly incapable, and the Negroes lacked the intellectual, moral and physical power to support them." His harsh appraisal found blacks "too ignorant to know how to better their condition even after the means of doing so—the ballot—was put in their hands."

The Harvard historian Albert Bushnell Hart also carried a sound abolitionist pedigree. The influential Hart served as president of both the American Historical Association and the American Political Science Association. He has been described as "a founding father of professional history" and a leading proponent of "scientific history." Hart was also the mentor and teacher of W. E. B. Du Bois, yet he considered the average black man a "moral and social cripple."

In 1910, Hart journeyed to the South to study black people and Southern society, because that was where more than 90 percent of blacks lived. His observations and research were published in *The Southern South* (1910). His trip carried him to the Mississippi Delta where he spent time with the senator and planter John Bell Williams and with the lawyer, planter, and archivist Alfred Holt Stone. Hart's conclusions about blacks were pessimistic. "The experience of the race in the Northern states," he wrote, "leads rather to negative than to positive conclusions as to their intellectual and moral power. Nobody can pretend that this movement [of 365,000 Southern blacks to the North] has improved the conditions of the Northern states, and the Negroes themselves encounter many hardships. . . . The situation of the Negroes in the North is frankly discouraging, both from their point of view and that of the Northern White. . . . Genuine friends and well-wishers of the Negro feel the irresponsibility of the race." The Harvard intellectual's summary of the race issue was devastating and offered little hope:

> The main issue must be fairly faced by the friends as well as the enemies of the colored race. Measuring it by the white people of the South, or by the correspondingly low population of Southern or Northern cities, the negroes, as a people appear to be considerably below the

Whites in mental and moral status. There are a million or more exceptions, but they do not break the force of the eight or nine millions of
average Negroes. Race measured by race, the Negro is inferior, and his
past history in Africa and in America leads to the belief that he will
remain inferior in race stamina and race achievement.

Theodore Roosevelt and Albert Bushnell Hart, while convinced of
black inferiority, did not subscribe fully to white racial superiority. Both
regarded the nonwhite Japanese with respect as a race.

CHAPTER TWENTY-ONE

From Cotton Field to Urban Ghetto: The Chicago Experience

ECONOMIC LAWS, not moral precepts, finally broke the chains that bound blacks to the cotton fields—though even economics, as we shall see, would not be strong enough to break America's racial legacy. The driving force was the labor shortage created by the World War I demand for troops and the interruption of the flow of white immigrants. As noted earlier, between 1890 and 1920 more than 18.2 million white immigrants had settled mainly in the American North, precisely where blacks were unwelcome. On the eve of World War I more than 90 percent of the African-American population still lived in the South, over half of them employed in cotton production.

When jobs beckoned, Southern blacks who wished to escape from the South were easily motivated to journey north. The nature of industrial work meant regular wages as opposed to the once-a-year unpredictable cotton payment. Yet another "promised land," the American North, loomed on the horizon, and Chicago, the bustling industrial giant, became the most conspicuous Canaan.

In a booming wartime economy, the number of unemployed dropped from 8.5 percent in 1915 to 1.4 percent in 1918. Employers were desperate for workers, even black labor. Fears of a black invasion gave way to the recruitment of Southern blacks by agents who offered free transportation. Between 1916 and 1919, 500,000 Southern blacks moved to the North; by 1930 another 1 million followed the steel tracks of the railroad, on their way to various Northern cities and the hopes they seemed to offer.

The momentum would continue. By the 1940s racial demographics had changed substantially. Between 1920 and 1940 the black population of Detroit grew from 40,000 to 149,000, Cleveland from 34,000 to 84,000, New York from 152,000 to 458,000. Still, New England's black population amounted to little more than 1 percent. Of 9 million people in New England, 90,000 were black. The cotton kingdom of the Mississippi Delta had a population of 400,000, of which 300,000 were black. Massachusetts had 4 million people and only 52,000 blacks, the same number of blacks that lived in one Delta county, Bolivar.

In the years bookending World War I, Chicago received a tenth of all migrating Southern blacks. The city became a natural terminus for blacks because of the Illinois Central Railroad, which paralleled the Mississippi River to New Orleans. Deeply involved in the cotton economy, the Illinois Central provided a direct route for rural blacks traveling to Chicago. As a consequence, Chicago's population statistics changed dramatically. After remaining stagnant from the end of the Civil War to World War I, Chicago's black population consistently rose in each decade of the twentieth century, from 44,103 in 1910 (2 percent of the total population), to 109,458 in 1920 (4 percent of the total population), to 337,000 in 1930 (9.4 percent of Chicago's population). It was Chicago that W. E. B. Du Bois selected as the setting for his 1928 political novel *Dark Princess*, a tale of the black migrants' political participation.

America's "Second City" was unprepared for these men and women who emigrated in search of a better life. Chicago, an anti-slavery stronghold in antebellum America, had had a miniscule black population of 1 percent at the turn of the century. Problems increased as soon as the population did. De facto segregation followed when black numbers became large.

In 1917 the *Chicago Tribune*, which did not extend its abolitionist stance to racial tolerance, called the black migration a "huge mistake" and shouted, "Black man, stay South." The *Tribune* described black migrants as "lazy, shiftless, ne'er do wells, sure to be a burden on the city." The newspaper often used condescending terms in referring to blacks, as in this headline: "Half a Million Darkies from Dixie Swarm to the North to Better Themselves."

As tens of thousands of blacks poured into the city, pressures rose for blacks to move beyond their traditional residential areas. Alarmed whites responded with bombs, threats, laws, and organized resistance. Between July 1917 and March 1921, whites exploded fifty-eight bombs at black residences in previously all-white areas. In 1919 a six-year-old black girl was killed by one of the bombs. As early as 1897, home owners in the Woodlawn neighborhood had coerced white landlords to stop renting to blacks. Even then, Chicago had a "black belt" that would eventually become a black ghetto. At the time the [Chicago] *Property Owners Journal* had launched a caustic salvo:

> There is nothing in the make-up of a Negro, physically or mentally, which should induce anyone to welcome him as a neighbor. The best of them are unsanitary, . . . ruin alone follows in their path. . . . Niggers are undesirable and entirely irresponsible and vicious.

In 1917 the Chicago Real Estate Board passed a resolution that encouraged whites on every block to defend their territory from black incursion. The NAACP challenged restrictive real estate covenants and theoretically won its case, but the Supreme Court did not rule that the racially restrictive covenants were illegal. Instead the Court in 1917 held that each case had to be tried individually. The result was a virtually complete quarantine of blacks in racially segregated Chicago neighborhoods.

For the most part, black housing in Chicago amounted to slum conditions. Toilets were located in "hallways, yards, and basements." Overcrowding was commonplace, and apartments lacked proper ventilation and lighting. Landlords did not make repairs for blacks' dwellings, which commanded higher rents than those for an adequate white residence. Health statistics were consistent with housing conditions: infant mortality, life expectancy, illegitimate births, and incidence of disease were disproportionately high in the "black belt." In 1925 the death rate for blacks in Chicago approximated that of Bombay, India. Vice and crime proliferated.

In every aspect of Chicago life from 1919 to 1925, blacks met with discrimination and ostracism. In the school system, principals practiced a form of racial segregation by assigning black students to a "substandard branch" that was 90 percent black. White parents in the Wendell Phillips school district formally asked for a new school because "white children should not be compelled to sit with colored children." There were frequent racial clashes at Wendell Phillips High School, which had a majority of black students. The "parks, playgrounds, and beaches" were "unofficially segregated," and violent means were used by whites to keep the parks segregated. Public accommodations, theaters, restaurants, and stores routinely treated blacks discourteously.

All these conditions were tolerated by blacks because of the possibility of employment. Before World War I, Chicago's major industrial companies—Armour, Swift, Pullman, and International Harvester—hired only white workers. But in wartime, white exclusivity was no longer possible. In 1900 approximately 65 percent of black men and 80 percent of black women in Chicago were domestics or servants. Only 8.3 percent of the men and 11.9 percent of the women held manufacturing jobs, most of them unskilled. But wages at the meatpacking plants and steel mills were attractive to field hands and sharecroppers. In 1910 blacks accounted for only 6 percent of the workforce at the meatpacking plants; by 1920, 32 percent of the workforce was black. As companies were forced to loosen their policies, factory work, both skilled and unskilled, became the main source of employment for blacks. The employment situation was plagued by layoffs and a rampant inflation that saw prices rise in Chicago by 75 percent between 1914 and 1919. Blacks were the last to be hired and the first to be fired. Was factory work a stepping-stone to a better life, or was it a stagnant position as an unskilled or semiskilled common laborer? For most blacks, a ceiling prevented upward mobility.

As the black population grew and as blacks became strikebreakers, racial friction increased. The racially combustible city received the spark that ignited a racial conflagration on July 27, 1919, when a black teenager, Eugene Williams, swam into the section of a South Side beach that was considered for whites only. The youth drowned after he was pelted with rocks. The ensuing violence lasted fourteen days and required the deployment of the state militia. Of 38 people killed, 23 were black; of 537 injured, 342 were black. The so-called Chicago Riot of 1919 had been preceded by numerous racial skirmishes. The *Chicago Tribune* responded with a plea for greater racial segregation:

> Despite the possible justice of Negro demands, the fact is that the races are not living in harmony.... How long will it be before segregation will be the only means of preventing murders?...

If blacks could not be confined to the cotton fields, they would be consigned to the urban ghettos.

Richard Wright captured Chicago's black experience in the introduction he wrote for the classic study *Black Metropolis: A Study of Negro Life in a Northern City* (1945). The authors, the anthropologist St. Clair Drake and the sociologist Horace R. Cayton, both black and both trained at the University of Chicago, presented a scientific appraisal of Chicago's black community and its relationship to the white community. Wright, a black migrant, had been born in Natchez, Mississippi, moved to the Mississippi Delta, then to Memphis, and then to Chicago. For him, "the most incisive and radical black thought" had come from Chicago. The black man, according to Wright, "wants to be free in a way that white men are free," but found an "[American] culture that crushes him." The American black, in Wright's view, was the victim of an almost "compete rejection" by American society. He concluded that "White America has reduced Negro life in our great cities to a level of so crude and brutal a quality" that hopelessness reigned.

Many of the topics explored in *Black Metropolis* had been treated earlier by the black sociologist E. Franklin Frazier in *The Negro Family in Chicago* (1932). Frazier's chapter titles were straightforward—"Desertion and Non-Support," "Illegitimacy," "Juvenile Delinquency," and so on. Clearly the social problems of blacks had migrated north with them. Wright, Drake, Cayton, and others noted the inability to form "stable, conventional, family units" as a legacy of slavery. Drake and Cayton cited the lack of an economic base for secure jobs in the North as the reason for "roving masses of Negro men" who left black women to support the family. The conditions of the Southern migrants, as described by these black sociologists, were directly attributable to

Southern slavery and segregation spawned in the cotton world. When slavery, legal segregation, and the cotton world disappeared, and when ghettos in the North and South persisted, sociologists would have to search for new reasons for the continuing plight of America's racial underclass.

Just as a labor shortage had created the need for slaves and later for free blacks in the cotton fields, so the twentieth-century migration of blacks was economically induced by a demand for labor. Yet racial overtones persisted. Cotton, disfranchisement, and de jure segregation may have been absent in the North, but repression and de facto segregation were not. The great migration would force white America to confront race yet again, but this time in a Northern context. It would introduce black Southerners to the reality of white "Northern racism, the business cycle, and class relations." Blacks would learn the "boundaries of American citizenship and opportunity."

Before the introduction of mechanization to the cotton fields in the 1930s, and its full impact in the 1950s, the Great Migration surrounding World War I represented a real threat to the structure of Southern cotton production. Until the 1930s the methods and technology of cotton farming were remarkably similar to those of post–Civil War America.

*

The post–Civil War experience of blacks in America began with Frederick Douglass's rhetorical question, posed in 1865, "What Shall We Do with the Negro?" White America's answer was simple, and resounding: keep him in the South to cultivate cotton. In 1875, Douglass posed another prescient query, "What will peace among the whites bring?" The answer was a booming affirmation of white superiority. The story of Reconstruction, despite attempts to idealize the potential of the era, reveals the heavy hand of political and economic expediency. Yes, legislation was passed, and yes, African Americans gained a brief influence they had never had before. But looking beyond these accomplishments we can see that Reconstruction was primarily a means for Republicans to gain black votes and an effort to solidify their hold on an unruly South. Those who would like to salvage the benefits of Reconstruction draw attention to the passage of the Fourteenth Amendment and its putative relevance during the civil rights struggle a century later. In fact it can be argued compellingly that civil rights advocates in mid-twentieth-century America could easily have relied on legal concepts embedded in the American political tradition and the Declaration of Independence rather than the Fourteenth Amendment. It can easily be argued that the "separate but equal" clause of *Plessy* was inherently unequal. In plain language, all Americans, it can be argued, should have equal political and civil rights.

It has been wistfully lamented that white America squandered an opportunity to implement black equality after the Civil War. But to assume that the moment was wasted is to ignore America's twinned realities: the prevalence of racial antipathy—a strain of hatred, disgust, and condescension that spread from the deepest Southern plantations to the most "enlightened" of Northern politicians, philanthropists, and intellectuals—and the country's overwhelming commercial priorities.

Historians, in an attempt to assuage the guilt of white America, have offered excuses and alternatives to the realities of American history. War weariness, the fatigue of racial reform, corruption in Grant's administration, the advent of an exaggerated materialism in the so-called Gilded Age—all have been proffered as reasons for the post–Civil War abandonment of blacks.

St. George Tucker observed in 1795 that a "comparatively very small" number of blacks could not be assimilated in Massachusetts. If that was so, how would it be possible for a large number of freedmen in the South to be effectively admitted into white society? It has been falsely assumed that abolitionism should naturally have led to a serious commitment to black rights. But freeing the slave and making him a political and social equal were two utterly different ideals: the former was the hope of nineteenth-century America, the latter almost unheard of. It is easy for Americans in the twenty-first century to assume that these ideals would be housed side by side in the minds of abolitionists, but if we take a long view of American history we see that it took an entire century from Emancipation to the serious struggle for civil rights of the 1960s. This gap is a sobering reminder of the prevalence of racial animosity in this country.

The slow course of progress is also a sign—though an often ignored one—of the powerful dictates of economics. For even if white America shared an earnest desire for the racial uplift of their black brethren, a simple fact remained: the backbreaking labor of politically disfranchised black men and women in the cotton fields was more valuable than equality. The importance of cotton in the American economy cemented a role for blacks both before and after the Civil War. An aggressively materialistic America valued cotton as an indispensable product.

Blacks were without a fundamental American trait: mobility. Stories of freedmen who walked six hundred miles to look for their families appeared during Reconstruction. In theory a freedman who walked six hundred miles would be capable of migrating to the North to flee oppression. Instead the freedmen journeyed laterally across the South; until a labor shortage arose, the black Southerner did not walk north where he was unwanted. By the 1930s, racial segregation was embedded in the law and racial partition was the norm of American life. Blacks were, in the words of the historian Leon Litwack, "repressed" and "quarantined," both across the South and in their new Northern ghettos. They were not just another immigrant group like the Irish, the Germans, the Italians, or the Jews, who had eventually moved into the mainstream. Their race consciousness was both self-imposed and outwardly reinforced by white America.

In the South the chronic need for cotton laborers meant that the presence of blacks was tolerated. And while they were needed, Southern state governments and individuals tried to prevent black cotton workers from moving north during the Great Migration. Only when mechanization arrived would white Southerners abandon their interest in black workers.

PART SIX

Cotton Without Slaves, 1865–1930

Slave labor is now gone and the legitimate sovereignty of cotton is an assured fact. Three-fourths of this great crop, which must be relied on to clothe civilization, and in the exploitation of which, two billions of capital are used, is raised in the South. It is a stupendous God-made monopoly.... —Edwin A. Alderman, president, University of Virginia, 1908

CHAPTER TWENTY-TWO

King Cotton Expands

AFTER the Civil War, America discovered with relief that cotton could indeed be grown without slave labor. And despite the destruction of the conflict, the South would produce exponentially more cotton than before the war. Although it did not regain the dominance of its prewar position, cotton nevertheless reigned as America's most important foreign export from 1803 to 1937.

Following the Civil War, the restoration of an internationally competitive cotton production system was seen as vital to the continued economic health of the United States and necessary for the absorption of millions of newly freed black laborers. The Freedmen's Bureau, for the most part, became an employment agency for cotton farms. Without promising alternatives, the freedmen ultimately remained trapped in the cotton world by white Northerners who wanted their votes but not their presence or their ownership of land.

The lure of cotton still mesmerized the agricultural South, which had hitched its economic future to the economic fortunes of that single crop. Wherever cotton could go, the agricultural South followed. Certainly industrialization emerged, but a large part of the South remained dependent on cotton. Predictable consequences followed. The black cotton laborer remained the vital cog in the cotton-producing machine. And most of the former slaves and their progeny would remain landless and politically disfranchised—chained to the soil and to an arbitrary wage system. There were, to be sure, black and white farmers who owned small farms, but we will concentrate on the large plantation owner and the black sharecropper, the two most visible actors in the cotton South from the end of the Civil War to full mechanization in the mid-twentieth century.

Paradoxically, the cotton business embodied a sophisticated international financial and trading system while cotton production, often referred to as feudal, remained nonmechanized. Despite an enormous effort by inventors and farm implement companies, cotton production remained impervious to mechanization until the successful experiments of the 1930s. Other major nineteenth-century American industries—railroads and steel—were influenced by technology and the ubiquitous tendency toward massive consolidation. But, as an example of its backwardness, cotton production fared poorly even by comparison with wheat farming, which by the 1850s had benefited from better plows and the widespread use of the labor-saving McCormick reaper. In 1800 it took 3.3 times the amount of time to cultivate an acre of cotton as an acre of wheat; by 1930 the ratio was 9 times. In 1930 the techniques of cotton production closely resembled the methods employed in 1865. Cotton still needed to be "chopped" and picked by hand; the mule was the only "machine." The result was a highly labor-intensive business in a society characterized by a racial caste system.

In a trading sense, however, after the Civil War cotton would become even more firmly established as the first truly integrated global industry. Cotton-trading exchanges were no longer confined to Liverpool, Manchester, New York, New Orleans, Memphis, Bremen, and Le Havre. Other cities—Milan and Osaka, for example—had active cotton exchanges, and private transactions took place in Barcelona, Alexandria, Shanghai, and Bombay. By the 1920s Japanese cotton salesmen, who had spent considerable time studying cotton growing in the United States, were traveling in rickshas down narrow streets in Osaka to offer cotton to Japanese textile mills.

After the Civil War the financial apparatus for trading cotton, as opposed to producing it, grew still more sophisticated. The advent of the transatlantic cable in the 1860s, the increased use of the telegraph, and the growth of rail transportation allowed a mature trading system

The Cotton Corner in Liverpool. After the Civil War the city's cotton exchange remained at the hub of international trading.

to develop. These advances led to a systematic effort to organize public information on the price at which cotton was transacted. In 1865 the U.S. Department of Agriculture began to publish information about cotton prices, cotton supply, and cotton demand. Cotton exchanges, particularly in New York and New Orleans, began actively trading cotton for future delivery—a valuable service for cotton mills and cotton participants.

Cotton production continued to grow because the world's population was buying more clothes made from cotton. The cotton textile industry expanded dramatically after the Civil War to meet this need, thus creating the demand for raw cotton. In America alone the number of spindles—the weaving unit in the textile process—increased from 5.2 million that consumed 422.7 million pounds of cotton in 1860, to 27.2 million spindles that used 2,232 million pounds of cotton in 1910. In the same period the value of American textile products increased from $115.7 million to $616.5 million. By 1910 the world's textile industry counted 142 million spindles. On the eve of World War I the measurable world consumption of cotton was 20 million bales. Postwar growth in U.S. cotton acreage, after a dip to 8.6 million acres in 1870, grew astoundingly, from 12 to 13 million in 1860 to almost 46 million in 1925. This led to a production increase of the "indispensable product" from 4.8 million bales in 1860 to 17 million bales in 1931.

But along with this impressive expansion of cotton output, risk remained fundamental to cotton production. From the earliest days of America's love affair with cotton, planters, laborers, and buyers alike had lamented the fickle nature of the crop and the many hazards involved in growing and selling it. The years after the Civil War were no exception as the all-important price of cotton remained a major determinant in the general well-being of the cotton South. The roller-coaster cotton economy continued. Before the Civil War, an increase in cotton production occurred within the framework of a steady rise in demand, which meant remarkable relative price stability over time. Over the next seventy-five years, the expansion of cotton acreage and cotton production met a harsher fate. Demand grew, but at a relatively slower pace than before. And occasional cotton shortages led to British "cotton famines." The cotton shortfall in 1903 led to the closing of one-quarter to one-half of Britain's textile mill production capacity.

The economic laws of supply and demand bedeviled the cotton farmer. While the supply of raw cotton continued to grow, the trend of cotton prices told another story. As one observer noted in 1904, "When southern cotton prices drop, every man feels the blow; when cotton prices advance, every industry throbs with vigor." From 1880 to 1890, acreage moved from almost 16 million to 21 million while production increased from 6.6 million to 8.6 million bales. Yet the price dropped to five to six cents a pound in the 1890s, and in 1893 a South Carolinian estimated that three-fourths of the cotton farmers were insolvent. A price rebound to seventeen cents by 1903 salved the farmer's discontent. The greatest acreage occurred in 1925–1926 when 45 million acres were planted and more than 16 million bales harvested. The year 1923 witnessed a price of 29 cents a pound, and the calamity of 1931 saw 17 million bales produced at 6 cents a pound. The statistics are straightforward, but the average price over time disguises the catastrophic price declines that wiped out farmers in 1873, 1893, 1920, and the early 1930s with five-to-six-cent cotton.

The statistics do not show the damage done by floods, droughts, or insects on individual farmers. Obviously cotton farmers were not the only American farmers to suffer during depressions, price debacles, and bad weather. Many of the grievances of the agrarian populist movement of the late nineteenth century were shared by all American farmers; but the racial component of cotton farming gave an added dimension to the cotton world.

The dictates of the natural world added another component of risk. For farmers using nonirrigated cotton land, weather caused enormous anxiety. Even prosperous times and locations, like the Natchez region, succumbed to eroded and worn-out soil. Even with fertilizers, cotton farmers faced soil depletion. Rainfall was required at critical times in the growth of the water-guzzling cotton plant. One farmer might receive a timely rain while his neighbor gazed wistfully at his dry fields. Flooding near rivers and on rich bottom lands raised havoc. The Mississippi Delta–born writer David Cohn knew that Mississippians feared just two things, "the wrath of God and the Mississippi River." He could have added: the price of cotton. Insects too were always a threat—first the army worm, then the boll weevil, either of which could destroy an entire crop.

Credit policies and accompanying financing determined the practices of the cotton business. When a farmer decided to grow cotton, he became a commercial farmer who sold his crop in the international market and was subject to the rules, rewards, and pitfalls of a business. Any notion of growing foodstuffs for personal consumption became subordinate to the cash crop. Credit became the paramount consideration; cotton and cotton society conformed to it. Cotton required credit and credit demanded repayment, which virtually required that the farmer grow only cotton, the money crop. Thus cotton credit almost precluded attempts to diversify Southern agriculture into potential food production. After all, supplies had to be purchased.

Cotton was not the sole culprit; all staple crops tend to reduce or eliminate food production as the farmer, like all Americans, tries to maximize income rather than produce his own food and grain. But once-a-year crop harvests mean once-a-year payment. With no income stream during the year, both planter and tenant must borrow. The risky cotton business becomes even more treacherous because of this reliance on one unpredictable payment at harvest time.

Although the South's agricultural methods were considered inefficient, her credit policies exploitative, and her labor system oppressive, American cotton production was feared and envied by the world powers. It was extolled as "the only natural monopoly of a world-wide necessity." Cotton production statistics reveal America's preeminent position. At the beginning of World War I in 1914–1915, the United States produced 16.5 million bales while the production of other countries paled in comparison—India accounted for 5 million bales, Egypt 1.3 million bales, and Russia 1.3 million bales. The value of cotton exports in 1913 was equally dramatic: U.S. cotton exports were valued at $1 billion, followed by India at $170 million and Egypt at $155 million.

In the period before World War I, cotton was critical to American foreign trade. In 1911 the United States exported cotton worth $639 million (including $28 million of manufactured cotton goods). The other leading export contributors lagged strikingly: wheat and flour $142 million, iron and steel manufactures $106 million, and copper manufactures $144 million. Since the positive U.S. trade balance was $489 million, cotton entirely accounted for it, aiding monetary stability and enhancing American borrowing capacity. The average annual trade surplus during the five years 1910–1914 was $514 million while average annual raw cotton exports were $551 million. Since the value of cotton exports exceeded the amount of the trade surplus, it has been suggested that "our debts . . . [were] paid in cotton."

Despite the primitive nature of American cotton farming, with its production and market risks and a racial caste system, prodigious foreign efforts could not supplant American cotton. At the end of the nineteenth century the British and the Europeans were still trying to rid themselves of their dependence on American cotton. The British anxiety of the 1850s recurred in 1902 when the British Cotton Growing Association was organized. It aimed at "establishing and extending the growth of cotton in the British Empire" in order to free "Lancashire from its dangerous dependence on the United States for raw material."

The quality of cotton in disputes between buyers and sellers in Liverpool was arbitrated by disinterested parties who were members of the city's Cotton Association.

The situation worried even the king of England. In a message to Parliament in 1904, Edward VII declared:

> The insufficiency of the raw material upon which the cotton industry of this country depends has inspired me with great concern. I trust that the efforts which are being made in the various parts of my Empire to increase the area under cultivation may be attended with a large measure of success.

That same year the English Master Spinner's Federation sponsored a convention of sixty-five European delegates who sought alternatives to the American cotton monopoly. Reminiscent of the 1850s, Europeans yearned for supplies from India, Egypt, and Africa. By 1910, Sir Herbert Dixon of Manchester had already registered pessimism over the prospects for Egyptian cotton. Its volume and quality had deteriorated. Twelve years of British efforts to develop and increase cotton production in India, Uganda, West Africa, the Anglo-Egyptian Sudan, and

An English sample boy in the Liverpool cotton market carries samples from one office to another.

the West Indies yielded 360,000 bales. Increased production from the empire did not materialize before Britain's textile industry succumbed to Asian competition and before Britain lost its colonies.

Germany was very much irritated by its need for American cotton. In 1902 the chairman of the Kolonial Wirtschaftliches Komitee (KWK, the Colonial Economic Committee) referred to German purchases of 320 million marks' worth of cotton from America as a "tribute payment." The Germans fostered cotton production in their West African colony of Togoland. In 1900 the KWK hired four black cotton specialists from Tuskegee Institute and sent them to Togo, seeking a "scientific rationalization and transformation of the indigenous Togo cotton growers' methods." Yet the Germans, who had created a sophisticated industrial sector, could not develop a viable cotton production business.

American cotton was always less expensive in the German and Liverpool markets. The Portuguese cotton experience in Mozambique was so harsh that in the 1990s, "peasants throughout Mozambique insist that 'cotton is the mother of poverty.'" In general, Britain and other European countries failed in their attempts to supplant the American cotton-production monopoly.

CHAPTER TWENTY-THREE

The Controlling Laws of
Cotton Finance

 FINANCE reduced the white planter and the black laborer to pawns in a business world ruled by profit and loss, not by the laws of an idealized agricultural utopia. Cotton production required financing for land, seed, equipment, supplies, and wages. In the world of private commercial activity, finance would ultimately determine the organization of cotton farming. Financial culprits, the credit system, and crop liens have long been identified by economists and historians as principal causes of the South's economic and racial woes. But these analysts are hard pressed to offer alternatives that might have developed in the real-world environment. Finance was not an afterthought; it was the driving force in shaping the Southern agricultural world that involved one payday in the entire year. Four million blacks were an integral part of the cotton world and distinctly absent from the industrial economy at the beginning of the post–Civil War period.

Because of its distinctive qualities, cotton farming prompted financing methods that were different from those of the modern business economy. Business corporations could be financed by the impersonal securities market and through bank loans, with or without collateral. Securities could be bought and sold within burgeoning capital markets by Europeans and Americans. The financing of railroads, the largest growth industry of the late nineteenth century, was largely a function of stock and bond markets. Publicly owned railroad companies that serviced cotton-producing areas were the closest (but still an indirect) connection with the financing apparatus of the securities market. Railroads that operated in cotton country, like the Illinois Central, derived enormous profits from cotton production, but unlike cotton farms they could be financed by stocks and bonds. The trend toward business concentration, a feature of the late-nineteenth-century industrial landscape, linked the securities markets ever closer to the machinations of Wall Street.

The *financing* of cotton production did not resemble the modern techniques of cotton *trading*. Cotton production required its own set of financing rules if it was to function. It did not follow the path toward concentration growing up around it. Instead a much-maligned financing system evolved to fit the particular needs and risks of King Cotton. Regardless of the size of his operation, a cotton farmer had to borrow. For money he went to the cotton merchant and the financial institution.

As noted earlier, before the Civil War, cotton factors played many roles—merchant, cotton broker, and lender. If a farmer/planter could not repay interest or principal, the lender extended the loan or foreclosed. The process of reselling the farmer's assets—slaves, land, livestock, equipment, and buildings—was subject to market risk and tempered the decision to foreclose. In times of a general price decline in cotton, a surfeit of land and slaves rendered the market mechanism dysfunctional. Lenders were left holding unwanted human or physical collateral.

Another important consideration was that lending to small farmers was cumbersome and treacherous. Large-scale farming operations were simply easier to analyze and monitor. In 1860 there were approximately 450,000 farms producing cotton in the United States, of which only 12,500 were of more than 500 acres. By 1876 the number of farms had actually increased, but the average farm size had dropped from 401 acres in 1860 to 229 acres. In 1876 there were 618,000 cotton farms, an increase of 37 percent from 1860.

A complex financing issue thus became even more difficult after the war. The lack of Southern capital, the absence of an effective

Southern banking system, the increase in the number of farms, the removal of slaves as financing collateral, and the general physical and political disarray of the cotton South contributed to the postwar financing conundrum. The actual value of farm land and buildings declined from $1.5 billion in 1860 to $764 million in 1870. Antebellum plantations that had been worth $100,000 to $150,000 sold after the war for $6,000 to $10,000. Slaves, as a major source of collateral and wealth, disappeared. A slaveowner had been able to borrow by mortgaging his "human property." Estimates of the asset value of slaves in the five leading cotton production states range from $1.6 billion to several billion dollars. Some sources estimate that slaves constituted half of all cotton wealth. But these statistics overstate the real value of slaves as an asset category and a financing tool. The figures are static in a dynamic environment. As we have seen, slave prices fluctuated with the price of cotton, which was subject to the whims of supply and demand. The aggregate number in the billions is unrealistic because any large number of slaves for sale would reduce their value. After the war, as long as free labor produced cotton, a revenue stream was generated and hence financing would be available.

Even the antebellum cotton factorage arrangement died after the war. The location of factors in the major Southern ports made sense before the war because cotton was transported almost exclusively along rivers to the ports, where it was loaded onto oceangoing vessels for shipment to Europe and the American North. After the war, railroads replaced the riverboats as the primary conduit for cotton. Inland merchants generally based at railroad stations were much better situated to provide local services to cotton farmers. The port-based cotton factors were thus brought down by the railroads.

The postwar conversion of slave labor to free labor—and the concurrent loss of slave collateral and cotton factors—demanded a new financial infrastructure. Into this void stepped new lenders—country merchants and, secondarily, moneylenders and banks. The merchants are regularly portrayed as Shylocks who forced farmers to abandon all for money-generating cotton. But no bank or merchant, foreign or American, would finance a cotton farmer without sufficient creditworthiness or without recourse to an asset that could be used as collateral in the event a farmer could not repay a loan. A conventional bank loan was not an option because of the nature of cotton farming. What assets did a cotton farmer possess? Land was an inadequate asset for purposes of lending until the end of the nineteenth century, when larger farms evolved and were able to use normal bank loans. The cotton farmers' only creditworthy asset that afforded practical marketability was their physical product, cotton. And cotton's attractiveness as a readily marketable commodity asset was further enhanced because of its imperishable nature. King Cotton would not starve for want of credit.

Because of his proximity to the cotton grower, the country merchant was best positioned to judge the competence and creditworthiness of his borrowers. In return for lending money and supplying the cotton farmer with seed, food, and clothing, the merchant demanded cotton. This meant obligating the cotton farmer to plant cotton and market his crop through the merchant. The merchant charged what was considered to be a usurious rate of interest, from 25 to 100 percent on loans and on markups of goods sold to the farmer. In effect the cotton farmer was charged twice—an interest fee on a monetary loan, and a credit price on goods that was higher than the cash price. Since there was no cash except during the fall when cotton was sold, purchases were made on credit.

The merchants, "once on the periphery of the plantation economy," moved to "center stage." As might be expected, their numbers increased substantially. The Natchez district counted 130 merchants in 1860, 218 in 1870, and 283 in 1880. The white landowner often served as middleman between the merchant and the black tenant farmer. In this case, the freedmen tenants would obtain permission from the landowner to purchase goods from the merchant, who would charge the landlord. In many cases the landlord would then mark up the goods sold to the freedmen. After the crop was sold, the landlord would pay the merchant for his freedmen's purchases, and the tenants would pay the landlord. The merchants' activities were thus predominantly local, with little opportunity to expand because of the time-consuming chore of managing poor credit risks. In the Natchez area this tiered system left the freedmen as permanent tenants, a mudsill class. By 1900 a mere 5 percent of black farmers owned land.

The backbone of the system was the notorious crop "lien" laws, which codified antebellum practices. Before the Civil War, planters had at times resorted to loans that were based on pledges of a crop or a crop about to be planted. In other words, the crop was mortgaged to the lender in return for a loan. After the war, too, a farmer would pledge his crop to a lender in return for credit—sometimes to more than one lender. But state governments soon introduced the crop lien law, hoping to encourage lending in order to stimulate much-needed cotton production. This law dictated that a lender was entitled to a creditor's crop before anyone else or before any other claim. The infamous crop lien was not specifically designed as a conspiracy to defraud farmers. The crop lien arose because it was needed; it evolved because lenders had no choice. If a repayment problem occurred, the crop lien made it clear that the lender with a crop lien would have first right to the cotton crop. Because of the fragmented nature of cotton farming, the terms of a crop lien—interest rate, amount, marketing terms for the cotton, and payment date—were flexible because no one knew how much cotton would be produced, when the cotton might be sold, or what expenses would be. Mississippi enacted the first crop lien law in 1867; it was optimistically called "An Act for the Encouragement of Agriculture." Most Southern states followed suit with similar legislation.

The economist Mathew Hammond described the impact of the lien: "When one of these mortgages has been recorded against a southern farmer, he has usually passed into a state of helpless peonage to the merchant who has become his creditor." Once his crop was mortgaged, the farmer could borrow from no other lender because he had no collateral of value. Because of the nature of cotton farming, few farmers were able to save enough money to free themselves from the perpetual money chain of the creditor merchant.

Historians have sanctimoniously vilified the merchant lenders and the lien laws without suggesting how things could have been different. The lien laws have been called a "curse of the soil," a "new evil," and "one of the strangest contractual relationships in the history of finance." This "new evil" was thought to have inflicted more "permanent injury to the South than the ancient evil" of slavery itself. Crop liens are blamed for the South's being held captive to cotton production and debt peonage, a perennial bondage to the lender. The cotton farmer, it is thought, was compelled to choose a total reliance on cotton, to the exclusion of diversification:

> The explanation for the persistent concentration on cotton after 1865 is that cotton farmers were effectively prevented from practicing self-sufficiency as a means of escaping the merchant's power. They were locked in to cotton production.

The creditor-merchant was accused of dictating terms. North Carolina farmers, in an 1887 survey, explained:

> We ought to plant less [cotton and tobacco] and more grain and grasses but how are we to do it; the man who furnishes us rations at 50 percent interest won't let us; he wants money crop planted.
>
> We shall be swallowed up by the commission merchants. . . . It is cotton! cotton! cotton! Buy everything and make cotton pay for it.

Cotton farmers spoke consistently of the forced addiction to cotton. One observer noted, "All that has kept them from [self-sufficiency] was trying to raise a crop that would bring money to pay their debts." In 1895 an Alabama farmer reported to a Senate investigating committee that "Cotton raising has grown to be a necessity more than a choice." If the cotton farmer had been left to his own devices, historians and economists assume, he would have diversified and would not have had to pay for his food.

But the stringent conditions of the South's postwar financial system came into being because, as C. Vann Woodward argued, there "was no other means of getting credit." Finance is amoral; it will respond to the theoretical opportunity to make money within an existing legal and cultural framework. Retrospective criticism of the South's credit system is without substantive alternatives that could have met the problems of a once-a-year payment to farmers, the risks of cotton production, the small-farm fragmentation of cotton cultivation, and the overwhelming priority of white America to reestablish cotton production. How could cotton laborers be paid weekly or monthly if the farmer had his money only once a year? What creditor would lend money if other creditors had a prior claim? The economic demand for cotton allowed a viable

but harsh system to develop. Interest rates may have seemed high
and the legal system may have seemed exploitative, but no alternative
presented itself. Cotton was too important to discard, so the crop-lien
system prevailed. As we shall see, technology, not morality or politics,
would finally revolutionize the cotton production system.

Did the merchant-lenders charge exorbitant or even extortionary
rates of interest? Practices varied among communities and merchants,
but even so, charges of 30 to 100 percent seem high. Yet the absolute
rate level does not appear high when the merchant's risks or actual
profits are considered. The American South represented a decentralized, cumbersome credit market that required protection for the
lender. An accurate measure of profitability in the financial world is
the number of competitors who enter a business. If cotton merchants
and lenders had been getting rich, Americans would have flocked to
these occupations in the South to chase wealth. The numbers increased,
but there was no mass movement. The much-maligned merchant was
plagued with a steady stream of defaults, indicating that his fees were
a reflection of his own risks and borrowing costs.

Just as before the Civil War, money flowed down from New York
and the Eastern cities, this time to the merchants and country banks.
Cotton profits traveled back upstream to the money centers. Historians
call the South's cotton economy a version of imperial oppression:

> The immemorial pattern of colonialism—the dependence upon the
> sale of cheap raw materials on a world market and upon buying
> back manufactured goods from protected industrial and commercial
> areas—continued to hold sway in the South despite the much-vaunted
> "industrial revolution."

In other words, the imperialist power, the American North, was selling manufactured goods in a protected market in return for cheap
raw materials, in this case cotton. According to this interpretation, the
cotton South, utterly defeated in war, now remained under occupation by Northern financial and commercial warriors. It suffered under
government-sponsored high tariffs and Northern industrial trusts that
imposed excessive, monopoly-generated rates. The resulting poverty
led to a general agricultural populist revolt and at times an alliance

between farmers in the West and the South. Federal appropriations in the form of land subsidies went to railroads and businessmen, not for Southern infrastructure projects or relief from drought and floods. In fact, as we have seen, the cotton South had been heavily dependent on the commercial North before the Civil War. In both circumstances, blacks were pawns in an economic game.

*

The lien system was onerous but a reflection of reality. Chief among the realities of the business side of cotton was its price. The credit system—regardless of its legal and social inequities—was tied to the price of cotton. The price of cotton and natural conditions, which the merchant, the bank, or the New York financier could not control, determined whether the cotton farmer was in debt or solvent. The price of cotton ultimately determined interest rates, credit charges for purchases, and thus the ability of the farmer to diversify. A long-term trend of stable and rising prices would have brought better terms and conditions for the farmer. Unfortunately the price of cotton was volatile, with no discernible upward trend in an environment where cotton supply was exploding. In 1894, for example, the production of 23 million acres of cotton throughout the South, when the price was 4.6 cents a pound, yielded less revenue than the 9 million acres cultivated in the panic year of 1873, when cotton sold for 14.1 cents.

The importance of cotton caused contemporary observers to focus on the elusive profitability of cotton production. In 1883, John Peabody of Georgia attributed the woes of the system to the price of cotton after the Civil War.

> I think the peculiar difficulties existing grow out of the fact that the people here were led by the high price of cotton just after the war into a craze of cotton-raising. . . . It was very easy to sit down with a pencil and figure out how many bales of cotton each hand would make, and what it would cost the planter to buy his corn and meat, and how many bales of cotton he would produce, and how much money he would make at 20, 25, or 35 cents a pound, and the result of the calculation was so encouraging many went into the business who knew

nothing about it. They usually went into it upon borrowed money, and
if it so happened that cotton declined in price, or some other disaster
happened to the planter, he was unable to meet his obligations. . . .

Peabody's comments could have applied equally to the 1830s or the
1920s. The optimistic projections he notes are pervasive in financial
history. Simplistic extrapolations may be found in crude calculations or
on sophisticated computer spreadsheets. The rosy scenarios are based
on price assumptions that may or may not be accurate. Cotton's past
episodes of glory and the hope of favorable prices provided a powerful,
long-lasting attachment to risky dreams of wealth.

Too, the post–Civil War price of cotton may have been affected by
more than temporary supply-demand imbalances. Gavin Wright has
attributed the "timing of southern economic spurts and relapses" to a
structural weakness in demand. Antebellum demand for cotton, in his
study, grew at a robust annual rate of 5 percent. Between 1860 and the
1880s, demand fell and "stagnated." Between 1880 and 1900, demand
grew 2.7 percent annually. From 1900 to 1920, the boom in the textile
industry prompted annual growth of 3.5 percent. The fickle 1920s saw
an anemic 0.5 percent growth. In light of the excessive supply of cotton and the relative waning of demand, one can understand the severe
price swings for the farmer who was wedded to cotton either by credit
or vision.

*

All roads from the cotton fields led to the credit markets, and the credit
markets led to New York. King Cotton was chained to the financial
world. The creditor would lend only to produce a revenue stream that
would pay off the debt. The world of cotton conformed to the financial
structure that accounted for the risks. Certainly no ameliorating circumstances were available in the nineteenth-century world. In 1899 a
Georgia cotton planter and merchant succinctly summarized the financial process in testimony before the U.S. Industrial Commission:

Question: How do they [Southern farmers] get supplies?
Answer: Through merchants.
Question: And the merchants?

Answer: Through the banks.

Question: And where do the local banks get money?

Answer: New York.

In 1922 a Federal Trade Commission report confirmed the preeminence of New York's position in cotton credit. The report found that 36 percent of all cotton loans came from New York—three times the amount supplied by New Orleans, the largest Southern banking center. New York retained its influence as financial king of the cotton trade through its banks and the New York Cotton Exchange. Southerners were still befuddled by the grip that New York and Northern banking centers had on cotton revenue.

In 1910 an Atlanta editor, Henry Reed, resurrected the hope of breaking the chain of dependence on Northern finance. He advocated the same measures as those of the cotton convention in the 1830s—"ample warehousing facilities" in the cotton South and a "great cotton bank and trust company, capitalized and managed in the sole interest of the cotton crop." He bemoaned the fact that "The new gold which cotton brings from foreign lands is of such vast sums that it is absolutely unwise to permit it to be returned to New York instead of to New Orleans. . . ."

Periodic slumps in cotton prices, particularly in the 1890s, caused the cotton South and the agricultural West to lash out at the culprits from Gotham. Senate committees became venues for endless discussions about the cause of cotton's price woes. The futures markets, high tariffs, and the demonetization of silver were prime suspects.

As in most economic crises, Wall Street was demonized along with the futures market and the abstractions of the market process. Agrarian radicals blamed the futures markets for manipulating the price of cotton. Brokers and speculators were the villains who reduced farmers to poverty by forcing prices down. The physical world of the cotton planter clashed with the abstract world of finance. In John Faulkner's novel *Dollar Cotton*, the scoundrel white cotton farmer Otis Towne is informed by the president of the New York Stock Exchange that "Supply and Demand controls the price of Cottons." In desperation and about to lose his farm, Towne responds, ". . . and supply and demand is them numbers them fellers chalks up on blackboards? . . . You fellers

don't know whut hit's wuth to grow things. . . . You fellers never put no
seed in the ground and saw it come through a plant with little branches
and little leaves on it. . . . They ain't even a bale of cotton setting on
that floor where them fellers is saying whut hit's wuth." But Towne's
frustration was no match for the laws of economics.

The panacea of crop diversification appealed to the idealistic observer but was never a realistic possibility as the need to produce cash
revenues intensified. When prices rose in the early part of the twentieth century, anger abated, then disappeared. Boom times brought
further increases in production, and financial memory was buried by
another bout of temporary prosperity for cotton.

The invisible hand of finance played a crucial role in dictating the
conditions of cotton production. The crop lien was merely a logical extension of the financial system. It was easy to mock this device as "one
of the strangest contractual relationships in the history of finance."
The humor vanishes under the matter-of-fact reasoning of a South
Carolinian in 1880: "A mortgage given in January or February on a
crop [that is] not to be planted until April is not taken as a first-class
commercial security, and consequently the charges on the advances are
heavy." A traditional banker would have been perplexed at the thought
of loaning money for an unplanted crop, pledged for a loan whose
amount was unspecified. After the Civil War the increase in cotton
supply and the moderating of demand exacerbated the risk profile of
cotton production. The foreordained path of the cotton economy was
due to financial logic, not Northern design.

CHAPTER TWENTY-FOUR

The Delta Plantation:
Labor and Land

 THE PLANTATION and the black sharecropper are the most compelling part of the cotton-and-race story. Some antebellum plantation owners managed to retain their holdings for generations after the Civil War; some lost their land. To be sure, cheap land allowed some black and white farmers to own small farms. Some whites became tenants, some survived as owners, some drifted into sharecropping, and some emerged as planters. Over time a racial labor caste system developed, which conformed to the realities of cotton finance and dominant attitudes about race. And it was inevitable that the fragmented cotton production structure, with its thousands of individual farms, would succumb to consolidation. Each cotton farm produced roughly the same product, except for grades, so the importance of keeping costs low and production high promoted the development of larger, well-run farms; but this consolidation bore no resemblance to that of the manufacturing world. In cotton, growth meant the purchase of more land and the employment of more black labor.

In 1881 both Henry Grady, the influential editor of the *Atlanta Constitution*, and Frank C. Morehead, president of the National Cotton Planters Association, expressed enthusiasm for the Mississippi Delta's potential. They thought the 20 river counties that abutted the

Mississippi River from Memphis to Baton Rouge could by themselves better the record American crop of 6.6 million bales produced in 1880. First and foremost among these counties were those of the Mississippi Delta. Southern visionaries touted the ability of these counties to produce their own grain and foodstuffs. Labor, it was believed, would gravitate quickly to the land. A rail system would provide efficient transportation. In short, "the cotton kingdom would become as efficient as any northern factory system," make profits as never before, and thus provide general prosperity for a New South. These were tall expectations.

The interaction between the cotton plantation owner and the black sharecropper may best be observed in the frontier environment of the Mississippi Delta. The Delta developed into a land characterized by large plantations with tenant arrangements for its black laborers.

An area comprising 7,200 square miles, the Mississippi Delta, the most fertile cotton land in the world, extends from Memphis to Vicksburg and is bounded on the west by the Mississippi River and on the east roughly by the Yazoo River. Almost 70 percent of the Delta was settled after the Civil War. Freedmen came there in another version of the biblical "Promised Land" parable. Land was cheap, and the unpopulated, vast Delta seemed to offer the potential for thousands of freedmen to own or rent land on attractive terms, without the need for confiscation or redistribution. The rich alluvial floodplain attracted settlers with an eye on cotton wealth. A diligent farmer could purchase land and sell timber to pay off his debt. First the land speculators came, then the railroads, then the permanent settlers, the white and black cotton farmers.

The Delta is truly the quintessential intersection between cotton and race. Cotton dominated the economy; blacks dominated the population. It was in the Mississippi Delta that cotton and culture combined to produce the musical genre of the blues, which has earned the region a reputation as a "primary taproot of black culture and history in America." It has been referred to as the "greatest single subregional contributor to the stream of black migrants to the urban North." As one of the spokesmen for the Delta Chamber of Commerce noted in 1938, more than 40 percent of all cotton produced in America bloomed within two hundred miles in any direction of the Mississippi Delta.

In this famous photograph circa 1900, J. C. Couvert captured a farm manager weighing cotton just picked. Note that the farm laborer is sternly monitoring his activity because she will be paid according to her production.

The Delta's potential was recognized soon after the Civil War. In 1870 the scalawag governor of Mississippi, James A. Alcorn, wrote of the need for levees to unleash the Delta's cotton potential, "England, France, Austria, Italy, etc. are united in a simultaneous effort . . . for the reversal of the triumph of American skill and energy which has made us superior in the cotton markets of the world." Opening the Delta would "swell the national treasury by hundreds of millions of gold dollars . . . aid in the construction of levees of the Delta of the Yazoo would insure America's cotton supremacy" and would benefit "every state in the Union." Other than the Mississippi River, the most serious problem for white plantation owners was the labor shortage—or, as cotton planter Leroy Percy identified it, "the supply of Negroes."

The state wanted money and immigrants. And to fill these needs, speculators and railroad developers eagerly stepped in, setting the pace for the postwar economy. In 1881 the state's levee commissioners sold 774,000 acres of Delta land to the Memphis and Vicksburg Railroad for 8.5 cents an acre. Earlier, land had been offered for as little as two cents an acre. The land speculator Thomas Watson purchased a half share in 706,397 acres for 20 cents an acre. In 1889, Augustus Hawks of England bought 10,000 acres in Sunflower County for $1.50 an acre.

A 1903 publication described the process of coaxing people to the Mississippi Delta, the final frontier. Planters and speculators would offer timberland "rent free" to black tenants "for three years." The tenants would keep all the cotton and corn they raised while they cleared timber and brought the "soil under cultivation." Timber production, the intermediate step between forest and cotton field, allowed the clearing process to be profitable.

The Delta's population expanded ultimately because of cotton production. Between 1870 and 1880 the black population grew from 44,000 to 88,712 while the white population expanded from 12,786 to 20,825. New towns sprouted; old ones like Vicksburg grew from 4,591 people in 1860 to 12,443 in 1870. Some promoters encouraged freedmen to emigrate; others sought to attract Chinese or European labor. Labor agents used hyperbole to describe the Mississippi Delta as a place "where cotton grew so tall it could be picked only from horseback" and where "money could be gathered from the trees." Prompted by their own bad crops and the promises of labor agents, thousands of freedmen migrated, particularly in 1873–1874, to the Delta from Alabama in covered wagons and on the Vicksburg and Meridian Railroad.

As we have seen throughout the postwar South, the settlement of the Delta's interior was contingent on the growth of rail transportation. The movement of cotton by rail rather than steamboat was essential. In 1882 the railroad builder Collis P. Huntington, along with the New York banker Richard T. Wilson, embarked on a scheme to traverse the Delta with a rail line that would run from Memphis to New Orleans. The goal was a lucrative business in hauling cotton to market. In the process the entrepreneurs purchased two small existing rail lines that owned 774,000 acres in the Delta. One of them, the Louisville, New Orleans, and Texas Railway, brought more freedmen to work the land, more settlers to own it, and more buyers to trade in cotton and related

Staggering amounts of cotton were transported by steamboat before railroads penetrated the Southern interior after the Civil War.

goods. As with all American endeavors, land and credit were the inducements to this brave new world.

The LNO&T's profitability and location soon attracted the interest of the giant Illinois Central. When Collis Huntington encountered serious debt problems, the IC took advantage of the magnate's vulnerability and in 1892 bought the LNO&T, which was now called the Yazoo and Mississippi Valley Railroad (Y&MV). Because of the IC's Eastern investors, New York's financial tentacles now extended indirectly to the Mississippi Delta, which the IC traversed with its rail monopoly. And while cotton production profits might be unstable, the IC's cotton country profits soared. In the years 1888 to 1892, local traffic increased by 117.2 percent. Even though no new tracks were added, gross receipts per mile continued to rise—from $4,111 in 1892 to $5,901 in 1898, even during the depression of 1893. The IC's president, Stuyvesant Fish, who along with directors of the IC and Speaker of the House of Representatives Joe Cannon owned a 10,000-acre plantation in the Delta, enthusiastically reported that gross receipts of the Y&MV were higher than the parent had earned "in any year from 1887 to 1890." In addition, the IC changed its credit policies to encourage large land purchases. From 1894 to 1897 the railroad sold almost all of its 579,000 acres for $6.18 to $7.32 an acre; in 1896 land was offered at as high as $15 an acre. The terms were a 20 percent cash down payment, the remainder to be paid in two to five years at an annual interest rate of 6 percent. It is important to note that a warranty deed was given with the initial down payment. This meant that cotton production could be financed via a mortgage loan rather than a crop lien. And the fact that the land plots were large was a key to obtaining bank lending.

Chicago's business ties with the South, especially the physical connection via the IC, prompted a reconciliation ceremony in 1895 between the white North and the white South. The purpose was to foster business rapport. The timing of the celebration coincided with the dedication of a statue in Chicago's Oakwood Cemetery to commemorate the Confederate soldiers who died at the notorious Camp Douglas prison camp nearby. John C. Underwood, a Confederate veteran, determined that more than 100,000 Chicagoans attended the dedication of the statue, which cost $25,000 to erect. The Mississippian Stephen D. Lee addressed his hosts: "We accept your friendship . . . we invite you again to invade us, not with your bayonets this time, but with your business. We want to hear in our land the voices of your industries." The Chicagoan Frederick Peck wanted "closer commercial relations and business union between citizens of our country, thus enlisting in a larger degree of investment of the capital of this section in developing the vast resources of the southern states."

The Illinois Central eagerly promoted its profitable Delta franchise. In 1910 the IC's marketing materials hailed the Delta as a prosperous plantation region:

> Nowhere in Mississippi have antebellum conditions of landholding been so nearly preserved as in the Delta. . . . The Negro is naturally gregarious in instinct, and is never so happy as when massed in large numbers on the Delta plantations.

The IC, of course, sought to enhance its own traffic by portraying the Delta in a positive image.

A Yazoo and Mississippi Valley Railroad bond. The line, owned by the Illinois Central (which was in turn controlled by New York capitalists), was the central transportation artery for the Mississippi Delta cotton kingdom.

Like Northern states, Mississippi did not want black labor. Cotton planters tried diligently but unsuccessfully to recruit Chinese and Europeans to work in the cotton fields. Efforts were made to foster immigration, particularly of Italians, but even Chinese—because of their reputation for thriftiness and industry—were considered more attractive than blacks. Labor agents promised to bring workers to the Mississippi Delta from China for a fee of fifty dollars per head. They would work for five to seven dollars a month. In June 1869, prompted by rumors, the hopeful white residents of Vicksburg eagerly greeted the steamer *Great Republic*, which was presumed to be carrying five hundred Chinese workers. When the boat arrived, there were no Chinese. Since the Chinese did not flock to the banks of the Mississippi River, Mississippi's white congressmen eventually "joined with their colleagues in other sections to exclude Chinese from our soil" via the Chinese Exclusion Act of 1882.

The Delta's population, cotton production, and land use soared after the Civil War. In 1860 the Delta's population consisted of 5,000

white and 45,000 black residents. By 1890 the population included
273,000 blacks who comprised 77 percent of the population. The 1920s
saw a decline in the black population from 414,000 to 306,000, but the
percentage of blacks in the population remained between 73 and 76
percent of the total. Cotton production rose accordingly, from 197,000
bales in 1880 to 873,000 bales in 1930, while land use expanded from
255,000 acres to more than 1.5 million during the same period.

Despite the explosive increase in black cotton workers, planters
were continually dissatisfied with their labor situation. They were ag-
grieved by real labor shortages, especially in years such as 1903, when
mills in America and Britain had to curtail production for lack of cotton. Planters' annoyance arose from their long-standing view of blacks
as poor workers. Despite notions that they enjoyed sitting atop a racial
caste system, planters would gladly have jettisoned blacks and the accompanying racial hierarchy if a replacement in the cotton fields had
been found. In 1893, William Yerger, the Mississippi lawyer for the
Y&MV, implored Stuyvesant Fish to encourage "frugal, white labor" to
immigrate to the Delta. Fish, in turn, recommended that blacks in the
Delta be tutored in proper habits and protected from their "simplicity
and childlike appetite." In 1903 the planter Charles Scott wrote to Fish
again about the "totally inadequate" labor situation, which had become
even more pressing because of insufficient black migration from other
Southern states. In 1905 the planter and student of race Alfred Holt
Stone described the black cotton worker to the American Economic Association as a "failure." Stone strongly recommended the replacement
of blacks with white Italians. Leroy Percy thought that Italian cotton
farmers made "$5 out of a crop where the Negro made $1."

In 1904, Delta planters tried to encourage Italian immigration by
sponsoring a trip through the Delta for the Italian ambassador, Baron
Edmundo Mayor des Planches. Although appeals were made to the Illinois Central, America's economists, and the federal government, only a
few Italians were enticed to the Delta. After a rough start at places like
Sunnyside plantations, the Delta Italians soon gravitated to the middle
class. Cotton production was "left in the hands of the Negro tenant."
Frederick Douglass's earlier observation remained in force: the black

cotton laborer is "as he is nowhere else, an absolute necessity. He has a monopoly on the labor market."

*

In the absence of slavery, various labor systems were used to cultivate cotton. A few landowners attempted to pay freedmen wages, but the once-a-year crop revenue and the inability to know crop production made cash wages impossible. Landowners devised a scheme of cash renting, in which "the landlord provided land, house, and fuel for a fixed rent per acre in cash or cotton." But the system that evolved to dominate cotton production was the "share" arrangement: the freedman was given an interest in the crop rather than cash. This relationship between white landowners and black workers was initiated by freedmen who wanted a more flexible work environment without strict supervision. In 1866 a freedman in South Carolina asked for one-fourth of the cotton production, food, and shelter in return for his labor. The plan thus evolved from these simple requests to an organizational structure throughout the South.

The share system took on several forms and was subject to negotiation. For example, share renting, according to one definition, was an arrangement by which the "landlord provided land, house, fuel, and a portion of the fertilizer" in return for rent of one-quarter or one-third of the tenant's crop. Sharecropping entailed the landlord's contribution of everything except half the fertilizer in return for half the tenant's crop.

For the laborer, the working year was tied to the cotton-planting season. The freedmen, now called "tenants," began to be "furnished" around March 1. Preparing the soil, planting, and "chopping" followed, ending in July when the crop was "laid by" or left alone to mature. The tenants then had no cotton-related chores until the end of August or September when picking began. Gathering the cotton lasted until November or December. When the cotton harvest was complete, the tenant worked for cash wages until the planting season began again. The cotton work year lasted about 150 days per year. Theoretically the tenant was bound to the creditor and hence to the land until his debt was repaid. As we have seen, this has been called "debt peonage" when poor black and white agricultural workers were consistently in debt if the creditors were fraudulent. But in reality, sharecroppers did move from farm to farm regularly without paying their legal or fraudulent debts. And after the Great Migration began, they had the option of moving to Chicago. By 1910, "92 percent of the farms [in the Mississippi Delta] were operated by tenants, as opposed to 63 percent outside the Delta." On these farms, 95 percent of the tenants were black.

The sharecropping system evolved naturally from the dynamics of cotton production—expenses, revenues, credit requirements, management control, and risk. If we look at it purely as a financing device, the sharecropping arrangement would be considered a normal transaction appropriate for risky ventures. A straightforward loan either is unobtainable because of credit risk or, if obtainable, would have a prohibitively high interest rate. The lender wants a greater return to compensate for an abnormal or high incidence of risk. The borrower, in this case the black tenant, generally had no choice, because he had neither the money to purchase land nor the skill to maintain it. Cotton farming would certainly qualify as a business that demanded some form of equity or higher return. A 1916 study of the Mississippi Delta concluded that the sharecropping contract was a reflection of risk. Based on data from 1913, the research indicated that landlords were better off if they used cash or share renters rather than day labor. Landlords during 1913 could make 6.6 percent from cash rentals, 11.8 percent from share renters, and 13.6 percent from sharecroppers. These numbers, which represent crop conditions and prices for one year, vary from year to year and farm to farm.

Many observers and scholars have offered judgments about the "infamous" sharecropper system. It has been vilified as a mechanism for racial oppression, or defended as fair in theory and the only available means of organizing large-scale, nonmechanized cotton production. It is instructive to examine the theory and practice of this labor system through the words of William Alexander Percy, David L. Cohn, Hodding Carter, and Gavin Wright. All four men were familiar with the origins, functioning, and abuses of sharecropping. All justify the economic rationale of sharecropping.

*

William Alexander Percy, scion of a Mississippi Delta cotton family, wrote extensively about sharecropping in his book *Lanterns on the Levee: Reflections of a Planter's Son* (1942). Percy, the son of Senator Leroy Percy, owned and managed the family farms. He attended the Harvard Law School, wrote poetry, traveled extensively in Europe, and entertained national literary figures, politicians, and academics at his home in the Delta town of Greenville, in Washington County. His book is touted as a classic portrait of the aristocratic Mississippi Delta planter. In fact it is an idiosyncratic memoir that reflects the literary skill and opinions of one man.

Percy's farm demonstrates the sharecropping system at work. His 3,343-acre farm, Trail Lake Planting Co., was the subject of a 1938 study, "A Social-Economic Analysis of a Mississippi Delta Plantation," by Raymond McClinton. The data for the study came from the auspicious year 1936 when twelve-cent cotton and a favorable growing season produced the plantation's first profits since 1929. In 1936, Washington County's population of 54,310 included 39,125 blacks (72 percent). The total farm population, 29,352, was 88 percent black. All the farm hands on Trail Lake were black; approximately 150 resident families (589 individuals) worked the land. Most were sharecroppers. Cultivation was divided as follows: cotton, 1,833 acres; vegetable gardens, 52 acres; pasturage, 50 acres; and corn and hay, 1,408 acres. Each family farmed between five and 40 acres. The planting company, which was divided into two farms, Trail Lake and Klondike, produced 1,542 bales of cotton. One of the farms, Trail Lake, yielded 495 pounds of cotton per acre.

The sharecroppers and the renters both made money in 1936. The sharecropping families netted an average of $479.34 while the cash renters averaged $643.34. All the tenants made enough to pay off their accounts. In addition, the tenants received "free water, free garden plot and pasturage, a monthly credit for six months to cover food and clothing, a credit for doctor's bills and medicine, and a house to live in." Percy calculated that his tenants worked 150 days a year. The markup for supplies at the farm store was 20 percent. Credit was extended via coupons that could be redeemed at the farm store. The study indicated that farmers were reluctant to give cash to tenants for "fear that the tenant will squander the money by gambling, or for whiskey. . . ." The credit allotments per family ranged from $6 to $32 every fifteen days for six months. The study noted that between ten and twelve families moved off the plantation each year.

Two managers were employed to supervise tenant activities in a very specific manner. One manager used "force and violence" when he was sufficiently "antagonized," the other did not. Approximately 95 percent of the tenants were literate. Several tenants subscribed to black newspapers, the *Pittsburgh Courier* and the *Chicago Defender*. A Rosenwald School located on the farm had an average daily attendance of 230 out of an enrollment of 350 tenant children. The school, which had four teachers, was in session for six and a half months a year and consisted of eight grades. Each teacher had the difficult task of handling 56 pupils. About 25 percent of the students failed each year. The number of students dropped markedly from 127 in the first grade, to 40 in the third grade, to 8 in the eighth grade. Black teachers in Washington County earned a monthly salary of $39.18 while their white counterparts made $103.90. The average annual expenditure per black pupil was $6.74, per white student $84.59. The farm was home to three churches with annual budgets, Mount Airy ($400), Porter's Chapel ($388), and Sunrise ($550). There were approximately thirty-six privately owned cars on the Percy farm.

The study concluded that the tenant on Trail Lake "has a fair home, . . . receives fair treatment and is given honest settlements." The study described the sharecroppers' plight as "cultural and intellectual" as well as economic:

> [T]he managers consider them shiftless and lazy that they have to be
> . . . supervised very closely. As a whole, the croppers are poorly educated,
> and their plane of living is low, varying from good years to bad years. If
> they make several hundred dollars one year, they probably spend it on
> worthless objects in the fall. The landlord usually justifies their position
> by pointing out that there is no other enterprise in the capitalist system
> that will take a pauper and extend several hundred dollars' credit with
> no security except the promise of a crop if it is made.

Percy's own account of the morality and practicality of sharecropping has been widely quoted. He defended the system as a "profit-sharing" arrangement between landlord and laborer: "Share-cropping is one of the best systems ever devised to give security and a chance for profit to the simple and the unskilled." He identified the problems of the sharecropper system as those of "human nature":

> The failure is not in the system itself, but in not living up to the contractual obligations of the system—the failure is human nature. . . . The white planter may charge an exorbitant rate of interest, he may allow the share-cropper less than market price received for his cotton, he may cheat him in a thousand ways, and the Negro's redress is merely theoretical. If the white planter happens to be a crook, the share-cropper system on that plantation is bad for Negroes, as any other system for Negroes. . . . If the Delta planters were mostly cheats, the results of the share-cropper system would be as grievous as reported. But strange as it may seem to the sainted east, we have a sprinkling of decent folk our way.

Percy knew the system was arbitrary. Abuses occurred because the black had no legal recourse. Percy recommended that blacks deal with the problem by boycotting "unworthy landlords." The government, he wrote, should "deny . . . benefits to the landlord who violated contractual obligations." Percy recognized that this was no equal arrangement between black sharecropper and white landlord, but he argued that such a thing did not exist in America: "The Negro is no more on an equality with the white man in plantation matters than in any other dealings between the two." Yet Percy also realized his dependence on black labor. His actions in trying to prevent black laborers from leaving Mississippi during the 1927 Mississippi River flood illustrated the essential nature of black labor in the Delta.

Greenville's nationally known newspaper editor, Hodding Carter, won the Pulitzer Prize for his editorials on tolerance while pointing to the complex, inevitable, and arbitrary sharecropping system:

> The worst evil of the sharecropping system was that it could be fair to the sharecropper in the best of years only if the landlord were honest, and profitable to the landlord only if the sharecropper were

diligent, the land productive, and the price of cotton high enough to give planter and sharecropper both a profit. Fair landlords, diligent sharecroppers, and high cotton prices were rare enough as separate phenomena, in conjunction they were extraordinary indeed.

*

Percy's friend David Cohn, the writer, agreed with Percy's assessment to some extent, but the cosmopolitan Cohn knew that the system needed to change. Cohn brought a national and worldwide perspective to the economic and racial world of the 1930s. Another native of Greenville, he studied anti-trust law under William Howard Taft at the Yale Law School, wrote speeches for Adlai Stevenson, and between 1937 and 1959 published forty-nine articles in the *Atlantic Monthly*. A lifelong Democrat and worldwide traveler, Cohn embraced the doctrine of free trade.

Cohn became a spokesman for the South, of the South, and to the South. He famously defined the geographical and sociological boundaries of the lands he knew best: "The Mississippi Delta begins in the lobby of the Peabody Hotel in Memphis and ends on Catfish Row in Vicksburg." Cohn knew that Delta land yielded three times the amount of cotton per acre than other areas of the South did. He thought the sharecropping system evolved naturally and that its problems derived from human nature. "Many evils of share-cropping," according to Cohn,

> flow not from the economics involved, but from the workings of human factors on both sides. It is obvious that the cropping contract is worth neither more nor less than the worth of moral integrity of the parties to exploit it. It is doubtfully true that some farmers in the Delta exploit their croppers. They are poor, usually ignorant and illiterate, the white man's word is law, and resort to the courts is a dubious enterprise. . . . Croppers therefore represent a rich field for exploitation, and some Delta farmers have exploited them as ruthlessly as possible.

For Cohn, "the majority of the farmers of the section [dealt] honestly with Negroes on their land." Black sharecroppers were "equally suspicious" of black and white landlords. Cohn cited Benjamin A. Green, the black mayor of the all-black town of Mound Bayou, Mississippi:

> Mayor Benjamin A. Green . . . says that there is no generalization one can make about plantation owners . . . some owners have a reputation for . . . "fair settlement." . . . Where the fair reputation obtains, sharecroppers . . . have made a fair living. . . . Where there is no such reputation "they catch hell." . . . In this respect there is no appreciable difference between Negro and white plantation owners.

In a 1937 article entitled "Share-Cropping in the Delta," Cohn suggested that the "national welfare would be promoted if thousands of croppers owned small tracts of land and lived in the tradition of a good life." But he cautioned that both black and white sharecroppers "are at present unfitted for the responsibilities and cares of independent ownership." He also believed that land "ownership was not a guarantee of success," for "acquiring land is much less difficult than holding it." Cohn thought black behavior required a "long period of physical and moral rehabilitation." His description of black farm laborers was unvarnished:

> The Delta Negro, with few exceptions, is utterly thriftless. Yesterday is vaguely remembered. To-day is bright. Tomorrow may never come. . . . And because there is no future, it is utterly senseless to save money for it. At "settlement time" in November or December, when croppers receive their share of the proceeds of the cotton crop, most of them immediately spend the fruits of a year's labor on secondhand automobiles, gasoline, gambling, whiskey, or aimlessly and gaily traveling about the countryside. . . . Then they will go along with little or no money for the next nine months. . . . A single household may contain five or six children born of various mothers and fathers. . . . The Delta Negro's sex life is a long moral holiday.

Cohn was echoing what Mathew Hammond had written forty years earlier. Hammond had described the black tenant as living in a "condition of lazy contentment which is the boon of the idle and improvident." Du Bois's description in 1908 resembled Cohn's. "Without

doubt," Du Bois wrote, "the point where the Negro American is furthest
behind modern civilization is in his sexual mores." Du Bois pointed
to the then troubling statistic: one-fourth of all black births were illegitimate. Zora Neale Hurston, in her 1935 review of Cohn's memoir,
God Shakes Creation (later reprinted as *Where I Was Born and Raised*),
praised his "grim courage" in exposing the "brutal, hideous truths, of
the cotton culture" and in "rudely brushing aside the traditional mag-
nolias and roses that shield the pig-pen." Hurston noted that "Negroes
or Southern Whites" would approve of the book. Indeed, Cohn declared
that "the white man at his worst outdoes any other man in barbarism
and brutality."

The Yale anthropologist Hortense Powdermaker concluded that
blacks had merely adopted the spendthrift habits of white farmers who
would splurge in boom times:

> The attitude of Delta Whites has been taken over by a majority of
> Negroes. During the boom years of 1918 and 1919, when cotton prices
> were at their height, some sharecroppers cleared $500 or more in a
> season. Usually they spent it on extravagances—automobiles, whisky,
> expensive clothes, jewelry—just as the white man was doing.

Powdermaker guessed that 25 or 30 percent of the sharecroppers "get
an honest settlement at the end of their five months of labor."

The classic study of black Delta agricultural laborers, *Caste and
Class in a Southern Town* (1937) by John Dollard, referred to "the de-
tachable conscience of the Negro." Dollard, a Yale sociologist, lived in
the Delta town of Indianola, Mississippi, for several months in 1934
to study the relationships of blacks and whites. When he examined
the fifty-fifty sharecropper arrangement between landlord and tenant, Dollard thought the landlord might deserve a higher percentage
because of the high risk and low (2 percent) returns of cotton farming.
On the question of defrauding tenants, Dollard concluded that "there
are honest and dishonest landlords." He noted that middle-class black
"informants" (interviewees) thought sharecroppers approved of the
furnishing of credit which removed "responsibility and the necessity
of forethought."

Cohn's solution was a federal government program that would provide rigorous supervision. The sharecroppers, he said, must be "recast and re-created":

> They must be taught sound methods of farming small tracts. They must be physically and morally rehabilitated. They must be cured of malaria and sexual diseases. They must learn thrift and industry. . . . This is a problem for the years.

Technology eventually intervened and made Cohn's plan irrelevant as blacks became displaced farm laborers.

*

The Stanford economic historian Gavin Wright has also evaluated the sharecropping system in his works in the late twentieth century. Unlike Dollard and Powdermaker, Wright has focused on the economics of the cotton business. The sharecropping system, he writes, evolved through a "market process." The system was not imposed on blacks by whites.

> [O]nce we know that the system emerged from a market process, we can be reasonably sure that the outcome represented a balance of forces. Sharecropping was a balance between the freedmen's desire for autonomy and the employer's interest in extracting work effort and having labor when needed.

Wright describes the financial aspects of cotton production as paramount. First and foremost, the sharecropping system was a credit system that resulted from the shortage of capital and the vagaries of cotton farming. What were the financing alternatives of financing? Real estate loans were not an option. The landlord cotton farmer could not pay wages because he received cotton revenues only once at the end of the season. Wright notes that the early clauses in Freedmen's Bureau labor contracts in 1866–1867 called for a "postharvest wage." Even the earliest contracts provided for "collective share agreements." Yet the much-acclaimed panacea of land ownership was less important than credit. Tenancy, according to Wright, was not the cause of "Southern poverty and the slow rate of progress in Southern agriculture during the nineteenth century":

> A more equitable distribution of land, a better credit system, perhaps even a different pattern of historical timing among war, emancipation, and cotton demand, might have provided more independence, more racial and economic equity, and somewhat better terms of trade for Southern cotton over the years. Independence and equity are by no means minor aspects of human welfare, but such changes would not have produced dramatic improvements in living standards and agricultural process.

Diversification, Wright suggests, was available to the "advanced agriculture of the North" but was not an option for the cotton South. Mechanization, when it came, initially proved detrimental to the black laborer. It pushed "tenants to a lower position" in terms of relevance and ultimately led to their displacement. As we shall see, Wright's hypothesis about independence and equity was tested by the all-black town of Mound Bayou, Mississippi.

*

Because of the poverty of black (and white) tenants, the word "sharecropper" detonates an emotional response. The sharecropping system, described by Clyde Woods as complete exploitation, has been blamed for the poverty of the agricultural South and the degradation and oppression of blacks. Woods, a black studies professor, issued one of the strongest indictments of the arrangement as one "wrapped in violence and fraud" and "mythical paternalism." Sharecropping, he judged, "was in reality a production system organized around institutional starvation, discrimination, violence, fraud, debt and enforced dependency." Blacks "who challenged the system of exploitation often found themselves or their family members imprisoned, beaten, or murdered."

But it was the cotton economy and America's racial attitudes, not the sharecropping system, that created black poverty. At its worst, abusive administration of the sharecropping system caused unimaginable hardships on blacks. The cotton world, slavery, segregation, and sharecropping have been blamed for a host of stereotypical behavioral problems that have plagued black America even after the Great Migration. Indeed the sharecropping system was arbitrary and highly susceptible to exploitation. It was also a logical development of the power of cotton within the financial, technological, social, and racial context of white America. With cotton production as the goal, sharecropping was a predictable outcome. To leave cotton production for factory work would have been a solution for blacks, but that alternative was not available until the labor shortages of World War I. Mechanization and chemical herbicides, not morality or justice, determined the fate of black farm labor.

Were the hardships of black cotton laborers egregious when compared to the working conditions of white Northern industrial workers of the same period? Harsh labor conditions were not confined to the South during the latter part of the nineteenth and early twentieth centuries. While work in the cotton fields was difficult, labor conditions in Northern factories were hardly idyllic.

These years witnessed a particularly virulent, unencumbered, materialistic business environment which allowed a few families to accumulate massive wealth that was ostentatiously displayed. The most conspicuous participants of the era—businessmen like John D. Rockefeller, Andrew Carnegie, and J. P. Morgan—have been called "robber barons" because of their ruthlessness in amassing fortunes by consolidating various industries into large corporate structures. Eric Hobsbawm has compared the robber barons to medieval lords whose economic strength placed them above the law. They employed "private armed forces" to dispense "private justice." Severe labor practices were characteristic of the business tycoons. Labor disputes were a common feature of the economic landscape, often escalating to violence.

Business historians and economists generally applaud America's leap to industrial preeminence as miraculous; labor historians usually denounce the process as a tragic example of unbridled capitalism, undertaken at the expense of its worker victims. But the hardships that were endured by the white immigrants—as miners, factory workers, or farmers—do not resonate with succeeding generations. Unlike black Americans, the progeny of impoverished white immigrants, for the most part, blended into a prosperous white America. The taint of their struggles and humble beginnings lost their emotional component as the past was buried in American materialism. Blacks had a different experience.

*

Was it possible for a black person or a black community to succeed in the cotton South if white oppression and a white-administered labor system were removed? Here we must look to a near-perfect test case, the Mississippi Delta town of Mound Bayou, an all-black community established by freedmen. If there was any chance for a successful black cotton-farming enclave to exist in a white world, it could be observed at Mound Bayou. It was populated by blacks and governed by blacks, and the surrounding land was farmed by blacks, with no white Southern intervention. There were other experiments in African-American agriculture. The Southern Improvement Company, sponsored by Northerners, leased land to more than sixty black families in Macon County, Alabama, in 1900. After a promising start in which the black farmers paid their commitments for nine years, the enterprise folded. These efforts proved little except that farming was risky. Before a generalization could be made, a farming venture had to exist for an extended period of time.

Mound Bayou, one of many all-black towns established by freedmen, was the best known of the all-black agricultural communities. It was the town that came closest to the embodiment of Booker T. Washington's philosophy of self-help, racial consciousness, and racial separatism. Mound Bayou residents called it the "Jewel of the Delta." Washington himself wrote, "Outside of Tuskegee, I think I can safely say that there is no community in the world that I am so deeply interested in as I am in Mound Bayou." President Theodore Roosevelt, who paid a personal visit to the community in 1907, described Mound Bayou as an "object lesson full of hope for the colored people."

The Mount Bayou experiment was an attempt to establish an economically viable black cotton-farming community within an area dominated by white farmers and white towns. Black separatism was viewed by the founders and the residents as essential for an acceptable existence with self-respect and economic opportunity in white America. The community became a highly visible symbol for the hope of black America, 90 percent of whom lived in the South and most of whom were tied to the cotton economy.

Mound Bayou was the creation of the Montgomerys, an educated, experienced, willful, and confident black family. Its patriarch, Benjamin, was born into slavery in Virginia in 1819; his son, Isaiah, was born into slavery in Mississippi in 1847 and died in 1924, at the age of seventy-seven, in the Mississippi Delta. During the period between the end of the Civil War and the demise of cotton farming in the 1930s, the Montgomerys became at one point the largest black landowners in America.

The story begins with Joseph Davis, older brother of Jefferson Davis, who was pivotal to the development of the skills and aspirations of the Montgomery clan. Joseph Davis, born in Georgia in 1784, in 1811 set out to make his fortune on the newly opened rich cotton land of what was to become western Mississippi. In short order, as a slaveholder he amassed land at Davis Bend, Mississippi, and wealth in addition to a thriving law practice.

In 1825, while on a trip in western Pennsylvania, Davis by chance shared a nine-hour coach ride with the utopian Welshman Robert Owen, who was responsible for the communal settlement in New Harmony, Indiana. The well-read Davis was familiar with Owen's writings; now he was influenced to adapt the notions of a cooperative environment to his plantation. It was still slavery, but a different form of slavery. Davis developed a vision of a cohesive, communal black society that he passed on to his slave, Benjamin Montgomery. As a child Benjamin had learned to read and write from his playmate, the white son of his owner. Isaiah Montgomery would later write, "We barely had an idea of what slave life was like."

Benjamin Montgomery proceeded to develop a myriad of mechanical, business, and intellectual skills. While a slave he opened a retail store, and the business expanded as Davis served as a guarantor for goods that Montgomery bought in New Orleans. White Mississippians traded in Montgomery's store, and the enterprising owner soon established his own credit credentials. Montgomery also acted as an agent for Davis in purchasing supplies and shipping cotton. He became the business manager for Davis's Hurricane plantation and his brother Jefferson Davis's Brierfield plantation.

On his 11,000 acres Joseph Davis established a form of "self-government" for the 345 slaves. (Although benign by slavery's standards, this arrangement nonetheless remained chattel slavery.) Davis instituted a judicial system whereby slave complaints were heard by a slave jury and slaves were allowed to testify. The court met every Sunday in a building called the Hall of Justice. There could be no punishment without a conviction by a jury of peers. Davis sat as judge but rarely became involved except to mitigate the harshness of a punishment. An overseer's complaint was also subject to the court's review. This limited authority led to problems with overseers and brought frequent turnover among them. Jefferson Davis adopted a similar court system at Brierfield. Only one other Mississippi slaveowner, A. S. Morehead, is known to have used slave juries.

During the Civil War, Benjamin Montgomery moved to Cincinnati and was technically emancipated, but he returned to Mississippi in the summer of 1864. When, after the war, he confronted the Freedmen's Bureau with his plans for developing a self-contained black community, an acrimonious relationship ensued. Meanwhile the Montgomerys continued to operate a retail store as they had before the war. Montgomery & Sons supplied 80 percent of the goods for the Davis Bend freedmen and charged a 20 to 25 percent markup on its goods.

When Joseph Davis received his pardon, his lands, which had been confiscated by the Union army, were returned. On November 19, 1866, Davis and Montgomery entered into an agreement whereby the former slave and his sons purchased both the Hurricane and Brierfield plantations. The transaction was kept secret because the Mississippi Black Codes permitted black ownership of land only in towns. Davis therefore announced that he was merely leasing, not selling, the land to Montgomery. After the law was changed on February 21, 1867, the deal was made public. The four thousand acres were sold for $300,000, to be paid in ten years at an annual interest rate of 5 percent in gold or 7 percent in paper currency. The experiment of a large-scale black community began with sixteen hundred freedmen who rented land from the Montgomerys.

Benjamin Montgomery immediately made it clear that his interests were economic, not political. He believed enfranchisement and political involvement to be distractions: "Regarding the suffrage question as of doubtful and remote utility, the discussion of it and other political topics as more likely to produce contention and idleness than harmony in the community, such discussions will be discouraged." Montgomery's goal was to "attain as much prosperity and happiness as are consistent with human nature." Joseph Davis, on the other hand, supported the benefits of black suffrage.

The Northern press, white and black, followed events at Davis Bend closely. In December 1866 the *New York Times* endorsed Montgomery's avoidance of political activity. The newspaper praised Montgomery's "common sense style," which was "practical and sagacious enough" to provide a successful model for freedmen. The *Times* was impressed with Montgomery's knowledge of freedmen, with "whose faults and foibles he [was] entirely familiar." The proper way for the freedmen to succeed, said the *Times*, was by "making themselves an indispensable industrial power."

The Davis Bend operation was subject to the vagaries that confronted all cotton farms—fluctuating cotton prices, unpredictable weather, floods, labor shortages, and insects—and were partly responsible for the Montgomerys' failure to make interest payments in several years.

Some of the results were gratifying. In 1870, Davis Bend produced 2,500 bales of cotton, which might have given the Montgomerys a $50,000 profit. By comparison, the entire cotton production of all black landowners in twenty Mississippi counties in the same year was only 6,141 bales. At the time the Montgomerys were reputed to be the third-largest planters in the state. On October 9, 1870, "Montgomery & Sons, Hurricane, Miss." won $500 for the "best single bale of long staple cotton" at the St. Louis Fair. In 1876 their cotton ranked first in the international short-staple contest at the Philadelphia Exposition. By 1872 the New York credit-rating firm of R. G. Dun gave the Montgomerys its highest rating, A No. 1. Dun "estimated their net worth at $230,000" in 1873 when only 7 percent of all merchants in the South had more than $50,000. Yet the New York agency revealed its attitude toward blacks with a backhanded compliment about the Montgomerys: "they are negroes, but negroes of unusual intelligence & extraordinary bus[iness] qualifications."

Despite their competence, the Montgomerys were able to pay only interest and not the required principal on their mortgage. Joseph Davis, who received weekly correspondence from Benjamin Montgomery, was lenient in extending the terms and even provided $200 a year for the "aged and infirm on the plantation." Jefferson Davis was not as accommodating. He declared that "the property is too large for the administrative capacity of a negro, and he must ultimately fail." After Joseph Davis died in 1870, Jefferson Davis challenged the Montgomerys, initiating a suit to repossess his land because of delinquent payments.

The Montgomerys' woes mounted. Their store in Vicksburg failed; turmoil over cotton prices pervaded the 1873 depression; credit losses accumulated; and Benjamin Montgomery became ill in 1875 and died in 1877. Jefferson Davis's case meandered through the state court system and was finally decided by the Mississippi Supreme Court in 1878 in favor of Davis. The Montgomerys lost their judicial appeal in 1881, and the land was sold at auction to Jefferson Davis.

Like other black families, the Montgomerys cast about for alternatives to Mississippi and the South for settlement. Isaiah and his older brother Thornton looked at and participated in black colonization in Kansas and the Dakotas. While in Kansas, Isaiah purchased 640 acres in Waubansee County for distribution to freedmen. Again the press followed the Montgomerys' activities, and the *Boston Herald* wrote approvingly of Isaiah's purchase, "Should [Montgomery's project] . . . do well, the frequently heard statement that the negro cannot thrive in Kansas will be disproved." Isaiah eventually referred to Kansas as a "fool's paradise" and ended any further involvement with the Exodusters. The Montgomerys decided that the North provided no Promised Land for black migrants.

Isaiah Montgomery later expressed his view that Davis Bend did not succeed because it was based on tenancy rather than on land ownership. Yet he adhered to his father's philosophy of the primacy of economics in an environment where political rights were unattainable. Isaiah was able to pursue his vision of a black-owned cotton community in the Mississippi Delta after he was contacted by the Louisville, New Orleans, and Texas Railroad, which had just completed a line through the heart of the Delta. The LNO&T could now transport cotton from the Delta to trading centers, but it needed cotton farmers and towns to settle along its line. Because of the prominence of the Montgomery family, the LNO&T sought Isaiah as an agent to sell land to black settlers. After visiting the designated site, Montgomery embarked upon his plan to create a black colony.

In 1887 he led fifteen Davis Bend freedmen to the settlement that he called Mound Bayou in Bolivar County. Montgomery was accompanied by his cousin, Benjamin Green, an astute businessman. In accordance with Montgomery's beliefs, the settlers would own the land. The LNO&T, as noted earlier, sold land in plots of 40 acres or more for $7 per acre. Payment terms were $1 down and five equal annual installments. Seven hundred acres were sold in the first year. The land had to be cleared such that selling timber, rather than cotton, became a means of earning cash. The first three difficult years saw the black colonists earn $8,780 by selling timber and harvest 379 bales of cotton on 655 cleared acres. By 1907, Mound Bayou had attained a fragile and superficial prosperity. It was a self-sustaining community with 800 families of 4,000 blacks. The colonists cultivated 5,000 to 6,000 acres of the 30,000 they owned. The land yielded 3,000 bales of cotton. The town contained a railroad station (with a small waiting room for whites), a timber mill, 13 stores, two cotton gins, a hospital, schools, and churches. The stores generated annual sales of $600,000. For Booker T. Washington, Mound Bayou became living proof that his philosophy of self-help in a racially separate community was achievable.

But Mound Bayou was nonetheless tied to the roller-coaster cotton world and had no financial infrastructure to absorb the attendant and inevitable financial shocks. When Montgomery defaulted on his mortgage payments, his land reverted to the Illinois Central, which had acquired the LNO&T in 1892 in its Yazoo and Mississippi Valley Railroad affiliate. The IC thought Montgomery was essential to Mound Bayou and "the best ally that we have in Mississippi, so far as selling of lands to negroes is concerned." A lenient renegotiated loan followed. Many of the Mound Bayou settlers also had difficulty in meeting their loan payments.

During the early years of Mound Bayou, Isaiah Montgomery committed the notorious act for which he is most remembered. As the only black among 134 delegates at the Mississippi Constitutional Convention of 1890, he voted for a constitution that codified white dominance and effectively disfranchised most black voters and some white voters.

President Grover Cleveland enthusiastically applauded the position of the only black delegate. Despite some Republican opposition, the North embraced Montgomery's stand as a way to end the "southern problem." Most of the response from blacks was scathing.

Montgomery's justification of his action prompted a harsh rebuke from Frederick Douglass, who recommended that "we must denounce his policy, but spare the man." Douglass called the speech a "disaster to the race." A decade earlier Douglass had demanded that "The South must let the Negro vote or surrender its representation in Congress." Yet in 1879 Douglass had questioned the readiness of blacks for public office: "Slavery was a poor school in which to develop statesmen," he said, "and colored legislatures proved this."

Interestingly, a decade earlier Douglass had emphasized the priority of economic over political power in a tone similar to that of the Montgomery family. He suggested that blacks must gain the respect of whites through frugality and hard work: "Other races, notably Jews and the Quakers, worse situated than [blacks], have fought their way up." Douglass especially respected the Jewish habit of saving—to "put money in his purse." The economics of the cotton field were never far from Douglass's thoughts. "Neither the Chinaman, German, Norwegian nor Swede," he wrote, "can drive him [the African] from the sugar and cotton fields of Louisiana and Mississippi. . . . The climate of the South makes such labor uninviting and harshly repulsive to the white man. . . . On the contrary, the Negro walks, labors, or sleeps in the sunlight unharmed." The freedman's labor in the cotton field was worth more than "sword, ballot-boxes, or bayonets. It touches the heart of the South through its pockets."

What were Isaiah Montgomery's motives? Certainly he sought the favor of white leaders in order to protect Mound Bayou. Its survival was his distinct priority. His fledgling black community existed in the midst of a dominant white environment that was hostile to the very existence of a black enclave. The forty-three-year-old Montgomery had seen a lot and lived a lot. He was conversant with white America's racial attitude toward blacks in 1890. He could expect no help from white Northerners. He was not naive in assuming that assimilation with whites was a possibility; a self-segregated community was his only option. Montgomery even boasted that "Not a single white person resides or owns property within [Mound Bayou's] . . . limits." Black political power had already been lost in the fallout from Reconstruction; black political presence was ineffective and on a course of inevitable disappearance. Most likely he felt that a symbolic protest, either in refusing to become a delegate or in assuming a role as a protest delegate, would be a futile gesture.

Montgomery is often associated with Booker T. Washington's maligned policy of appeasement. Yet the choices for Montgomery and Washington were either militant protest as individuals outside the South, or attempts to improve the plight of millions of black cotton farmers within an existing system. In reality, both Washington and Montgomery had no alternative if they wished to build black institutions in the South, where blacks were entrapped by white Northerners and white Southerners. Most of the time Washington and Montgomery were adapting to the world in which they lived. In bowing to the "power realities of [his] time and place," the historian Neil McMillen wrote, Montgomery realized that "conciliation was a more promising path to black progress than confrontation."

Mound Bayou's experiment in racial partition represented the most important attempt by blacks to achieve economic, social, and civic independence within a white-dominated economy. It was necessary to create a town with viable mercantile concerns, an educational system, financial institutions, an appropriate municipal government, and functioning contacts to the surrounding white environment. The Delta, with its cheap, fertile land, provided the venue. Cotton was the commercial linchpin that would determine the colony's fate. Survival meant developing a commercial and financial infrastructure to support cotton production.

In a revealing letter to Booker T. Washington, Isaiah Montgomery outlined another bold agenda—to establish a credit company that would loan money to black farmers. It would further the expansion of a black-owned "vast territory" that would include most of the northern part of the Mississippi Delta. The area would consist of parts of Tunica, Coahoma, Quitman, Tallahatchie, and Washington counties. Mound Bayou would be its financial and industrial capital. Montgomery's scheme encompassed more than a multitude of black yeoman farmers with "forty acres and a mule" or a modest, black self-contained community. He envisioned a large economic unit that could function as an independent black political entity. Isaiah Montgomery, like his father, knew that political power meant little without economic muscle.

The focal point of the Montgomerys' economic plan was the proposed Mound Bayou Oil Mill, a facility for crushing and processing cottonseed. After much fanfare the cotton mill was built in 1912, but by the 1920s it was out of business. Despite national publicity, white Northern philanthropists provided Mound Bayou with philanthropy but not investment. The exception, Julius Rosenwald, who later helped found a school in Mound Bayou, assisted the cotton oil mill and the credit company, but he did so because of the significance of Mound Bayou. He crossed the line from philanthropy to investment and in effect mingled humanitarian and business interests.

The fluctuations of the cotton market severely bruised Mound Bayou. Its shallow, fragile, and short-lived prosperity has been exaggerated. Because of national publicity, Mound Bayou became a symbol of black hope, but it never developed into a healthy economic community. The town became economically moribund in the early 1920s. Both its bank and its loan company failed. Great swings in the price of cotton were a large factor in the community's demise. The white Delta towns were subject to much of the same trauma caused by the cotton economy, but a more secure financial infrastructure allowed them to survive for another forty years.

Montgomery's legacy draws both ire and praise. He has been vilified by blacks who look at his support of the Mississippi constitution of 1890 as an ultimate betrayal. He is also belittled as an elitist. In contrast to these criticisms, Mound Bayou's historian, Milburn Crowe, revered Isaiah Montgomery. The elaborate tombstone erected at Montgomery's gravesite was a gift from Delta white men. Walter Sillers, Sr., an influential white planter and a friend, delivered a eulogy at Montgomery's funeral. Sillers remarked that Isaiah Montgomery was "one of the greatest of his race, a man known throughout this great nation as one of the most thoughtful and helpful leaders of his people."

Like Moses, he carried his people from recent slavery to their new freedom in the wilderness, and under his masterful hand, the wilderness blossomed, and farms and homes sprang up around him . . . for he was the first to draw the color line in Mississippi; and he would sell the lands in the territory of Mound Bayou to none save the people of his own race, knowing best for every race to dwell unto itself.

Mound Bayou and the Montgomery family saga provide an abject lesson in the futility of black economic hopes after the Civil War— even with black ownership and black political control. Mound Bayou was a real experiment, in a real place, at a real time. Its viability was predicated on racial separatism and the always unpredictable cotton market. Despite glowing rhetoric, Mound Bayou demonstrated the limits of racial independence in a white economic world. And in the commercial world, racial separatism just couldn't work effectively. Mound Bayou showed that economic interaction with white America is a prerequisite for commercial existence.

*

How efficient and how large could a cotton farm be under a nonmechanized sharecropping system? For the answer we need to look no further than the Delta and Pine Land Co., located in the Delta counties of Washington and Bolivar. The cotton production methodology of the times placed severe limits on a farming entity's organizational structure. A cotton farm, no matter how large, could not be recast as an a modern business corporation. The Delta and Pine Land (D&PL) story is a brew of international trade, large-scale cotton farming, meticulous record-keeping, the vagaries of the cotton market, scientific agriculture, and sharecropping.

The story begins with the perennial threat of a cotton shortage at the British mills. The British were forever searching for a reliable supply of cotton. Into this void in the early twentieth century stepped an entrepreneurial Michigan native and graduate of the University of Michigan Law School, Lant K. Salsbury, who orchestrated the land deal that enticed British investors into the Mississippi Delta. After being attracted by the Southern timber business, Salsbury moved to the Delta and fell under the spell of cotton. He managed an 8,000-acre farm in the Delta before joining with the aggressive and formidable planter Charles Scott of Rosedale. Their unsuccessful effort to finance a 21,000-acre purchase through Eastern or Southern sources prompted them to solicit British money. In 1911 the persuasive Salsbury journeyed to Manchester and coaxed the directors of the Fine Cotton Spinners' and Doublers' Association Ltd. to the Delta to examine the huge parcel of cotton land.

The Fine Cotton Spinners (later Courtaulds Ltd.) were a consortium of fifty firms that employed thirty thousand workers and owned four million spindles. The prestigious textile conglomerate's offices were on St. James's Square in Manchester. The consortium was keen to secure a predictable supply of fine-staple cotton, a situation that became even more acute after the 1903–1904 cotton shortages reached "crisis proportions." Many mills "were forced to close or go on half and quarter time."

The Fine Cotton Spinners were in a receptive mode when Salsbury appeared with his offer of a large tract of land, and a group of directors from the textile firm traveled to the Delta. The chairman, Herbert Dixon, and "a canny Scot," John McConnel, with his handy slide rule and whiskey flask, were among the representatives. The hospitable Delta planters enchanted the Brits with geese hunting along the Mississippi River. The Brits liked what they saw, eventually purchased 38,000 acres for $3 million, and in 1911 established the Delta and Pine Land Co.

The Fine Cotton Spinners had a vision of a vertically integrated company that included a "scientific super plantation." To implement this strategy, D&PL hired Early C. Ewing, a plant geneticist and a graduate of Mississippi A&M (later Mississippi State University). After college Ewing had studied under the legendary botanist Herbert J. Webber at Cornell University.

Corporate planning then encountered the precarious world of cotton farming. Floods in 1912 and 1913 damaged crops, and the pesky boll weevil proved to be a valiant and destructive guerrilla warrior. Although it had been designed to provide its British owner with both cotton and profits, D&PL did neither. Its much-touted efficiency yielded no profits. Yet the company was producing excellent seed varieties, had an organized approach to its sharecropper system, and succeeded in controlling insect pests. Still, after sinking $3 million dollars ($95 per acre) into the land deal and spending $1.5 million on other expenses, the British failed to make any money. Over sixteen years D&PL paid only one dividend, a 20 percent payout in 1920. The company did not show a profit until 1917. The cotton market crash of 1920 caused even greater troubles. Herbert W. Lee, the future president of the Fine Cotton Spinners, had originally opposed the purchase of D&PL. Now he was outspoken and sarcastic about being conned into the deal by "American salesmanship."

Faced with a huge loss even if they were able to sell the land, the British had no choice but to try to make D&PL profitable. By the standards of a cotton farm, D&PL could be categorized as efficient. In the 1920s the company's cotton acreage expanded from 12,000 to 18,000 acres. Cotton production rose from fewer than 5,000 bales in 1924 to 15,198 bales in 1925, then fell back to 12,500 in 1926. Yields per acre rose from 152 pounds per acre in the disappointing year of 1923 to 406 pounds per acre in 1925. Then 1926 saw the cultivation in the United States of a record-breaking 45,000 to 47,000 acres, good weather, and little insect damage—but also a ruinous fall in cotton prices. The cotton farmer was caught in the supply-demand vise. D&PL managed to survive the price decline as well as the disastrous Mississippi River flood of 1927. That year Oscar Johnston, a practical businessman and lawyer, was named president. He immediately realized that the flood would bring a cotton shortage. The astute Johnston purchased cotton futures at 14 cents a pound and sold them for 18 to 22 cents a pound, making a profit of $200,000.

A 1937 *Fortune* magazine article, "Biggest Cotton Plantation" described the operations of D&PL with a combination of praise, bafflement, and revulsion. *Fortune*'s investigation provides an unparalleled view of cotton farming within the racial world of the 1930s, in this case the "biggest cotton plantation" in America, located on the "best cotton soil" in America.

Johnston had inherited a losing operation and had shown a profit in six of the nine years between 1928 and 1936. The numbers for 1936 were extraordinary. D&PL had produced 15,000 bales of cotton with an astounding average yield of 638 pounds per acre. The cotton was sold for a "premium price of 13.25 cents per pound." By comparison, in 1936 the American cotton farmer on average received 11.9 cents a pound and produced 187 pounds per acre. D&PL's scientifically developed cotton-seed was the envy of the world; D&PL sold more cottonseed for plant-ing purposes than any other company. Its longer-staple cotton made it especially valuable to mill purchasers. Foreign sales amounted to 3,500 tons of cottonseed to China, Greece, and Argentina. In 1936, D&PL had operating profits of $518,000 and a net income of $153,000.

Johnston's management style featured meticulous records, account-ability, scientific research, and a corporate reporting structure. He hired twelve managers, each responsible for approximately one thousand acres and one hundred sharecroppers. The managers supervised and gave detailed instructions to the sharecroppers. Johnston gave no orders to his sharecroppers except through the managers, who rode horses around the farm daily and knew all the sharecroppers in their units personally. Johnston and the corporate officers met four times a year with the managers. Each manager lived on his farm unit and received a house, $150 a month, and a potential 10 to 15 percent annual bonus. Science provided a cottonseed that produced 20 percent more cotton than the average and matured six weeks earlier than normal. Insecti-cides were sprayed from crop-duster airplanes.

The resemblance to a modern business corporation ends with the functioning of the sharecropper system. D&PL furnished goods and supplies to more than one thousand black families totaling five thou-sand people. The company also owned one thousand mules that were managed by an independently wealthy elderly Scotsman, Mac Mc-Clure, who worked "on the biggest mule farm" because he liked mules. The sharecroppers worked on "halves," which meant they received half the cotton they raised. A "three-quarters" arrangement implied that the sharecropper had his own mule. Johnston generally would not allow "three-quarters" because he did not think the sharecroppers cared properly for their mules.

The sharecropper received credit in the form of scrip, which could be used only at the company store to buy food, clothing, and essen-tials. Cash was not paid because of the sharecropper's propensity, as *Fortune* put it, to "blow it rapidly for unnecessaries such as whiskey." At D&PL the sharecropper worked an average of 125 days a year cultivating cotton; during the rest of the year he might work for cash wages of one dollar a day for the company on farm-related projects. The sharecroppers' school for children was open five months a year. A hospital with a doctor was available for a charge of nine dollars a year. The sharecropper received a house, free fuel, a half-acre garden plot, and a payment for half the expenses of fertilizer. In 1933 the average sharecropper received $220 in credit and $185 in cash, a total of $405; in 1936 he used $200 in credit and was paid $320 in cash, a total of $520. *Fortune* noted that "When a cropper has a deficit at the end of the year, D&PL, as is the general southern custom, writes it off, clears the debt."

According to *Fortune*, "a very important factor in Mr. Johnston's success" was "the intangible of his treatment of labor." The Socialist party of Tyronza, Arkansas, thought that Johnston was "better at administering his [sharecropper] contracts than any other planter studied." The abuses of sharecroppers by unscrupulous landlords were well known—excessive markups for goods, fraud in determining cotton production and sales, and manipulation of allotments under guidelines established in the 1930s.

While calling sharecropping a "national disgrace," *Fortune* offered no alternative: "[A]ny practical solution of the problem is hard to see and, even if seen, hard to preach. . . . It is probable that at Delta and Pine, you see sharecropping at its best, or say, its least objectionable."

On "settlement day," the payday after the cotton was harvested, D&PL workers were accosted by used-car salesmen, prostitutes from nearby Greenville, bootleggers, and a host of opportunists. Of the 1,000 sharecropper families, 280 owned cars. A sharecropper's entire year's pay was "apt to go in a moment." Four to five homicides—blacks killing blacks—occurred each year at D&PL. *Fortune* wrote of the "sexual carelessness of the Negroes," which planters said was "one example of the general irresponsibility which makes [sharecroppers] dependent on the responsibility of others." A thousand cases of syphilis were reported at D&PL between 1930 and 1932. The $14,000 cost of treatment of the venereal disease was shared by D&PL and the Rosenwald Foundation, and was administered by the resident physician. The company distributed a half-ton of yeast to prevent pellagra, a disease common among sharecroppers but rare at D&PL.

Sharecroppers could use their credit scrip only for food. D&PL continually pressured its tenants to grow vegetables on their half-acre plots. The company maintained "better than average cabins with tight-fitting walls, grooved and tongued floors." The company did not supply screens because "the croppers normally punch holes in the screens to let the dogs in or throw trash out."

The planters interviewed by *Fortune* reverted to a consistent theme: a "lack of thrift and initiative" among the sharecroppers, who they indicated had made enough money to buy land but invariably returned to seek a sharecropper contract. Delta planters contrasted the blacks with the Italians, who had started in the Delta as sharecroppers and had "become Memphis doctors and lawyers in the second generation or otherwise improved themselves." Johnston compared the living conditions of D&PL tenants favorably to those of "the masses of city labor."

In 1939 a Harvard study group led by David B. Dill added scientific evidence about the effectiveness of D&PL policies. The researchers found that a "good diet and excellent medical care accounted for the low death rate and superior health" of blacks at D&PL. The *New York Times* noted the importance of Dill's work: "The Harvard experiments not only teach a valuable physiological lesson but [also] point the sociological moral that working for an enlightened company on a sharecropping basis need not be another form of slavery."

Supervisors or managers brought a measure of structure to the process, but cotton farming was not comparable to a modern business enterprise. Profit, as always, was the goal. Laborers worked in family units in a decentralized manner on specific outdoor plots of land. There was extensive personal contact between a landlord or a manager and a tenant because of the individual nature of tilling the soil on a specific piece of property. Whether this boss-tenant relationship became one of condescending paternalism, responsible paternalism, or ruthless exploitation depended on the people involved. Relationships in an agrarian community are personal. In 1937 the clever Oscar Johnston could debunk the prospects of a mechanical cotton picker because it could not pick cotton cleanly and missed cotton as it moved through the field. He still saw greater production as demanding a corresponding increase in sharecroppers. This is the antithesis of modern industrial logic. Andrew Carnegie would have been appalled at the suggestion that a cotton farm was a modern business entity.

The history of D&PL through the 1930s illustrates both the possibilities and the limits of cotton farming. Within the succeeding generation, technology would obviate the need for most forms of manual labor, which had been required since the cotton boom of the early nineteenth century. Yet the dichotomy between the sophisticated world of cotton finance and the primitive world of cotton production remained stark. Although cotton could be grown at D&PL and elsewhere by hand and animal, cotton could also be represented in finance by futures contracts, traded on a multitude of international exchanges, regulated by standardized contract laws and exchange rules, and secured by government and private loans. Even at its best, as in the case of D&PL, cotton farming in the 1930s remained an extremely labor-intensive and technologically backward business which bore a striking resemblance to antebellum cotton production. A centralized office may have made management decisions about work schedules, applications of fertilizer, proper insect control, maintenance requirements, crop distribution, and the timing of cotton sales, but the actual cotton cultivation was done by hand, hoe, and mule.

CHAPTER TWENTY-FIVE

The Planter Experience in the Twentieth Century

WHILE economic growth, financial activity, and industrialization produced large individual fortunes in the North after the Civil War, the South's cotton economy limped along at the mercy of the price of cotton. In 1937 the Southern editor and historian Jonathan Daniels called Memphis the "Paris of the plantation country ... sitting above a gambling land, the Cotton Kingdom." Memphis, of course, was the "metropolis" of the Mississippi Delta, its financial, social, and cultural capital. The Delta's population was reputed to contain a layer of rich cotton planters and an overwhelming majority of poor black tenants. The large, impoverished underclass was real, but planters were scarcely rich. An occasional brick home whose front was adorned with white columns dotted the landscape. These conspicuous edifices were referred to as Southern mansions and supposedly demonstrated vast sums of cotton money. Energetic towns sprang up in the Mississippi Delta as commercial centers to serve the cotton business. The towns boasted brick buildings, banks, railroads, cotton gins, stores, and doctors and lawyers. They were adjuncts to cotton production and thus too were exposed to the whims of the international cotton market, the weather, and even lowly insects.

Planter affluence has been greatly exaggerated, either as compared with that of Northern businessmen or absolutely. Delta cotton wealth was ephemeral. While land purchased after the Civil War for as low as a few cents on the dollar rose to $16 in the 1890s, $40 to $60 before World War I, and $125 to $455 briefly after the war, the intervening years were a violent roller-coaster ride. In no way could the income from farms justify the sometimes lofty land prices that were buoyed on pure speculation. No great fortunes were amassed; no large philanthropic foundations arose; no dynamic financial centers developed. European aristocrats, looking to shore up their meager income, did not flock to the South to find wives among the plantation belles.

In 1908, Leroy Percy, a former senator, Delta cotton planter, and attorney for the Illinois Central Railroad, estimated that "Ninety-five percent of the planting operations of this section of the Delta are carried on borrowed money. . . . Easy credit has been the curse of this section." The availability of credit had allowed "men without experience, ability, and pecuniary resources" to become large-scale cotton planters. The price of cotton and a good growing season dictated a pliant credit market. Within a few years after Percy's comment, the cotton business fell on hard times during World War I and then resiliently, but temporarily, reemerged. The Delta planter had to possess gambling instincts.

Cotton production had to adjust continually to credit availability. The Delta cotton planters' credit, just as we have seen with the intriguing role of the factor in antebellum New Orleans, could be rolled over during a bad year at the discretion of the lender. In the Delta it was bad form to foreclose. David Cohn explained the personal nature of cotton finance in the Delta:

> No creditor was so boorish as to sue a debtor. If one had done so, he would not only have faced social ostracism . . . but would also have set off a chain reaction and destroyed himself. Everybody, therefore, owed everybody else until a good cotton crop came along and there was an all-around scaling down of debts.

For an outside creditor who was accustomed to recourse in the courts, it might be difficult to enforce a foreclosure judgment or even obtain one.

In New York a financier might have to foreclose, refinance a loan, install new management, or even take over a company. The cotton creditor did not have this flexibility unless circumstances were dire over an extended period of time. The outlook of the indebted cotton planter could be summarized by Cohn's folksy black friend who said, "It ain't what I owes that worries me. It's gittin to owe." In other words, the *availability* of credit was a concern, not the debt itself, which was a fact of life. Cotton could always be sold and a revenue stream established, so some form of credit would eventually be forthcoming.

The dramatic fickleness of cotton prices may be illustrated by one extreme example. In 1919 a Delta planter, LeRoy Allen, sold his first hundred bales for 50 cents a pound. As the price rose, his tenants complained that he had sold too early. In 1920, Allen purchased an additional farm with partners for $360,000. Cotton was then trading at $1.25 a pound. Two of Allen's partners declined to sell the cotton at a price that would have netted $45,000 in profits. They also turned down opportunities to sell at 87.5 cents a pound. Allen finally began selling at 31.75 cents a pound. The price continued to plummet to 12.5 cents a pound. Allen ended the season with less than $100 in assets. Remorseful, he observed, "Planters whom I have known to be in excellent financial condition before the 1920 collapse had either lost their property or were struggling to hold on in a struggle in which the odds were likely against them."

The precariousness of the cotton cycle left few unharmed. Abe Isaacson, a former Talmudic scholar in Russia, wrote a personal account of the turbulence of the cotton world in his memoir, *From the Russian Ghetto to the Mississippi Delta* (1942). Isaacson had experienced hard-bitten poverty in a Jewish ghetto in frigid Russia. He was without antebellum emotional or cultural baggage when he decided to settle in Clarksdale, Mississippi, in 1914. For the next thirty years he owned a retail store that catered to black customers. He recalled the pitfalls of credit and cotton prices:

> During the time that I resided in Clarksdale, Miss., since the year of 1914 almost every merchant that I found there . . . [habitually patronized] the bankruptcy court where they were well known to the judge, referee and lawyers. . . . During the boom years of 1918 and 1919,

people in Clarksdale made so much money that they did not know what to do with it, in fact Clarksdale counted ten or twelve million-aires among its citizens, that is they were worth that much on paper, counting on selling cotton and land at top prices which were prevalent at that time.

However, when 1920 came along and the crash occurred in the market, people sold cotton at four and five cents per pound that could have [been] sold at sixty or seventy cents had they acted a little sooner. Land values dropped in the same proportion, and land that the owners didn't want to part with at four hundred dollars an acre was sold under the hammer in foreclosure, and in tax sales. Thus, in the year 1920 a great upheaval took place in the Delta and almost every body involved from the biggest planter to the small merchant . . . mighty few escaped from getting towed under the economic whirlpool that brought the mighty from their throne.

The cotton world was hardly static. The dynamics of environment and market forces—price, supply, demand, and the ability to buy and sell—render estimates of alleged planter wealth dubious.

CHAPTER TWENTY-SIX

The Long-Awaited
Mechanical Cotton Picker

COTTON PRODUCTION and black labor were thrown together because of technology—or more precisely because of the lack it. Until the 1930s the extensive use of fertilizer was the only significant technological improvement in cotton production. Black labor was the preferred choice because it was the only alternative. Cotton production could not be mechanized despite the expenditure of a prodigious amount of effort and money.

Until it was displaced by the tractor, the stubborn mule represented the primary machinery for cotton farming. This diligent creature pulled the plow that created the rows in which cotton was planted and weeded. It was impossible to produce cotton on a plantation without mules. It is impossible to discuss cotton production without describing the crucial role of the mule. During the explosive growth of cotton production in Mississippi between 1850 and 1860, the Mississippi mule population increased from 54,547 to 110,723 as the amount of cultivated acreage surged from 3,444,358 to 5,065,755 acres. Productivity remained fairly constant because cultivation ranged from 20 to 22 acres per mule (or horse). Essentially the mule was the engine of the cotton industry until the advent of the mass use of the tractor in the 1940s. The American mule population, which had risen to 26 million in

1920, declined to 4 million by 1958. Although cotton was not the sole factor, the price of mules doubled between 1899 and 1905, and tripled between 1899 and 1918. The importance of the mule over so long a period compellingly illustrates the absence of technological progress in cotton production.

America needed a new inventor to solve the vexing, labor-intensive problem of picking and weeding cotton by hand. Even nineteenth-century contemporaries knew that cotton production needed to be made more efficient. In 1881 the *Scientific American* described cotton planters as "not remarkable for economy or efficiency."

> A device which should do for cotton picking what Whitney's gin did for the work of freeing cotton lint from the seed would give an incalculable impetus to the extension of cotton culture. The demand for such an invention is urgent. . . . Already a crop amounting in value to three or four hundred million dollars is every year made difficult to secure . . . any rapid increase in the crop is prevented by the lack of workers at the critical season.

The article cited the enticing estimates of "Special Census Agent Hilgard" of the Mississippi Delta. The rich land, he reasoned, could easily produce 2.25 million bales with the aid of a mechanical cotton picker. The state of Mississippi, as a whole, could harvest 5 million bales, an amount equal to the average cotton crop for all of the United States in the preceding five years. The article then listed twelve recent patents for cotton pickers, accompanied by their drawings, to show the efforts that were being made to build a mechanical cotton picker. Inventors from Brooklyn, New York (1870), Canton, Ohio (1872), and Bridgewater, Massachusetts (1867), along with Southerners from Louisiana, Arkansas, and North Carolina, received patents for their versions of the cotton picker.

The earliest patent for a mechanical cotton picker was issued in 1850 to Samuel S. Rembert and Jedediah Prescott for a machine that used spindles to pull the cotton from the bolls, thus leaving the cotton plant unharmed. (Ninety years later, the spindle became the basic design element for a workable machine.) Other techniques involved static electricity and pneumatic tubes. Between 1850 and 1930, enterprising inventors and promoters received 750 patents for mechanical cotton pickers. Many were fakes. In 1870 a huckster bragged that his machine could be substituted for the "fingers of Sambo." He added that "the machine did not vote, go to circuses, barbeques . . . just when it was needed in the field." In 1894 the *Jackson Clarion-Ledger* excitedly reported that a mechanical cotton picker had been tested in Yazoo County, Mississippi, and "Picks Ten Bales a Day." This proved to be false.

The process of invention required an obsessive commitment. In 1885 the Chicagoan Angus Campbell began a frustrating twenty-year struggle to design a cotton picker; Peter Paul Haring of Goliad, Texas, began a thirty-year journey in 1897. Major farm implement companies put their resources to work. The International Harvester Co. of Chicago purchased existing patents and spent $4.5 million dollars on a twenty-five-year research project. One of its first tests in the 1920s ended with its mechanical cotton picker capsizing in the middle of a cotton field. John Deere and Co. of Moline, Illinois, entered the fray in the 1920s to compete with its rival. Skeptics appeared early and often despite serious and well-publicized development efforts. In 1937 a pundit remarked that "A successful cotton picker has been just right around the corner of the last eighty-seven years."

The first workable mechanical cotton picker was invented by John Rust, a quintessential solitary entrepreneur who tinkered with his design in his garage. A self-taught mechanic, Rust worked with his brother, Mack, who had a mechanical engineering degree from the University of Texas. Over several years the two Texans' experiments by trial and error resulted in a mechanical cotton picker in 1931 that harvested one bale of cotton in one day. In 1934 the Rust brothers' company, Southern Harvester, relocated to Memphis, the strategic center of the cotton business. By 1937 the Rust cotton picker was harvesting thirteen bales in one day and making national news. When the Rust Cotton Picker Co., as the firm was now called, attempted to produce the revolutionary machine commercially, financial risk intervened. The company went bankrupt, and the larger farm implement companies, like International Harvester, reaped the benefits.

Similar to Eli Whitney's gin, the Rusts' mechanical cotton picker carried with it enormous social and racial implications. John Rust was

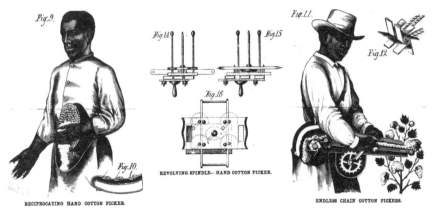

PNEUMATIC COTTON PICKER.

As the cotton market expanded, numerous attempts were made to invent a labor-saving device that would pick cotton. Above, clockwise from upper left, the Reciprocating Hand Cotton Picker, the Revolving Spindle Hand Cotton Picker, the Endless Chain Cotton Picker, and the Pneumatic Cotton Picker. But cotton production stubbornly resisted any form of mechanization, and plantations remained dependent on black labor. *(Scientific American)*

well aware of the possibility that millions of black (and white) share-croppers might be displaced. Unlike Eli Whitney, however, he was concerned with the human consequences of his invention. He established the Rust Foundation "to promote the well-being of humanity" without discriminating on the basis of "race, creed, or color." The Rust brothers were not interested in massive wealth, so they restricted the compensation of any employee or officer of their company to no more than ten times the income of the lowest-paid employee. John Rust hoped to eliminate "the great field of hand labor [that was] . . . the greatest source of child and woman labor in America" without harming "their friends and neighbors, the planters and the tenants."

The social revolution was interpreted differently by W. E. Ayres of the Mississippi Delta Experiment Station, a joint federal and state venture. In a letter to John Rust in 1934, Ayres expressed himself in terms of emancipation:

> We sincerely hope that you can arrange to build your machine shortly. Lincoln emancipated the Southern Negro. It remains for cotton harvesting machinery to emancipate the Southern cotton planter. The sooner this be done, the better for the entire South.

After the Rusts were out of the picture, in 1942 Fowler McCormick, chairman of International Harvester and a scion of Cyrus McCormick and John D. Rockefeller, publicly announced that Harvester had developed a commercially viable mechanical cotton picker. He emphasized the enormity of the task of developing the machine:

> The International Harvester Company has been experimenting with mechanical cotton pickers for approximately 40 years. It has proved to be the most difficult designing and engineering job in the modern history of agricultural machinery. Up to now we have never said that we had a successful cotton picker.

International Harvester had more pecuniary objectives than the Rusts. In another historical irony, the Chicago-based company would hasten the migration of blacks to Chicago and other Northern cities by mass producing a well-designed mechanical cotton picker that would displace black farm workers.

Practical as well as technological obstacles complicated Harvester's efforts. In a 1946 internal memorandum, the company predicted that a sharecropper family could farm one hundred acres rather than twenty-five if the farmer/owner used a mechanical cotton picker. But Harvester noted the need to manufacture mechanical cotton pickers quickly. It was concerned that laborers returning from World War II

Delta Station men in the fields with what appears to be a mechanical cotton picker. Successful trials of the mechanical picker in the 1930s led to a revolution in production and the displacement of millions of farm laborers. *(Courtesy of Delta Research and Extension Center)*

would reestablish the hand-picking system. The company cited cotton production figures of 9 million bales for 1945, suggesting that even this small number would not have been achievable without the use of prisoners of war who were used to pick cotton.

Harvester also worried that planters might be reluctant to use mechanical cotton pickers because of their "so-called obligation to labor." If planters were "forced to invest in the costly maintenance of families . . . the acceptance of the mechanical cotton picker will be retarded seriously." But when planters embraced the new machine, Harvester was able to increase production. Between 1948 and 1963 its market share of all mechanical cotton pickers rose from 30 to 64 percent. Over time the relative costs of hand labor versus the mechanical cotton picker completely eliminated the human field hand.

CHAPTER TWENTY-SEVEN

The Abdication of King Cotton

COTTON AND RACE were linked by three acknowledged monopolies: America monopolized cotton exports, blacks monopolized the plantation labor system, and the cotton South, by default, monopolized the working life of much of America's black population. Within a generation after the end of 1930, all these monopolies evaporated. The cotton economy came unglued. American cotton production fell victim to a number of factors that spelled the end to cotton's independent power and the beginning of cotton's dependence on government subsidy and control. The year 1937 marked the last year that cotton was the leading American export. Technology finally triumphed in 1931 as the first successful demonstration of a mechanical cotton picker was performed at the Delta Experiment Station in Stoneville, Mississippi. During the 1930s cotton production became a permanent ward of the federal government—as it is today—except for a few aberrational periods such as World War II. Cotton production would henceforth require permanent government subsidies in the form of price supports or loans.

The economic priority of reestablishing cotton production in the South after the Civil War eventually gave way to the crippling problem of overproduction. The Great Depression of the 1930s and the implementation of the U.S. government's misguided tariffs further hastened the demise of King Cotton. The effects of the depression were myriad.

From 1935 to 1939, cotton exports dipped to 46 percent of total exports, from as high as 50 to 60 percent a few years earlier. This decline is noteworthy when we consider that overseas consumption during this period actually increased by 69 percent.

The ever-important price of cotton reflected the laws of supply and demand. World War I shortages moved the price to 35.5 cents a pound in 1919, which brought huge new acreage into production. As the price dropped in 1920, cotton farmers turned to a "burn-a-bale" strategy. Farmers in Oklahoma and Louisiana responded with a voluntary acreage curtailment. Cotton sold at 17 cents a pound in 1929, the year of the stock market crash; the price plummeted to 9.5 cents in 1930 and then to 5.5 cents in 1931, the lowest level since 1894. The depression prompted Governor Huey P. Long's plan, a "Cotton Holiday," which banned the planting of cotton in 1932. Only South Carolina and Arkansas acquiesced. Texas, the most prolific cotton-producing state, passed more moderate legislation to reduce cotton acreage by 30 percent in 1932 and 1933. In desperation, Governor Bilbo of Mississippi and the legislature of South Carolina promoted Texas-type legislation. The arrogant overconfidence of Mississippi, the largest cotton-producing state on the eve of the Civil War, had given way to despair: one day in 1932, one-quarter of the entire state was auctioned for delinquent payment of taxes.

Expansion had led to oversupply, which was beyond the capacity of the states to rectify. The scope of the disaster was greater than in previous cotton crises. The federal government stepped in to rescue the cotton states as well as other agricultural sectors with various programs designed to control supply. In 1933 the Agricultural Adjustment Act provided a "plow-up campaign" that compensated farmers up to $20 an acre for plowing up cotton that had already been planted. The poor mules were made to walk on cotton plants they had always been conditioned to avoid. The intent was to reduce production in order to elevate the price of cotton. Henceforth the federal government would be involved with cotton farming, which became no longer a private industry. King Cotton had been reduced to a beggar.

Within a generation after 1930, black and white cotton workers were caught in a technological vise. As it so often does, technology created a

As late as the 1930s, cotton production depended on the reliable but inefficient mule. In 1935, under government auspices, these same mules were used
to "plow up," that is, destroy, cotton to reduce supply. (*Delta Research and
Extension Center*)

revolution in cotton production, bringing labor-intensive cultivation to
an abrupt end. Following the mechanical cotton picker, the final blow to
labor-intensive cotton production came in the 1950s with the creation of
the chemical Diuron, an herbicide that removed the need for "chopping"
or weeding cotton by hand. The displacement of workers changed the
labor dynamic. No longer did white cotton planters need blacks as laborers; they were jettisoned without even a nod to paternalism. The sharecropper system had evolved out of a particular combination of American
economic and racial forces: the abundance of freed slaves in the South,
the dominance of white economic and political power, prevailing white
American concepts of the utility of black labor in the cotton fields, and
an inability to mechanize cotton production. This constellation of forces
was now obsolete.

Times changed quickly. No longer were cotton farms filled with
black sharecroppers and their shacks. Mules and the farm equipment
of a bygone era disappeared. Sheds for tractors and mechanical cotton
pickers replaced barns and mule stables. The many black churches that

After World War II, tractors at last replaced mules and manual laborers in the cotton fields. *(Benjy Nelken)*

dotted the farm landscape were abandoned as blacks moved to Southern towns and cities and to cities in the North. High unemployment resulting from the displacement of unskilled farm laborers remains an enduring feature of the cotton plantation landscape. The coincidence of the advent of technology, the civil rights movement, and the end of legal segregation has left blacks in the plantation world groping for an economic identity.

The aggressive materialism that cotton farmers pursued was merely a variation of American commercialism, with a racial component. The racial caste system of the cotton plantation South was finally dismantled by economic and technological forces. The reign of King Cotton as an economic juggernaut ended, but its ugly human legacy remains among a great many black citizens who are unprepared to function effectively in the modern world.

Cotton, deemed to be so vital that it was instrumental in causing the Civil War, that the Confederacy placed an embargo on exports, was deemed expendable on the eve of World War II. In 1941, before Pearl Harbor, the United States attempted to bankrupt Japan by placing embargos on strategic material, such as oil and steel. Although Japan needed cotton and Japan was "America's largest foreign customer," no embargo was possible because of the glut of cotton in world markets. The Department of Agriculture noted that "Surpluses of cotton throughout the world are abundant to the point of being burdensome. . . . Cotton [growers] will face impoverishment or disaster [if an embargo was imposed]." In the eighty years from 1861 to 1941, cotton descended from an indispensable product to a surplus commodity. It was replaced by oil as the eventual strategic resource in the post–World War II global arena. In many ways, cotton had been the oil of the nineteenth century.

*

This journey through the vicissitudes of the cotton world has demonstrated again and again that the near fateful power of economics in human history cannot be denied. The destiny of most black Americans was tied to the cataclysmic explosion of cotton production in nineteenth-century America. The pursuit of money saw no bounds in solving labor shortages created by the demands of cotton production. The association between cotton and race began in earnest with the invention of the cotton gin in 1793 and with the possibility of a profit explosion. This link between white cotton and the black laborer, a fundamentally economically determined event, simply grafted a race-based slave system onto a new gold rush, cotton. And even after emancipation, the extent of white Northern racial animosity and the absence of Southern labor alternatives dictated that, more often than not, blacks remained in the fields. The abolition of slavery left the freedmen in the cotton fields under a new social system predicated on the ever-present need for black labor. The connection between cotton and race began to unravel only when another labor shortage, this time during World War I, trumped prevailing white Northern racial animosity. The complete decoupling came only with two technologically driven events, the practical advent of the mechanical cotton picker in the 1940s and the successful adoption of herbicides in the 1950s.

The consequences of this productive but unholy marriage of cotton and race were twofold: a powerful American advantage gained by a virtual monopoly of world cotton exports, and American's most serious social tragedy—slavery and the racial caste system endured by black America. Before cotton went the way of all monopolies, it had a profound social, economic, and political impact on America.

Once considered royalty, cotton now survives on government handouts. The mid-twentieth century technological revolution reinforced cotton's inevitable tendency toward large-scale farming operations. Expensive machines, chemicals, and irrigation required major investments that could be provided only by large producers. In an historical irony, the cotton states, America's most conspicuous adherents to the political theory of states' rights, now are able to produce cotton only because of support from the federal government. In another irony, American cotton producers, now armed with technologically advanced equipment and agricultural chemicals, face stiff competition from primitive cotton producers in countries like China, India, Pakistan, Uzbekistan, and those in West Africa. In America a ten-thousand-acre farm that might have required the labor of a thousand black families in the 1930s would require only a few workers today. And yet foreign cotton-exporting countries today successfully compete with America, for the most part because of their own subsidies, tariff barriers, proximity to textile mills, and often harsh labor practices.

Few sympathize with the modern dilemma of the American cotton farmer, whose federal subsidies are lambasted by editorial pages as ideologically diverse as the *Wall Street Journal* and the *New York Times*. One may recall the glory days when the *New York Times* in 1865 expressed a common sentiment that critical restoration of cotton production after the Civil War called for black labor managed by white brains. And with copious amounts of Northern racial antipathy, a racial caste system, and a huge effort, American cotton regained its command of the export market. But cotton's demise in the last seventy years has left in its wake many rural Southern communities in dire economic and social straits. Large areas like the Mississippi Delta, once hailed as a cotton kingdom, are now characterized by large-scale farm operations, decrepit towns, a majority, often struggling black population, and economic hopelessness. In the last few years cotton has suffered a further blow as the surging price of corn has prompted a shift from cotton acreage to corn production. Of course, cotton farming has been declared dead before—especially when synthetic fibers became competitors in the 1930s. If the price of grains drops precipitously, cotton farming may yet again rise. Likewise, American innovators are always at work. Currently a farm family in the heart of the Mississippi Delta, perhaps latter-day Eli Whitneys, are refining a ginning process that may create new markets for cotton.

What is the legacy of cotton for African Americans? Slavery and its descendants—legal segregation and sharecropping—are blamed for persistent black poverty, educational shortcomings, and destructive behavioral traits, from high rates of illegitimacy and single-parent families to a disproportionate incidence of crime. Even when the prerequisites of black plight did not exist in the North, the devastating inheritance remained for many Northern urban blacks. Where slavery, legal segregation, and sharecropping did exist in the South, their disappearance has also failed to eliminate the black underclass. After generations with no connection to the cotton field, African Americans may be found among the elite in almost every aspect of American life, including the 2008 election of Barack Obama to the presidency. A large African-American middle class has developed. But a tragic, seemingly permanent underclass of African Americans continues to inhabit our nation's cities and rural areas.

The problems of black education, family structure, and behavior have perplexed African-American scholars from Du Bois to the present. As black cotton laborers moved to the urban ghetto, did they bring along the legacy of cotton? In 1932 the pioneering African-American sociologist E. Franklin Frazier wrote of "family disorganization," "desertion," "juvenile delinquency," and "illegitimacy" among blacks. In 2007 two black scholars at Harvard University, Orlando Paterson and Henry Louis Gates, Jr., called attention to the staggering 70 percent rate of illegitimacy in the black community as well as the disproportionate number of black men in jail and the high rate of school dropouts. These statistics, they pointed out, are worse than "anything achieved at the height of the Jim Crow era." Poverty, acknowledged as a progeny of slavery, segregation, and sharecropping, has also presented itself.

Is the legacy of cotton subject to a statute of limitations? This legacy is an American rather than a Southern issue. Typically, the blame is now spread more generally: white American prejudice, the black community's lack of leadership, and government inattention. Until the black community organizes a massive grassroots effort, in a process reminiscent of the self-help philosophy of Frederick Douglass and Booker T. Washington, the black underclass will never enter America's economic and social mainstream.

White America deals with its history of racial animosity through collective guilt, but though white guilt may soothe the conscience, it has real-world limits. While white America abolished slavery and helped dismantle legal segregation, it is reluctant to admit African Americans to economic equality without concessions to assimilation and education. The polarizing concept of affirmative action is still considered necessary to enforce racial quotas or guidelines in employment and universities. The feeling of white remorse does not prevent de facto residential and school segregation. And white guilt stops short of seriously considering federal laws to provide African Americans with reparations in recognition of their historical treatment.

For more than 150 years, America benefited enormously from cotton picked by African Americans. The economic world of cotton needed a workforce, and white America designated African Americans for the role. America no longer needs cotton, but it still bears cotton's human legacy.

Appendix

1. Cotton Prices in Cents per Pound, Weighted Average, 1800–1860

Year	Price	Year	Price
1800	44.0	1839	7.9
1802	14.7	1842	5.7
1805	23.0	1844	5.5
1811	8.9	1847	7.0
1815	27.3	1850	11.7
1817	29.8	1851	7.4
1822	11.5	1856	12.4
1830	8.4	1859	10.8
1835	15.2	1860	11.0

Source: Stuart Bruchey, *Cotton and the Growth of the American Economy, 1790–1860: Sources and Readings* (New York: Harcourt, Brace & World, 1967).

2. Movement of Slaves in the Old Southwest

Population Changes

GEORGIA

	White	Free Colored	Slave	Total
1790	53,886	398	29,264	82,548
1810	145,414	1,801	105,218	252,433
1830	296,806	2,486	217,531	516,823
1850	521,572	2,931	381,682	906,185
1860	591,588	3,500	462,198	1,057,286

MISSISSIPPI

	White	Free Colored	Slave	Total
1800	5,179	182	3,489	8,850
1810	23,024	240	17,088	40,352
1830	70,443	519	65,659	136,621
1840	179,074	1,366	195,211	375,651
1850	295,718	930	309,878	606,526
1860	353,901	773	436,631	791,305

(1800–1810, Mississippi Territory [present-day Mississippi and Alabama])

Cotton Production, in Millions of Pounds

	Georgia	Mississippi
1800	10	0
1833	88	70
1839	163.4	193.2
1849	199.6	194
1859	312.3	535.1

Source: Bruchey, *Cotton and the Growth of the American Economy.*

3. Breakdown of Population in Selected States, 1800–1860

NEW YORK STATE

	White	Free Colored	Slave	Total
1790	314,142	4,654 (1.4%)	21,324 (6.27%)	340,120
1800	556,039	10,374 (1.8%)	20,343 (3.47%)	586,756
1860	3,831,730	49,005 (1.26%)	0	3,880,735

NEW YORK COUNTY

	White	Free Colored	Slave	Total
1703	3,745		630 (14.4%)	4,375
1746	9,273		2,444 (20.9%)	11,717
1790	29,661	1,101 (3.3%)	2,369 (7.1%)	33,131
1860	801,095	12,574 (1.54%)	0	813,669

Source: Edgar J. McManus, *History of Negro Slavery in New York* (Syracuse: Syracuse University Press, 2001). In 1746 there was no distinction between "Slave" and "Free Negroes."

CONNECTICUT

	White	Free Colored	Slave	Total
1800	244,721	5,330 (2.1%)	951	251,002
1810	255,279	6,453 (2.5%)	310	262,042
1830	289,603	8,047 (2.7%)	25	297,675
1840	310,856	8,105 (2.5%)	17	318,978
1850	363,099	7,693 (2.1%)		370,792
1860	451,520	8,627 (1.9%)		460,147

OHIO (statehood 1803)

	White	Free Colored	Total
1800 (NW Territory)	45,028	337 (0.7%)	45,365
1810	228,861	1,889 (0.8%)	230,750
1830	928,329	9,568 (1%) (6 slaves)	937,903
1840	1,502,122	17,342 (1.1%)	1,519,464
1850	1,955,050	25,279 (1.3)	1,980,329
1860	2,302,838	36,673 (1.6%)	2,339,511

ILLINOIS (statehood 1821)

	White	Free Colored	Total
1810	11,501	613 (5%)	12,114
1830	155,806	2,486 (1.6%)	158,292
1840	472,806	3,598 (0.8%)	476,404
1850	846,034	5,436 (0.6%)	851,470
1860	1,704,323	7,698 (0.4%)	1,712,021

INDIANA (statehood 1816)

	White	Free Colored	Total
1800	4,577	163 (3.4%)	4,740
1810	23,890	393 (1.6%)	24,283
1830	339,399	3,629 (1%)	343,028
1840	678,698	7,165 (1%)	685,763
1850	977,154	11,262 (1.1%)	988,416
1860	1,339,000	11,428 (0.8%)	1,350,428

WISCONSIN (statehood 1848)

	White	Free Colored	Total
1840	30,749	1,185 (0.6%) (11 slaves)	30,945
1850	304,756	635 (0.2%)	305,391
1860	777,710	1,171 (0.2%)	778,881

MICHIGAN (statehood 1837)

	White	Free Colored	Total
1840	211,560	707 (0.3%)	212,267
1850	395,071	2,583 (0.6%)	397,654
1860	742,314	6,799 (0.9%)	749,113

IOWA (statehood 1846)

	White	Free Colored	Total
1840	42,924	172 (0.4%)	43,096
1850	191,881	333 (0.2%)	192,214
1860	673,844	1,059 (0.2%)	674,903

KANSAS (statehood 1861)

	White	Free Colored	Total
1860	106,579	625 (0.6%) (2 slaves)	107,206

CALIFORNIA (statehood 1850)

	White	Free Colored	Total
1850	91,635	962 (1%)	92,597
1860	361,353	4,086 (1.1%)	365,439

OREGON (statehood 1859)

	White	Free Colored	Total
1850	13,087	207 (1.6%)	13,294
1860	52,337	128 (0.2%)	52,465

Source: U.S. Bureau of the Census.

4. Cotton Prices per Pound in New York and Liverpool, 1860–1865

	New York (cents)			Liverpool (pence)		
Season	Low	High	Average	Low	High	Average
1860–1861	10	22	13.01	6.5	11.625	8.5
1861–1862	20	51.5	31.29	12.25	29	18.37
1862–1863	51	92	67.21	20	29.25	22.46
1863–1864	68	189	101.5	21.5	31.25	27.17
1864–1865	35	182	83.38	13	26	19.11

Sources: James L. Watkins, *King Cotton* (New York: Negro Universities Press, 1969); Harold D. Woodman, *King Cotton and His Retainers: Financing and Marketing the Cotton Crop of the South, 1800–1925* (Columbia: University of South Carolina Press, 1990).

5. American Cotton Expansion

	COTTON ACREAGE	COTTON PRODUCTION (bales)	AVERAGE PRICE (cents per pound)
1880	15,921,000	6,606,000	9.83
1890	20,937,000	8,653,000	8.59
1900	24,886,000	10,124,000	9.15
1910	31,508,000	11,609,000	13.96
1920	34,408,000	13,429,000	15.89
1930	42,444,000	13,932,000	9.46
1931	39,110,000	17,097,000	6

Sources: U.S. Bureau of the Census, *Historical Statistics of the United States, Colonial Times to 1957* (Washington, D.C., 1960); Woodman, *King Cotton and His Retainers*; C. Wayne Smith and J. Tom Cothren, eds., *Cotton: Origin, History, Technology and Production* (New York: Wiley, 1999); Timothy Curtis Jacobson and George David Smith, *Cotton's Renaissance: A Study in Market Innovation* (Cambridge, England: Cambridge University Press, 2001).

Notes

Part One. Slavery in the Making of the Constitution

page

7   "There is no Congress": Quoted in Wilson E. Lyon, *The Man Who Sold Louisiana: The Career of François Barbé-Marbois* (Norman, Okla., 1974), 46.

7   "mortified beyond expression": Quoted in Carol Berkin, *A Brilliant Solution: Inventing the American Constitution* (Orlando, Fla., 2002), 28.

7   "authority or rather the influence": Quoted in Edmund S. Morgan, *The Birth of the Republic, 1763–1789 (Chicago, 1992)*, 12.

8   ". . . the States were divided": Quoted in Joseph J. Ellis, *Founding Brothers: The Revolutionary Generation* (New York, 2004), 91.

8   "Madison's motivation for his warning": Gordon Wood, "Reading the Framers' Minds," *New York Review of Books*, June 28, 2007, 64.

8   "An Ethiopian could as soon": Quoted in Melvin Drimmer, "Was Slavery Dying Before the Cotton Gin?" in Melvin Drimmer, ed., *Black History: A Reappraisal* (Garden City, N.Y., 1961), 110–111.

9   "lust for gain": Quoted in Catherine Drinker Bowen, *Miracle at Philadelphia: The Story of the Constitutional Convention, May to September 1787* (Boston, 1986), 202–203.

9   "Tobacco was known": James A. B. Scherer, *Cotton as a World Power: A Study in the Economic Interpretation of History* (New York, 1916), 147.

9   "Slavery in time": Quoted in Christopher Collier and James Lincoln Collier, *Decision in Philadelphia: The Constitutional Convention of 1787* (New York, 1986), 232.

9   "the abolition of slavery": Quoted in Paul Finkelman, *Slavery and the Founders: Race and Liberty in the Age of Jefferson* (New York, 2001), 26.

9   "and though the period is more distant": Quoted in Ellis, *Founding Brothers*, 94.

10   "could insist on abolition": Morgan, *Birth*, 141.

10   "nefarious institution": Quoted in Collier, *Decision*, 229.

10   "Morris also introduced": Ibid., 234.

11 "It exported cattle": Ibid., 234.

11 "A crafty debater": Berkin, *Brilliant Solution*, 52

11 "different as the interests of Russia and Turkey": Collier, *Decision*, 111.

11 "abolish the importation of slaves": Ibid., 231.

11 "In any event, he observed": Bowen, *Miracle*, 202.

12 "Indeed, his financial dealings": Forest McDonald, *We the People: Economic Origins of the Constitution* (New Brunswick, N.J., 1992), 47.

12 "What enriches a part": Bowen, *Miracle*, 202.

12 "it was better to let the Southern states import slaves": Finkelman, *Founders*, p. 28.

13 "the three-fifths clause": Gary Wills, *"Negro President": Jefferson and the Slave Power* (Boston, 2003), 1–13.

13 "without the indulgence": Ibid., 56–57.

13 "never confederate": Finkelman, *Founders*, 18–19.

13 "produce all mischief": Collier, *Decision*, 234.

14 "Even though some Southerners": Ellis, *Founding Brothers*, 95.

14 "The moment this plan goes forth": Bowen, *Miracle*, 258–259.

14 "is it possible to deliberate": Ibid., 259.

14 "the greatest single effort": Ibid., 279.

15 "I wish the Constitution": Ibid., 280.

15 "no barrier in winning approval": A slavery exclusion clause was included in the Northwest Ordinance, passed by Congress in the summer of 1787. This document provided rules for the settlement and eventual admission to statehood for the Northwest Territory, the region west of the Appalachians and north of the Ohio River that would ultimately encompass Ohio, Indiana, Illinois, Michigan, Wisconsin, and parts of Minnesota. America's aggressive land expansion was thus given legislative credence.

15 "the importation of blacks": Collier, *Decision*, 188.

16 "Franklin also asked": Claude-Anne Lopez and Eugenia W. Herbert, *The Private Franklin: The Man and His Family* (New York, 1975), 291–302.

18 "A committee of employ": Benjamin Franklin, "An Address to the Public from the Pennsylvania Society Promoting the Abolition of Slavery and the Relief of Free Negroes, Unlawfully Held in Bondage," November 9, 1789, Series I, No. 45559.

18 "I have no doubt": Harold G. Syrett, ed., *Papers of Alexander Hamilton*, Vol. II (New York, 1961), 17–19.

19 "[Cotton] . . . has not been cultivated": Syrett, Hamilton, Vol. XIX, 443–444.

19 "by which slavery": Ulrich B. Phillips, *American Negro Slavery* (Baton Rouge, 1966), 123.

20 "Washington probably supplied": Phillips, *Slavery*, 283–286.

20 "When he became president": McDonald, *We the People*, 71–72.

20 "Like other slaveholders": Lewis Cecil Gray, *History of Agriculture in the Southern United States to 1860*, Vol. I (Gloucester, Mass., 1958), 616, 911.

21 "to return to Africa": Gary B. Nash, *Race and Revolution* (Madison, Wisc., 1990), 57–83.

22 "Edmund Morgan has written": Morgan, *Birth*, 142.

22 "needed free and mutual commerce": George E. Baker, ed., *The Works of William H. Seward*, Vol. IV (New York, 1853), 168.

23 "Abraham Lincoln's earnest wish": Allen G. Guelzo, *Lincoln's Emancipation Proclamation: The End of Slavery in America* (New York, 2004), 26–27.

23 "As the historian Joseph Ellis": Ellis, *Founding Brothers*, 101.

Part Two. The Engine of American Growth, 1787–1861

Epigraph: Quoted in William J. Chute, *Damn Yankee! The First Career of Frederick A. P. Barnard: Educator, Scientist, Idealist* (Port Washington, N.Y., 1978), 192.

27 "Thus within one man's lifetime": Henry Hobhouse, *Seeds of Change: Five Plants That Transformed Mankind* (New York, 1986), 141.

29 "Between 1787 and 1807": Douglass C. North, *The Economic Growth of the United States, 1790–1860* (New York, 1966), 41.

30 "From 1800 to 1860, cotton production provoked": Ibid., 67.

30 "David Cohn places cotton": David L. Cohn, *The Life and Times of King Cotton* (New York, 1956), 88.

31 "Northern businesses": Stanley L. Engerman, "The Southern Slave Economy," in Harry P. Owens, ed., *Perspectives and Irony in American Slavery* (Jackson, Miss., 1976), 84–85.

32 "It was then packed into bales": Timothy Curtis Jacobson and George David Smith, *Cotton's Renaissance: A Study in Market Innovation* (Cambridge, England, 2001), 326.

32 "the Southern counties of New Jersey": Gray, *Agriculture*, 687.

33 "I involuntarily happened": Mathew B. Hammond, ed., "Correspondence of Eli Whitney Relative to the Invention of the Cotton Gin," *American Historical Review*, Vol. 3, no. 1 (October 1897), 90.

33 "It is generally said by those": Ibid., 100.

34 "By the summer of 1797, thirty of the Whitney gins": Ibid., 104.

34 "He then gave the impressionistic rendering": Charles S. Sydnor, *Slavery in Mississippi* (Baton Rouge, 1966), 181.

34 "Cotton gins were consistently improved": Stanley Lebergott, *The Americans: An Economic Record* (New York, 1984), 169.

34 "One of his biographers": Jonathan Hughes, *The Vital Few: The Entrepreneur and American Economic Progress* (New York, 1986), 131.

34 "New Englanders played a significant role": John Hebron Moore, *The Emergence of the Cotton Kingdom in the Old Southwest: Mississippi, 1770–1860* (Baton Rouge, 1988), 57–59.

36 "Engels worked in his family's cotton business": E. J. Hobsbawm, *Industry and Empire* (Harmondsworth, England, 1972), 184.

36 "Raw cotton, in fact": Scherer, *World Power*, 4–5.

36 "Liverpool shipping tonnage": Frank Lawrence Owsley, *King Cotton Diplomacy: Foreign Relations of the Confederate States of America* (Chicago, 1959), 8–9.

37 "In the 1830s, raw cotton accounted for": Hobsbawm, *Industry*, 56–96.

37 "The overall cotton industry production": Owsley, *Diplomacy*, 6–7.

37 "British and American Raw Cotton Trade": Stuart Bruchey, *Cotton and the Growth of the American Economy, 1790–1860: Sources and Readings* (New York, 1967), Tables 2A, 3A.

38 "The Manchester Chamber of Commerce": Owsley, *Diplomacy*, 3–4.

38 "The peasants": Ibid., 3–6.

39   "Rich, inexpensive Louisiana": Gray, *Agriculture*, 681, 688.

40   "Just as significant": Scherer, *World Power*, p. 150.

40   "His personal obligations extended": David J. Libby, *Slavery and Frontier Mississippi, 1770–1835* (Jackson, Miss., 2004), 38–39.

41   "The total purchase price": Alexander De Conde, *This Affair of Louisiana*, (New York, 1979), 161–175.

41   "Eventually the British owned": Richard Sylla, "Emerging Markets in History: The United States, Japan, and Argentina," in Ryuzo Sato, Rama Ramachandran, and Kazuo Mino, eds. *Global Competition and Integration* (Boston, 1999), 427–446.

42   "The Indians blinked": John Ray Skates, *Mississippi: A History* (New York, 1979), 80–83.

43   "In 1831 the land auctions": A. M. Sakolski, *The Great American Land Bubble: The Amazing Story of Land-Grabbing, Speculations, and Booms from Colonial Days to the Present Time* (New York, 1932), 232–254.

43   "Everybody is speculating": Quoted in Ibid., 233.

44   "Money is plenty": Quoted in Mary Elizabeth Young, *Ruffleshirts and Rednecks: Indian Allotments in Alabama and Mississippi, 1830–1860* (Norman, Okla., 2002), 115–139.

44   "The Georgia Company Association purchased": James W. Silver, "Land Speculation Profits in the Chickasaw Cession," *Journal of Southern History*, Vol. 10, No. 1 (February 1944), 84–92.

44   "They could not sell the land": Moore, *Emergence*, 19.

44   "The returns over the life of the company": Young, *Ruffleshirts*, 149–150.

45   "Bemoaning speculation that": Roy M. Robbins, *Our Landed Heritage: The Public Domain, 1776–1936* (Lincoln, Nebr., 1962), 61–69.

45   "A plague o' this cotton": Quoted in Scherer, *World Power*, 191.

46   "Further planned extensions to Cincinnati": Scherer, Ibid., 202–203.

46   "The steamers on the rivers": Quoted in Gerald M. Capers, Jr., *The Biography of a River Town: Memphis: Its Heroic Age* (self-published, 1966; Chapel Hill, 1939), 79, 105.

46   "The *Memphis Commercial Appeal*, in 1847": Ibid., 133.

46   "Men might flame with malaria": Cohn, *Life and Times*, 103.

47   "in 1850 only 12 percent of the farmers": Skates, *Mississippi*, 93.

47   "Charles's grandson and namesake": James David Miller, *South by Southwest: Planter Emigration and Identity in the Slave South* (Charlottesville, Va., 2002), 19 n20, 155.

47   "In 1811 he managed to put down": Roger G. Kennedy, *Architecture, Men, Women, and Money in America, 1600–1860* (New York, 1985), 346–352.

48   "Talk of 35 percent returns": Bruchey, *Growth*, 113.

48   "To sell cotton in order": Harold D. Woodman, *King Cotton and His Retainers: Financing and Marketing the Cotton Crop of the South, 1800–1925* (Columbia, S.C., 1990), 135.

48   "I have been trying": Quoted in Gavin Wright, *Old South, New South: Revolutions in the Southern Economy Since the Civil War* (Baton Rouge, 1986), 26.

48   "By 1860, 360,000 white Northerners": Fletcher Green, *The Role of the Yankee in the Old South* (Athens, Ga., 1972), 5.

48 "Mobile, which exported cotton": Robert Greenhalgh Albion, *The Rise of New York Port, 1815–1860* (New York, 1970), 104–105.

49 "The state banks": Green, *Yankee*, 130–131.

50 "The scholar and future president": Scherer, *World Power*, 150–151.

51 "He thought that if gold": Frederick Law Olmsted, *A Journey to the Back Country* (New York, 1860), vi–viii.

51 "One historian of cotton": Scherer, *World Power*, 199.

52 "Eighty thousand may have traveled": Phillips, *Slavery*, 190.

52 "In 1832, Professor Thomas Dew": Scherer, *World Power*, 151.

52 "The slave migrations to Alabama": Michael Tadman in Walter Johnson, *Soul by Soul: Life Inside the Antebellum Slave Market* (Cambridge, Mass., 1999), 225.

52 "One source calculates": August Meier and Elliott Rudwick, *From Plantation to Ghetto* (New York, 1998), 57.

53 "Cotton, the money crop": Robert William Fogel, *Without Consent or Contract: The Rise and Fall of American Slavery* (New York, 1989), 44–45.

53 "They remained low": Gray, *Agriculture*, 666. Note graph in Phillips, *Slavery*, 371.

53 "A Georgian noticed": Johnson, *Soul*, 6.

53 "The old rule of pricing": Quoted in Robert Sobel, *The Money Manias: Tales of Entrepreneurs and Investors During the Eras of Great Speculation in America, 1770–1970* (New York, 1973), 90.

54 "White cotton can": Quoted in Johnson, *Soul*, 83.

54 "As historians and market participants": Sobel, *Money*, 80.

54 "The state legislated": William K. Scarborough, "Heartland of the Cotton Kingdom," in Richard Aubrey McLemore, ed., *A History of Mississippi*, Vol. I (Jackson, Miss., 1973), 328–329.

55 "Through the nineteenth century": Ibid., 329–330.

55 "By 1860 there were 773 free blacks": Ibid., 331.

55 "Most fugitives returned": Ibid., 339–342.

56 "*DeBow's Review* offered these rules": Paul F. Paskoff and Daniel J. Wilson, eds., *The Cause of the South: Selections from DeBow's Review* (Baton Rouge, 1982), 20–57.

56 "Resolved, that the people": Quoted in Sydnor, *Slavery*, 240, 242.

56 "The treatment of slaves": Janet Sharp Hermann, *The Pursuit of a Dream* (New York, 1981), 18.

57 "His views were conditioned": Ibid., 143.

57 "Examples of slaves": Ibid., 18.

57 "Pemberton, she related,": William J. Cooper, Jr., *Jefferson Davis, American* (New York, 2000), 49, 128, 229–239.

58 "He vilified Jefferson Davis": R. J. M. Blackett, *Divided Hearts: Britain and the American Civil War* (Baton Rouge, 2001), 122, 132, 225.

58 "By the 1850s, idealistic Northerners": Olmsted, *Journey*, 351–352.

58 "The levee along what": Quoted in Robert W. Harrison, "Levee Districts and Levee Building in Mississippi: A Study of State and Local Efforts to Control Mississippi River Floods," published by Delta Council, Mississippi Levee Commissioners, Board of Levee Commissioners for the Yazoo-Mississippi Delta and Mississippi Agricultural Experiment Station (October 1951), 7–8.

59   "Slave labor cannot be substituted": Sobel, *Money*, 77; Cohn, *Life and Times*, 64–65.

59   "Slave ownership was skewed": Carl Degler, *Out of Our Past: The Forces That Shaped Modern America* (New York, 1959), 163–164.

59   "During the Civil War": Drew Gilpin Faust, *The Creation of Confederate Nationalism: Ideology and Identity in the Civil War South* (Baton Rouge, 1989), 73.

59   "Cash for Negroes": Quoted in Emory Q. Hawk, *Economic History of the South* (New York, 1934), 254.

59   "The scope and profitability": Libby, *Frontier*, 64; Sobel, *Money*, 69–110.

60   "Judges encouraged participants": Jenny B. Wahl, "The Jurisprudence of American Slave Sales," *Journal of Economic History*, Vol. 56, No. 1 (March 1966), 143–169.

60   "Her biographer reported": Catherine Clinton, *Fanny Kemble's Civil Wars* (New York, 2000), 162.

62   "The roller-coaster cotton business": Albion, *New York*, 114–115, 236.

62   "The entire credit structure": Woodman, *King Cotton*, 41.

62   "Southern factors": Cohn, *Life and Times*, 112.

63   "The Mississippi cotton planter": Woodman, *King Cotton*, 119–122.

63   "From the beginning America": Sylla, "Emerging Markets," 433.

64   "The single fact": Bruchey, *Growth*, 67–71.

64   "Indeed, revenues": Davis Rich Dewey, *Financial History of the United States* (New York, 1924), 230.

65   "But the antebellum period": Sydnor, *Slavery*, 189–199.

66   "Let the public believe": Joseph G. Baldwin, *The Flush Times of Alabama and Mississippi: A Series of Sketches* (New York, 1964), 59–60.

66   "The weakening price of cotton": Dewey, *Financial*, 230.

66   "You may tell your government": Quoted in Niall Ferguson, *The House of Rothschild: Money's Prophets, 1798–1848* (New York, 1995), 374.

66   "The price per pound dropped": Moore, *Emergence*, 20; Gray, *Agriculture*, 697.

67   "In the New Orleans slave market": Hawk, *Economic*, 251.

67   "On paper, slaves may have accounted": Wright, *Old South*, 19–20.

67   "Debtors, in many cases": Skates, *Mississippi*, 85

67   "Mississippi is ruined": Philips, *Slavery*, 372; Cohn, *Life and Times*, 116.

68   "[I]f the United States wants": Bray Hammond, *Banks and Politics in America: From the Revolution to the Civil War* (Princeton, 1985), 548.

68   "But the Southerners George McDuffie": Thomas Payne Govan, *Nicholas Biddle: Nationalist and Public Banker, 1786–1844* (Chicago, 1959), 321.

68   "Soon after, Biddle realized": Robert Sobel, *Panic on Wall Street: A History of America's Financial Disasters* (New York, 1972), 32–76.

68   "His bright and accomplished mind": Quoted in Hammond, *Banks*, 533.

70   "By merely supineness": Quoted in Woodman, *King Cotton*, 128.

70   "Skilled at marshalling statistics": John McCardell, *The Idea of a Southern Nation: Southern Nationalists and Southern Nationalism* (New York, 1979), 123.

70   "New Orleans, the Cresent City": *DeBow's Review* (July 1849) Vol. VII, 12, 37.

71   "For Gregg, the South had to": Paskoff, *Cause*, 122–130.

71   "Much of the 'negro cloth' was manufactured": "Negro cloth: Northern Industry & Southern Slavery," Myro O. Stachiw: Merrimac Valley Textile museum,

September 1, 1981. Published in conjunction with the exhibition at the Boston National Historical Park, Boston, Mass.

71 "Dependence on Northern capital": Woodman, *King Cotton*, 172–173, 149–153.

72 "To accomplish this the Cotton Planters' Association": Ibid., 140–150.

72 "The truth is that the cotton crop": Quoted in Scherer, *World Power*, 231.

73 "He anticipated the correlation": Joseph Holt Ingraham, *The South-West by a Yankee*, Vol. 2 (New York, 1968), 86–87.

73 "Both before and after the Civil War": Scarborough, "Heartland," 322–327.

74 "Referring to the extraction": Degler, *Past*, 110.

74 "We cannot help the matter": Quoted in David M. Pletcher, *The Diplomacy of Annexation: Texas, Oregon, and the Mexican War* (Columbia, Mo., 1973), 334.

74 "In this he agreed with the expansionist Mississippi senator": Stephen John Harnett, *Democratic Dissent and the Cultural Fictions of Antebellum America* (Urbana, 2002), 121.

75 "It is easy to foresee": in Reginald C. McGrane, *The Correspondence of Nicholas Biddle, 1807–1844* (Boston, 1919), 328–333.

75 "A little-known Democratic congressman, David Wilmot": Charles Sellers, *The Market Revolution: Jacksonian America, 1815–1846* (New York, 1991), 426.

76 "Provided, That, as an express": Quoted in Charles Buxton Going, *David Wilmot: Free Soiler, A Biography of the Great Advocate of the Wilmot Proviso* (Gloucester, Mass., 1966), 98.

76 "Wilmot had favored": James Ford Rhodes, *History of the United States from the Compromise of 1850 to the Final Restoration of Home Rule at the South in 1877*, Vol. 1, *1850–1854* (New York, 1919), 89.

76 "When territory presents itself": Ibid., 174.

77 "Wilmot's racial antipathy": Sellers, *Market*, 426–427.

77 "When Daniel Webster, the anti-slavery Massachusetts senator": Scherer, *World Power*, 218–222.

77 "When Daniel Webster": Rhodes, *History*, Vol. 1, 143–153.

78 "Wheat, which was slave-grown": Gavin Wright, "Slavery and American Agricultural History," *Agricultural History*, Vol. 77, No. 4 (Autumn 2003), 527–552.

78 "The economic historian Gavin Wright": *Slavery and American Economic Development* (Baton Rouge, 2006), 86.

79 "Efforts to use slave labor": Robert S. Starobin, *Industrial Slavery in the Old South* (London, 1970), 191.

79 "The Tredegar Iron Works was chartered": Charles B. Dew, *Ironmaker to the Confederacy: Joseph R. Anderson and the Tredegar Iron Works* (Richmond, Va., 1999).

81 "Examples abound of failed private": Phillips, *Slavery*, 376–377.

81 "As the business historian George David Smith": Jacobson, *Renaissance*, 54.

81 "The South's slave-produced cotton exports": Scherer, *World Power*, 242.

82 "The British anti-slavery organization": Adam Hochschild, *Bury the Chains: Prophets and Rebels in the Fight to Free an Empire's Slaves* (Boston, 2005), 193.

82 "The most ambitious plan": Thomas Prentice Kettell, *Southern Wealth and Southern Profits* (University, Ala., 1965), 31.

82 "Livingston wanted to replace": Niall Ferguson, *Empire: The Rise and Demise of the British World Order and the Lessons for Global Power* (New York, 2002), 35.

83   "[Cotton] . . . constitutes the structural weakness": Owsley, *Diplomacy*, 11.
83   "I hold that the pursuit": Starobin, *Industrial*, 216.
83   "Still others dreamed": Eugene D. Genovese, *The Political Economy of Slavery* (New York, 1967), 256–264.
84   "This 'Gulf Coast imperialism'": Rollin G. Osterweis, *Romanticism and Nationalism in the Old South* (Gloucester, Mass., 1964), 172–185; Robert E. May, *John Quitman: Old South Crusader* (Baton Rouge, 1985), 236–252; McCardell, *Idea*, 273–275; and John Hope Franklin, *The Militant South, 1800–1861* (Urbana, 2002), 105–124.
85   "Although geographically a Northern metropolis": Albion, *New York*, 95–96, 112–114.
86   "Many New Yorkers": Ibid., 96, 59, 87, 100.
86   "The 'Southern' trade": Philip Foner, *Business and Slavery: The New York Merchants and the Irrepressible Conflict* (Chapel Hill, 1941), 6.
87   "Yet New York continued to benefit": Albion, *New York*, 114.
87   "The city of New York": Abram J. Dittenhoefer, *How We elected Lincoln: Personal Recollections* (Philadelphia, 2005), 1.
87   "When Southern planters defaulted": Foner, *Business*, 1–14.
87   "Northerners were well aware": Woodman, *King Cotton*, 170.
88   "The *New York Post*": Quoted in Foner, *Business*, 168.
88   "Having learnt that some insinuations": Quoted in Albion, *New York*, 257.
88   "As commercial people it is": Quoted in Foner, *Business*, 148.
88   "New England shared in the trade": Kettell, *Wealth*, 60–61.
89   "The native Southerner": Ibid., 50.
90   "Slave traders often used": Warren S. Howard, *American Slavers and the Federal Law* (Philadelphia, 1963), 51.
90   "I know of two ladies": Foner, *Business*, 164–168.
90   "Slave traders openly discussed": Earnest A. McKay, *The Civil War and New York City* (Syracuse, 1990), 14.
90   "One slaver, the *Wanderer*": Albion, *New York*, 212.
90   "W. E. B. Du Bois later described": W. E. B. Du Bois, *Suppression of the African Slave Trade, 1638–1870* (Baton Rouge, 1969; first published 1896), 178–179.
90   "Jay presented a petition": Foner, *Business*, 167–168.
91   "Jay's address was bitterly received": *New York Tribune*, September 30, 1859.
91   "The root of the evil": Foner, *Business*, 167.
92   "In the decade before the Civil War": Ibid., 33, 34, 43.
92   "Indeed, in 1860, New York voters": McKay, *New York*, 22.
92   "They delivered a petition": Foner, *Business*, 248–274.
93   "If New York gives the money": Ibid., 263–264.
93   "We do not believe it is either wise": Howard Cecil Perkins, ed. *Northern Editorials on Secession* (Gloucester, Mass., 1964), 435–438.
94   "Horace Greeley's *New York Tribune*": Ibid., 359–360.
94   "Lord and Taylor would inform": Quoted in Foner, *Business*, 208.
94   "According to Wood": McKay, *New York*, 33–34.
95   "That either the revenue": Charles Adams, *When in the Course of Human Events: Arguing the Case for Southern Secession* (Lanham, Md., 2006), 24.
96   "The swift change in the attitude": Foner, *Business*, 297–308.

97 "When the confederacy's president": Foner, *Business*, 169–310.

97 "In fact, the issue had already been raised": David L. Cohn, "Southern Cotton and Japan," *Atlantic Monthly*, Vol. 198, No. 2 (August 1956), 237.

98 "To begin with, slavery as a labor": Genovese, *Political*, 43.

98 "Despite the faults of the Southern system": Wright, *Old South*, 56.

98 "But at the opposite end of the spectrum": Phillips, *Slavery*, 401.

99 "No power on earth dare": Quoted in Drew Gilpin Faust, *James Henry Hammond and the Old South: A Design for Mastery* (Baton Rouge, 1982), 347.

99 "[W]ould any sane nation make war on cotton": Scherer, *World Power*, 239.

100 "The meetings were co-opted": McCardell, *Idea*, 138–139.

101 "The legal status of slavery": Marshall L. DeRosa, *The Confederate Constitution of 1861: An Inquiry into American Constitutionalism* (Columbia, Mo., 1991), 141.

101 "If the price of slaves comes down": Gavin Wright, *The Political Economy of the Cotton South: Households, Markets, and Wealth in the Nineteenth Century* (New York, 1978), 150–154.

103 "Georgia's Henry L. Benning feared": Charles B. Dew, *Apostles of Disunion: Southern Secession Commissioners and the Causes of the Civil War* (Charlottesville, Va., 2001), 32–33, 65.

104 "[W]hat our system of labor works out": *New York Times*, March 1, 1860.

104 "Shall I tell you what this collision means": Frederic Bancroft, *The Life of William H. Seward*, Vol. II (New York, 1900), 458–459.

Part Three. The North: For Whites Only, 1800–1865

111 "And whereas we are willing": Quoted in Edgar J. McManus, *A History of Negro Slavery in New York* (Syracuse, 1966), 23.

112 "Thus only 16 blacks": Leslie M. Harris, *In the Shadow of Slavery: African Americans in New York City, 1626–1863* (Chicago, 2003), 119.

112 "In 1860 and 1869 state constitutional conventions": David N. Gellman and David Qigley, *A Documentary History of Race and Citizenship, 1777–1877* (New York, 2003), 199, 259.

112 "In each case, black inferiority": McManus, *New York*, 184.

113 "The gritty job of crawling down": Harris, *Shadow*, 72–95, 217.

113 "These jobs, rather than stepping-stones": Ibid., 217.

113 "Everywhere Negroes were shunned": Quoted in McManus, *New York*, 188.

113 "Lydia Maria Child, a prominent abolitionist": Harris, *Shadow*, 198–199.

115 "The Manumission Society also recommended": Ibid., 140–141.

115 "In 1859 the historian Thomas De Voe": Ibid., 263, 268.

116 "We find ourselves crippled": Gellman and Quigley, *Citizenship*, 236–248.

117 "On no other issue can we be so unanimous": David Quigley, *Second Founding: New York City, Reconstruction and the Making of American Democracy* (New York, 2004), 63.

117 "Black political equality was defeated": Ibid., 64, 68.

118 "Seward desperately wanted California": Ernest N. Paolino, *The Foundations of the American Empire: William Henry Seward and U.S. Foreign Policy* (Ithaca, 1973), 29, 5.

118 "the only element of discord": Quoted in Bancroft, *Seward*, Vol. II, 444.
118 "The great fact is now fully realized": Quoted in John M. Taylor, *William Henry Seward: Lincoln's Right Hand* (Washington, D.C., 1991), 122.
118 "He asked rhetorically": Bancroft, *Seward*, Vol. II, 449.
118 "When he invited a former prisoner of war": Taylor, *Seward*, 255.
118 "By 1865, in a cabinet meeting": Ibid., 254.
119 "I am ready to leave the interests": Bancroft, *Seward*, Vol. II, 455–456.
120 "Alaska was not": Paolino, *Foundations*, 105–108.
120 "In a speech in 1870": Ibid., 40, 35, 29, 17, 30, 36.
121 "According to the historian, Peter Hinks": Peter Hinks, "A Privilege and Elevation to Which We Look Forward with Pleasure: The Connecticut Academy of Arts and Sciences and Black Emancipation in Connecticut," in Connecticut Academy of the Arts and Sciences, *Voices of the Republic: Connecticut Towns, 1800–1832*, Vol. II (New Haven, 2003), 107.
121 "His son Charles Griswold": Albion, *New York*, 77, 114, 241–249.
122 "Connecticut has left an extraordinary record": Christopher P. Bickford, "Taking the Measure of Human Happiness: The Connecticut Academy of Arts and Sciences and the Statistical Account Project," in Connecticut Academy, *Voices*, Vol. I, 1–19.
122 "This inquiry, possibly inserted by Webster": Bickford, "Measure," 12.
124 "[T]hese people . . . are": Quoted in Hinks, "Privilege," 113.
124 "Why should we leave this land": Horatio T. Strothers, *The Underground Railroad in Connecticut* (Middletown, Conn., 1962), 38.
125 "The same Simeon Baldwin": Hinks, "Privilege," 114.
125 "The law was upheld": Strothers, *Railroad*, 184.
127 "Meanwhile the *Jackson Mississippian*": David G. Sansing, *The University of Mississippi: A Sesquicentennial History* (Jackson, Miss., 1999), 77.
128 "I was born in the North": Quoted in John Fulton, ed., *Memoirs of Frederick A. P. Barnard* (New York, 1896), 253.
128 "Barnard knew that the slavery issue": Ibid., 252.
128 "When the war came in 1861": Ibid., 279.
128 "On June 13, 1861, Barnard's last sermon": Ibid., 282.
128 "Barnard attributed": Chute, *Yankee*, 192.
129 "Abraham Lincoln supposedly remarked": Joan B. Hedrick, *Harriet Beecher Stowe: A Life* (New York, 1992), vii.
129 "The background for her story": Ibid., 70.
130 "Stowe's enlightenment had limits": Frederick Jager, *A Scapegoat in the New Wilderness: The Origins and Rise of Anti-Semitism in America* (Cambridge, Mass., 1994), 232, 138, 200.
130 "Even his fellow slave catcher": Harriet Beecher Stowe, *Uncle Tom's Cabin* (New York, 1994), 55–57.
130 "One of her characters explicitly states": Stowe, *Cabin*, 160.
130 "For Stowe it is": Ibid., 285, 291.
130 "I might mingle in the circle of whites": Ibid., 373–376.
131 "Frederick Douglass brimmed with indignation": Hedrick, Stowe, 235.
131 "Of all vague unbased fabrics": Ibid., 247. For a disappointed Frederick Douglass's response, see *The Life and Times of Frederick Douglass* (London, 1892), 290–291.

131 "She stayed with him": Harriet Beecher Stowe, *Palmetto Leaves* (Gainesville, Fla., 1999).

132 "Harriet Beecher Stowe's foray into cotton farming": Harriet Beecher Stowe, "Our Florida Plantation," *Atlantic Monthly*, Vol. 43, No. 259 (May 1879), 642–649.

133 "The two other major cities in the North": James and Lois Horton, *Black Bostonians: Family Life and Community Strugggle in the Antebellum North* (New York, 1999), 73, 78, 2, 3, 5.

133 "Frederick Douglass in 1862": James M. McPherson, *The Negro's Civil War: How American Blacks Felt and Acted During the War for the Union* (New York, 1991), 259.

135 "Ninety-four percent of the free black population": Leon F. Litwack, *North of Slavery* (Chicago, 1961), 91.

135 "It did not take long": Eugene H. Berwanger, *The Frontier Against Slavery: Western Anti-Negro Prejudice and the Slavery Extension Controversy* (Urbana, 2002), 32.

135 "Cincinnati, the major trading city": Carter G. Woodson, "The Negroes of Cincinnati Prior to the Civil War," in John H. Bracey, Jr., August Meier, and Elliott Rudwick, eds., *Free Blacks in America, 1800–1860* (Belmont, Calif., 1971), 72.

136 "In 1829 violence erupted when": "Banishment of the People of Colour from Cincinnati," *Journal of Negro History*, Vol. 8, No. 3 (July 1923), 331–332.

136 "Blacks in Cincinnati found solace": Woodson, "Cincinnati," 79–80.

136 "The city's 'black laws' stood": Berwanger, *Frontier*, 43.

136 "Peter Clark, a respected black community member": Eric Foner, *Reconstruction: America's Unfinished Revolution* (New York, 1988), 471–472.

137 "Ohio indulged in the": Berwanger, *Frontier*, 54–55.

137 "The Ohio Democrat": Ibid., 126.

137 "The Republicans George Julian (Indiana)": Jacque V. Voegeli, *Free but Not Equal: The Midwest and the Negro During the Civil War* (Chicago, 1969), 20, 22.

137 "Ohio senator John Sherman": Ibid., 28.

137 "In June 1852 he worried": Ibid., 18.

137 "He spoke of the impossibility": Ibid., 27.

137 "After emancipation Senator Sherman": Ibid., 37.

138 "Chase, the Ohio senator": Ibid., 22.

138 "In 1873 he sought to hire": Hans L. Trefousse, *Benjamin Franklin Wade: Radical Republican from Ohio* (New York, 1963), 311–312. Hans L. Trefousse, "Ben Wade and the Negro," *Ohio Historical Quarterly*, Vol. 68, No. 2 (April 1959), 161–176. Voegeli, *Free*, 45, 182.

138 "The hundreds of thousands": Voegeli, *Free*, 6.

138 "farmers and mechanics were not": Quoted in Ibid.

139 "We have no special affection": Quoted in Ibid., 29.

139 "There is but one thing": Quoted in James M. McPherson, *The Negro's War: How American Blacks Felt and Acted During the War for the Union* (New York, 1991), 250.

139 "A referendum that called for": Wright, "Agricultural," 540.

139 "why should we bring among us": Quoted in Berwanger, *Frontier*, 24–25.

140 "His particular concern was": Ibid.

140 "In August 1862": Ibid., 25, 32, 45.

140   "Republican congressman Owen Lovejoy": Ibid., 133.

141   "It was the presence": Quoted in Voegeli, *Free*, 64.

141   "In 1863 the Republican governor": Ibid., 86.

141   "The truth is, the nigger is an unpopular institution": Quoted in Voegeli, *Free*, 28.

141   "Let it not be said": Quoted in Berwanger, *Frontier*, 136.

142   "As an example, the historian George M. Fredrickson": George M. Fredrickson, *Big Enough to Be Inconsistent; Abraham Lincoln Confronts Slavery and Race* (Cambridge, Mass., 2008), 84.

142   "Colonization, according to Jacques Voegeli": Voegeli, *Free*, 112.

142   "Lincoln approved a plan": Ibid., 44. See also William B. Hesseltine, *Lincoln's Plan of Reconstruction* (Chicago, 1967), 91–94.

142   "In August 1862, Lincoln told": Ibid.

142   "One such plan presented by the promoter": Jay Monaghan, *Abraham Lincoln Deals with Foreign Affairs: A Diplomat in Carpet Slippers* (Lincoln, Nebr., 1997), 272.

142   "Republicans John A. Bingham": Voegeli, *Free*, 25.

142   "Equally distributed among": Ibid., 66–67.

144   "The *Tribune* hoped to allay": Ibid., 130, 163, 27, 87, 25, 112, 7.

144   "The *Tribune's* opinions paled in comparison": Ibid., 8, 6, 126.

144   "Indiana, admitted to the Union in 1816": Berwanger, *Frontier*, 20–21.

144   "Governor James B. Ray": Ibid., 23, 25, 31–32.

145   "Article 13 spelled out Indiana's": Ibid., 45.

145   "But the scheme failed": Ibid., 52, 55–58.

145   "In the 1850s he spoke": Eric Foner, *Politics and Ideology in the Age of the Civil War* (New York, 1980), 78. See also Voegeli, *Free*, 1.

145   "Another Indiana Republican": Voegeli, *Free*, 23.

146   "Since racial animosity was so": Richard W. Leopold, *Robert Dale Owen: a Biography* (Cambridge, Mass., 1940), 272,

146   "In 1863, Owen was appointed": Ibid., 362–363. See also Foner, *Reconstruction*, 68–69.

146   "The Anglo-Saxon race": Quoted in Voegeli, *Free*, 180–181.

147   "Such marginalization apparently": Ibid., 59.

148   "If blacks could vote": Berwanger, *Frontier*, 36, 53, 42.

148   "Republican senator James R. Doolittle": Hesseltine, *Plan*, 92.

148   "In 1863 the Wisconsin Assembly": Voegeli, *Free*, 85–86. See also Eric Foner, *Free Soil, Free Labor, Free Men: The Ideology of the Republican Party Before the Civil War* (New York, 1995), 289.

148   "In 1853, Wisconsin received the following": Robbins, *Landed*, 135–136.

148   "The recruitment efforts": Richard H. Zeitlin, *Germans in Wisconsin* (Madison, Wisc., 2000), 5.

149   "[T]he negro belonged to a": Quoted in Berwanger, *Frontier*, 32–33, 38; Voegeli, *Free*, 162, 165.

150   "In Iowa, where the black population": Berwanger, *Frontier*, 32–33, 54.

151   "Ultimately the anti-slavery Wyandotte": Ibid., 97–118.

152   "White Californians were as": Rudolph Lapp, *Blacks in Gold Rush California* (New Haven, 1977), 186–209; Berwanger, *Frontier*, 60–77.

153   "Oregon is a land for the white man": Quoted in Berwanger, *Frontier*, 78–79.

154   "For the most part": C. Vann Woodward, *The Old World's New World* (New York, 1991), 122.
154   "Tocqueville famously wrote": Alexis de Tocqueville, *Democracy in America*, Vol. 1 (New York, 1945), 342–452.
156   "Later, because of French colonial emancipation": Seymour Drescher, trans. and ed., *Tocqueville and Beaumont on Social Reform* (New York, 1968), 137–173. See also C. Vann Woodward, "The Price of Freedom," in David G. Sansing, ed. *What Was Freedom's Price?* (Jackson, Miss., 1978), 101.
158   "Even Senator Charles Sumner": Voegeli, *Free*, 58.
158   "Northern treatment of free blacks": Leon F. Litwack, "The Black Abolitionists," in Drimmer, *Black History*, p. 143.
158   "Seargent Prentice of Mississippi": Sydnor, *Slavery*, 252.
158   "In 1864, Frederick Douglass did not": Voegeli, *Free*, 145.
158   "In June 1862, Illinois soldiers": Bell I. Wiley, *The Life of Billy Yank: The Common Soldier of the Union* (Indianapolis, 1952), 40–42.
158   "As the war progressed": James M. McPherson, *The Causes and Comrades: Why Men Fought in the Civil War* (New York, 1997), 117–125, 175–176.
159   "The participation of approximately": Dudley T. Cornish, ". . . Even the Slave Becomes a Man . . . ," in Drimmer, *Black History*, 270.
159   "The black abolitionist minister": Litwack, "Abolitionists," 213.
160   "As the historian C. Vann Woodward cogently wrote": C. Vann Woodward, "Freedom," 113.

Part Four. King Cotton Buys a War

161   "Cotton Prices": James L. Watkins, *King Cotton* (New York, 1908), 30. In Woodman, *King Cotton*, 227.
164   "The future president of the Confederacy": Cooper, *Davis*, 3–8.
165   "On the morning of March 11": Robert Duthat Meade, *Judah P. Benjamin: Confederate Statesman* (Baton Rouge, 2001), 166.
166   "The *Philadelphia Press* logically": Charles Adams, *Course*, 65.
167   "To the slave-holding states": Quoted in Owsley, *Diplomacy*, 16–17.
168   "Charles Francis Adams, son of the American": Ibid., 19.
168   "Russell, in turn,": Ibid., 20–21.
168   "During early cabinet meetings": Richard I. Lester, *Confederate Finance and Purchasing in Great Britain* (Charlottesville, Va., 1975), 5.
168   "As one cabinet member, Leroy P. Walker": Meade, *Benjamin*, 166.
169   "This was a daunting task": Cohn, *Life and Times*, 124.
169   "Davis preferred to hold": Owsley, *Diplomacy*, 30.
169   "According to one of his biographers": Cohn, *Life and Times*, 121.
170   "South Carolina, for example": Owsley, *Diplomacy*, 35.
170   "Arkansas placed a limit on cotton": Cohn, *Life and Times*, 124.
170   "A local citizens' organization": Owsley, *Diplomacy*, 35–38.
170   "The embargo was popular": Ibid., 34–50.
171   "As the spectators witnessed": Cohn, *Life and Times*, 125.
171   "The Confederacy's propaganda arm": Owsley, *Diplomacy*, 47.
171   "In the first half of 1861": Cohn, *Life and Times*, 131.
172   "It has been estimated that": Owsley, *Diplomacy*, 49.

172   "Britain's mills experienced no shortage": Ibid., 134–135.
172   "The burdensome inventory of cotton textiles": Ibid., 138, 544, 549.
173   "Every family had passed through": Quoted in Cohn, *Life and Times*, 131–132.
174   "The American North": Monaghan, *Lincoln*, 287.
174   "In the fall of 1862, Lord Palmerston": Owsley, *Diplomacy*, 346.
174   "By January 1864, England's": Ibid., 146.
174   "With the notable exception of the mill workers": Ibid., 552–553, 557.
175   "Frank Owsley judged that": Ibid., 547–549.
176   "In practical terms the embargo died a natural death": Ibid., 42.
177   "The *Economist* prophesied": Lester, *Purchasing*, 26.
178   "One historian described": Owsley, *Diplomacy*, 187.
178   "Contemporary Southerners knew well": Ibid., 36.
178   "Gladstone, speaking for himself": Cohn, *Life and Times*, 137.
179   "This was the same Palmerston": Robert Kagan, *Dangerous Nation: America's Place in the World from the Earliest days to the Dawn of the Twentieth Century* (New York, 2006), 216–217.
179   "Yet in September 1862 he was ready": Owsley, *Diplomacy*, 341–342.
180   "After the *Trent* Affair": Robin W. Winks, *Canada and the United States: The Civil War Years* (Lanham, Md., 1988), 52–53.
181   "Palmerston capitulated when faced": Owsley, *Diplomacy*, 401–402, 411.
181   "Canada stood at the intersection": Robin W. Winks, *The Blacks in Canada: A History* (Montreal, 1997), 270–271.
182   "The peripatetic pro-Northern English journalist": Winks, *Canada and the U.S.*, 17, 62–63.
182   "Canada's anti-Northern leanings": Claire Hoy, *Canadians and the Civil War* (Toronto, 2004), 254–263.
182   "In a direct reference to Canada": Winks, *Canada and the U.S.*, 166, 318.
182   "By adding another chapter to the restriction of free black mobility": Winks, *Blacks in Canada*, 308–312.
183   "In the same year, Sir Wilfrid Laurier": Hoy, *Canadians*, 114. Winks, *Canada and the U.S.*, 11.
185   "In 1863 one of Cooke's agents": Dewey, *Financial*, 319.
186   "By October 1, 1864": Hawk, *Economic*, 400–423.
186   "The South's task of financing": Douglas B. Ball, *Financial Failure and Confederate Defeat* (Urbana, 1991), 82.
187   "But when the Confederacy suffered": Ibid., 74.
187   "Gladstone, Britain's pro-Southern": Lester, *Purchasing*, 10.
187   "As finances worsened into the spring": Ibid., 19–21.
188   "The South moved farther along the path": Ball, *Failure*, 132–133.
188   "but the concept behind it remains prescient and brilliant." The world of European international finance had to wait one hundred years for another dual currency bond when Sir Siegmund Warburg proposed a Eurobond denominated in sterling with an option to convert to deutschmarks. The idea bore fruit with the issuance of a 5 million sterling loan for the city of Turin in 1964. See Niall Ferguson's forthcoming biography of Warburg and the creation of the Eurobond market.
188   "Indeed, President Lincoln took an active interest": Monaghan, *Lincoln*, 297.

188   "After being authorized on January 29, 1863,": Judith Fenner Gentry, "A Confederate Success in Europe: The Erlanger Loan," *Journal of Southern History*, Vol. 36 (May 1970), 182.

190   "By one estimate the South raised": Ball, *Failure*, 79.

190   "Erlanger bonds were also conspicuous": Lester, *Purchasing*, Appendix III.

190   "It may appear somewhat": Quoted in Owsley, *Diplomacy*, 376.

191   "Such a sum . . . would have": Quoted in Cohn, *Life and Times*, 139.

191   "It would indeed have been feasible": Ball, *Failure*, 1–17; Lester, *Purchasing*, 56.

193   "Lieutenant Colonel J. W. Mallet": J. W. Mallet, "Work of the Ordnance Bureau," *Southern History Society Papers*, Vol. 37 (Richmond, Va., 1909), 1–20, in William B. Hesseltine, ed. *The Tragic Conflict: The Civil War and Reconstruction* (New York, 1962).

194   "The blockade was difficult": Richard E. Beringer, Herman Hattaway, Archer Jones, and William N. Still, Jr., *Why the South Lost the Civil War* (Athens, Ga., 1996), 56–63.

194   "The crew and the backers of blockade-runners": Stanley Lebergott, "Through the Blockade: The Profitability and Extent of Cotton Smuggling, 1861–1865," *Journal of Economic History*, Vol. 41, No. 4 (December 1981), 867–888.

195   "Risks of injury, loss of life": Time-Life Books, *The Civil War: The Blockade* (Alexandria, Va., 1983), 91.

195   "Here's to the Southern planters": Hoy, *Canadians*, 260.

195   "The first official government-owned": Thomas Boaz, *Guns for Cotton: England Arms the Confederacy* (Shippensburg, Pa., 1996), 48.

196   "According to one source": Ibid.

196   "The well-known British shipbuilder": Lester, *Purchasing*, 109–110, 197.

197   "Stanley Lebergott calculates that": Lebergott, "Through the Blockade," 884.

197   "Cotton valued at": Ibid., 199; Owsley, *Diplomacy*, 248, 265–266.

197   "Eventually the South attained": Lester, *Purchasing*, 135–147, 194, 199; Boaz, *Guns*, 15–16; Cohn, *Life and Times*, 130.

198   "Meat purchased in Boston or New York": Boaz, *Guns*, 65. Lester, *Purchasing*, 194.

198   "At Vicksburg, 31,600 prisoners": Ulysses S. Grant, *Personal Memoirs* (New York, 1999), 299–300.

199   "At the onset of the Civil War": Adrian Cook, *The Alabama Claims: American Politics and Anglo-American Relations, 1865–1872*, 15; James Marquis. *Biography of a Business, 1792–1942: Insurance Company of North America* (Indianapolis, 1942), 197.

199   "The legendary *Alabama*": Lester, *Purchasing*, 216.

199   "As the *Alabama* sank": Philip Van Doren Stern, *When the Guns Roared: World Aspects of the American Civil War* (New York, 1965), 289–290.

199   "Most of the premier fleet": Owsley, *Diplomacy*, 555.

199   "After the Civil War": Cook, *Claims*, 38, 76–81, 147–148, 159.

200   "Capital requirements tempered the belligerent": Ibid., 239–242.

200   "In effect the American Civil War": Winks, *Canada and the U.S.*, 376–377.

201   "Northern regulations for dealing": Rhodes, *History*, 281–302.

203   "The mathematics of the trade": Ibid., 290.

203   "They could be bought": Ludwell Johnson, *Red River Campaign: Politics and Cotton in the Civil War* (Kent, Ohio, 1993), 49–50.

204   "Among other embarrassments": Grant, *Memoirs*, 210.

204   "The extent of the illicit trade": Johnson, *Red River*, 51.

204   "General Daniel E. Sickles wrote": Rhodes, *History*, Vol. V, 292.

205   "Hundreds of thousands of bales that": Edwin G. Burroughs and Mike Wallace, *Gotham: A History of New York City to 1898* (New York, 1999), 899.

205   "The fall of Memphis": Capers, *Memphis*, 153.

206   "As early as the fall of 1862": Woodman, *King Cotton*, 213–214.

206   "As cotton reached an unprecedented one dollar a pound": Rhodes, *History*, Vol. V, 289; Capers, *Memphis*, 154.

206   "Union officers participated": Rhodes, *History*, Vol. V, 301.

207   "Thomas Knox, who leased a plantation": Thomas W. Knox, *Camp-Fire and Cotton Field: Southern Adventure in Time of War* (n.p., 1865), 299.

207   "Sherman summarized the unbridled competition": W. T. Sherman, *Memoirs* (New York, 1990), 288–289.

207   "The irate General Grant did": Leonard Dinnerstein, *Anti-Semitism in America* (New York, 1994), 32.

209   "Massachusetts governor John Andrew": Voegeli, *Free*, 58–59.

210   "The governor's real agenda": Ibid., 174–175.

210   "The West had to face a similar situation": Ibid., 59–61, 107–110, 176.

213   "The area along the Mississippi River": James T. Currie, *Enclave: Vicksburg and Her Plantations, 1863–1870* (Jackson, Miss., 1980), 56–57, 75, 81.

213   "The government would receive": Knox, *Camp-Fire*, 226.

214   "The majority of the lessees were unprincipled": Ibid., 233.

214   "An ex-slave later recalled": Currie, *Enclave*, 55–82.

215   "The lessees were driven by cotton money": Ibid., 58.

215   "General Oliver O. Howard, head": Ibid., 79.

215   "Thomas Knox discovered several": Knox, *Camp-Fire*, 236–237.

215   "In 1866 the experiment of leasing cotton land": Stephen Joseph Ross, "Freed Soil, Freed Labor, Freed Men: John Eaton and the Davis Bend Experiment," *Journal of Southern History*, Vol. 44, No. 2 (May 1978), 213–232.

216   "Fraud was not limited": Currie, *Enclave*, 68–69.

217   "If the war had proved": Woodman, *King Cotton*, 216.

Part Five. The Racial Divide and Cotton Labor, 1865–1930

224   "Frederick Douglass rhetorically posed": Foner, *Reconstruction*, 66–67.

225   "Radical Republican Charles Sumner": Voegeli, *Free*, 176–177.

225   "In Mississippi alone": Skates, *Mississippi*, 107.

226   "Reconstruction has even been called": C. Vann Woodward, *Tom Watson: Agrarian Rebel* (New York, 1963), 53.

227   "Grant wrote that his": Cohn, *Life and Times*, 141–142.

227   "On June 13, 1865, Grant submitted a pardon": John Hope Franklin, *Reconstruction After the Civil War* (Chicago, 1963), 33–34.

227   "The federal government did not even": R. F. Nichols, "United States vs. Jefferson Davis, 1865–1869," *American Historical Review*, Vol. 31 (April 1926), 266–284.

227 "But before his trial for treason": Cooper, *Davis*, 566.

228 "Lincoln did, however, espouse the": Gabor S. Borritt, *Lincoln and the Economics of the American Dream* (Urbana, 1994), 172, 189.

228 "In the judgment of Frederick Douglass": Eric Foner, *Forever Free: The Story of Emancipation and Reconstruction* (New York, 2005), 57.

229 "In April 1865 the New York Chamber of Commerce": Woodman, *King Cotton*, 246; George Ruble Woolfolk, *The Cotton Regency: The Northern Merchants and Reconstruction, 1865–1880* (New York, 1958), 52.

229 "In 1865 a U.S. Treasury official": Woolfolk, *Regency*, 25, 52, 56.

230 "At the same time": Ibid., 46.

230 "The Radical Republican Thaddeus Stevens": Quoted in W. E. B. Du Bois, *Black Reconstruction in America, 1860–1880* (New York, 1992), 198.

231 "The federal government received another": Cohn, *Life and Times*, 152–153.

231 "As the historian John Hope Franklin writes": Franklin, *Reconstruction*, 40.

231 "The *New York Times* endorsed": Gerald David Jaynes, *Branches Without Roots: Genesis of the Black Working Class in the American South, 1862–1882* (New York, 1986), 23.

232 "In 1865 a key member of the Boston Board of Trade": Ibid., 8–11.

232 "For East Coast financiers": Sobel, *Panic*, 161.

233 "Northern businessmen responded to the postwar": Woolfolk, *Regency*, 119.

233 "It wasn't long before the Northern states": Ibid., 141–174.

234 "New York City's commercial journals": Sven Beckert, *The Monied Metropolis: New York City and the Consolidation of the American Bourgeoisie, 1850–1896* (Cambridge, England, 2001), 161–162.

235 "Secretary of State Seward wanted the freedmen": Foner, *Reconstruction*, 219.

235 "I bid the people, the working people of the North": Quoted in C. Vann Woodward, *American Counterpoint: Slavery and Racism in the North-South Dialogue* (Boston, 1971), 170.

235 "He may have inadvertently acknowledged": Hesseltine, *Plan*, 116.

235 "The high price of cotton": Woodman, *Life and Times*, 247–251.

236 "Southerners who visited New York": Woolfolk, *Regency*, 76.

236 "The Boston Board of Trade passed": Woodman, *King Cotton*, 252.

236 "In the fall of 1865 former governor": Lawrence N. Powell, *New Masters: Northern Planters During the Civil War and Reconstruction* (New Haven, 1980), 6.

236 "In the winter of 1865–1866 it seemed": Lawrence N. Powell, "The American Land Company and Agency: John A. Andrew and the Northernization of the South," *Civil War History*, Vol. XII (December 1975), 295–308.

237 "Always present was the desire": Ibid., 300.

237 "Early on, in 1861, he offered a harsh": Edward Atkinson, "Cheap Cotton, Cheap Labor: By a Cotton Manufacturer" (Boston, 1861), 6.

237 "At the close of the war": Perry Bliss, *Life and Letters of Henry Lee Higginson* (Boston, 1921), 239–248.

238 "His financial and moral adventure": Ibid., 250–251.

238 "On November 15, 1865, Higginson outlined": Ibid., 252.

239 "Higginson's idealism was tested immediately": Ibid., 255–259.

241 "The final financial accounting was dreadful": Ibid., 256–262.

241 "Other groups of prominent white Northerners": Powell, "American Land Company," 46.

243   "On January 16, 1865, General Sherman": William S. McFeely, *Yankee Stepfather: General O. O. Howard and the Freedmen* (New York, 1994), 47.

244   "The order conveyed no title": John David Smith, "The Enduring Myth of 'Forty Acres and a Mule,'" chronicle.com/weekly/v49i24/24b01101.htm (February 21, 2003).

244   "But these isolated experiments": McFeeley, *Stepfather*, 42.

244   "The language of the act": LaWanda Cox, in Ibid., 4.

245   "In September 1865, Thaddeus Stevens": Du Bois, *Reconstruction*, 198.

246   "General Olivet Otis Howard was appointed": Foner, *Reconstruction*, 133.

246   "He wanted blacks to": Ibid., 158.

246   "Howard was echoing": McFeely, *Stepfather*, 110.

246   "General Howard initially": Ibid., 82, 252.

246   "General Howard thereupon forbade": Powell, *Masters*, 13.

246   "While the Freedmen's Bureau": McFeely, *Stepfather*, 311.

247   "Samuel Thomas, assistant commissioner in Mississippi": Foner, *Reconstruction*, 161.

247   "In the absence of clear standards": Woolfolk, *Regency*, 70–75.

248   "In 1901, W. E. B. Du Bois identified": W. E. B. Du Bois, "The Freedmen's Bureau," *Atlantic Monthly*, Vol. 87, No. 521 (March 1901), 354–365.

248   "The bureau did somewhat ameliorate": Foner, *Reconstruction*, 152.

249   "Racial violence soon ended any": McFeely, *Stepfather*, 273.

249   "after the Civil War, racial animosity": Whitelaw Reid, *After the War: A Tour of the Southern States, 1865–1866* (New York, 1965), 481.

249   "White Union troops under the": McFeely, *Stepfather*, 273.

249   "In 1865 the Union chaplain": Ibid., 74.

250   "Eaton wrote to President Lincoln": Broadus B. Jackson, *Civil War and Reconstruction in Mississippi: Mirror of Democracy in America* (Jackson, 1998), 41.

250   "The Memphis race riots": James Gilbert Ryan, "The Memphis Riots of 1866: Terror in a Black Community During Reconstruction," *Journal of Negro History*, Vol. 62, No. 3 (July 1977), 243–257; Altina L. Waller, "Community, Class and Race in the Memphis Riot of 1866," *Journal of Social History*, Vol. 18, No. 2 (Winter 1984), 233–246.

250   "The commanding Union general, George Stoneman": McFeely, *Stepfather*, 278.

250   "A congressional investigation ensued": Ryan, "Riots," 243.

250   "Despite warnings of violence": McFeely, *Stepfather*, 284.

250   "General Philip H. Sheridan, who had expressed": Ibid., 285. See also James G. Hollandsworth, *An Absolute Massacre: The New Orleans Race Riot of July 30, 1866* (Baton Rouge, 2001).

251   "When not hosting riots": Skates, *Mississippi*, 11–113.

253   "America's postwar calculus was based": Hesseltine, *Plan*, 121–141.

254   "This was, after all, the America": Franklin, *Reconstruction*, 74; Woodward, *Counterpoint*, 174–177.

254   "In the North, blacks were faced": Foner, *Reconstruction*, 472.

255   "He was quite explicit": McFeely, *Stepfather*, 233.

255   "In 1866, Roscoe Conkling, a New York": Woodward, *Counterpoint*, 169–170.

255   "A variety of federal legislation attempted": Ibid., 170–171.

256   "Southerners quickly read between the lines": Ibid., 173–176.

256 "The Civil Rights Act was": Franklin, *Reconstruction*, 202.

257 "Later, as with other events": Foner, *Reconstruction*, 577.

258 "Most federal expenditures under": Quigley, *Founding*, 88–89; Woodward, *Counterpoint*, 182–183.

258 "In order to combat the Ku Klux Klan": George Sinkler, *The Racial Attitudes of the Presidents from Abraham Lincoln to Theodore Roosevelt* (New York, 1972), 156–157.

258 "In 1871 he suspended habeas corpus": Richard N. Current, "President Grant and the Continuing Civil War," in David L. Wilson and John Y. Simon, eds., *Ulysses S. Grant: Essays and Documents* (Carbondale, Ill., 1989), 3.

258 "Yet the Radical Republicans": Foner, *Reconstruction*, 148.

258 "There were 200,000 troops in the South": Current, "President Grant," 5. See also William Blair, "The Use of Military Force to Protect the Gains of Reconstruction," *Civil War History*, Vol. 51, No. 4 (December 2005), 388–402.

258 "In 1869 there were only": Franklin, *Reconstruction*, 120.

259 "In 1942 the Mississippi Delta planter": William Alexander Percy, *Lanterns on the Levee: Recollections of a Planter's Son* (Baton Rouge, 1994), 274.

259 "Grant confessed that he": John Hope Franklin, ed., *Reminiscences of an Active Life: The Autobiography of John Roy Lynch* (Chicago, 1970), 173–175.

260 "The present difficulty in bringing": Sinkler, *Attitudes*, 177.

260 "In his final message to Congress": Ibid., 175.

261 "The picture of Reconstruction": C. Vann Woodward, "White Racism and Black 'Emancipation,'" *New York Review of Books*, Vol. 12, No. 4 (February 27, 1969).

261 "The fervency of abolitionism": Jaynes, *Branches*, 23.

262 "As one freedman poignantly put it": McPherson, *Negro's*, 297.

262 "The propaganda tide was give a boost": Heather Cox Richardson, *The Death of Reconstruction: Race, Labor, and Politics in the Post–Civil War North, 1865–1901* (Cambridge, Mass., 2001), 107.

262 "I incline to think": George F. Hoar, *Autobiography of Seventy Years*, Vol. II (New York, 1906), 160–161.

263 "Horace Greeley, the eclectic anti-slavery": Foner, *Reconstruction*, 503.

263 "His Wisconsin colleague, Senator Timothy Howe": Foner, *Free*, 212–213.

263 "A disillusioned and chastened Senator Howe": William B. Hesseltine, *Sections and Politics: Selected Essays by William Hesseltine* (Madison, Wisc.), 68.

263 "Despite his bargain that secured": Sinkler, *Attitudes*, 197–242.

264 "The most significant of the initial": Edward Mayes, *Lucius Q. C. Lamar: His Life, Times, and Speeches, 1825–1893* (New York, 1974), 183–189, 513–519.

265 "He was a far-sighted man": Hoar, *Autobiography*, 177.

265 "The Northern Press wrote": Josiah Bunting III, *Ulysses S. Grant* (New York, 2004), 140; Cohn, *Life and Times*, 149.

265 "Even the black soldier who": David W. Blight, *Race and Reunion: The Civil War in American Memory* (Cambridge, Mass., 2001), 194–195.

266 "Most conventional discussions of the Exodusters": Nell Irvin Painter, *Exodusters: Black Migration to Kansas After Reconstruction* (New York, 1992), 54–68.

267 "White city and state officials": Robert Athearn, *In Search of Canaan: Black Migration to Kansas, 1879–1880* (Lawrence, Kans., 1978), 45, 53.

267 "One of the leaders of the black exodus": Foner, *Reconstruction*, 600.

267   "In May 1879, Frederick Douglass famously recommended": Frederick Douglass, "The Negro Exodus from the Gulf States," *Journal of Social Science*, Vol. XI (May 1880), 1–21.

268   "Kansas could be a": Athearn, *Canaan*, 74.

268   "Most of them destined for": Sidney Ratner, James H. Soltow, and Richard Sylla, *The Evolution of the American Economy: Growth, Welfare, and Decision Making* (New York, 1993), 304.

268   "Between 1879 and 1881": Richard H. Zeitlin, *Germans in Wisconsin* (Madison, Wisc., 2000), 4.

269   "Grant's appointments to the Supreme Court": Peter Irons, *A People's History of the Supreme Court* (New York, 1999), 198–215.

270   "The newspaper proposed": Richardson, *Death*, 150–151, 215.

271   "Senator Don Cameron of Pennsylvania": Sean Dennis Cashman, *America in the Gilded Age: From the Death of Lincoln to the Rise of Theodore Roosevelt* (New York, 1988), 189.

272   "In 1929–1930, Mississippi spent": Neil R. McMillen, *Dark Journey: Black Mississippians in the Age of Jim Crow* (Urbana, 1990), 73.

272   "Gavin Wright has written": Wright, *Old South*, 123.

274   "White America—educators, politicians": James D. Anderson, *The Education of Blacks in the South, 1860–1935* (Urbana, 1990), 72, 272.

274   "Along with praise came Northern money": Ibid., 86. See also David Levering Lewis, *W. E. B. Du Bois: The Fight for Equality and the American Century, 1919–1929* (New York, 2000), 136.

274   "Wallace Buttrick, executive director": Anderson, *Education*, 89–92.

275   "Blacks would contribute": Daniel J. Boorstin, *Hidden History: Exploring Our Secret Past* (New York, 1987), 207.

275   "The black novelist Richard Wright": Quoted in Anderson, *Education*, 149.

276   "White America's acceptance of the Klan": Milton Mackaye, "Birth of a Nation," *Reader's Digest*, January 1938, 103–105; Leon F. Litwack, "Birth of a Nation," in Ted Mico, John Mille-Monzon, and David Rubel, eds., *Past Imperfect: History According to the Movies* (New York, 1996), 136–139.

277   "The Ku Klux Klan was resurrected": David H. Bennett, *The Party of Fear: The American Right from Nativism to the Militia Movement* (New York, 1995), 208–214; Clyde Woods, *Development Arrested: Race, Power, and the Blues in the Mississippi Delta* (London, 1998), 90.

277   "The Klan met with pockets": Percy, *Lanterns*, 225–241; "Address by Senator Leroy Percy, Greenville, Miss., March 18, 1922," *Houston Chronicle*, March 19, 1922.

277   "The racially inspired brutality of the vigilantes": Stewart E. Tolnay and E. M. Beck, *A Festival of Violence: An Analysis of Southern Lynchings, 1882–1930* (Urbana, 1995), 119–165, 272–273; Jessie Parkhurst Guzman, "Lynching," in Allen D. Grimshaw, ed., *Racial Violence in the United States* (Chicago, 1969), 56–57.

277   "The only broad conclusion": Beck, *Festival*, 119–165, 272–273.

278   "Roosevelt, the man of action"; Sinkler, *Attitudes*, 378–447.

279   "In politics, Teddy Roosevelt": Owen Wister, *The Story of a Friendship* (New York, 1930), 115, 253–261.

279   "Another representative of Eastern intellectual life": John David Smith, *Slavery, Race, and American History: Historical Conflict, Trends, and Method,*

1866–1953 (Armonk, N.Y., 1999), 37; John David Smith, "Frederic Bancroft's Notes Among the Negroes: Writing Contemporary History in Bourbon-Era Mississippi," *Journal of Mississippi History*, Vol. 66, No. 3 (Fall 2004), 227–264; Frederic Bancroft, *A Sketch of the Negro in Politics, Especially in South Carolina and Mississippi* (New York, 1885).

281   "The Harvard historian Albert Bushnell Hart": G. S. Borritt, "Introduction," in Albert Bushnell Hart, *Salmon P. Chase* (New York, 1980), xvii.

281   "Hart was also the mentor": David Levering Lewis, *W. E. B. Du Bois: Biography of a Race, 1868–1919* (New York, 1994), 112.

281   "In 1910, Hart journeyed to the South": Albert Bushnell Hart, *The Southern South* (New York, 1910), 62.

281   "The main issue must be fairly faced": Ibid., 100–105.

283   "When jobs beckoned, Southern blacks": St. Clair Drake and Horace R. Cayton, *Black Metropolis: A Study of Negro Life in a Northern City* (New York, 1945), 99–100.

284   "Between 1916 and 1919, 500,000 Southern blacks": Ratner, *Evolution*, 304, 418.

284   "Between 1920 and 1940 the black population": David L. Cohn, *Where I Was Born and Raised* (Notre Dame, Ind., 1967), 23–24, 332.

284   "As a consequence, Chicago's population": Drake, *Metropolis*, 8.

284   "In 1917 the *Chicago Tribune*": William Tuttle, Jr., *Race Riot: Chicago in the Red Summer of 1919* (Urbana, 1996), 104–105; Allan H. Spear, *Black Chicago: The Making of a Negro Ghetto, 1890–1920* (Chicago, 1970), 40, 202.

285   "As tens of thousands of blacks": Tuttle, *Riot*, 61–180; Spear, *Chicago*, 211, 220; Drake, *Metropolis*, 179, 186.

285   "For the most part": Tuttle, *Riot*, 164; Spear, *Chicago*, 192; Drake, *Metropolis*, 659, 203–205.

286   "In every aspect of Chicago life": Spear, *Chicago*, 205–206, 44–45.

286   "All these conditions were tolerated": Tuttle, *Riot*, 133; Spear, *Chicago*, 29, 151, 157.

286   "Blacks were the last to be hired": Drake, *Metropolis*, 83, 218–232; Spear, *Chicago*, 227–228.

286   "The racially combustible city": Spear, *Chicago*, 216–217. For other American race riots, see Tuttle, *Riot*, 11, 25, 29.

287   "Richard Wright captured Chicago's black experience": Drake, "Introduction," *Metropolis*, xvii–xxxiv.

287   "Many of the topics in *Black Metropolis*": Drake, *Metropolis*, 589. E. Franklin Frazier, *The Negro Family in Chicago* (Chicago, 1932), xvii, 149, 179–180.

288   "It would introduce black Southerners": James R. Grossman, *Land of Hope: Chicago, Black Southerners, and the Great Migration* (Chicago, 1991), 8–9. At the end of our period in 1943, General George Marshall, whose name is attached to the Marshall Plan, opined on the complexity of America's racial dilemma. Marshall told reporters that he "would rather handle everything that the Germans, Italians, and Japanese can throw at me, than handle the negro question." John Dower, *War Without Mercy: Race & Power in the Pacific War* (New York, 1986), 173.

289   "St. George Tucker observed in 1795": Litwack, *North*, 15.

290 "Blacks were without a fundamental": Foner, *Free*, 8.

290 "Blacks were, in the words of the historian": Leon F. Litwack, "The Bicentennial and the Afro-American Experience," *Journal of American History*, Vol. 74, No. 2 (September 1987), 315–337.

290 "They were not just another immigrant group": Spear, *Chicago*, 223–225.

Part Six. Cotton Without Slaves, 1865–1930

294 "In 1800, it took 3.3 times": Donald Holley, *The Second Great Emancipation: The Mechanical Cotton Picker, Black Migration, and How They Shaped the Modern South* (Fayetteville, Ark., 2000), 14.

294 "After the Civil War": Alston Hill Garside, *Cotton Goes to Market* (New York, 1935), 151–169. It should come as no surprise that this interconnected, international trading cotton world produced William L. Clayton (1880–1965), a cosmopolitan cotton businessman who became the chief architect of the post–World War II Marshall Plan. Clayton, a Mississippi native and principal of the world's largest cotton brokerage firm, employed contacts and experience for the State Department. It was Clayton who understood the need for economic reconstruction of Europe. See Gregory D. Fossedal, *Our Finest Hour: Will Clayton, the Marshall Plan and the Triumph of Democracy* (Stanford, California, 1993).

295 "These advances led to a systematic": M. B. Hammond, *The Cotton Culture and the Cotton Trade* (New York, 1897), 292.

295 "Cotton production continued to grow": Scherer, *World Power*, 348.

295 "By 1910 the world's textile industry": Ibid., 424–425.

296 "As one observer noted": Wright, *Old South*, 59.

296 "From 1880 to 1890, acreage moved from": Woodman, *King Cotton*, 343.

296 "A price rebound to seventeen": Jacobson, *Renaissance*, 81.

297 "Credit policies and accompanying financing": Cohn, *Life and Times*, 270.

298 "Although the South's agricultural methods": Scherer, *World Power*, 311–313.

298 "At the beginning of World War I": Ibid., 422.

298 "The value of cotton": Ibid., 337.

298 "in the period before World War I": Ibid., 399–401.

298 "Despite the primitive nature of American": Robert Leon Brandfon, "Planters of the New South: The Economic History of the Yazoo-Mississippi Delta," Ph.D. dissertation, Harvard University, 1961, 398–422.

300 "In 1902 the chairman of the": Allen Isaacman and Jean Hay, *Cotton, Colonialism and Social History in Sub-Saharan Africa* (Portsmouth, N.H., 1995), 81.

301 "American cotton was always": Ibid., 81–91.

301 "The Portuguese cotton experience": Allen Isaacman and Richard Roberts, *Cotton Is the Mother of Poverty: Peasants, Work, and Rural Struggle in Colonial Mozambique, 1938–1961* (Portsmouth, N.H., 1996), 1.

303 "In 1860 there were approximately": Hammond, *Culture*, 129.

305 "As might be expected": Michael Wayne, *The Reshaping of Plantation Society: The Natchez District, 1860–1880* (Baton Rouge, 1990), 150–196.

306 "The economist Mathew Hammond": Hamond, *Culture*, 149.

306 "Historians have sanctimoniously": C. Vann Woodward, *Origins of the New South, 1877–1913* (Baton Rouge, 1964), 180.

307 "The cotton farmer, it is thought": Roger L. Ransom and Richard Sutch, "The Trap of Debt Peonage," in Robert Whaples and Dianne Betts, eds., *Historical Perspectives on the American Economy* (Cambridge, England, 1995), 277–279.

307 "Cotton farmers spoke consistently": Wright, *Political Economy*, 173.

307 "In 1895 an Alabama farmer": Ibid., 182.

307 "But the stringent conditions of the South's postwar": Woodward, *Origins*, 180.

308 "Did the merchant-lenders": Ibid., 184–187.

309 "In 1894, for example": Ibid., 185.

309 "I think the peculiar difficulties": Quoted in Wright, *Political Economy*, 173.

310 "The fickle 1920s saw": Wright, *Old South*, 56–57.

310 "All roads from the cotton field": Woodman, *King Cotton*, 354–356.

311 "In 1910 an Atlanta editor": Ibid., 356–358.

311 "In John Faulkner's novel": John Faulkner, *Dollar Cotton* (Athens, Ga., 2000), 222–231. See also the description of New York cotton trading in Du Bois's 1911 novel about cotton, *The Quest of the Silver Fleece* (New York, 2004), 166–170.

312 "The panacea of crop": Woodman, *King Cotton*, 338–343.

312 "The humor vanishes under": Ibid., 357.

312 "A traditional banker would have": Frank E. Smith, *The Yazoo River* (Jackson, Miss., 1954), 176.

313 "Some antebellum plantation owners": Wayne, *Reshaping*, 75–109.

313 "In 1881 both Henry Grady and Frank C. Morehead": Robert L. Brandfon, *Cotton Kingdom of the New South: A History of the Yazoo Mississippi Delta from Reconstruction to the Twentieth Century* (Cambridge, Mass., 1967), 17–21.

314 "It was in the Mississippi Delta": Tony Dunbar, *Delta Time: A Journey Through the Mississippi Delta* (New York, 1990), 5.

314 "It has been referred to": James C. Cobb, *The Most Southern Place on Earth: The Mississippi Delta and the Roots of Regional Identity* (New York, 1992), x.

314 "As one of the spokesmen": Lawrence J. Nelson, *King Cotton's Advocate: Oscar Johnston and the New Deal* (Knoxville, 1999), 194.

315 "In 1870 the scalawag governor": Brandfon, *Kingdom*, 70–74.

315 "Other than the Mississippi River": Ibid., 217.

315 "The state wanted money and immigrants": Ibid., 107, 111.

316 "In 1889, Augustus Hawks": Ibid., 154.

316 "A 1903 publication described": John Solomon Otto, *The Final Frontiers, 1880–1930: Settling the Southern Bottomlands* (Westport, Conn., 1999), 40.

316 "The Delta's population expanded ultimately": Brandfon, *Kingdom*, 97.

316 "Labor agents used hyperbole": McMillen, *Journey*, 259–261.

316 "In 1882 the railroad builder, Collis P. Huntington": Cobb, *Southern*, 80.

317 "The IC's president Stuyvesant Fish": Ibid., 335.

318 "The terms were a 20 percent": Ibid., 204.

318 "Chicago's business ties with the South": Blight, *Reunion*, 203–204.

318 "In 1910 the IC's marketing materials": Cobb, *Southern*, 98.

319 "Since the Chinese did not flock": Cohn, *Life and Times*, 154.

319 "The Delta's population, cotton production": Otto, *Frontiers*, 113–118.

320 "In 1904, Delta planters tried to encourage": Brandfon, *Kingdom*, 193–243.

321 "In 1866 a freedman in South Carolina": Hammond, *Culture*, 132.

321 "The share system took on several forms": Cobb, *Southern*, 99–100.

323 "Percy's farm demonstrates the sharecropping": Raymond McClinton, "A
     Social-Economic Analysis of a Mississippi Delta Plantation," master's thesis, Uni-
     versity of North Carolina, 1938. President Franklin Roosevelt, in 1938, paid his
     three black farm workers in Georgia $20 per month each. A black farm worker on
     a fair, well-run Mississippi Delta cotton farm earned more than FDR's employees.
     Frank Freidel, *F.D.R. and the South* (Baton Rouge, 1965), 68.

325 "Greenville's nationally known": Hodding Carter, *The Angry Scar: The Story
     of Redemption* (Garden City, N.Y., 1959), 246–247.

326 "Cohn became a spokesman for the South": Cohn, *Born and Raised*, 12.

326 "He thought the sharecropping system evolved": Ibid., 127.

327 "Cohn cited Benjamin A. Green": Ibid., 342–343.

327 "In a 1937 article entitled": David L. Cohn, "Share-cropping in the Delta,"
     Atlantic Monthly, Vol. 159 (May 1937), 579–588.

327 "Cohn was echoing what": Hammond, *Culture*, 159.

327 "Du Bois's description in 1908 resembled": Frazier, *Family*, 3.

328 "The Yale anthropologist Hortense Powdermaker": Hortense Powdermaker,
     After Freedom: A Cultural Study in the Deep South (Madison, Wisc., 1993) 76.

328 "The classic study of black Delta agricultural": John Dollard, *Caste and Class
     in a Southern Town* (New York, 1949), 115.

328 "On the question of defrauding": Ibid., 121.

328 "He noted that middle-class black": Ibid., 402–404.

328 "Powdermaker guessed that": Powdermaker, *Freedom*, 86.

329 "Cohn's solution was a federal government": Cohn, "Share-cropping," 588.

329 "[O]nce we know that the system emerged": Wright, *Political Economy*, 85–86.

329 "Wright notes that the early clauses": Ibid., 87–102.

330 "Diversification, Wright suggests": Wright, *Political Economy*, 179–180.

330 "The sharecropping system, described": Woods, *Development*, 92–95.

331 "Eric Hobsbawm has compared the robber barons": Eric Hobsbawm, *The Age
     of Capital, 1848–1875* (New York, 1996), 144–146.

332 "There were other experiments": James G. Hollandsworth Jr., *Portrait of a
     Scientific Racist: Alfred Hold Stone of Mississippi* (Baton Rouge, 2008), 264–265.

332 "Outside of Tuskegee": Quoted in Louis R. Harlan, *Booker T. Washington: The
     Wizard of Tuskegee, 1901–1915* (New York, 1983), 224–225.

333 "Its patriarch, Benjamin, was": See Hermann, *Dream*, and her *Joseph E. Davis:
     Pioneer Patriarch* (Jackson, Miss., 1990).

334 "The four thousand acres": Currie, *Enclave*, 121; Hermann, *Dream*, 109.

334 "Regarding the suffrage question": Quoted in Currie, *Enclave*, 123.

336 "Isaiah eventually referred to Kansas": McMillen, *Journey*, 49.

338 "Yet in 1879 Douglass": Athearn, *Canaan*, 234.

338 "The economics of the cotton field were": Douglass, "Negro Exodus," 2–4.

339 "The historian Neil McMillen wrote": McMillen, *Journey*, 300.

339 "It would further the expansion": Ibid., 188.

339 "Not a single white person": Quoted in Ibid., 186.

340 "He crossed the line from philanthropy": Peter M. Ascoli, *Julius Rosenwald*
     (Bloomington, Ind., 2006), 159.

340 "Like Moses, he carried his people": Quoted in Florence Warfield Sillers, *His-
     tory of Bolivar County, Mississippi* (Jackson, Miss., 1948), 592–593.

341 "The story begins with the perennial threat": Nelson, *Advocate*, 1–44.

342   "the Fine Cotton Spinners'": Brandfon, *Kingdom*, 398–402.

343   "A 1937 *Fortune* magazine article": "Biggest Cotton Plantation," *Fortune*, Vol. XV (March 1937), 125–132, 156, 158, 160.

346   "In 1939 a Harvard study group": Nelson, *Advocate*, 109.

346   "Supervisors or managers brought": Cobb, *Southern*, 101.

349   "In 1908, LeRoy Percy": Ibid., 132.

349   "No creditor was so boorish": Quoted in James C. Cobb, ed., *The Mississippi Delta and the World: The Memoirs of David L. Cohn* (Baton Rouge, 1995), 72.

350   "In 1919 a Delta planter": Cohn, *Southern Place*, 133.

350   "Abe Isaacson, a former Talmudic scholar": Abe Isaacson, "From the Russian Ghetto to the Mississippi Delta," 1942.

352   "During the explosive growth": Moore, *Emergence*, 51.

352   "Essentially the mule was the engine": William Ferris, *You Live and Learn. Then You Die and Forget It All: Ray Lum's Tales of Horses, Mules and Men* (New York, 1992), 2.

353   "Although cotton was not the sole factor": Wright, *Old South*, 120.

353   "In 1881 the *Scientific American* described cotton": *Scientific American*, October 1, 1881, 211–212.

354   "In 1870 a huckster bragged": Cohn, *Life and Times*, 151.

354   "The process of invention": Holley, *Emancipation*, 37–53, 87, 104–116, 120–121, 202.

358   "The Great Depression of the 1930s": Cohn, *Born and Raised*, 305–306.

359   "Cotton sold at 17 cents": Holley, *Emancipation*, 55.

359   "Farmers in Oklahoma and Louisiana": Ibid., 57–58.

359   "The federal government stepped in to rescue": Ibid., 59–61.

361   "Cotton, deemed to be so vital": Edward S. Miller, *Bankrupting the Enemy: The U.S. Financial Siege of Japan Before Pearl Harbor* (Annapolis, 2007), 144–145, 209.

363   See also the description of New York cotton trading in Du Bois's 1911 novel about cotton, *The Quest of the Silver Fleece* (New York, 2004), 166–170.

364   "In 2007 two black scholars at Harvard": Orlando Patterson, "Jena, O.J. and the Jailing of Black America," *New York Times*, September 30, 2007; Henry Louis Gates, Jr., "Forty Acres and a Gap in Wealth," *New York Times*, November 11, 2007.

Index

A NOTE ON THE AUTHOR

Gene Dattel grew up in the cotton country of the Mississippi Delta and studied history at Yale and law at Vanderbilt. He then embarked on a twenty-year career in financial capital markets as a managing director at Salomon Brothers and at Morgan Stanley. A consultant to major financial institutions and to the Pentagon, he established a reputation as a foremost authority on Asian economies. His *The Sun That Never Rose* (1994) remains the definitive work on Japanese financial institutions in the 1980s. Mr. Dattel is now an independent scholar who lectures widely. He lives in New York City with his wife Licia and two Parson Russell terriers, Winks and Rosie.

3 1143 00927 1413